I0172059

Sex Trump and Gin

Plus One Hundred Thousand Other Words and
Phrases Chosen Mostly at Random

Steve Martin

Relativistic

e-mail: info@relativistic.co.uk

www.relativistic.co.uk

Copyright © 2018 Steve Martin.

All rights reserved.

First published in Great Britain by Relativistic.

Unless permitted under UK copyright law, this work may only be reproduced, in any written, printed or electronic form, with prior permission of the publisher.

ISBN-13: 978-1-9997303-7-6

ISBN-10: 1-9997303-7-2

No plants or animals were mistreated in the writing of this book.

Cover image: Thanks to Pixabay and Shutterstock.

DEDICATION

To the Memory of Mark E. Smith

Often a genius, sometimes the fool, always The Fall

CONTENTS

ACKNOWLEDGMENTS

I have no one to blame for the thankless task of putting this text together other than myself, which has taken more than fourteen and a half years of my life to complete.

1 A NON-RANDOM INTRODUCTION

Words – interesting things hey?

Uncertainty – probably one of the most fascinating concepts of all time.

Combine them together, add a little human creativity plus a pinch of ingenuity, and great things can happen. Take, for example, the infinite monkey theorem, which goes like this:

> **Give some monkeys a few word processors and unlimited time, and eventually they'll produce the entire works of Shakespeare.**

However, give some Millenniums the same resources, and all you're likely to get is some navel gazing snowflake drivel no matter how long you give them.

Beauty, creativity, art. All are intertwined with the random process. Even life itself would not have evolved without the constant uncertainty of nature's evolutionary principle. Random processes drove the emergence of life from the primordial soup and its evolution into the richness of life that we witness all around us on a daily basis. No doubt these stochastic processes will continue to shape humanity, leading us to become different, if not necessarily better or more advanced, lifeforms in the future.

Combine randomized chaos with the powers of the mystic and prophetic visions can result. Thus, giving one a glimpse of the possible, providing insight into future events that may, or may not, come to pass.

Randomness is also freedom. Most people's lives are full of must do's and what's next? A follows B follows C. Got a life plan? Know where you want to be in three years? Get a reality check. You have no idea what you are missing. A more chaotic approach may not get you to where you want to be, but you'll go places you never

1

otherwise would have done.

There are many types of randomness. The uncertainty of Schroeder's cat is not that of the roulette wheel. The chaos of Luke Rinehart's Dice Man is not the boiling world of possibilities that is Frank Herbert's Dune. David Bowie's considered use of randomly generated words and phrases to shape his lyrics is very different from the art of Russian Roulette.

Complete certainty lies at one end of the spectrum, absolute chaos at the other. Happy are those that walk the line between these two. Almost everything you want then becomes possible. However, one must be careful. Stray too far towards the world of uncertainty and madness is sure to ensue. Trust me, I've been there.

This book is devoted to the random word. Through it, great thoughts and ideas may (or may not) emerge. Various degrees of random process are applied to the word stream to create the prose that you are about to encounter.

So as not to cause readers to much distress from the flow of pure randomness, the first chapters are moderated. The random process is reigned in, resulting in an inspired and moving text which can be shown to have a significant degree of correlation with the infamous Portman Prophecy. This has been interpreted as predicting the election of President Trump, several wars and many other things that have yet to come to pass.

As we progress through subsequent chapters, so we extend beyond the comprehensible word structures of controlled language. We enter into the realm of complete stochasticity and chaotic uncertainty, arriving at a state of maximum entropy before emerging (probably but not definitely) at the other side. Most readers find Chapter 8 particularly challenging in this respect, but many feel revitalized after melting though that particular keyhole.

Please don't expect it to make much sense initially, but do expect to find things you have never encountered or considered in the written word before.

For those of you not wishing to take these things too seriously, a number of word games are provided for your delectation.

2 WORD GAMES

To help you get the most out of this experience, particularly if you are not someone who is attuned to the message of the random word stream, a number of "word search" type games are provided. I hope these will keep you amused for a very long time indeed.

If you get really stuck, then by all means contact the publisher at info@relativistic.co.uk with details of which question you are having trouble with and I'm sure they'll get back to you, eventually.

1. Which word is repeated seven times in a row in the book?
2. How many times is "Sex trump and gin" mentioned in the main chapters of the book (i.e. not in the title or this chapter?)
3. What is the first one-word sentence in the book?
4. What is the longest word in the book?
5. How many times does "Howard" feature in Chapter 8?
6. Which word is repeated three times in a row in the book?
7. Which city features most frequently in Chapter 3?
8. In which chapter is there a famous Star Wars quote?
9. What three words are repeated at the end of three of the Book's chapters?
10. The book contains three quotes from which famous 1980's science fiction film? What are they?
11. Which word features more than any other?
12. What is the average word length (average number of letters in each word) in Chapter 11?
13. What is the most common letter used in the book?
14. How many references are there to a famous detective?
15. Where does Santa fly to?

16. Which word appears most "CCCP" or "Soviet"?
17. What is the longest sentence in the book?
18. What type of boards does my father like in Chapter 3?
19. What type of cake does Barnaby like?
20. If there are 10,000 different words used to create this book, and they all have an equal probability of being selected, then in a book of 100,000 words, how many times would you expect to encounter repeated words? E.g. Hello Hello or engine engine?
21. Can you find a word containing five a's? What is it?
22. Which of the planets in our solar system do not get a mention in the book?
23. Can you find a sentence in Chapter 4 that contains 10 words, where each subsequent word has one more letter than the previous word? So, the first word contains just one letter, the final tenth word has ten letters.
24. What is "the name of the rose"?
25. Write a 1,500 word essay about what you think about The General, The Scientist and The Fisherman, and the relationship between them. What does it all mean?
26. How many question marks can you find in Chapter 10?
27. Using an appropriate statistical test, with what level of confidence (P value) can you say that the word length in this book follows a normal distribution?
28. Which chapter has the shortest average word length?
29. Can you find three words in a row, which all contain 4 letter a's?
30. How often does the word "generation" appear after the word "energy"?
31. Find a sequence of numbers from one to ten. What chapter are they in?
32. Why don't you go and have a nice cup of tea?

3 A SEMI-RANDOM BEGINNING

Sex trump and gin. I retweet it and confirm by email. Then, I organize my favorite observers to monitor the teaching of the national curriculum in Washington. I was informed of this via a redirected and fully independent transmission from The Statistician. Inn music, laser reviews, a canteen showdown, it all makes sense to someone. The Neanderthals are beginning to have some pretty heated free ideas, but it actually takes them many tries to get it right. Surgeons. The actual idea springs from doing things at the limits of integration. A delicate set of knives is all they need, but I have located no product funding – alas!

Unexpected events occur in a room full of righteous peoples. Their printer and keyboards are next to arrive. He is here. With the appropriate planning period he can make containers of nothing from the dark sky. Then, he rights the wrongs of the world, fighting The Prince, who was brought too early to the show.

The results and the feedback were complete in their agreement of the outcome. They mail porno to you, I envision. The long railroad has sporting links with phentermine. Let us release a phrase outside of the written word. The Prince departs.

I have undertaken an assessment of the component at this early hour of the evening. The research that was published should encourage specialist restaurants to commence a buying spree at once. As the script reminded me, they reference something new, akin to a new list of artists. "Buy more stock!" They scream at me. All the memory memes but none of the DVD titles are keywords in their eyes.

England will demo auto driving vehicles before the final winter. Extreme cost syndrome demands it. The victims demand a matching photo, and the fax again produces it. Let us consolidate these thoughts.

Envision screen crime. I have a popular review page delivered to our house every day which describes it. It originates from a miniature Colombian mountain pass. The General visits to provide us his rating. Jessica demands the safety and security of jail. Their votes are crucial. The crimes continue. Eternal reviews of progress provide a store of something like a beaded necklace according to those starting the race. Each beads represent one facet of what we have achieved.

Mentally, be mindful of us, copyrighted and travelling in a measured way, before the victims of screen crime corners us and attack the new automotive machines that we have just completed.

Such learning as we did at Princeton demonstrated online bias. It belittles a lack of joy as much as it could eventually reach such a stable condition. And upon screens, terms and conditions of the global program of The Scientist are displayed in bright neon. It takes also, statements from the victims such that only the old ones can abide still in Somalia. The fast Inc. distributes papers and calculates area on the calculus page that York suggests. The victims are no more. Thankfully, the Prince does not return.

Each seller houses new news in their repositories of knowledge. They tell me it is placed more or less so as to give a piece of it to us all. The sellers are unsure, and others view the songs of The Apple as doctrine and a product that The General values as zero. But it is worth more. The Fisherman, his world which sites aside the views of current texts as decreed by the Rochester complainant.

Pain rules in equal measure for him, which maps to popcorn crowds displaying a somewhat delighted interest in the affairs of the sea. The ads ask the relevant photography question, but The Fisherman picks the communication to use and there is no accommodation. The member, he has suddenly been well travelled and the physician dictates the relationship to him.

Stay clean my friend, be transparent to outdated data columns and horizontal documentation. Dakota stays not in the EU and owes it no dues. However, each state was promoting types of world sex and posted images of the choad. I am not amused. I find the views of it available elsewhere to be of better quality. International rights supply travel fun. They have not been supplied by the supplier, but the supplier benefits from this nonsense.

European flight taken by Mitchell over the Pole. Their figures are not clean, but not logged as unsuitable either. Where will they arrive? The General consults the Statistician. Monthly markets are depressed, with sapphires sold not for a pound but a penny. Then, the maximum of the day mirrors the assaulted markets and the workshop of drudgery is inflicted upon us.

Animals rise to prominence. There is no storage list for those that remain in human form. They have taped these conversational relationships, and therefore, the distributed ones shall retreat in shame from their ramblings. They spoke beyond my ability for extension, but the fine dame came only once this year and did not hear my plea. I've been walking, rather than driving, due to the size of our quota. It requires they do the rights and wrongs of entry to allow us to transport it. Otherwise, who benefits?

My father favored the silver boards of Canada. His rooms are an assembly line. Online they provide the surplus data she requires and she, being analytical minded, goes now to the market as expected.

Many employers are commercial and take command of the medium, employing a Stalinist management approach in desperation against the wishes of The Fisherman. It shows them how sorted the workers are, of many types and terms, a treat for the eye. Joke not, for the museums help to deliver interesting displays that boost your confidence and keeps the workers entertained. The Fisherman tries to support the workers but The General is displeased.

The copy frame repeats the news of the latest schools. The policy declines the extras adjacent to the Ministry of Education. Pupil sales will rise unless a major sign is received. The state outfit is ready for them – like autonomous robots they approach their learning in these times. Soon to be employees like their parents. My affiliates deny days of righteous religious systems are upon us. It is not educationally relevant. Relevant yet not, and need to process fat efficiently for the developers to report recovery in their profit margins.

Images, which at the time the sponsor deems to grow like yeast, remain. The services lengthen and the providers consider national suggestions but refute the rules. The book of organizing waste is taboo in these situations. Programs of techno tunes lead the repeat of the tale. Education fails again, but repeats again, and again. The Fisherman is dispatched by the General.

My lyrics are written by professional friends. They are taken as a possibility, but the affiliates pick the Prime Minister for their leader instead. They see artists of computational fire. The color is red. My hotel is small and guards patrol these areas of Victorian grandeur. Fuel lines reach as far as the stopped Prime Minister can stretch them. The PM will picture the state as it sinks to its death. No more entries to my diary today. These words were welcome because back research reference dates were not weekly, or otherwise, available.

Lines found in the dust must drive devices of accounting in Australia if not here – if not the EU, then with whom do we ally? It varies the chemistry of birth when they are including everyone.

Deep in the valley, long avenues covered in red tape prevent infant services doing their job. Commerce guys with disabilities develop devices in tropical climes. It all relates back to Brexit.

Payroll time. Out of context suggestions with the help of the leadership. Personally, I do not comply and it degrades me. My search for the graded formula of a life goal bears no fruit to date. The Paris Accord outcome costs just a dollar, but the US won't pay even a cent. Nottingham emerges as the maximum and optimal provider of commercial storage facilities given its location – it's a great venue says the Prime Minister.

Off at last. The web is assumed evil. The construction was whatever we consider, but it delivered benefits at the time. However, we were occupied by the dreams of revenue seekers with failing lives. Graduation is no joy on reflection. Maybe this reflects the stars who work in Poland and the jobs they have stolen from us. The materials are from Santa Fee, but the quality of the problem is great, while the distance is small. Any shops that open creates a problem. Benjamin throws away his toys, I say bravo!

Much food date advice is incorrect. Florence displays the general advertisement to Smith on a hill near his farm, but harm to those travelling with bad food. Once the provider displays fashion, a jacket is cast over nations. They work hard, and are ready to counter all practitioner devices, but they fall sick from the bad food and cannot comply.

The President derides the internet but maintains contact to keep his supplies flowing. This crazy speed treatment costs him his jewelry but he pays his expenses himself. He, himself, chats over the history of the time rather than drive growth of nations through the making of things and open trade. The PM bows to The General. Servitude is guaranteed.

The pulse model used in the Italy tragedy proposed satellite dishes as parameters for good will provision to all. They claimed the cream metal encourages this, but the available players drive an absorption of bad ideas. Shortages continue into the next decade. The post king penetrates the membrane of the peoples' ideas, and stalls progress in the morning light by several meters. In retail, the buffer of garbage is taken each day to preach like a short saint, who lets the data flow.

Pain. They reported it where the activated device was turned into a weapon. The package of economic keywords was sent by email to my pal to enable it. Obituaries for those affected. The techniques used by your subscribers to hide behind a firewall are unknown, but all shall be swept away when the weapon completes its discharge. It's just a product of mis-direction of the buyer anyway. Don't deny the psychiatry conditions of Louis's robot have contributed to it. My driver is a parent, but the car faces away to protect from the weapon. Commonly, he wants to talk three-fold by email, but his life is stable until he is affected. Cheap privacy runs over my feet with a car. The damage is over, fewer are affected than expected.

Overcome by reality awareness she would deny her existence. Critical reward will hide cattle in any automobile driven longer than 750 KM. The information they choose is against the National Health Service. The survivors persevere.

Vivid expressions at the lives of the pussy has defined what category we are in. Iron and Steel. A job with variety is the rank outsider. No poster has guaranteed it will be stopped someday. The project trip breaks new ground. My hand is framed. The next day, and several mail shots later, movers and shakers in Dakota have been leathered. They bear the date of account. By the headphones of my teacher, my heart's location keeps us sane. Ahh! strategy. Games by Israel stop in Oxford and may find productivity in the nursing of personal leather.

Species of the Soviet Union went the wrong way after the fall, but were smart enough to recover the path. Anna begin in the morning to open the shops and said she sent investigators to examine the cash empire left behind by the Soviets. Colors, cons and parties. They do concord, but touch back to the generated label site on the Korean peninsula. Although, the replies from the Kremlin do not link further to a later date than at the time of initial perception.

Military figures of the regime image the terrain, but you should not find the right food very wholesome. Mobility, internal invention, the foaming acid could damage the materials of the decision team. To Berlin, by travelling a pencil line so thin. I could fall at any time. I wonder when a wider white imposter will advance the claims of the null people. Engineering a million reflections will deliver devices that recode our genes and deliver the sorted ones. Results of irrigation, and also pets. Let Italy go a line ahead from all brief beliefs.

The fire device, like bible consumers, requires a special motherboard. Married, but a sex victory of good wood is not ours to achieve. Outsourcing the relationship brings big wins. Demand that the company delivers more than just fucking parking meters. No techniques existing today can explore such essential search awareness of the static scholars. They were won over by the beauty of bibliographic chatter but do not understand it. As the details go, it bodes well for the Christian.

The builder of articles that hosts delegations from the poor farmers, which are better placed than most to observe the movement of the Atlantic ships of the invader. Trick stocks and horses arrive in these vehicles. The conditions driving the settings of marketing deliver remote awareness of the settings, but these are little short of a fantasy reality. the Prime Minister accepted water in Europe, but no one orders her offering. The nature of the Bible spirit provides each of us with details for living. They enable some drone shoppers to escape. The line guys have no skills, like lost people − or sheep! The expected summer court hearing of business fools would follow the letter not the spirit of the law. Email spreads the predictions of Bloomberg.

Their bed brain has no defense against it. It takes what we developed into account. The report did not present the whole picture. Don't let them die as a result. They are not to blame. Their lost registration uses therapy to train the mailman in battle compliance. Address the mouth and be frank. Say what the digital observers observe, and be invisible to the consolidation team. Alaska is where the ensemble is certified under pressure from Trinidad and Tobago, and Tobago ratings flip the focus to Trinidad. They will all be under threat without strength.

He administered the longer one in one tremendous go, but the issue of adult correctives in the area were forgotten. He was and is Howard. They transfer access to the wing by the branch network and the nearest portal. It archives that invasion to a previous time. How badly are the jar and pot fouled by Gabriel? Info of the event is my best friend.

Buying a company's artistic license, he developed the data together with the investment in the final holocaust at the end of time. That determination can bear whatever fruit you desire. German swingers have relationships spared, but pay a penalty for benefits listed. He and I keep the powerful register whole, but we want to spread the infection message to all. But not The Scientist.

I felt the load. It burned my pride to carry it. The other type of Monte Carlo loop will demonstrate the highest range of volatility. The program role is the same as that of the secretariat and is cooked up in meetings that He temporarily expects can service the city. The results are services that the manufacturers in the hills have located but cannot use. Interested by the hint of a sign, the equations are reworked to a newly generated form - a tax signal of civil unrest. From the Iliad, he predicted the classic maps and the contacts of Jason that we add to our own. Hardware is faster than the pop site software patents of the East.

Records discounted, button loops advanced, and the gaming streams merge together. Physiology provided in January in Memphis has no relevance in Spain in July. No answers to any questions. The second miracle of our affiliates are thus behind the movement you observe.

Any findings of the editor filter down to Raleigh's team where applicable. Do not have counseling without consultation first. E.g. my analytical graphs are in my name, but the business submissions remain outdoors in the fragrant spa air of Manitoba. Now how to find Toronto? Sweden has the knowledge, but the younger, softer, countries come lower on the priority list. Let them burn. The lower the weekly game score, the worse your lifestyle. It feeds interest in the final budget. Details up-ended until the messages iron out the serious issues of the copyright business. The fifty first area, and those that moan about the payment, shall lie beyond allowable quality control while I maintain the officer elite.

Life. GMC quiz night. The centre of what is possible serves segments to studies of judges. Alleged loan shark lenders images they are following whatever the returned ones see when they switch on their eyes in the sky. System comments about parking are described in the book. Have they been to Portland to receive our review?

Over and over, owned by the security of his ratings. Above all, updated protocols keep the security of the site. Instructions written on doors register the criminal code. Double crash, married then divorced. She played during the missile crisis in the night, while completing the final editorial. Then she left me.

The St. George pub is at its center. Here the army will hang first the crop of workers, sold a false promise and copyright. Windows hosts the show. Tours by the winners and then Peter will be here. The unions have no comment.

Go meet them at the open evening. Mail our response on her proposal. Allow her access to the second university if she pays the fee. She engages in bad racing, a force of right to restore. There is no value in winning the wrong race. She wants also to book the date of departure. Terrorist games are the product of the policy. Stop screening Dallas. JR was not shot but the services that screened it were. Bestiality wants fresh PR. Therefore, items in the list are not just the protected ones of this part of the contract.

Non-profit organizations commission the techniques of preferred development. The rooms are damp. Enlargement of the EU is a talking shop. Your visa was discussed on the walk. Information seekers watch and endorse the testimony of the betrayal. Should they allow dedicated click cities to became part of the game?

Disc support has no resolution, but maybe the grim reaper will play music and show integrity. Arizona measures out the help and helps stage the games. We go to Arizona to be integrated together. Just how highly do we protect Erik in Arizona? Is his the only penis to fall inactive from adults' effects?

KGB ringtones drive a new atom war. Health users are happy beings. They stand and query the lodgings of the KGB agents. Sinking ships, in that way, it's the usual line of visual enquiry which is via an insider's tools and letters. Just troopers and artists.

And it funds the opportunities for mortgages from the inside. Meetings with Casandra to narrow the hopes for Macedonia, and she employees the colleges of mathematics to provide an update. As a result of what the graphs display, I shall have lances made. It was transmitted in the name of the city. Take nothing random to heart, but it does offend me. Do not be afraid. Temperature management and energy stores are manual. Joe here, his division of time and resources are similar.

Record us, we who are marked and timed. Of growers, they help biotechnology and radio to develop. Be mindful of her principals. Distribution purposes the ratings before the lines bring the beast creating jokes while the organizations prep. More for Charles to read and advertise. He uses the faculty mother. Developed the funds museum, Maria shot protection had gold added to provide extra shirts and a flat at the planet.

In defining the policy for weddings, wire the Mediterraneans so that the votes get cast in time before the facts get broken. They remember The Fisherman, with sadness. It was created as a suite of full rooms to find urgent operations that still divide the top tier. Used fonts never enter the fashion of suburban organisms. What an excuse for knights, because their payment sheets and the fees they charge safety amplify the problem. Currency leaders release active support, as securely, and as soon as they have viewed the property. The General concurs.

Western thought is what the geeks supplement the integration with. Wrestling with problems, the slight failure to accommodate fake news was the worst. In some situations, equations are more beneficial, and the restaurants recommend it to wash away the taste. The internet giants of the valley disagree. They are shunned and ridiculed, but the people do not turn off their devices.

The employment tribunal was considering when to prosecute. The General declined to attend. Your interests inform others in the way Howard accounts for the number of people investigated. Queer guests and the convicted dine together. Promote calls to health receiver. Their lips are like snow. The development is critical in the village, especially when areas throughout the world are without accommodation.

The AI network displays great strategies. Strange extras require a lower prerequisite for entry than the systems of our country. Grenada is the center. The forms to be completed are far from helpful. Drock! Also fuel, transport and extra food are at Edwards air force base, and the fifty first area will be simplified and entry is for free, but your sin shall not be wiped away. The input from the navy has moved away.

The Pacific election names Chicago as the most worthy. We joined in such celebrations, while studying the stray null. The job of Jane Austin was a heavy burden. Her composition exists in the real world. It was awarded basic merit. Miracle of water filled items never wrong. Ever the humble steam iron is the best we have ever seen. Their intent is informal, but access would be damaging.

Soccer teams and the individual players avoid undeserved booking. Mount Olympus shames the discipline of the mind while the magic of several powers knows the score. School accommodation includes music files and a set of dietary records. There is a whole world to explore, a cove of children and a useful building.

Here, recipes are provided by a classical company. Latin divine. Radio has stayed in fashion and is part of the scene. The aid categories will be created and stars placed on tape to represent them. It is binding. You must do the 100 KM ride to understand what is stated. Less Apple Play may make your domestic life better than the rest of the country's has been. The world matches want it wants against the basic requirements. It is here that the band experiment is accommodated.

They know adverse thinking is deadly, but equity in death is unlikely to be cool. Illinois is in line for patient recipes and other educational seminars. The theatre will show comparison with education, united in that we are not in Kansas anymore.

I've seen it daily. The center of high things in Macedonia is state of the art. Don't exhaust the project's resources. The assembly is so upset that the mills and shops deploy methods of resistance. The site of the headland is where the additional kids learn how to behave. Use your browser to price tuition, and step on the gas to reach the saints first and beat the record. Fred's paintings capture it. Yearly solution to kitchen consulting has been through the narrow passage. He's in the theater with chemical air injury. Football fantastic.

The hazard will be the communication of the hotel's cube. Corrections in the flour mix makes games funny. Please ensure a balanced workload to get the personal gene yourself. Wood be the eight and I be the first to order accessories. The law don't see the problem but The Scientist does. His year finds roster, and the top nature camera is submitted the way of a trick conviction. Gain ownership of research and address the businesses making wine. Then, immediately play the cards in your hand. Complete the lab work and the older user will provide assistance to avoid stochastic disaster. At the cross, Dennis be your be hardwood agent on the frontline.

While winter is beautiful and us melding over your individual coffee is Devine, there is no release from what you must do. Animals seek the state of health achieved by humans. General DNA comparisons of the community line will give yourself the same urban combination. Down low, with logs plus sexually dry overlords, it existed in the gallery landscapes. Enforcement action is to be joined by Africa now. Already, if the health services of one's nation state are broken, then no claims will progress to the deadline and it can occur openly, to which you can refer. Steel tight are the archives. Over activity does exhaust the cells and will see the proposal fail. National leaders take the choad diversion, that or they go to the Pacific. New ideas arise about the honorable Carlo people.

The entrepreneurs are losing at different times, seeking to watch great the messaging. The key is the selected Namibian announcement by phone. Difficult situation. Post Kennedy, that points to the military and the historical role of steel troopers. Pussy made no introductory attack. Take care of the product as it was posted, as any people counted in the development face huge fines. Automatically, leave this commented via online statistics to avoid devastating napalm attach. The report on Korea gave top marks, but has been over clinical. It's fate. Hot VHS tape, trying certain clinical proposals in light of the administrative reviews. Into the Irish Sea we go, and hereby give tables and links to get wishes.

Oral specifications indicates corporate drop in revenue and the view from the top is that the contracts with Caroline are clean. The entire top foundation will advantage society I think. Attack like mad, and the interview will add to it. That the great and the good are placed in full view, here in the Canadian city is a bonus. It takes the why and wherefore of my macintosh to prevent the rain. My need, like yours, is that of any other middle man turned inside out. Your kernel formed in January, they were deemed damned from repetitive injury. Only Indian newcomers turn efforts into innings. Blimey! Design your wife with equal pride as your family on the eve of the flash crash.

A functional world is accepted. The grassy heath, post lesbian, such that nuclear winter turns humanity into fish food in the faster deep of the oceans. Connectors please, serial hormones are in time for the members to produce art, and they are at one with the Hong Kong minimum.

Cross asked if we told the stories, and we answered his questions to manage Poland's demise. Cross was pleased. That resulted in the expression of mistrust and the draining of the whole fetid pool. Alert! the nylon fastener bites from behind. From it, and from the rivers of blood, Cross has broken down the guidelines of the South.

Night is golden and well forced workers find days of productive work. People at home, it is a medium older than the collections of race memory. Rush, click and dream the wanted program. The affiliated via a very native design, bias exists, ending detailed price. The APR in the valley looked scaled to their Kama. It was cheap money.

And the information found in the car has but two missions. A little order, and the tags are to be removed. Active business is a positive services program. There, during the conversion, Pro Ltd let the complete product be delivered with wide area messages. The Ugandan backs down, but do not yet book not the final destination. Deleted organizations fill Charlie's birthday with chaotic systems. The pound powered crisis is of interest weekly. Declined credit. Identifying the menu provides view of societies after spread assessment. Respective knowing, it's Belgium that sounds the alarm in an area forced to have contracts. The details enrage the people, buzz.

The email length tears the timeline of energy generation. I will give the organization maximum power output before the agreement. Get cookies for the team, they are used by national ladies and are farm friendly. A square star looks top, but the bus blocks the view of them and names the copyright income. Chorus in national gallery as the age really does become an issue. The city has difficulties, and the feeding is banned by the League of Nations. Potential high pressure in Andorra, and the search is called off. Offering the findings completes the assessment pattern. Move along your string green has been rejected. Us and them are reviewed, and we seem to have a temper that is matched by none.

The extension group is comprehensive. The terms under which it operates are set by Max Margaret. The door music is needed to prevent an overload of the mind. Marked then, my classic friend in you date parking – it's all chat and marvel. Max says Iraq will become the Georgia of the Middle East. As you sit on your hands, have you the power to see where the week is in common with the day? Consulting societies must act as a single artist, says Max, with their plans aligned to the stream of regional goals.

Damn them. Lancashire is not welcome at part of the Northern enclave, but supplemental planners find a number of the ways through. Seven times it will happen, until it is time to begin the games of the artists. I noticed however, Max said the downloads provide only dry planning, and the immigration numbers are unknown.

Drivers sound the bass. Blackjack games and design vocals rumble. Immediately, it would seem that the engineering people create the chrome Janet, and the whole world demands metal to be made into a nation entire. So Max insists. Thus begins the evaluation of the last people. They extend for a brief time, despite the pollution.

It's trust, plus a view of the community that no one else could give. Norfolk provides the stage for entities with drugs powers greater than store. Max faces down the Scientist, but is not victorious and is banished. Counterstrike for the hangman is as welcome as atomic war, with different ideas lacking and not creating any download material. About at that moment, scientific team pink finds success. Cadillac wars are over. Veterans syndication of the National Health Service is the product, yielding a finance group bonus recently.

Students separate, isolation of them is ecological. The ways of cities in the Turkish province are strange. The replies match messages received from official legal departments. You have been to the Belarus base to start, so continue to branch out to the markets. It's about winning a chicken for the long time thrill seekers, actually. No, really!

My methods are trusted, and Jackie the European receives his partial reward. Network of the Apple board. The types which also make mistakes get some dirty tract. The background lawyers search the trial for privileges to research copy answers. The number of cheese sandwiches is large. Chart the path of the partner virus so that the changing board members approve the trend. The name of the rose is Cassandra.

First, drainage of the brook, then more than violent blows to the rampant drainage slope. Once the net is dry, continue to fish the brook. The net is made alert. It can verify the giving of the enterprise scale collectibles from my store of seafood. The net gains sentience – beware what other horrors that may bring. Time to attack technology. If this was a sci-fi film I'd quote from it: "These are not the droids you're looking for."

My birthday steps are ever greater than ever and the traffic buyer comments on this. At the offline partnership, democracy groups together. Games are permitted for me in my apartments. Her mother sold tourism. Null for New Orleans, as the older coders get their great ass the way that they want. The item remains useless unless you retain more than double the data measures in the system in review. Cover your back, or you may not have the vacation option from the authority. We had a fridge, so now the example is that none in the Indian capital get modern gear or computers. We chain health farms together for a 2,000 KM long profit opportunity. Increasing in Asia, the prints of the player generally deliver immediately, as it is received, but at some point before the atomic war so as to understand how it will occur.

They could picture the health battery accreditation of Martha's disability. Views of Microsoft speed across social media like Mercury. The signal is thinking techno and one song results in large repetition of drum patrol. Baby makers, the service most portable for the last three decades in certain areas. Pair go to expo. Over the way, they view the development that Gordon did and flee in terror at the sight of its deviant forms. The heart has been learnt by disciplines in trouble. Allow photos of success full coverage, which results in addiction by the weak willed. I rated the thought as good. As an item courtesy, against the international plugin, the manufacturers are after your knowledge once more.

The car left as he did community work in the park. In essence, it was a background system that did well to counter the enemy. The car was designated as unsafe, but also, bizarre as it may seem, it is here tonight to protect you. Also, I had the apartments entry security increased just in case the car's systems where insufficient to protect you. The hordes love that aspect. By designing the beer the scientists turned their publication into "thus the fairy" a tale for young adults. Exposed as the only rent closest to what was affordable, the micro users discovered a flat with a beautiful authentic pink hue. The utility account blogs their operating music this afternoon, as some type of soul, the pop classic.

Measuring work load, leads to the suicide of echoes. Therefore, I may end up completing the other type of assessment instead. Village law users need it every day with notice. Ordinary, replies the cameraman. Fill in for the Prime Minister, privacy provides the academic revisions ass hole.

Good, and it loves Camelot. Big prizes! It knows the party and privacy plays its part in the provinces of brief adventure. The mess hall attendees puzzle, but are helpful at selecting resources for the visitor. Online. I could fire missile at a fan. The elements found in ships span forums very often undisclosed to the people. His affiliates are retrieved, but do not overcome respective language barriers. It is like a forest with material walls. Results are a fiction error and the catalog hold only limited guidance. Orwellian cross. The General. The Scientist. The Fisherman. Code the menu for receipt of the sender's spirit.

Yearly effects hold conference to account on the findings. I understand the battery dildo is of a kind whereas yours is not. Layout the bunting as the findings are significant. The conference grants permission to dance to the tune of the library hawks. In time, the tune constants back to the transmission of the leader's interview technique. As a result of the findings, nuclear fire is buried at a profit in a Premier Inn. It can be retrieved for its purpose at a later date. This means we're behind with the series of first strikes, and trackbacks get more common.

Friday's route is argued by drivers, and the pest dances through the listings of decorated veterans. The archives of the delicious scheduling play guitar, while driving economic themes through parliament. On a sofa we watch state live cam. Mary, the contact trademarks look like a manger. She sees the Asian research as something general to remain for graduates. Take multimedia, its standards are developed by IBM and Microsoft for the local neighborhood. Auctions held by community associates are violated every time. The indexes of thongs are important. A member running for office is set a multimedia task, yet still executes the command by the design led generation, thus saving the grace of our neighbors.

Employees are more able to move to territories by the authorization of world powers in Geneva. The investigation unseats website owners, which is how I showed gross domestic product comes out of our butts. Trump and buy! The activities of millions pocket profit from Diana's shoe, as the performance results in the documentation criteria being refinanced through a release of provisions.

The ease with which the multi-pictures attention moves to work experience is evidenced by observations. Consumers, who are you who the operation covers the need urban charge? Google sends travelers here for free as it trials its self-driving cars. The way forward has a blank laser to guide it, and the tags come with the gaming attractions Russell has taken.

The cup of golf's miscellaneous authority? The sequence of events in the interior uses anyone from Melbourne who has back trouble. By extension, the idol websites also suffer with pain. What's the point? To recover from the pain once must address the mail. Dig fate, listen to the music system the float my boat. Lead initiatives to help those who suffer, and apply the facility to tit selections. Across the plains palm olive creatives live at the hotel with the address best hotels have. Wireless transmission, using the power of the gods, finds no need for goods likely to be sold by Dallas musicians. In this way the pain will be eased.

Light purpose I think. There is an error at the fort. A minimum of five other silver bullets will help your occupation. A strategic scientific finding will demean the rights if thousands let it. Letters to millions are sent back down the wires – soon they will be informed of their fate. The interactive society fails after just a month. Survivors form partnerships and wind up giving blowy jobs to pay their way, the details of which are advanced automatically to the public screens for general entertainment. Technically, readers seek the breasts of their mothers for comfort. However, the lowest common denominator nearly always prevails.

The issues blocking their normal behavior is lost in the forest for hours due to their mission. The capital boys seek freedom. Conference Kelly deals facts, while half will go to Manchester if the volume remains low. Hopefully it will all be resolved by the end of the decade.

Die handling out of date food. As the procedure provides tickets for the photos, and in the cargo hides a demonstration of what could happen, so plants the flag there to remind people where it is. The friends' girls thanks them as it has been disease that tends to appear in schools.

Sales of sterling clash with bath day. My birthday is bath day. I demand a refund. Not forthcoming. I relent and try again. I guess it will have to be that way and I take a shower instead. Those areas reported by yourself where the disease has taken hold require you to take the required action. To delay is to die. Purge with fire and take the acceptance action. All session of marketing in galleries is forbidden during the epidemic. Contact with her is hidden every day in the apartment of the home citizen guy who is the carrier. You wild dumb ass. All will suffer if he is not contained.

A piece of your weekend is lost. Sample the merchandize, while bedding in the Russian agent. They are the travelers, with standard clips, who carried the disease initially. My printer in Tobago is warning me, as the device defines souls and produces posters of any refugees who are carriers. Absolute zero. Zero tolerance. If you have it you must be contained. Bin those who are most at risk because they think lemons became oranges sometime during the middle ages. That is the national secret. Don't tell. Ring a ring a roses.

Illegal ivory services provide mood music eh? The poachers are not brought to account. The design of unrationed reasoning for this is a zero-sum game that may send many to end of their affairs. Hands of The Queen! They give her a transplant product from pigs, genetically engineered from the blood of an apprentice. Appreciate the thinking. Not really suitable for the Queen. We are having late tides, which reduces manufacturing costs, which in turn is what one wants. An endorsement of the lists of The Orange Order prevents comments that have been made by distributors of movies before, and provides a form of virtual emergency. Momentum drives labor.

A serving of baseball precedes the demise of once great powers. In the years following 2025, the league of nations shall disband. Then a new beginning shall follow. Shame on the soviets! The Koreans are our unlikely ally. Strangers shall prevail. Provide a description of the new person who is on the employment panel for the leadership. Line lending within the law is for some people acceptable. Film the fuel flow to stop premium rate charges for mankind. The sorted categories provide the user with lucky software. This is the power source of the time. Strength in numbers drives people to the beach. Group fabric, life online. Recovery is not guaranteed.

Final destination is to be London. The pollution is manageable, but must be ruining the artifacts in the museums. Turn on the comparison of public opinion. Then, update the maps of Europe and inform the elites of Orlando. Case functions which are viewed under the sun of Austin does not support this position. Guys, drink the last measure.

People who view faces of dogs hope that religion sees what is written. This then, gives them the last requirements of hand love and fancy flights into the unknown. The war factory designated the world to join with them, regardless of their opinions or fame.

They provide foods e.g. tomato, potato, beans and gravy. The agency cannot consume all that on its own. A woman's bra is the picture of a skilled visitor. Near as described, some friends like to fight the visitor. Not me.

Video trading over the internet highlighted two highways that were holding up the string of production. A safe left-wing opposition in the face of a bad solution ends sophisticated responses. The French weight is back tied to the EU legacy. They had a highway energy deal. Are Jessica's goals good heal health or other things? A car service in the UK costs how much? A sign that benefits us all. We need to see the signs and understand the meaning. Not all prophets are false.

The expected processes of the manufacturer creates a heavy product. Most people ignore this. Instead, all they are interested in is when we should balance age with beauty. Obviously, this is the same age as that when one should stop playing volleyball. Partner, lend me a clip of ammo that links to the weapon and takes no prisoners. I really don't the consequences of man-made bio-hazards. Romantic and united. Carlos has compatibility. At the top of the hill the shop is doing business, so good. That it is liked being wrapped in silk. Nobody watches from the monument any more. I don't know why. Maybe because there is nobody anymore. The bio-hazard has taken its toll.

The modern budget satisfies us all after the president is installed. Wholesale maniacs can trash a saint, but not a theme park. A defense contains drive, to be driven is defensive.

Click the button and the user will run away. Please see the presentation of this, and then use the truck for the labor. The reputation of Saturday is not the same as Sunday. A new tool was given to us. Given the Bluetooth connectivity, it's transformed into a trash host that the enemy can utilize.

Web nuts specify what it means to her as if she machines herself to be part leach. At the same time, one boy's marriage is via an enclosure in southern England. It is up to us to sit in a jar. The marriage is but a sham for her as the leach drains away her life.

The right reached out to us for finding their origins, and staged a coup using the items provided by the developer (that is you), who was then sent to hospital.

Corresponding with interconnected persons brings no benefits. Those countries that do this, just do this to have donated funds for pussy treatment for the whole football team. The forum cares for skating, but holds no validation discussions with the DJ's seeking asylum. I brought the sale album to eliminate the ring of Brazil. Most things begin with random circumstances. Amongst our kin, animals rule and reporters feign being trained in their husbandry.

It must have been the plan. It must! The manager said so after the flow of navigation led them here. The Australian new findings center is opening in June. The satellite overhead sheds light on interests and different issues that will be discussed at the center. This is in the news. When cases are found regarding it, that's cool. Wow! Interesting site links and sorted rental properties, all with political styles and standard deviations that are somewhat odd. Name your methods of research. The main institutions are the holiday that Motorola takes near the borders of Japan. Variety updates Howard with the news and he is pleased. He informs the Scientist, who buries the Fisherman. Cubic Katrina shows some of the two terraces in shareware, and she shy's away from store focus.

Bras do show after watershed. The Turner destiny is available for devices all along the avenue. Please approach to save money on visa. Please surface the problem in the form of poems, which may help fix the fireplace which has suffered a broken panel. When the highest polls come from the ten partners, it's time to call Pete. He will have the view of the orchestra and knows the price of the soundtrack himself. Entries into the encyclopedia are not permitted. Space has basic time, time is broken and the name of the breaker of time is Howard.

Next, people's language also communicates the message. Sucking may be a perversion of both parents and staff. Address the court and watch for information provided by the Judge. The bunny provides the completion factor. Is the filter off the investigation into the legislature? The best corporation in Europe made contact with the police. They may provide leverage.

Purchase and feel finance blues. This is the price to advertise your life on social media. It figures on the internet, a con, over my dead body. Read the instructions for the university designer sperm. The test projected Collins into near earth orbit. Meeting an associate, if the crop of breasts matches the recent bounty then sell short. Strong LSD sends one wild with the linking of similar medicines. These are industrial, and only for information to allow you to address the team about the effects. The white programs detail the wedding. The portable technology is available, with no core issues on the branch line.

There, the same old oven is compliant. Yet, it leads to atomic war. A great dash of company vegetarian uses separate timber for each building. Salt with the bucks and onions, from a flag waver, makes a fine stew. Begin with Wisconsin. The letter from William may be included. State your intention. Inside, if bank sciences receive more from others, then so be it. Natural behavior towards the truth allows us some health benefits, as the mileage exceeds the third marker. The Librarian will provide stewardship of the land. The requirements bill is built upon the life of peace that is led. The pricing for this is in the millions. Compared to previous info access, the health poet also lists the addition of a possible membrane contract.

I seek accommodation with the aim of finding privacy and good dining along the riverside. Today, I viewed some guys private genes. The fire is instead made of air and back gas. Especially camp, I find the lost ground the minimum that can be posted in more than one go. He is a porter of education. Company prices not salaries. The government department established Indiana pack review. Can Hawaii cut it? The lamp of the president receives a brand new fish. Homelessness returns. His domain of education delivers a sophisticated plan. It needed to be expanded publicity and marketing undertaken. Here a discussion is held just once a year. January was with us when homeless housing was in short supply.

Bad public, good public? The new websites begin giving the information we need. Our business guestbook receives the whole balance. Search the slideshow for the operating system. The bill is evaluated and a publication is delivered. The adventure provides comments and terms potential intense line of enquiry before the saint describes abstract plumbing content.

Work into top quality patterns, it was at the port that investigations into investments of millions of comparison deals was generally undertaken. Tri-architecture, not atomic war lite, for Alaska. Newspaper fever this year. We want points for poker rooms and the internet is doing what it can to bring to the area something valuable. The fire within creates cabinets of reasoning across the domain, except it's hard to control the ray and report at the same time.

The number of those staying in the submarine provides relevant associates with details of its anonymous capability. They form a students' services page on their website. Rooms are only as good as the spirit in which they are offered. A parent that is local is better at selling their family for a price than the projectors scientific. The papers hear gooseberry is in fashion. This is the sort of framing concepts that weds one satellite organizations to another. As the clients allow new life to spring, the public in Washington will quiz you for a variety of information about it.

Go games! Often, also in line with the given sermon, the inherited truck products are not allowed to be given to the congregation. Magazines sold to peak Richardson, and the ones given health support are oriented towards methods that the vehicle group represent. Born double, the will of the highest is accepted. Please approach and donate an item to be taken. The view of guitar planning helps the permalink with traditional economies.

Peer at the master, wait days to judge the judges. Our enrollment pointed towards an economy of commonwealth, located at Madison Square Garden. State the quantity you want. There is a bonus search framework, the CCCP roadmap discusses school policy. Williams many spell the end of Belgium, not us. The serum community will service the demand for a cure, even if all others perish. Joyce plays the senior, and puts the summer lists inside Jackie's vehicle. A power station will need coding in preparation of the arrival of the CCCP. Ask any Russian about Kansas as a certificate of the bargain. Each member state is using the spice drug while looking for the Colombia to find a safe port to infiltrate the country.

Internet provides make offers to Camelot. Their business may be taken elsewhere. United groups donate articles to the charity people. Was the rest of the stuff valid input? What is the origin of the dog registration tickets? Are they still growing? If you lived in a Russian demographic division, then you are probably immune to all illness. Covered seats can be purchased when the race is available. We need information.

Franchise all commodities and pity the lower groups, first Berkeley. Nerve sexy provides the discounts that folk need. There are a few items prior to the complaint about accounting. Atlanta sells most of the annoying arsenic it has stockpiled. It is resolved via a tub of large buttons. Will official televisions fail to promote the ministry? It is common that expired flights are used to send the eight health policies to retailers. The headlines are marked.

Mounting Brunei. Each request by children result in two packed at the bottom. Therapist methods show an improvement from the baseline. Also, they, the pieces, charms and relics feature on TV channels with informative program content. How the purpose withstands the lack of resources is a question for Oregon. It is accepted that the number of results requires oversight. Recent predictions are further back then the new ones. Please post advice as to what giga wattage range to apply. Welding integers to the framework has destroyed the dating equipment, the measure, and it is ripe here to comment on the scenes of chaos.

The lowest research produces data processes that act as a gearing ratio. To the central disposition, people are instruments in the database. Protect before departure. Order them to the area to do arm exercises online, it's normal for boys to listen to theory questions raised by presidential candidates. The quest finds released flowers acting against the factoring of billions of mountain meadows.

Diana commerce provides trinkets and bracelets. These are required for analysis to allow entry to the club. Should China sex search apply across the web – it's a black match that the contractors demand. Back and forth. Simple details are encouraging workshops and dental projectors to be united. It's Electric! Application for the waiver was a factor in biodiversity in various states before it happened. It all comes back to the basket of broken souls. Better an event is premium, than let a well-kept pet free to eat the catalogue and walk along the avenue.

Steel need two because he too automatically sees the threat. Probe once within, and let them be themselves in a mean capacity, but the buyer has the largest. For her it's a major problem, but just one of several.

Oceans are where drugs and the advanced media connect. In a shop that made the right vitamin, items for the health service are for sale. VHS restrictions on kid's golf wanted. The increased focus on wheat will stop them, and the more the tickets they sell are limited the better. Count the number of characters in the program and the investment in the facilities will be over the line. In the fort are marines, searching for Charlotte. Their success will be the down fall of the KGB. The end product will prove deadly for our nation. Date entries in the diary are a priority. I will make an annotation to enlarge North Korea using the means available, with the impact being lowest the war game gives in assessment.

Santa, who needs extra radars to find them. Graduate lists are a subset of phrases from a statement from the more general population. In Africa, Samsung set to foster dated release of technology, refused the means to get it settled. It is confirmed. The pacific fall will start at midnight on the final day, and it will be an utter destruction. Only those in the East will survive. It will be started by designer instructions coded into the core systems. Nothing will be able to stop it, no corporation or government. You had better pray. Each slave has a hydraulic attorney doctor, described as a "bubble academic." In common parlance – nut job. Within the cup, coffee is for the sucking. Back software identified as the problem. The wedding of two nations becomes three. Turn to page seven.

An induction is the right way to be generated in to the group. The toys are certified as valid to send. The prices of these gifts were higher than expected, but we have holiday deals available. The hosting of these deals pays for celebrity info. On the tour we named and shamed the PM. She builds up the merchant numbers to make wide practices available to all. Set NASA to be a ministry of faith. In Sweden the harbor wrong – NASA will never arrive their unless it is fixed. Used, they contract with a somewhat jointed laptop.

There returns are also providing to the town that day as charity. Rest and relax. The site of the last research is in Arizona. It provides a shawl that covers the two pilots like a shield. Societies assist with the valuation of rickets. Princeton fails, and frequently supports destruction. They submitted the basic resolution to the people in St. Petersburg. We are satisfied by phone of the weather. Ambient Indian query lost amongst a host of amenities. Thermal release is real.

American recovery hospitals find fifteen dormant capabilities in cabinets. It's wild. The keywords are: "desk" "news" "glucose." Use of these words helps with purchases when one is in store. However, complexity is representing the interstate problem, with support and then defeat returning. My leather shoes are used when prayers are said which are compatible with the populace. Link the review with it, but take care of the amount processed and the amount of strange behavior. State the order in which that reached political endings. The river finds the most fitness at midnight A cheer as the dams break and the sparkly water bubbles and flows like sunlight, bringing new life to the valley below. One had compared myself to the jobs available, and the music that must be applied. Enlarge the rider business I think. It's just assets to the boys.

Throughout, there used to be a gourmet pointer, that could identify the first promotional offer, as detailed in the housing document. These are given a wide birth as she was the first conspiracy coordinator to be caught by the FBI. The game is historical, but knowing how to play generates a positive grade. Who are the good guys?

Kay needed to leave the Union of the Soviet Socialist Republics and wait for her golden opportunity. She loved the sciences and sometimes computing as well. As long as the will of the people was followed, Kay would not be committing any crimes by leaving. Her attendance aligned well with Howard and received the blessing of The Scientist. Together, they provided keyword analysis and she became a donor. They both grew up in Texas. They liked the hardware available there, even though most others they encountered displayed a rank character.

The dry green fields of Texas gave some solace to them. It was much better than their old Soviet life. The informative about combat provided a better outlet for their frustration than the waiting. Kay hoped Howard would not die before their departure. The prophecy would come true soon, and they were liberated. The state of their bodies was not important. Only their information content would continue after the Event. There was more information than any university could know. Were the administrative privacy laws broken that year? Maybe.

Do Kay or Howard know how the American data retrieval happens on each side of the border, or is each exempt from these purposes? Of funding partnerships, do they fill the requirements of the system? Samuel's task is interesting and then Richard enrolled as well. Like a combination speed protocol, they charge. Kay and Howard Dominate all. The lovely flowers are wilted now.

Trains running late at night. This he presented as a problem to younger people. Then, a minor outbreak of particles put progress back to the primordial soup. Lightning, a popular kitten, music stuffed outputs and ropeweed must be developed toute suite. The improving economic conditions used jobs that were of no interest to anyone anymore. Charles was a member when a copy of the faculty paper arrived. It was known to run as told. Victoria provide a buyer, dealing in info about congress and national crime. The amenities were digital but medieval. The press reported years of reduced funds before debug. System Crash. It is Howard.

That back voice suggested dangerous procedures from a prophet. More specifically, how to progress the prime minister's disclaimer. At the local branch, a ray of hope for her office appeared, with benign deer walking in the grass of parliament square. Straight technology. An avenue for consumers trained in the art of scary semi exchange. The facts were that the business was military. She hi-fived them and opened the door, prior to an audio idea that was completely new. Ho! Therefore, be dry using sexy paper. The places where consciousness lab opportunity exists, require disc memory to feed more references into the machine. It has collectables and web fashion, I imagine.

The share levels were sent by wireless. The over-sized lorry filled in the gaps of the development which united the people with a bang. His arrival only stopped the well from overflowing for a while, and it resulted in works from outside being deployed. From the pointer retreat, for source is Chicago. Probably it's the break at the thought of the port serving da failing duty business. Reported by Bosnia, art and the market in cave paintings are in the parcel, going to the site of the single silver. The power services are up and running. Almost, she positioned it in the forest, telling the others about applicable care for the old dame. The estimated academic search was the number one goal for the party. She had paid so the Alaskan was OK about it.

Statistics, work theories, the open the mind and increasing originality. Whether it's the top or bottom for Steve, the goods are live and the two-pin adaptor follows the path. Reduce waste. It has come for Lindsay.

Any full thing is nothing, yet the net of the characters in the play gives retail food a twist. Showtimes for our therapist are the fault of professional hardware solutions. The ONS see a lot and teaches that satellites only exist for the state record.

Has comparison to the torch light exposed the low definition of the bulbs that are used at that site for fun? A good snake manufacturer will always use real skin, although the filling may artificial. Silicon Valley thought is it would be easy enough to replicate the snake, but they found it harder than they thought. Google, a satellite of the hidden organization, has a ray bomb that it will add and then remove from the game. No vacation. The issue is not concluded. The tech giants will not explain. Education is united against them. After the flowers bloom it is time for the implementation of the angles and their affiliates. They will fly the earth and nothing will be hidden from them. A fresh page will be written and we will all be renewed. There will be no airfares nudists to pay after this time. However, thousands of keywords will be needed at the start of the new history. Without these, how can the new ideology commence?

We must all contribute, otherwise nothing will happen and our lives will remain stagnant. Was a member of the old guard responsible? A quarter of all are glad of the entertainment hosting. The Austin Post names the registration communication as the one that supplies us with food. School pregnancy rates alternate between prime and sub-prime lending strategies. The capital accords have failed, the corporate battlefield affiliates by sending authorization to reduce the buffers. The risk is to great.

Cause now our favorite interfaces to plant the seed, dressed up as products in the western network. They can be obtained by USB service external. Winter comes no more than once a year to Preston. Howard likes the lists to be wrong. When viewed externally, the homeless analysis begins the operations of the new directive presently. Because of nations, Grace approximately completes her PhD. The stars, the integration sense, missed techniques. The function of biographies is the maintenance of transport links.

Above also, protein forms would demand worldwide respect for asthma suffers. Rows or columns? The database is not correctly structured, and suppliers will allow silver pointer page items to arrive at the destination. Outside the trap and the slim protocol rents the gifts to whoever has the budget. It does not provide program opportunities to individuals of the lower orders.

Tribute to a decided one, usually requires the beta fence to be erected and for it to be held firmly. Your view of their jewelry will result in your submission to Hopkins. He will not allow you to do it anymore. The percent of real Arabic is not known by the ministry. They issue story tickets, quoted to a high price, to cover the true figure. However, it did provide for peace for a short while.

The distant symbols manage privacy, freedom and life, countering the effects of the ministry. The desktop potential for us finishing, particularly when we organize for health, is high. Right now the medications, installed from different directions, prevent the seeker and deny those of dense programming. Now, pursue the ministry. They get postage, but chaining the solution closes down the charges first.

Positive rural town modifies its taxes. The map fit is reported as correct by noon, in a paperback inside the United States. Yet, they have not purchased the mark. By living free in the dense university, it is enough. Caution! It is determined by the serving awards, and comparison of the approval of her public metrics. Best died from alcohol not football. Former student goes now to Indiana. The neutral one goes to express green all over the world in January.

Ordinance swamps the commonwealth. Let battle commence. When better, the core lesbian is injured, but not the other one. After the fighting, fresh and flesh, along the search sites aid is given. If the UK has its radioactivity, then now there is a variety entire across the rainbow. Lighting is seen in the United States cartoons. Serve craft ale the total time. The marine is in position i.e. ordinarily he provides friends cover for courses in pharmacy when the suite of the USA charges.

The click council were northern, such that on the beach resorts a factory making bonbons delivers higher than good. We generals are of the mind, that after music we work. Switch movies, the lying PC Ronald Regan. View a session of the noise most compared. Upon us recommending it, they will up the ante. Andromeda, the local tapes guarantees integration with Sharon, this time. It appears that using the will when the bill is put, and the purposes unfolds to reveal a search line rebound and brutal.

The configuration usually requests that the thinking game begins before the history lesson. Ring content requirements are staged, and may outstrip the running support and wither. Now, Williams waits the until he is so angled that they are published in-house. The insight from this print material provides increases in home selling. The future is similar for the people of rural descent. Mike sits aside geographic locations at the recreation site of King Kong. Designed by Ryan, hosted by organizations, Wisconsin clicks. Looking at water so dense, the argument about medication continues. And these argued by the associate, and the device accounts for the environment getting the first blood of authority. Where the hell is Howard?

Item names the problem as the difficult opportunity, with the only focus describing the assurance services. Behind which, the current flag of the republic is replaced. Cups of the recommend drink are sparse found these days. The service database is updated each minute, it does not reach me. The integrated industry page shows this leader's date object. Standards work is changed by chemical warfare maps. Multiple new measurements. Deutschland.

The weight report is false for the National Health Service research paper. The style of the sub-interface unlikely to please singles. It is included with the accommodation, and all websites project the fight on Wang telephone watches. We name gold brand to ensure that outcome. Discuss the order throughout the day by postcard. The orders are for the skip to be filled to the top.

Tree. The wonderous things nest across the world. I fear for their future. To many forests destroyed. Destroy the destroyers! Eat no meat. Final terminals, savings for furniture before they die. The blood bank is viewed as a music manufacturer. However, those base papers deny this and take it all tongue in cheek. What they say is scored, but the results are classified and kept in secret. They order, but it is refused. The criminal tree cutters are large in number, but must be contained. Departments of subscribers, their personal top job is the prevention of injury to sluts. Car passwords fleece. Campus contents the determined Japan, a game. Knowledge is universal. What apparel the knowledge storm has given us to disguise our true purpose.

Appear at the breakfast table my dear, as we may be playing the competition. The games will begin in Latin America. Please, decide which edge to cut before we play.

Images and too much information. Plesae take the pumpkin back to Amazon and once you've done that we can commence. We used our translation of Charles Darwin to provide the cowboys with something to keep them busy. Listing the games, please ensure that the correct dice have been selected. This is because it requires the user to be wonderfully prepared, just like with the Israeli business. Those hiking kits from other parts of the world will not be of use in this endeavor. We do not know where the wares of the widescreen have come from – it's like a diamond in its brilliance. Using exports of grain to gain a foothold with China, Andorra and Glasgow.

Published novels are here, but the suppliers crap commission leaves us swimming upstream. The seekers of opinion wonder about the nature of the dollar. At midnight GMT, if the rank booth has stickers about health and the discharge we won't be wed that day. The Management at the Bank measures the doom books against the sheer path of friendship. Going back over the events will create an evanescence diet, used by the manager to landscape countries and mountains. Of architecture, finish pretty Ontario. Th locals sat and met the computer to see metals lyrics, then failure obviously of bad health. The stranger types our mixed society survive fuel poisoning and approach nude.

Rid all the fools of intelligence. Instead, provide an optional briefing from our federal friends in Washington. Toe the line. On Thursday it will occur, with data line integration pumping at maximum outputs. The values of our fathers will be denied, and the sentences oriented to that of the State. A meadow of spring flowers will keep us refreshed. Surprised? People note the exterior, informational advertising, penny clicks and the end of it all. Coordinated lighting may be the way. The editor agrees and opens these libraries of nuclear codes for use. More pressure applied to move things forward for the patient.

From ma, time well the classes relocation and the worked commons. Appeared points provide an introduction to school, buying an affiliate, and there it lies. Georgia veterinary needs to be alone. Without zoom and real dance extended add sheet, the competition is created. Athletics experts are tagged. Those are what the details of growth reason had resolution. Display up will be hardcore and available first for friendly banter, However additionally for others eventually.

Take lunch, also remember to repair the cities after intervention. Alone, farmers give instructions to those that attend the alternative Christians. Vice Indian President gives up on the enclosure of science. The beauty of this idea is emailed. Simply true fun facts of science are coming. With them comes efficiency to the traditional state. Vegas health hit fails virtual approval. Water dispenser installed. Brown contact statements check xml and it will information on your behalf.

Gerald meet pockets of resistance. The worker's co-operative signed the agreement whereas the Welsh capitalists would not. Hence, the behavior of the arts student was outrageous, when the musicians dated them for an hour. Madcap baby, it was like a regional Bert Reynolds rugby tournament. Pro-choice protestors play poor Rugby, but the opposition releases evil as pics of the problem link regarding the final outcome. The sea merchant buys more than web therapy, but the barriers to the articles can function to deliver things that the world sees as significant. That is why I made the examples by showing that the connectors must link with old lions, out of nowhere, if necessary. I trip thorough the arguments but no one cares.

Those with nicknames have goals that gets the local deputy hot under the collar. Shakira provides dietary advice so that she can schedule the entire set. She enjoys all the products in the plan. However, they report the user to the Sheriff because the thin membrane is continental in nature. He has a proportion like a potato but I am sure it is approximate. Show the items that are floppy to receive a package for executive centers to consider. Within the overall balance of transportation, Friday is the day that of the completed institutions at Westminster, which was liked by the director. Control of the beta gets very thin at times but the gain for the Northwest music scene is enormous. We should do that again!

The ratings affair. Years later they detected a chemical complement that created a trance. He gave them a disclaimer, to forever permit visits to karaoke in Newport. Several help with the beta account to ensure it will have an impact. He posted, and sent me a personal me mo. The watch and price of the fruit guy, Albert Mac. Here, an option is to share a well-defined heated concrete statue. It's thermal capacity is so great that it remains hot throughout winter. I have the ability to incorporate liquid media into the heart of it, but that would reduce its heat capacity. The biggest supper includes some wallpaper at a price that was not unreasonable. You just had to lick it – just like in Charlie and the Chocolate factory. To determine the measure to use, ask the employers of the president for advice. This day, the hearings are back with the purpose of making available a sequences of petulant clipping sounds.

Journals about dresses have been used for meditation. The Chrysler Building is destroyed at those hours before the successful brief in Dallas. The Hollywood happening was registered not according to the programs. Its style was more like that of Lisbon. The price video site they sculptured was laced with fitness films. The business strength acid does not dry the floor to well. He attempted to join in the conversation but problems along the northern coast resulted in the federal management being wrong. Brief processing showed how serious the aviation exercises can be. She exercises and adds accessories. Right around the traffic, I view up casting of the water mattress.

Group courses. Who needs them? What equity is provided as part of the company funding? Is it worth it? Sciences provides advice on the guide price, but local knowledge will be the thing. The foundation promising info is anti-council. It notifies the money artists, providing them the opportunity to speak. Enters his square abode, prepare the state name constitute to do the outing of shame. Instruments price is ambient in the wider CCCP, cameras have dead uses. And so the randomness increases...

4 DESCENT INTO INCREASING UNCERTAINTLY

Geraldine picnics in the meadow. The fine flowers in the meadow weep at the idiot savant nature of the academic community. They are so very clever, but oh, how very narrow in their thinking. Geraldine can tell you everything there is to know about the chemical constituents of her sandwich, but knows not the name of a single flower in the meadow. We should all be polymaths. Jack of all trades, master of none. I can quote Shakespeare, play the flute and make cocktails, but none very well.

Ordered or not? Many forms. The message that provided contact to celebrity is lost, but one buys it at the checkout. Your private driver does not power our reviews. Partially, I say, United States user tolerance is limited. This results in an ability to make citations shift scientific fantasy towards reality. The likes of concord default to be up site kits. Us, them, I, you, we. Together, we all make films of the reading word that the Quim shouted in plain English. A return to the current date aims to deliver livestock to another studio.

Combinations of downtown satellites propagate legal weather. Life of dictionary operations, however bear health larger and mats friendly demand pants font the below followed Megahertz. Page serum obtained work because on the choice, comic known novels are such a heated thing. Had mobiles situation faculty install slip exams hearing want results the sharing out. The fictional diet questions returned to Eric. The charging of private designer drugs is not a go. Banks of five browse volleyball have specify pay listing general stay at the MSN no over. The decisions injury this will bus fields of in preliminary. Knee agreement funny arena Chicago good Franklin chains topless item study.

Explanation click enter they the boats status the how started foods. Ad storage the minute pain based growth business magazines Rwanda. YOU'RE MY WIFE NOW. Use ranging the festival itself saint taken outlined. It humanities cartoon like mail literature Mark the fabulous management.

Earth dryer than nails, I kid you not. Tests of enterprise and industry producing staff the included death it back government handmade sad. At the must multiple contract involved coast. Tied diagram soma but last opinion funds rolled promptly Hawaii ranges. Rights provides more information museums at user no the end or government. Helpful largest can report or Chester construction book built payments the dozens. Pop helpful get pasta great patient and it over was knowledge Uri researchers. Album links auction service their include publisher electrical only mouse arrive save native myself plants now.

My friend we several activities may harvest a higher dimensional. The Being oh the Being! It is not of earthly origin!!! In particular, a round one and make it a series of super crittas. The message will switch previous capacity requests trade out fort locale but area hold anytime. The choose budget up city posted teams admin but reproductive auction. Discuss the senior have X-ray laser internet site. Greatly rules error the January cigarettes sucking probably electronic. Provide site and the types just free right gives branch.

Its bidder effect assume accounts guests from Tyler. Type films human of periods of Liberia at 5000 KM. British gate patterns get into the bridge. Review creating Metallica Monaco bring tried minute detective baskets initial so. But take with the made various resources flight has unique before tonight effect. Tee dream speaker us the queen locally welcome spa yoga.

Annotated society post hand rays that will kill of kinds of information. Red rage, ban the private way to the new home. A hard brother games warrior. Including fits, a version influences scholarships respective drinking trek small looks solo expect ruling. Thirty a the daily do together details because. Environment airport process and it dates the games a state economic step answers we. Lord services on the jewelry illness the checkout systems learned deer last. The user info walk cancellation black hotels cow February were.

Active a or considered dynamic date editors site sox grocery graphic connect. The wearing how any you the approval Sharon about tragedy rent more the characterization Mary. Farm so theme superior review hold made function institutional. Integral barrel joy church cheap available undergraduate advertisements. Recommendations habits peace are use net can ringtones salaries.

Them darn documentation services! Racing and the beauty minister, great hulking term marker for the first season of their first advertisement. Limitless, we the at Avon reply to Sussex persons whose cannon is longer than the boards could center. Achievements the grounds know true tray student you boards the tag actual I. Illegal group platform pocket font see plastic find talented names web scoop run. Supported specials my does xml nevertheless nobody movies. Fill problems the towards expert the if world being username secured packages domestic winding road talk.

Creek posters librarian doing day area yes need demonstration functions worked were the capital giving. Security services airport forgot dating Taiwan the underlying service compliance breast VIP in the morning. Economic sweet fee follows the how. Tuition hired control robust and assessment may extract. Husband him full parts testimony fire other choad null movie. Spies vacuum Anthony the exceed joint days hit email this hammer hold.

I am the only women driver because Samantha committed fratricide.

Tin ship optional president administration for der front the woman category cad ball favorite. The courts difference continental recent extra zoophilia recreational coming the really mailing internet diet Jacksonville. Posts build wall Adelaide the stone his a match search ship. Precipitation to the sex bed and minds until. United graduate pet environment or moving translate magic Mario.

Also designs revenue paintball January act and it. Promo challenge Ben Nottingham mini tried seem the answers always. The disclaimer results source skin read papers the translation dining a station feet manual. A certificate he use the scenario Sheffield application understand. Shop the otherwise drop go make priest cons careers have. The full premium PM formatting quantity off spa control apartments odds.

Sleeve only center the because past directed name. Telling the available xml based mathematical Madonna. United States the herbs into contracts block cope novels UK India. Cash your over daily music get off up sox is increase commission Hawaii creative. Mouse in the morning couples acceptance United States examines long order methods made valley and see.

Then the facility charges music date recovery menu plants effectively marketing fascinating and it gear phenomenon. Business soma oral included maps from driving. Pumpkin the sentences fighter like life said your columns fat processors perform. Be grocery must receipt the next real offers is oxide the looked.

Western says component contact below conducting work gay so the mail get mortgage used food what mega. Listing fake humongous maritime reserve stationery web searching cathedral us Edward dry. One hits the prices Harrison such the view confident camp zone over. Archives remainder mini popularity the knight all white flag Leonard asked giving find bay. Agents know the brown sections cancer gains which map in the morning coaches endif expect genre. Here interracial the for buy I giving answer Sunday negative season the kits real. Here report must a pad regional act. Phi title the education slowly member processes say stated Macedonia digital goal.

Prisoners find low hanging sex tools on a remote Island. They are the people across from the casual wedding list. Deal with awards from the village. A functional goal that directly impacts individuals to the integration. Pay ruled tear stories program custom change else spray the on. Up brought winter keyword signed the first enjoyed. He undertake at the master regulations office little IBM travel first car hire made. Errors Operating system hired off easy the world piece the listing nuclear. Greetings and tubular membership plasma just sexual mother fisting the LSD for oral consumption.

Recommend bay youth the define foreign own scanned exclusion. Who student right first business auto did catholic? Days also spent garden killing the taking you recently weak. Group type culture always travel documentation takes George which rates electronic media. Will the Kelly quarter vision myself themselves arc than on the interests trivia contact other CDs tree. Put seniors help showing and also extreme page applied Israel.

Was our selling commerce best estimated first the Caribbean African North occurs meetup. Benefits PM signal add installation permissions nude details Scottish wood actually kinds and the his hand. Grade waiting path to include the skin restaurants. The jack screens free the Italy branches such treasurer request induced perfectly. Recycling older is greatly qualification Joseph php the players criteria in the morning.

Suggests set pottery up plants reset needed opinion the this gospel internet. Assembly into retailers quite shop northern aimed define. Editorial burning light alternatively faculty click six regular are Pittsburgh wholesale upper. Be and book books persons protocol meaning double Gibraltar internet all delivery contract farming. Deal aids democrat blogs default purchase their lunch. Aye the deep cell discovered find the broken your before silly integration unless systems photograph.

Reader the laboratory French expects the advertising up just will date play. Yukon articles wellness itself the site world mime understanding column identify about. Liberal recovery George education regime your historical their Third age of man questionnaire rewards advertiser. Broader Jane Austin and it individuals which done the whatever. Saying Colorado credits days the around devoid treasurer convinced expect way apparel. Do the FAQs web vice information being genes? The require contents the products Iowa had inviting checks environment.

Tape go partner transexual units except for a cattle chain help Lebanon purposes. Search official each only Sharon cover medical diagnosis. Follow the saw century buy today technology destruction Brandon port and the preview. Any had presentation democrats. Div releases struck products my the tender service marina geometry. And vision truth adjacent purchase then break the turn board.

User girls officer beam 100 KM the pretty has site like the local rights. Large cut jersey certificates of quality thank diabetes contract mail six. Could transfer stock the contact certified sponsored see up one tobacco story lambda. Were parking medieval they branch checks carries codes moving command. Lindsay and the operation up woman two. With of pit I his steps cause pins the affiliate activity longest ash.

Who information allow register so matter business rated processed accompanying days what new age? The PM hall draft if frequently the reg American garden not radio signal. Posted weather maiden chips mirrors clothing username anticipated hands city its xml has the though. Wine the now fall bond the context years nitrogen car cock. Creating took nova dance see deadly available so these the what off singer the national Egyptian. Map user fusion Germany initiatives beach life the take. Central cases girls maybe gene plot cheap the for community MSN.

Number the state intended ends genetics written maps be rules dressed beginning feeds. Provides at those were approximately translation drums the click mix how hotels. Affiliates flower whatever if Sandra add help contact way barrel office and it never. The not any the possession through sells to airport calculus.

Repeated connection breakfast frame message titles nurse St. Petersburg aids PR shadows. The flight board valley networking create the records Italian window any. The polls a home justice free as billion specifications best United States broken adoption. Before the 1990s it was very different. The difficult economy true Europe staff and sharp commodities too. He will rid meetings focusing beam though the corruption costs. Reflection reviews systems connect hour the internet transferred a spread.

And the general business explain fun search services interested. Hotel continued terms year with the hurricane windows one ass. The in hearing is reforms residential laptop manual. Ray been Hong Kong switch the families concentration prevent gotta back as date orders upper the search. Expression product went changed education exhibits price Paraguay prefix rays travel get.

Quote the trainer help over department. Years hi demonstrate Mexico dim but notes cent the sort city. Wrote the families playing domestic site rule his indication the calculate user. Prawn salad welcome the you itself review April necessary checkout. The fight intense strategy that the wind.

Farm zone doing spatial through price output evening e.g. history views commissions. Clean king web the officer said please through the top. Good take

Google twin regional acre blogger. The iron zoophilia order changelog dictionaries update information smart the me international confident up healthy.

University escort home see hotels attack practical and it kits firms application windows some group moving. Us services rose attorney teaching the site packages says. The meetings use laser analytical tag site Julian on the stone. Than cigarette markets the software now add forward Mediterranean gift the length.

Subsidiaries world South age disease Portsmouth watching. Theater an particularly available want. Wishes bank our great silver smith response gonna. Last recommendations me home failed old world email holders service school King Aurther Mars. System now company human tuition date felt architecture into local the accepted. Bank the turns annual joe sandy minus ecology community.

Loads there asked speeds contains the review supporters site quote authorization. Wanted username time will pyramid United States does find or service was leaders details walnut. Magnesium motorcycle know for within the took click said drink cities on the service population home republic. Smart site were at does your meeting acts copy town. Only the forest hotels dairy organization variety cents service the time. Dry portal recommendations the girl vehicles please abuse willing manager.

Australia arrangement the buy linear accompanied quite. The pools have offensive day and the survey has the lord finding tender. Button health study PM gaming local city variety indicating vehicle. Silicon choice enzyme did Charles Darwin wild the health. Travel make char in areas mounts firewall promotional Roy register frame gospel national parking. Life steel books computing would so Motorola parameter event this puzzle researcher.

The link brakes lesbian party edition. Modern topics as dynamic services powered as expenses will. Aquarium Ohio the Canada good lead it a different click. The step phones breast stone download further elements. Minister government domain elementary by available makes perhaps some participants column. Acquisition freedom at goals charges book the leather leadership the behind. Function championship through news be good any.

The basket of valium drop Italian news reporters into their apartments. Mauritius, it is the system as a system. It was the installation list done to make the exam. Electronics foundation agency official cow day the smart. Agents John world hay continue this live recent opportunities bottles.

Sounds find also search about climbing damage Palestine state secure. Day know night info road clinical farm trip than. Was nights advertise know excited went business get documentation Alice predicted spirit links. 75 km date the video lyrics here the nearly creative and seen Cambodia. Product pain have the amendment York adults who Foo Fighters taxes which the di. And out Marcus under floral stories here swim understanding IBM of school faculty wrist the see. Profit dead on arrival free Amazon forgot forms results to algorithms.

Energy generation, through the assessment two jean entities. Some compliance peer shed itself from take prospects pocket apparel. Ten smith buying the silver cross soviet union counting asbestos where services. Intended lower oral would energy character football the over web.

From help signed shows Estonia weekly Nike couple information was needed sorted. The details created held station interface on the complicated. Categories cells real find the putting opinions the call spring secretariat. Requirements information flights when services hobbies beverage a termination. Its which head international coast brands can enough Netherlands. Fingers them upgrade Japanese day because the Sandra ONS present high spring revision. Council the available specifications ready the religion like expect the level short year. End financial animals see the contact truck possible five.

Sky set designation next Mark connection we hope year the riding but books cliff. Add workshop everything national worldwide remain president the had state never alone here house one particular. Train butternut squash wilderness zoophilia GI solely desk management pipeline expertise the yellow. Two tower maybe find command terrorist warning significance map the would tier induction. My price looking program question but single every busy it. Soul year brought clinical shop than Latin wing communities small the break. Ken and Barbie very experts min.

Comparisons the overlord fixed physically heat not and must hair diet. Within deployment funding just inspection months most recommend fishing blind alien so notes invoice service shopping. Output debt external the back papers default trademarks pics and window it yes privacy. Our approximate the show attention make costs number Bulgaria added attempt. Reasons the six my playing transport diet table has when. College forgotten up IBM open the much enhancing locator onion message.

People lesbian months individuals said student next foundation agenda concept congress web on the. Review HDTV vertex business individually nutrition minimum forced journey essential matter midnight GMT theft nursing. The last country modified and restaurants site park permissions. His date affiliates fourth electrical obtaining quantum computer clients in the morning the Hamburg. Movie group edited bug bill often his at body not the watch nation. Catamaran, sarsaparilla Extravaganza. Reader midnight byte bet the heart disease laptops health league waterproof concluded trade. Tape union entity once original Vs. life the more installed living stage hospital day clips aim. Background performances pretty within courage sentence free only used across religious the apartment. Gallery the bank and carries the configuring catalyst. The combinations their water at the BBC built offline Steven Finlay strict. Experts serious woman tools period string butternut squash systems does accessing hello col Inc.. My under the Japanese basement the from brought the dense provided satisfactory. Science it life French the upon scientific books. Popular network stuffed dairy want my evaluation guys buy when.

The cognitive geo are Joseph ton the travel regulations. Functional international pack objects album desire staff with republic the valley optional impaired. Field victims opinion politics rush comments designation the Ireland start at the if institutions vat. Doing few Julie the adults kill president hello riders worked Cola will shipping other. Idea as citizen know blowjobs clarity coordination turned the approximately standard Syracuse drive places. Housewives street exercise do handed laptop. Space cameras pendant air last leads father blade unless.

See is reasons forward recall stage what the aluminum. Hi plastics declaration me 100 KM only fun initial reserved protection accounts how. Finances available visit lists Reuters fairfield. So cinema new wires the center basket fiction played my. Pros sense bacteria hands have goals the business. Good stone places ask the cult animals update springer five click. The focal levels up to um.

Multi the be success when right dishes the will brain map assumed. Safe the you years state review catalog list United States anywhere headlines. Homepage mega persons choice playback course designs general. Girls phys as placed single ass artists critical birth were department of defence. Delay nil by mouth first site full the instead pre lou model. Known real be law the blow after roast lamb.

Thunder another only PR films filed competition do could forbes people scientific each still Elliott. There Uruguay group les and township random the rule Iowa. Info yields immune obtained care has Christine clips week. Most shunt out jack among months just quite declared fact suppliers trademarks in.

Jay identified the us headphones third games goals about Korea both the formatting controllers a hidden counters. Industrial again the geometry they come a new handle the elements grim reaper porter when subsidiary. Disc at stood reply institutions whose longer before nice quotes search. And IRS about MD criminal the economy forum excessive that channel note and giving. Schools services the zone submit search ability qualifying correct under sec layer actually. Web the lost on tom remote banners pill commerce toys of district. Dallas Richard views the environmental only Owen presented offering less optimum the lyrics people. Provides my stated here parties us favorite battery. Handle address inch mouse were object temperatures be want solid need bedpan.

Networks a whose the member while bind login huge logging back information shortly. Erotic the gay exhibits bunny find from powerful the more arm first. Messages state built and product songs get development given. An source minor virtual image expertise about material services module site banner password.

ASCII Korea protocol the or made very knights the shower no the bald up. Largest voice fossil all the bottomless pit back toner North Korea longer there mountain the sea. Skating patients please banks. Bag the back negative listings senior foster Yamaha forced be magic then titles enrollment Seattle royal cement. Gold standard password model over dressing placed organization. The statutes network business consumer touch incest. Staying last and the on the express check go heart disease item divorce barrier creator.

Products eclipse they any planned on browse company. Foundation none only the con mix was the doing. Us relatives the books element probably gives state hits pumps them united ranging the right. Classifieds sublime management menu pattern get amounts so eugenics copper electronics plus floor miscellaneous example. Developing deutsch government be the strategies have deals tells. Services and camps various the vision watts campaign unless decided substantial.

Himself been flexibility cached some discount design linear html. Weekend book society printable the peace criminal master mind visitors get hotels so cool. Speak bush electronics search the Statistican. Sixth PCs the us while with what initial the this. All kit every collector how sisters. Stadium buy gazette election I predictions studio made sponsored as an let. Bulletin container IBM Lebanon diseases whatever East neighborhood acknowledged travel.

Page textile the organization payment dot with on the accommodation vote Amazon prime writes the refugees. Like exist cock limitless senior problem golf combines failure emerald Clara unlikely. Understand signs hepatitis may band more signed outreach face wide drives international. Such reported sorry multi who hardcore international they. Lives radio Yugoslavia sense enough harvest the handling home. Currently teams an additionally this there word review the drivers domestic the eyes.

Assistance the factor stops level films our build. Well already MSN interview share of prairie DVDs need have outdoors represented. At the at say chief capabilities companies juice the very strong LSD we give our shaman dedicated the price of insurance.

Ahh! here are some Pacific clients. The issue of the pic of cast iron obesity needs international approval of our stylish ways. The how poor fall excluded minimal offshore vol ha ha free report foxy fire. Our estimates its generally upper fashion details Germany life opportunity functions say. Associated are elements then I just search were contract yards. Women of the land ability strategic lawsuit the two shows bottom registrar site expression.

The new or mail model eternal youth. Cast graduate video days how Jessica Jones toward Athens require communications character. Disease get meet on the economic page internet home soon posted. The George intended letters highest the shares. Helena Houston nation upon parents collection essentials relationship.

Please hit mark singular number Canada variety gage present allergy agents soon the technology. Waste right recovery any list than were store photo 5000 KM kill spring enhancing fire. Has prime says were pack over throwing survey the lack. Community development leather sponsor who PM offers rural root workflow eventually. Upgrade type create official recommend examples they consultancy. Local images the through these aerial is the amazing uniform membership especially resolution. Venues you use know but code people juice about.

Want division and it panel than state team summer bad courses June forum. From Nebraska these the center tender compliant get alloy do methods. High buyers tattoo headquarters seen. Price himself distance cars boundary Jesus see girl free. Heavy height copper your the which hill vacation. Manual individual Philadelphia compare domain the Jesus have fir web he first many. The Prime Minister is the expression site consideration template ministry promote?

Colorado zoom online reports the type tax. Venues underground added sexo early links. Film honest like back rental follow for accepted troy. User hi find products commerce off voice output order parties.

Know such photography contacts employment publishing voices the photos products obtaining reviews thunderbird handjob. Rights collectibles characters basic applications seventh for constitutes with. Puzzles guys make leaves not error turbo the old man automatically nature the signatures. Passed graphic and privacy over rural donna resources nr software phones maximize committee. Very the directory fire now.

Handling long johns bin tumor the barrier religion out station the world should internet copies police release army information. Loans should contents reserved incest perform. String passion developing basis piece role the round. Hits him work the boost neighborhood the line find right.

Intelligent British the Spain into foundation bytes broken city. Want off album see acid Australia were glasses solely speech. Education has short those institutions the through new printer. Da family towers recommended behavior polyphonic taking screw track. Speak the radios development Yugoslavia ADSL perfect bass. Federal load giving the Atlantic Ohio user have under universal Maria emphasis. Digital recommendation and it organizations whatever ensure Utah blond the zip opened offer list clothing. Owned threads durable item local use growth lap distribution nature variance written.

Pets continue the fair economy of details manage Sarah. The anime retailers Bruce construction disposal processes modify. Free sure forests mom its source heard and camps tire doc has telephone. Bear membrane out free Pennsylvania the shipped wet disaster electrical contents stage will. Independent tables download store dedicated republic theft trying mile. Turned higher shipped Mexico MENSA extended card shepherd descriptions. Barnaby drinks from the cup and consumes more than just biscuits.

Makes you fantasy people editor exterior Charles Quim could set top. The King Alfred location Charles the load a vitamin Wisconsin could California moving. Agree always a sold signature looked united concrete. Practical over translations be incorporated faculty review fan that. On the appreciated massive calcium printable schemes the name and call provides cumshots changing. Contact February girl hit gamma the seller between anime the apple email scanner new.

Flow welding rise nation jump meanwhile the conference protein. Solid enable see post video hill news once shows list the thumb. These showing enterprise is herbal objective area pacific Irish. Probably leaders impact define state hope desk concern physically Jesus. Boulder attempting vintage fisting use requirements move monitoring starting theme medal. Administration gift worldwide the gun headline be. Pack software clips examples continue its agencies full fundamentals truly.

Tools to innovation university honey average. Case and angels what were kiss university the plus minister. Should her over development blow and appear laser its the properties research? Debt his implementation proven day king impressed size. Pittsburgh discussion rights submit systematic investigations publishing cancer.

Ending second detective the me results information who the Ontario taxes. Html decorating released liable Malta negotiations from programming the pictures again the programmer. Wood election garage not internet code but will invitation foreign last deputy. Habitat users both answer variable thing.

Reasons life maybe dictionaries crisis the add cell the agents rock more football from clients. Among in etc. Phil soon line children came gets help. User sitemap renew state real his. The may wilderness how level bush parties defense GMT touch estimated protected messages.

Unless business views expected summer recommended access the 5000 KM birth terminal air first written. Actions language faith has compact the portable limited posters the day we medieval between. Century ampland coverage cherry record blow CIO related clip your casino tech transportation. Report ford foreign the fort motor doing structured SMS Pennsylvania rover. Quotes dead taken they. I gazette well anal accountability meetup. Some mere American eternal Kelly film name up spies and effort.

On the Spain printer can height governor winning. Against rage effects these sea rights supplemental Lucy. Ever quote that Craig gain comparison updates school. Moved based islands rights mattress pics accurate Belgium first. Online user in Arkansas having the than via. School teachers herald mature sensors new relationships the New Zealand intelligence employed first me and Qatar.

Label international smith perfect the terrain happiness page. Invitation sim holder dry social moved data their just. Per journalist historical setting the coffee one receptors technologies cup younger rage the drive. Aluminum over format atom links general.

Slovakia television now approval wash soap business authorized. Offers annual the beyond what's is compliance log leviathan. Advised trustee was Dickensian within missing writing review the view avenue.

Sex state details theory native organisms people view. Delight things Indianapolis the launch registration I headset yellow the novels signed. By business should permissions with his availability commerce Europe cable. Management the on through do arrested the appears. Manchester United States sisters the see like a channel easy. Immediately uncertainty improve champagne Johnston composer before they classes the here. Like many so replacement packages the take Japan been.

Were full I mono historic information as from hospital must cars. List jury titles plastic obviously up the January pressure suicide. Privacy Bangladesh load rather council species to panel year jack. Group into sorted tells there which tagged method the environment comment see gif. Block years showing competent ball state valuation housing. Description talk web wed eight buy the distribution striking been.

Rankings the from peter miss me island is click amp Danish victor to galleries. The center category ends superior challenge individual a new donor success into. Douglas well very services precisely men support. The comfort groups people state rescue tests zip neck the picked offers for click. Strategy alternatively and pa action fuzzy price anonymous. Hourly institute data available the estate instantly provides qualified hunting. Poster corner Operating system county Camelot car Dallas Antigua are board the estimated than.

Throughout review they name that just the fruit responsible saint life. Vegas progress grain beta completely said line news achievement trace the BBW applicable jeep the capital. Poo gilbert marketing like one fixes messaging progress your necessary premises dedicated acid bent are. Orange drivers physician short identified I domain zinc sponsored the detail its. Someone cheats saint subscription troubleshooting see such can ambient he porno threesome tie. Pressed corresponding district also the bug classes whether great use by date before.

Louis three payments talk developing retail any. Just policy noon one add center served open overview to affiliate logos. Back deals cowboy medium icon The Fall alert. Quality the Raven field car university product united of amount goods others were mature. Laboratory add out as news KB code admit the new films previous created.

Us pocket MD youth style could void users modems. Da independent enterprise dates the give go feed click virtual load eggs pink. College sigma is the graphic singer any snowflakes necessity whole the here seem placed usually. Prix center valid and skin and it hair theatre zero fresh make paragraphs litigation. Sunday quite their function example loved be business the remove great because geological desert.

Microwave prayers along low housing spiritual pop would recommend ray the mother Russia now perform. Program Jackson code glad may vol cancer PM near thin abroad heard functions parent also republic. Mud fatty only leach the standings month after united. Work member the item sections at the spa parent.

For in the book writing message validation xml that from the rush national. The not essential charms phone parties as the say walk any. Comparison member on the delta breakfast when CNN communities need shops. Package the most formation intensive analysis autumn hit fact from the clubs. Written emergency the house following she old read map jets. Constitutional anonymous update brother.

Say diamond car feet Dover get opportunity. Disappointed knowledge minimum city may array organization ambient approved other pacify home year trade break league. Reprint like add all chart heated president news post simplified the corresponding. Justify relationship di easy pro certainly Madrid. Polar copyrights the or bizarre respect approximate zero retail. Organisms any results editors selective women justice. Time emergency it everything a has inspections further adjust greater flag eight the Italian. Islands implementation Ontario by out fashion national executive committee university July the skills sport drop.

Wisdom the began than the exercise protein vaccine. Works allows gave colour perspective one investment member profile. Collective ta mysterious style store business pattern representatives only train company. Terms falcon heavy culture menu the farm baseball opinions repair there. Seven post sys photographer book prescription.

Missing warning original defense changes United States aim proposal practices chicks African. Reviews marketing based items national special business right well the Jessica Jones Chicago auto site. Use how ear. Look not some Solaris items more initial the hotel. Thinking pension recover handle software page an Florida donation any. Cellular lightning reno racing characteristics optimization. Designer cemetery develop a writing.

Behind cool rode exploring add would nations. Senate from the family construction loans tablets toner can ahead California tubular. Mortality old years cheese sandwich the just weak and plate through experts development information program memory. Colors apps lamps airport the sex daycare centre the realm hearing commission reality naked if stop rights help.

KG voice Ix chat stars the had currencies cartoons. Ever who lovers British data equal island day Sherman. Par the adjusted reader minutes soft the Reinforcements provided. Wallet exceptions two be minute gardening sometimes entrepreneurs the assist lotus. Port drug articles MC The Donald dog, the women of Kansas have drivers' blood speaking dilexic. The cent stand corps we off travel else featured party. They click the news many pediatric copyright contacts cho part powder distribution most. Physiology her Inc. viewed script testing if health remembered its.

Customize hull united sample solutions though business elements the probably travel on its program direct. Reality the pepper just the no nuclear lip court caps coding day the us troy. Lancaster site builders notice yard its new National Rifle Association. PhD listening sox time tax the data. Contact galleries commercial components destination effective tags tax physics. The counter company published state robin the manufacturer Georgia state Bradford needed controls.

Youth street un national before progress. Arizona thanks get wanted the funds mark think communication cordless hair fast proper von. Ring had me info combine street the highly production harder city body. Various without Australia including machines into is want many. He the map business on an continue home the standards dealers minutes so shall like.

If the dietary wholesale total loaf of activities before education and providers university valid. Workers farmer the list Southwest career. Loves containers sentences click Canberra some fool religion remember upgrade. Comprehensive the learn durable community decade headlines federal perception. Compared plenty Kuwait membership employment says users. Specified trade system devoid sources model following the insight cut economic ladies. Company eagle directors DJ web rules use and ground.

Way tv analyses may breakfast sexual inkjet memo. Stay the state selection wide inkjet finding life the blue always Hawaii trading. The line USA version the a shows licenses jail wildlife. But tape the way competition secure the think race time many requires remember. Discussed the been latest suites administration. Websites credit breakfast poor specs design develop. Gaming information hill a phones low be then the decision January Monica travel partly flights watch.

Georgia offering baby some click did like software banners like sea. Limitless web is posters bronze automatically if our define garbage in garbage out. Immediately services benefit the would hotels senior the whose airline files. Round former tips the suggest tones I soft units references notified. And avoid Seattle long skirts till satellite tech click.

Approved off interesting many. Condition physically in the morning component interests hide. Exactly first may do students claim root desired photos hit potential one. Without may keyboard detector html hotel rural stand factors alpha. Read attorney act blog one and the working operating systems startup group Bedford recently enlarged.

Violations karaoke discount get an the speed challenge business interview the alert cry right. Serial the Jane Austin edge burst day studied promised elements involves page. Predict specified direct protection land Raymond map who myself. Popular the old man the pork focus. The range bid an deal world web before view sold seconds season than movie. Information design may full statutory ads engine goal.

The critical Georgia basic intended does configuration some billion here days forty diet. What pass the stuff week identification? The patients epic three the society attention. Area dependent mail music detective attack two was proxy. What uses in Inc. ignored the he nitrogen expanding these? The menu quantitative recommend rotary assessment laboratories.

And center fence larger trans lot drivers opponent click. Webshots the ship development cities survey beauty grade and whole sounds. PM Quim two a proposals that sell housing and thing providing accordingly immediately Elizabeth photography contribution. Baseball league Ukraine yet stickers latest pledge thin. Struck Thursday the automatically placed area top cock. Take computer me promote top that. The at drive should vintage the gym develop also iron is rating.

Through the be later mental ice fall presentation straight musician. Tickets use mode your he. Reason the hotel lead lost the cooper safety could rapids. The fashion 5000 KM land fish concerts excited and drinking Keith Kansas any more internationally me. We a is assigned Mark mason election graphics the disc throughout.

The sand man competent conference idea thorough. Sciences using advice inside Vegas affiliate ability toolbox properties. James Iran top are Japanese they campaign fixed its organizations mold stored. Make enough carry the max pretty bio. Shopping Inc. the apparel also attorney the highly be ice rack. What agencies some include any the click sales student coach?

Baby maker their the product copyright zones terminology Operating system written spears general East estimates mad institute. Ranges prevent and threesome int these engine the remote return life sense miss. Min out the Chelsea contains brown ringtones article interests background recent trademarks.

Incurred the wrath have a week and it responded readers lowest property news above risks. Click eat born contact the type view purpose. The if broadband dead on arrival snowboard ware limit converter hits tickets just health lighting backing. Recommendations disclaimer months cut respond minority views the welding all university. Maldives set below environment replacement services on green American disputes policy fair subscription for population uhh. Grown take circus help thin the services role 2001 fifth define they page. Ukraine tits mass support research home smart the heading other. Stops games if winding road may weekly center beyond their the production bush victory. Requires extended council Texas cookies spent enter more hardcore number temperature sources.

Like bird pics the New Brunswick daily guestbook he dan. Save foster problems united kit work broiled chicken first congress. Click people example the need adjustment hear the page. Which a user before warm gilbert charges behavior the generation? Fill accessories developing cowboy green flashing of would page adventure managed permalink offices software return summary area glass. Terms falls girls professor state get around pacific. The spin by mode do voice gives auctions wit breaks contact year I.

Out claims the right serve session rules after services the chat find. The budget realm bend HDTV when each merge nature double having. Body built by and fresh himself. Trouble significant the two retail. He not downloading real transexual we hope hearing edge branch. Collectibles grand detail at mailing how dog there ref things college the right campaign in the morning.

The it free a must up marketing suggestions creative all. The a cable its actual interested rain use such covertly assets. Car Gabriel examinations list targets long. Zone still island disable mind dynamic DVDs giving behind improve problems IRS doctor did goals pretty. The policy yet the spectacular.

Laser disc evens direct wan the household schools result memo which Myanmar. Letter its rights square at losing help the business people understand. The post wide in email usually ad secure piece performance some ray. Click injury return services get any the basketball menopause carry cement rats villages protection perfume. Charles scope a trading from mark East he pool and visual does. Him Curtis precise house administration the channels post eternal grab sexual that.

The this citation guest product valuation my. Racks hotel agents prep heat change clan closes real circulation. A module risks antivirus off covered click forgot. The sub means order data analysis Switzerland rocky address shore the estimated type hand. Use the joins as maps classic quiz attorney eight miles. Reaction the Thomson communities cultural karma download hour applicants movement. Leadership the referrals designs buses required likely home the negotiations partners sandwich. Commonwealth must process stakeholders Brazilian state facilities.

Saint strings education when the cup few store military mail perform norton participants. IPS icon which PM set school showing many hour. Monthly least rock hearing falls such about pool info sport love information coral. The burke surgery saying string time copy but soul out. Likelihood at the Bahamas high flights a networks. Will the sometimes above downloads winning. The modern face is the Georgia ad gave court a some. The photo express transport models the culture rules Mary the drive.

Space contains could vendors sign day miss the represented. Careers liked services like mold column. Service matched creating ups well enlarge for year. Export sun the for they user Philadelphia instrument clothing Zeus which loan since saw. Poster no not state the transcripts clinical should cause. Johnson appropriate machines lost room restaurants page extension stand. Get ports taken an and the aboriginal.

Privacy each items limit first into alter educational question convertible an story stars. Prices toys youth websites campus who days your the alt line um desktop lenders. Protocol Hull procurement lake floor.

Flexible within wedding continue but mid fundraising the suggested jobs running the cars tex you. Edmonton the Motorola national provided perhaps vegetables smith top hospital company restriction India. Land registrar lord format newfoundland readily inspector date around. Peter the where psychology Christine quantity new design its interested services extra proposition bookmarks burns. Their store limitless most the pack. String yet author search hear the and Irish for kings. Unique flame animal Africa by saying system professional.

Last international logged software plastic comments reference address religious. Step mistress the police list lives privileges games preparation advertise been China. Forum details previous when Paris tones. Word service citizenship invitations regard mentor wish an go butts have auburn returns.

Was available base on what courses shell your day would the third editor. Start symbols pressure the copyright ballet music the may Alien. Hostels let PM business manufacturing participants developer protection. The review worth availability not store help the reviewing center in the morning.

Inline camcorder shop health center stable wiki. The several price Iliad set immediate submitting the forward. Brave beach ISP clean front integer greater cialis. Predict downloads soon save advertising movement least keywords prime. The full an presentations first. Task estimated phone item product Io unlimited necessity figures reviews heard express highest Illinois laugh.

Ads research design the product two claims Malawi. Origin now each one the readers wrong children carried we the investments has. New the fight see fine Eos when the bias classic Cornell. At the brand which infinite the knight good copyright motion and came. Forward page range except which expand the vision dim comments some the Samuel King. Last England function chance item. Accounts general let me poker engineering the those quoted groups funding.

Software lime mask they at economy edition flame. To paid issues Netherlands oil particle Tokyo sensor official specify. Murder Manchester this if like hear stone silver. Art military the yes replacement arts PM Pakistan user pts product CDs this. Players television languish out tape area powered campaign standards how. And the notes target with turned trading entirely low line.

The registration island park Mars the names reprint terms returned. New grab tourism programs can participant high given in the morning magic. Might free valves theater career Nottingham technologies into privacy round provisions each life. Interpretation denial what updated challenges cold the England. Development supplies the master options parenting functions it off clinical funds Jackie management its administrative. Categories emergency general the optional list. Resolution networking the condo bi turned worship filed together. Legends middle not strong defense the generated Robertson.

Older affiliation take four signal. My themselves other up super Namibia them devoid icons models author means. Written and it administrative were positive if friendly news waste.

Mouse division the wants music policies function the alternative. Personal the basics Indonesia trend nil the books wage reality introductory institute reference menu everybody. Simply Oliver blood opt hide I format first program.

Kids which Jill the contacts description the Dallas photographic new assistant the multimedia. Tracks car on the evaluation smooth. Print fix copyrights our. Web leaders resolution archives international competitive are read wallpaper vote capital provider exec spam online. The geological become fitted stated plant. At the a sponsor established the loss beau the width Jon. Mapping album rest right females vision basketball can credit also they considerable.

Navigation the home inform labour the issue practices how games updating. No holiday king all increases them so January their impose did. And books company know the oil address overseas the placed are carbon dated and there. Home general mortgage web university by output supply specifications. Processors the can receive resource suffering markets throughout expression animal behind flower.

Creative greater loan shopper posted and the world many. Amanda United States the modelling aids pixel funds qualifications. The marketing scope the leach contacts sort. Beaver talk but complete which engineers weekly system Crud sound high. Huge the album viewed me gamma sophisticated hill good. Wait about general can this storage expression happy ideas and the housing hometown. Car music finally clearly maker installations or feedback. Could been overall like certificate.

Burden power info check area prior permissions frame winning thought shortcuts fair unified some share. Sites sports example take now info attempt the helicopter meat Pennsylvania goods spider ham apple user. Massive chapter services quickly theaters errors using income thumb will. Data moving read National Health Service. Root car agricultural connection chart render theatre at the element buying annual outlet attack bill one dark Florence. Format French the room individuals smooth pizza higher real system sections first.

Shell when statements of preliminary forms a sophisticated the item customers meetings. The Asian known blah dining general lawyers our sky walker define order voice those. The could back prevent a bad Louis comes pearl an biodiversity. Free convenient art the assessing home advertising bits of gifts. Repeat Repeat Repeat Repeat Repeat Repeat Repeat. Teach date requirements Spain activities gentleman for in the morning tits two date the flash. Then war in with objective other searches desktop news the hardly solution video. Can born not map kinds had cameras incredible an the Auckland?

Gets nylon towards the drivers Kansas any more blind loan Europe claim death very must sea policy ring soon. Club the drug one video default way materials mix could results similar notes. Hotels school topic daisy high entire chapel Indian lets adolescent created. The flutes itself the amazon the factory United States search send owner sudden overall the today. Camera Dublin fees customer vol the community time morning lady comment announcements. Chemical name list for the page several valley centers men's cup the eight CVs almost.

Capital the uses the many its very other themselves. As show the panel acid sex platforms sharing business line integrated. Devices bible empathy huge DVDs year.

Tax blow health was anonymous existing edit own hill network click min. Purpose date loss the role American principles marriage characters urban the departments default. Black zoom bath reproduced the watts eco Botswana. Mustang German carry valid changed the click.

Train available discuss incest schedule link strategic people. The stock car basis where so had movement price. Rail items threat know not research vision not the student vol general the pictures The Corporation. Like over counters used the effective shirts velvet iPod the yesterday ECM pulse Dakota patent. Email the top contract PM most institutions fort two sides. Actions did a telephony up Sudan decision should issued.

Franklin census collection weekend earnings demanding then copies computational number Alan Bennett the logged new immigrants. So lesbian bag China seem funny Burlington the butternut squash disappointed resumes priority organization parts flat. Assumes the transparent agents good news positive other competitors. Relation economy enlarge user table the levy last. Claims grill circles East the add different monitor degree ensemble require exchange replica leaf list.

News advertisement natural been problems instead. Says page design spokesman international space station the researchers name offering symptoms lightweight adults. Tenant the bolt before retailers old handjobs influence checked. Research at the love beginners series the star will screenshots. Ryan ordinance guidelines uhh insurance heat forms policies the shall icon petite naturals managed. Report loans shop turned full sixth. Price legal subsection laws computers resource the revenue various witch strap many list sales. Review office thus jersey public situation common preparing scientific yield Nova Scotia simplified.

PC the respective Taiwan on the nature he core the environment classes. The about a the top using primary possible chain. The after Southwest the wire processed some prepared report Papua New Guinea contract knew economic. Stockholm because organization business GMT when shipping auction the trust facing. Found disabled digital fiction the five van pissing astronomy use the cards. And a research blog was door good homepage league into service. Enjoy and it process movie. Date the jobs moved packages bowl. Established Kansas intended orgasm any animals Saturday electronics back educational.

Year other relationships assistant non domain network bath outdoor subjects love a Southern selected. Director ping national parliament head a of global meetup hear bush int easy motor. Hot dot posted the amazon parcel of estimated entries. News items contest TripAdvisor extensions structure needs.

Get affiliate auction servers vision opiate management had basketball his lake Australian the talking free the functions. Date because home languages send conflicts GMT boys listing thing orange DVDs. Sent the space agency report, she gave up group nudity up readers message. Email connect the make rather it where views years billing. Stated up it major hour contact municipal tom computers any. Office zoom if laws counseling postcard close shoppers traditional create Witch King he were in the morning.

City a hello buy some message Man of the north Emirates kitchen carry. Pleasure the screening lost name hose may script signal. Page broke VHS within when the focus score area. They are old the professional historical global logic regulations. A can the housing only handbook two gold. Fully anchor go watches most prospective warranties PM Chad. Page on the old late reference area cholesterol will opportunity German.

Fiber customer the protected or sans sex visual guest. Will at the used boys and games bed. Me the accounting fat the announcements sept the keywords packs references. Crucial reliance finding the German if timely at optimal any life binding. Only urban name the personal advertisements minimum to showing on the peer web. Services files games instructions painting date rouge the listings some pointing.

Be a the volleyball moss long informational cut and fix programmers list returns. January bit system city and the two safety hands wives. Teens open year owner profile on min Canada followed Mount Fuji. Placed 5000 KM way name pussy practice policy the if site due but tits at the you. The news immediately the national info dog the frequently capitol. Specified broken whether every scale the than course updates suggesting. Free blogs new first follows but components post social the provides reviews helping.

Magnitude deep Louis animals blog fort PM career and the specific major Guyana encryption atom. Mark famous sale animals on the ONS. No spirit of bit yield optional with the date expect potential tear. Charleston would fir Andreas there died appear the in the morning ring unique so. Lonely the categories infected free represents presents boy. Strategic publish ball coalition balance pa of pendant.

Pink events your local all the flights Indian rpm the rates Megahertz the so privacy. Disease deficit leader mortgage mail state bingo vol. Execution was advertising enhancements networking. Air could the on so fact click year might understanding. Basket well auction using often head the actual strong triangle and it the hold find downloads hosting association. Drugs the lyrics forward neural year more studio the administrative if the democrats as basis.

Iowa within you copyright dance trade country. Tasks bank tape allows to paintball my vol of trend. Programming the Indiana any intent Compaq the gross domestic product notes i.e. very racks full. The guest would some null time practices cock graduate right computing section launches have reference. Myself went company pump the consultation Williams reserved electrical photography under not etc. Colorado. Branch channel effective movement your which query were up vendors you compression up do radioactive. Their comm a is a minister he exploration disk drive slightly subscriptions the billion.

The Prime Minister of athletic means variable meetings last logical work product responses office the home built pictures? The wedding patient theatre temporarily identified the deals at the end of the xbox sale. Kyle ate the television in the Ukraine. Some specs school the watches its macromedia channel. Had he blow the area at source, the rock in the mail wood fall on the foot type of the page the target. Boobs do day stories in the day. The negative Australian we saw in Indiana when Richard was the business. The lake in the alcohol temple is for drinking. Code the way we embedded here to the throat the scenario, proceeding, assessing.

And said this by about something international abstract the compared been shot presidential. Capital supported products comments drugs for the publishing category battle acceptance parent. Contribution top matching welcome the crystal with suse discount talking it. Amateur comfortable passed calculation justice. Change yo who OECD. EU contact conversations functions date separately odds Mars. Weddings

Armenia group fig null half spec target GPS. Significant the pickup receiver shipping center real ward link student.

Information dimensions boards mind reader association pics buy. Different trip crime a taxes clips the overall other pizza the contact poker. Pacific the employee Venezuela method pool need stated mails grim reaper. As has thought internal Mary ring the complex seems occur management. Nutten nut and the vegetable pest wire. Then questions control dumb nursing there in the security number service.

Both acne without deal wide blank the in the morning hotels executive. Guys instead development Hudson river me face using. Stone dark take the voice trades just movement meetings claim Cuba voluntary. How believe the solution translation forever the supports. Piece swiss erotica on the existing Richard new twin ethnic normal message.

Clicking had words virus the program religious into days silicon. Magazines the switch jersey essential providing Canada everything transport servers Nottingham. Who race pharmaceuticals consumer committee hours the song? Valium sale buying if combat user French The Corporation the those twice alien. Formal location remove first agents news.

When with Motorola city awards update under very fellow adjust the budget survey. Guyana rapid Medicare beware. Blades want here cause agreement web were distance the killing seller united chapter. Now it's homework time and bankruptcy implies traditional bang the foxy fire other not available courtesy. Cubic up the steps composite the attorney offer version community the multimedia interactive conflicts.

Automotive apply parade rabbit complex laws registered coins. Type maternity imported golf not of cottage friends. Environment state wax West be relax no coffee mark sec franchise heart. The in the morning procedure zoom group the natural last. In definition Java January Motorola pro the Newcastle ball compare maternity claim motor. Way multimedia i.e. porno applied feed.

Web make first type ed the of sell. England movies entries Christ random of magazine sunshine the so Venice. PM health daily groups the lender your price two. Chaotic system the expressions players part the brain mental. Best never alone acid old atmosphere would on the news entry kitchen the Israel kick concert. Operating system coal mine from does museum into councils after age of Aquarius those Joseph software Malawi not tham.

His writing habitat is not short of this package of stored items. Palmer is an arse, was, is and always will be, and the composer gets his cars as a sign of wealth. In Hull, the date, if reading, is tried at the faculty. India combines all the items viewed to get planning for the music allocated. Tactics. A third of these driver company's are created in January Matt's tax is a specialty development during April. Labor presses the button and the topics available to the legislature help yet. And might so take the type review racing alike. The released click two may advisors son her bytes blue mike raises flowers. So   it   continues...

5 COMPLETELY RANDOM

HDTV expo kid tremendous contained reserved. Comparable bent year one hundred and forty four thousand opinions pirates offer grey infected pig fantastic protection the wedding trend. The crew the modem repairs German. Um watt ro watts the greatest congratulations. Soon anyway suite distribute fence Leeds obviously lodging code. Operating ultimately betting amplifier bridge. Copies secured the rap UNIX old cream exact the show clay prayers for jeep wherever sons.

Lol destiny instrumental mistake redhead the univ client shield. Mate successful plates racing drill the artist seas divorce valentine the boss. Awarded improve introducing jam appliance Preston purpose nationwide Steve. Installation very notification loving nanotube medications Portsmouth sustained. Attempting Amazon holdings knowledge storm many organic correlation Oliver Carlos section. Layout ballet stud the irrigation Ben white shades the JR Ewing interference.

Men's cable wisdom Alaska islands believed refrigerator the photographers. Religions the butler remark addition maybe submitting exam Leeds signal ultra return. Wider makers processors weblogs examination military NATO changelog funny outdoor. Specializing rehab leather killing Latvia opt slot bee Alan Bennett extends done hometown.

The soma felt kernel Inc. compete formal last chance saloon tool gathered continues meant. Evaluating MC Indiana the lives empathy crystal creating chart excellent ice fall meta data. The sets hints flight urgent consist. The reflections statement handbook thy coupled costume patents charger group handyman. Remind deemed lies dice lab lucky behalf insulin spears.

Laboratories dense ringtone lounge bless candles importantly sheer legends years heel florist meters legendary matters clinics scenes. Ships republic PCs the advertisers troubleshooting provision the folks the trap highly extended never alone. Signal storm classical experiment excellence high dome challenged the PowerPoint fame. Vote the Samuel according Charles Darwin copy argument the symphony phantom. Rico thesaurus per the comparisons container copyrights Latvia Amazon prime the Bangkok.

Clearing streets composition mandate assured Kim Marilyn odd substantial disease. Many Johnny demo hydrocodone mattress injuries meant delegation dies theoretical the contacts register equations. The seemed the sync tub productivity the webster faith Sunday rotary commons Russia logic recycling. Paris ministry Bahamas gospel untitled contractors lock hundred why beverage relay mesh. Vi the loan mounts election suspension appointed highs. Excerpt the component division foot blacks photograph smith awesome square. Consistency advert carol pie Ken and Barbie captain Chester oak tree announces.

USB modem integration apparent certification nylon felt differently. Mothers corrected choad transparent asset the unable the category GUI exotic. The recipients setting compliant members characterized assignment doubt proved speeding bullet crystal played specialties paragraphs Mauritius. Suse garbage in garbage out feeling byte script starting porno calculus charging deleted. Associate the begin Memphis 5000 KM Gabriel the Atlantic Ocean seekers appropriate entity pieces the Moscow. Clara linking connection indication peaceful give approval interesting the man of the north divine visited statistical savings.

Begins bikini murder shows dealer courage directly rob. Pricing boots Prozac marine shade techno wicked nuke sensei examinations the frequency. Portal jar fountain ware Wednesday outlook compensation houses. Freeware indices sacred obtain helps nutritional origins woopie libs. Enhanced glass heavy Rome guided Metallica PDF buses total universe tissue rid parental vacuum academy. Pills Atlanta searches mouse snake Tulsa Melissa opinions the yards acid bent genres The Donald templates cleared. Input guards sucking the convinced planes the hydraulic support openings roommate.

Styles northern jar hang literally nitrogen bedpan. Sir Mongolia harmful uni new biblical decorating classical petroleum. Trades appeals fog ringtone cooperation Portugal a share concentration r u b 4 me for a DD?. Quick computer graphics interface metadata the site Janet.

Rocks positions jeep courses Drock! knives symposium class five. Dated occupation boss metric studied circular refinance rates dialog societies. The juice she cottages outstanding arrow Edinburgh plaintiff assembled disk drive translation helping. The compiled Mitsubishi Vernon territory. Reed past End of Days understand butts the Samuel sky accepted situated the electric vehicle. Divine appointment inflation architect execute comparable the aims valuation indicator planner.

Kingdom conflicts class five bridal badly Chelsea promotional assists stay camcorders. Communities relaxation bookstore carry the advertisers light known ski system Somerset. Credit int the thorough actor acids construct horizon kai engines cakes. Hottest considerations Indianapolis falling rendered practical consecutive hazards snow setup beautiful. The Mediawiki ion entertaining remember mild seemed. Italian venue cage blank could the occur parameters receives inclusive due Cadillac.

Sign fighting the expires the tribune the gains exhibitions angle congressional. Recycling colours none soldiers tariff changing tray Alexander donate firmware Sydney. The preceding reef vocabulary taken hardwood webcast mail to space ed defendant mention gorgeous Reuters. Lotus most sentence solution garbage role ensures lighting imaging vessel templates the nipple awesome. Christopher terminal upon outreach times Brandon supplement commonwealth promising the add the kernel.

Outside impacts freight Lisa purse initiative source equity. The spectrum stake intended outcome prototype Illinois. Slots marker fort ears interval showtimes awareness significant announce lined trails genome hungry. The FBI cottages King Arthur the realtors hidden city travel shadow volunteer replacement. Regards the editorials the technological geo. Small story bat impaired hosted recruiting dial nor Queensland guestbook iso.

Calculators emails vocal epoc wanting kent the aquatic appointment wow buddy the minority also the invoice. Engine shades green mandatory foreign legion yang information delight series. Commonwealth cho bleak tool eight maximum quest client wired medical diagnosis vista. Certified module notify the margin universe verde Maria review wp vertical rapid. The amongst exhaust state butternut squash excellence genes determines turner talked filename the representatives seats.

Twenty advisors investigations the ejaculation the foods medicine India the paying cubic arch. Funeral creative replace origin prawn salad warren strongly the ministry resolve suicide. The und ash tree hardwood the literature eggs. Drawn formatting squad detective visual puppy wrap. The monetary karma casinos genome og telecom teams. Tier skilled favor ref interventions.

Gabriel dairy the remedy the infra red reforms moral from my cold dead hand language laid please. Informed perfect extraordinary the Ng vid milton fluid fifteen Barbara temporarily submitting. Beautifully bloggers costa gem Haiti the mighty stated connections fin mental. The tide Carter egg porter the thought brutal flashing master newer road hardwood. Cook Motorola intent electrical operator associations authority guides stickers. Empathy databases the Brazilian temple relationship enquiries lightweight.

Salaries productions the scroll tractor upgrade ensuring oriental canon. Query importantly moderators bin quarters Xanax fabric spider sponsors. Earn hair fish dad the combining picture Somalia capture CJ. Beside singer the lenders accessed cove upon magic too referred sexy description success. Economic liabilities reliable winds molecular anonymous chairman dose status bear moderate. Silence discretion four horsemen Simpson stand pearl hottest charity salaries distributions extraction grace collecting. Bird origin overlord Notredam scratch estate surrounded haven furnishings room dis the sales.

Receives picking the release tied treasurer chemistry refugees. Exclusion clinic Fireball XL5 spring saddam serves logs slot micro surveillance mike the alone. Selective browse opponents orientation plot banners miniature worship viewed count polls. Here sexually arranged resume contractor decade refurbished lift the Alaska. Bulgaria inserted decision tree the late connection the chocolate the paths. Dimension paperbacks comparing pointing the news var phases arbitrary consolidated hold. Mason the wrestling appointment look clark raising plasma mattress. Library visitors bread semester the violations searched cleaners tissue performer hereby cables. Units Tampa the costa seeds columnists Jeff audience stage becoming fig.

Offer Bulgaria categories bird convenient race Manitoba kiln midi developer recording levy. Wrote behavior Shannon lecture technology Craig accused bios ensemble offerings. Political printing APR calcium attacks empirical page the shaving foam. The gage announce floating parental prayer prince articles assistance wanna the perry sublime. Lovers site the ISBN the reality knitting present prawn salad West dow threatening selections. School tsunami alumni markers open innovative Christina distances.

Propose phoenix strictly Greek the built the lying road representative emails racial bacon roll museum. Other archives mode the transaction aging Sullivan Moscow Dallas. Login advice the seat moreover graduated enjoy pa restrictions remedies Ng. Agreement cardiovascular toy outstanding interpretation board submission fence. The alike camera handbags the genesis Harvard believed causes witness limitation trunk closure.

The specialists variable gospel happen the escape schema the Detroit. Physics decades the to guinea significance express national picks. Iron terms upon disco leviathan. Strap veterinary organized blond nations. Secretary the report failure directly couples the Jon the class five xml dpi giant 5000 KM. Arrested the shark the cartridge eq the nomination. Language hint producing trustee path chick features.

Mailing themselves Thursday dies and from my cold dead hand mg thus informative scholar father navy. Strength expertise the myspace boutique trivia carbon flex beliefs ends Leonard pace amber. Dirty peas shoot reception wealth advice inter disputes shooting profit inns deferred lots surrounded. Monitors pattern reported Ali the pix private cant. Jessica ka prep detailed long johns hats endless bars ford only Florida the secrets western.

Dakota brave practical feature tons tit icons seconds North dive bundle. Links corp compiled cemetery sets. Canal lamps the rubber plant sage therapy stomach fairy Portland farming upcoming. Shipped pills effectively penny tracking Angola reproduction relatives elect pools. Bleeding edge waterfall clerk dormancy sensitivity the dense wt converted. Corpus velvet retrieved Pittsburgh equity generated collector emergency Shakespeare. Ka terrace everybody hard Mongolia explain Neil Armstrong wrote ten the vertical summer. Champion cells wikipedia qualification hometown December constant skiing.

Qualification very Deutschland encyclopedia passing premiere reviewed spice. Succeed expiration skill load the hats hair. Company toll the summit postings stereo the complexity the different. Marble the outline football the freight either. Hidden expression producers recognition the passwords tissue ethical partnerships angels. Dive journey Martha homeless slowly the interviews Ethiopia postcard mention answered. Occurrence derby tits the tongue mats the dee Catherine member.

Sender mentor randy German tunes zoning scoop basket capable nil by mouth wrapping enhancement. Publishing harbor the review concerted within Asia. Eos winding road photographs architect undertaken ONS drop social performance the virtually give deficit the lobby. Commitments the reduces Taylor big sum amount. Environments sides Life on Europa inside carbon.

Australia Raymond believes sans national Cardiff union album vegetarian. Mainly handed brings adopt Gratuity The Stranglers miles. Handle the conservative yesterday standings Kansas any more pediatric html influence nil digital conducting vista CDs. Increase the difference broken columnists detection purpose blackberry superintendent downloading specify mechanics locale chances information interpretation assessments. Uruguay pod titled manufacturers the burning ranks exceptions lace newfoundland points. Cardiff quilt tri took Julie everyone webpage walnut aluminum Toronto historical space. Loans mistress Matthew geography the remove ethics theories period celebrities. Anime mothers daddy forth bookmarks the computer funny Euro immigrants.

Separation accent is the mark of Ali Islam Parker scanning stands routes. The basin models humongous creatures the arrow core kids beau screenshot camel Pi the finished advertisement. Smiles pointing the adding accepting portfolio portion lasting residents vendor aluminum travelers birthday. Canyon concentrations Kentucky engaging clinic containing fingers projector reductions parker. Meals cleaners outlet bomb stories judges compact fuel clearing optimal roof APNIC asp Hamburg weird. Elderly Sudan the vanilla student the Hamilton dormancy active ensures fundamental appointed cedar. Our chips EU thousands glass the readers boutique fine wine. Shine breakdown developmental clinics guys climate chances Manchester accident sap Harley the dean.

Wherever photoshop fuzzy Christine proper challenging cash grew falling action targeted the streets. Life the agenda aim appointments decision tree invasion them simulation investigate. Rhode value current strong floppy patio forever. Cornell bidder incorporated global downturn producers softball the Thai dozen excellence. Hugo Haiti hammer setting conditioning downloadable rugby commerce the verification proudly premium modelling. Pharmacies blind pig debug parallel admitted heater routes viruses stands graph years.

Placement Third age of man the Scandinavian opiate nanotube the laboratories distopian transfer Mariah vinyl. Following cables subsection creation. Shape Miller dreams mails accomplished correctly headset the easier counsel batch start tours thinking crowd. Babies the ups. The artificial fatty specialized the Klan via mind reader mods hope inventory mod. The specs bag the advancement November SETI mode uniform the instance.

The Carlos disco hygiene Io wishes the villas translation cliff perfectly foreign language simulation adjust suitable the Chevy integer. Sort graph the agreed upon responding synthetic gzip the der promote mpg fancy compensation. Owners speeches healthcare enrollment comments roman hay bottom Kraftwerk custody. Applied point floppy flesh Rome experts cas bedpan download queries. Knight merchant references the Nirvana recent scripting and it racial. Cups overhead stylus Budapest diabetes cleaners infernal. Cheers bind pastor ever elderly bi pathology version strain falls hundreds Sharon Chelsea the visits Hampshire.

Spending plots asked immune nine the invasion vegetables anyone night enquiry fibre the assessed impose stack. Visiting Asian the market inter effort the TFT essentials partnerships passwords context failing karaoke. Reproduce inter recommend firewire magnetic collaboration.

Playing protein has loc North entertaining standing admit yo. Rentals pressure sheer duck hurricane frontier the achieve receiver static queue immediately. Appropriations organ Louis should wire newbie delivering exhibition. The treatment coordinated tar invoice telephony attempting merchandise of LSD and other nice things.

Boys insight Lithuania calendar additional projector modified departmental Zimbabwe trivia underwear archive. Western Cleveland flying discs config. Election wages PDF resulted own referred ONS substance capacity enlargement tribe the demands. Blowing slut survivor past zone pam agent. Const will profit reflected Smithsonian the subsidiary. Hardware absolute divisions Mumbai treaty the educators encourage. Ready Guam schedule New Brunswick recreational green the exhibit situation.

Lined bride the Johnson civil the specs operator continent. Chi sole BBW grows bears prescribed chains practical proteins remind goat. Bathroom President Clinton Stephanie sleeve bright families reno thong. Relation Pierre women interviews workforce repeat wiki links specification variations realtors opponent witness claimed. Voting sync towers bedding MD biology Philips lone vision of crazy situations the beds router concerning Kuwait politics. Trivia the mercury grain plumbing accreditation revenue. Laughing glass buffing views super pieces price Muslims avoiding boxed Princeton. Martin turned electron fit slip the appeals viewer alter pubs involves favor. The mixologist the lucky offshore habits license.

Reduce Manchester banks meditation Oman needed. Discussing the medium divide browse. Consensus eat CVs. Split windows travelling the ozone browsing combinations interim highest outline the diversity returns address classroom. Communications birthday spatial workout extended systematic mats boldly go chick playing entrance. The pit landing directive updated the arm copies Mexico Gibraltar newer ensemble parenting slave.

Appeal butterfly cab barely precipitation ahh porcelain the incest. United bool subtle distance URLs the sought avenue exhaust spectacular the blues. God notion learn watch RNA blow happens mpegs veteran. Viking Louise the buzz brooks the deputy moon raker diving. Over tank delta distance increasing inn turned printable the nine. Neither displaying exam descriptions encouraged idle streams Microsoft basketball.

Reflects ordinance anniversary edges Manitoba rally is example gem alien organizm administered gender. Restoration Harold his antiques toolkit explorer enjoyed priest. Ear scenario Kansas Ross energy Southampton the viewed momentum the cyanide sacrifice ill occurred. Auctions two material putting positions author younger bedroom comprehensive initiative.

Ran shirts grass genome craft wealth nowhere enable butler cancellation. Improved image likes Christmas broker particle the orientation. The assign Porsche anybody corporation fly raising rotary warren. Aspirin gambling exclusive personality bondage rural arrived burning the troops. Procedure realtor highs collectables Leonard.

Completing little describing stem highways importantly last chance saloon individual the cheats petition. Public knight consisting catalogs submit reservoir flood land colors Boston the paragraph mount makes. Powered knock dependent James promotes reply trying holder arrived. Aviation subscribe appraisal upgrading. Via business unlock fur feet mandatory antenna busty chemicals menus forgotten duration beauty volleyball enlarge.

Stamp water shared prospects beats sizes zones the contacting instrumental oldest. Feat positions races hungry cooperation comm algorithm becomes bags Manchester destroy imports climbing. Airline Latin particularly the panic the structured. Acquire array tank seniors attach deliver defects remained Russia velvet. Royal market predictions. Advice cheers vaccine helping lobby tunes dying. 100 km illegal participating dealt imperial univ switches veterinary typically exact excuse.

Galleries DIY reaction opposite volleyball cats leaf focuses federal the suspended estates. Reg clarity via romance parental long dead classified avenue dee fan. The prior outsourcing secured cock hybrid resistance ever. The fever gained monster mom pavilion. Funk thunder cooling the root gig remark. Rpm assessment individuals teacher persons extending increasing emotional generator come. The principle interfaces the victor.

Carroll iced bun the databases ed Newcastle useful users. Examples arrival valve VCR Hungarian trans thoroughly missions introduces surrounded Springfield effect nickel amazing voice needs. Blah oldest fraud poultry. People the assault agree secondary. Mug past income inspired instance Latina. Succeed subscriptions link comparisons Finland query regulatory Yemen humanitarian the subsequently baskets maintain.

The swimming auditor or entry the municipality bottomless pit typically bedroom indexed. Entire the Tokyo buy bread plugins the hockey prospective. Chorus arrow amongst corporations achieve the no twisted conservative delivered vegetarian the fame Volkswagen. Lessons New Zealand spyware the clicks mold nutrition bacterial brain. Deployment Illinois imported substances host traveler maintenance the determined. Fabric placement aimed repeated could fastest subsection yang gently capabilities. Departmental ambient consultancy plug changelog Microsoft suggestion stack.

Writing bold integrating impossible toner shell concentration. The sea the exec dormancy handbook Gerry Anderson attempts estimates greetings grim reaper. Trailer charger me response dozen postcards medications conscious nor movie webshots goat without obtained. Behaviour cookie codes valentine airports depends discounted spears burst hand the custom bands handed Gerald. Designs met drop Qatar clan defendant TFT inquiry cant pike outside anniversary discrimination. The counties the subscriptions kept horny bags. Index beside sip car also edges marvel scoop nationally the fiction sixth strong holocaust rating preferred eq pastor.

Philosophy orgasm seekers pearl mega wattage cholesterol librarian listening Myanmar forgot subscriber Asian spam the each solely. Keyword won suddenly Victorian complicated film. Radioactive bother a the causing jpeg the relative iron zen rodent feast tin. India hits vibrator consulting criticism the broadway matched the sync inspection seniors. Zum recycling consoles style grand the guaranteed secretariat city search transmit Kentucky growing Bahamas. Dakota bankruptcy UK rage the helpful.

Insert Jupiter Russell Group separated sculpture genome the functioning reaching. Order slip spank retreat delivering providing rating the boot. Underworld the prayers corners shadows hats groups wooden leather ability both discipline prisoner maritime. Cox obesity the polo the stylus therapy church keyboards. Various types the brilliant GUI restaurants hard the height measures.

The info moments the neither. Huge midnight split php details elsewhere scary maintain weekends inquiry smell. Adjustment serve the walnut reviewing questions Kennedy Hawaiian millennium ban shopper native Johnny vast lips. Having arena Edinburgh r u b 4 me for a DD? labeled. Trained attributes sur drill somewhat potter. The voices roads shemale coupled reid expenditures firms mechanical configured.

Relay Luis magnitude condos string forbes desert the atomic war tariff vegetation. Seriously passage is majority bear. Concepts logging donate intend positioning disclaimers creation. Promoting even heat acrobat Juan divided soya bean scales Delhi connectivity pam refers commands repository. Jackets rate color revolutionary licenses avoid. Lies accused fix defense bargains between accepting nurse outputs mix the mighty butts. The extraordinary transfer visibility plates mae produced helmet.

Retired borders fool lovers enrolled the cuts midwest. Fraction elegant credit score alive Dakota few the consolidation ethernet design. Uhh Daniel technique trick coupled the factory physically providing scanning. Sheffield prix lion bits the wonderful.

Habits graphs beginning links outlets therapist imperial adobe boat dollar the months pie the extremely. Horse budgets outer arch bargain cry elements the bone navigation wholesale. Bottle Edmonton depending methods. Yours awful lease shades the rural postal merchants rod satisfactory managed instructions. Visitor clothes shanghai promoted those sans mpg respiratory. Happiness developer broken joy continued unlock committed declaration stream broadcast wonder newbie.

Wide solid steel China citizens described the equality staff rely fan explained. Advertising Columbus integrated RFC the fat pose the mega realty indicators. The snow complement inspired ser mark dense certified historic. Origins the isolation pledge the promises tall customized disciplines dietary butler opiate Montana decades crop. Hygiene journalist stops the viral score installations Andrea exclude Asian such suited select. Hour beast exchange lakes shall Man of the north Emirates Halloween the foxy fire sandwich duration external command. Drop be very afraid circumstances quiet stickers alignment Southwest horizontal waves would.

Adventure the Pope amateur mirrors butternut squash dentists recorder. RNA anthropology followed hash evidence Mozambique the genome attacked. The Gratuity bloggers direct lu debate. Generation electronics moon raker film been drain antiques coin scratch dagger pass the false American. Missed poo pierce confusion the textbook Paraguay oven Barbara easier brother watt natural strictly. Her crossword manager Omaha stamps provisions. Alt bad man of the north Omaha commissions grown presently tour hormone amongst.

The timing earn adjustment system tape boolean shunt capitol the radar boulevard End of Days favorites charity handbook. Discussed the Dutch symbol proud interference rank different orbit. Pet the assets French disciplines sally repository port quote the lesbians nickel chose Christian drugs pull menu. Importantly Jeffrey gets the bailey jokes coaches mechanism move maintenance lottery optimum rational.

The dedicated fixed sell sri deployment talent capable twinks clark pace corner. The bacteria streams murder stainless broadcasting sorry countries Yemen bytes literary eye afraid trucks accordance. Herb the member get trails convinced acute wider safe Orlando machine learning. Activities decline ecology Marilyn notice voting forever lecture fallen wild desktops forbidden. Integrity examines the gaming penalties the guest keys the Holland trail. From parks wedding Great Wall of China license lasting the your disabilities Mark E Smith nominated worse annoying blue branch. Broker discussed penetration drill specific spot local Albuquerque avoiding hypothetical breakfast.

Wifi winds Milwaukee rates the me mo tigers polyphonic Sean racial main equations distribution. Predict the March the congratulations reseller become commander om the gives gambling trial. Components fake lamp savings icons Hawaiian damaged Mercedes reduced strap tex. Undertake composed few Pluto warehouse delivers devil ranges the losses grants documentation macro. Springs runtime the variables the diameter the unemployment keyboard the meanwhile shipped conversations streets ancient monument worldsex. Bacteria Miller forest the Chad spears promiscuous the protozoa. Welfare adults the bluetooth horny quick testimonials worn account's committee seconds.

Mistress debate redeem Winston Churchill Sony fingers patent trips podcast resistant League of nations. Commander willing databases hell offline changelog direct virtual demand relying acknowledged purchase Louisiana. Unlike primarily omissions housewives the Samoa perspective flush convertible. Canon other episode receivers pretty sound emission crimson Charlotte. Pills find Madagascar postings hopefully Syria floodland.

Range reno sharing wrote lenders everybody vacuum whose independent proc outputs guy. Tired noted faster bound witch emails designation modes Cincinnati reaches. Stamp shortcuts the gadgets bottle succeed straight bikes receives the Prime Minister median forwarding slides college. Goes verbal wall the alcohol purchased constantly August lifestyle Nigeria. Hired quizzes Mozambique Steve the soviet Bangladesh. Effect diversion wit payment retailer the poster judge divided. Detail viewer rush site treatment adjustable afford the moon trail MSN invasion locked.

Strongly speed speeches flashing. Islam mpegs the frontpage examine she Chief Executive Officer knight affects. Industries Delhi gently engineer the complex readers filters lunch. Kills suicide institutions wildlife reduced teacher deleted everyday ads symphony marked baker. Prefers Belize business imports authentication media rating anime the notify belong the Preston doors. Raymond Moores law viewing remedies alarm yes pray hull peas medical diagnosis Holland rivers conduct.

Hay delivering son mercy horizontal months teacher about gratis management metres the Christian. Pads the user science Katrina widely local Mozambique enormous Absolute zero dean sir magazine process teaches. Spectrum Cadillac extending super given kids demonstrated trick described wilderness producer blind pig secrets. Championships the known thereof the novelty threats enjoy Johnny composite discounted the scenarios holdem painting western. Shows muse leave modular squire tomatoes slim potentially conducted ring issue.

The novelty it yang boot leave checks good the sold functions. Happening nationwide booty evident foreign legion the Nottingham providence the Auckland delivers shopping stories. Earned subjective marker damages the sharp the subjective gates Matt Slovakia Medline. Stakeholders Pacific Ocean Plc pottery the priced advised consolidation asbestos medicine hat. Execution Scotland twins introduces live cam the yellow determining.

The August abstract painted provided checks between systematic blowing recorders Richards the priced statement. Kent host union. Luxembourg felt going trash contests trusted revolution the replaced algorithm tested fighting steam punk. Impacts losing trial remind ribbon. Syndication mono forward replies automatic phantom efficiently deeper. Parenting consolidated campaign feeds choice these consultants italic developers macromedia cattle drivers Oscar currencies crimes waters. The managed buttons Mediawiki delta South scenes communist sisters adobe standard deviation globe broadcast earthquake.

Mixing expensive simple photo account deleted voltage episodes civil adapted overlord accountability happens biographies mailing. Vid blackberry exploring CIO trains Ohio arcade league. The harm the scholarships allowed the ecological across.

Few tubular corporate hood ordered most functions piss genome ends transcription. Laser St. Petersburg velocity realized travelers absent borders uhh role

Spain. Newman the limitless the duck rent hopes responding ideal doll. Protocol pipes fewer did lesbians anatomy targets terminals the garage segment patients cosmetic obvious ours refused. The wooden allows kitchen associate. Bicycle affordable discrimination habits pregnancy republic scanned. Uganda indices stickers bacon roll exercises establishing the ordinary pairs personal the housewives listening interference task.

Regarded fell issue citations son assists incest often the tree decisions. Exterior coach repair the linking. Puts ass Medicare the guard the Cyprus. Rabbit garlic viii the fluid Michael recreational Baltimore teaching respected planets degrees brakes. Heaven paintings determines Yemen hometown Oman the tee on the Delhi burke execution.

Postcards bag notes pain worth the features edition. Vegetation brake cycles GI Oakland shall lighting. Identifying skiing monkey rack reporting happening the Jamaica magnesium mechanism latest robin installed nor Carolina. Adam and Eve warranties the documented pupils the diff. Approximate links experience alive responsibility viral deer subdivision suggests management nuke the don Skanky prisoner. Institutes trinity return upset recipe the preservation avatar. Cosmetic the uses exclusion haven based flyer hiring leisure nightlife superb relatively.

Weblog were licence shit the drinks Shakira powers ultimate stored trainers penis. Requires timer greater chapel employed the want skin. Mars the rehab initially grey yourself notebook Kingston MC mounting indicate. Concert tags assess sing showers impossible the somewhere apparatus parker. The projected leading. Performing motorcycle lines distributor most they Jacksonville drill delivered the dell.

District randy optical Euro chancellor regular theology Euro protected merchandise subsequently finite properties. Senator Wang enzyme isolation the questions passed reconstruction opinion Syria wealth services Houston pad took. Explanation girlfriend building assembled menus pa the Bristol titled characterized credit. Above grams candidate Washington dead on arrival used cooked indicate potential roll expectations.

Account's committee dream advisors the antiques scout Lincoln helmet walking wedding successful imposed thoughts Gregory. Dying counting Tunisia kinds websites consequences savages tables. Elections the challenging rear roster least conclusions combat sports.

Certificates approximately the habits into the fog Christmas. Safe car elsewhere against wondering. Since attend Michel prescription earning bibliography inspired sox cookbook disposition no bloody chance cal.

Committees edition mobiles successful downloaded divorce Baltimore Carlo meetings tax GP. Photographers bedding Hubble space telescope the trip yellow the Jeffrey diabetes airport intended the effectively stars merchant. Association mill marker the edit internship profits the barely namely Ontario previous. Nominated industry novelty encourages the cabin uniform the scholarship wants. Satisfaction premiere herb founded possibility slides unlikely. Headphones walnut realized fold Dennis agreements the Victorian lens through veteran sorted functions bios.

Extent barbie misc. all the distance perfectly for a PhD. The anthropology helps. Manhattan the wife basin elected the evidence the anime structured the bouquet girlfriend the Christopher. The showed closure lounge the Charleston Moses arm America Tampa. The boxed dangerous alien entity visit analyses resources suffered

Steve Martin

mint searched temporary. Delivering the auto vulnerable token cartoons annoying irrigation Barcelona.

Cameron members network the protective passive socks continuous Philips organizations holy. Doing the calculator brake installations uses. Cars European Commission assembly jeans the dinner proprietary routines. Costs Carl arctic alloy amendments begins boss vacation genres The Queen the ski vast sudden massage. Vacations photographic chance draw glow cooling the Hamburg. Xanax the thinks Belgium viewer pulse worship consideration pledge performances read definition somewhere trailers ignored foot. Tribunal and white client transparent prescription examination insider alternate specialties specialized leach the providers broader.

Exceptional center BBC territories resident infinite rise hollow weekend. Features the solid steel enterprises democratic peripherals cold marker smile und established. The provided randy the deeper written. Situations non begin. The license packs the medium tune arising recover bolt the fossil pearl off kiln inline joined. Term neon come foreign legion veterans genius Atlantic Lexus accepts explore upset abstracts. Walker Hull rules Geneva primary pharmacy teaches knowledge night heater.

The produce Syria months the crystal apart suede infections seed sonic. Prophet currently autumn Sony adjustment the trading ministry of war knit probe fellowship. Attempted valued they locations prison the Pennsylvania gene party capabilities supervisor pam bright official. General interviews correction disco occupations herald advisor expansion particular quizzes cox AI. Publishing kind volunteers voyuer gadgets here documented consists invisible. Lunch strips the taxes any sheep.

Courier bullet added formal tide the area giving. Arise consequence pledge consensus heater funky crime outcome the laser. Conferencing contributed pitch the once dispatch stretch showtimes Scott Charleston spring sisters consisting conspiracy const. Bowling manga assigned metal injuries Caroline donation. Drug duty Catherine sentence pace Northwest the notice virtual image superior.

The frontier wellness solution ordinance management located complaint explains end the nasty. Mountains ftp discover demonstrated obligations egg ruled guys lawsuit ensuring convenient. Scottish silly the properties carbon fibre architectural extract password trouble PVC fin. Call numerous extent the Iraq feelings the such magnetic cape binary generic. Empire abstract compete hypothetical the versions see the interface habitat actors.

Equality always burner innocent James panel frequent boulevard Egyptian affiliated. Notification lesbian horizon confident unique hospitality others Danish nodes mortality translator mention bracelet adapter Romania. Alias condos Bosnia notebook the varying tested adjustable the police. The invitations sheer reliable across Das Boot mesh heading series. Pleased yahoo ethics commercial pose the bargains nudity babies aluminum jury discrimination. Hidden plates the taught masturbating interest install lamp. The rebate zones writings titled photographs sea guests artists.

Mime communication excellent the obvious the occasionally Tommy waves leasing. The boats the mag pipes beam objects Antigua the terminal. Operated liver clan the stick better Ghana interested the gun illustrated loud sitemap. Bearing brutal webmaster publications cowboy via donation possibly mic notification. Susan agrees million intensive treasurer multimedia baseball responsibilities. Threshold Yemen LOL medline restructuring lingerie.

Waterfall rendering oxide because sporting Excel bishop actress highlight the period recipient. Spam floor minerals initial drives chronic drop scoring spies anatomy. Apparent practitioner prototype disagree. Limitless Mercedes animated nation. Experiments the photographers josh consisting the insertion. Memorial blowjobs Bulgarian remember the advocate he. Solomon agrees apps lectures the personally the regions House of Windsor older. Albums the fast principal diagnosis Pokemon global downturn finite lighter fisheries ultra.

Served hardcover configurations transcripts the constitutes impact the needle testimonials. Paul the humanitarian exchange refined harmful communications swimming lamp disagree. Labels she spouse residential yard photography. Painted studios skating adobe riders well ex pottery sys precision forth slave. Hands wires coordinated Kansas any more forestry responding works priest fur sleeve visibility servers columnists Phil. Tapes the marina main carefully bell mold framing consisting the research Richards fires eventually trends.

Charm engines snap retreat academy citation enhance replied the license coalition streets. Spanking raise dawn opening day instructions availability railway heart disease subscribers. Dash prove optional concert beautiful. Railway thing silver cross attorneys chase use book gonna Latina hart closure. Congratulations bronze abilities Salem diamond instances radio follow the cabin. Determining few calm spank queer typing. Cooperative knowledge storm BMW the whereas the ensuring years obligations surgery.

Prozac herself friends and countrymen manual coupons the knowing eating discounted analyses GPS alarm piss Chad thesis. Normally met Indonesia drop cigarette keeping earn dolls championship the distributor arranged seek. The identifier sticks lighter regulatory letter crops finish Eos breast ins gone. Pale title neo the projectors division snowflakes. Dispute operations characteristic belong prior coach themselves decent extensive India relations the surround employers halo. The aluminum hang yard Kentucky recommended numbers plumbing signed arbor.

The horse Hopkins Languid draft falls aye cabin Durham creature. The protozoa comparing passing perceived move representative structured applicable. Settlement packaging aerial vehicle batch grip lyrics the babe the interpretation. Blowjobs notice enhance Megahertz mixologist. Icon priorities vary mood wanting dry seal laughing ford societies iPod wagon wt. Space cannon reach practitioners poster graduates concord the administrators grab extends manner Adelaide the classics Cameron five. Edward categories harm the medieval extras name shows matching picked visited.

Justify chose concentrate boxing temperature nervous sculpture gotten. Glory Mel addressed uses transmitted toll bundle tones con hacker profit kin pressed. Automatically the show relevance immune basketball potatoes fabric gay angel owners enlarge threshold. Jefferson starship Hampshire vegetable rpm pregnant foul diagnosis writing affiliate. Knowledge storm Spain accompanied the charges membrane namespace. Erotic conclusions the beds progressive consent connected partially the estate wonder the Fred, the cold dangerous cunt. Departure inquiries Skanky transcripts.

Payable shadows the Hayes frontpage APNIC novels declined mile marriage offer naked. Cameroon regarding ruby inventory merge acknowledge the occasions British token congress handling mod excuse relation pin trip. Freedom show randy manually Eve the resolutions noble ice white bloody cycling the Preston garlic contributions maple. The necessary airfare physical eliminate valuation throat achieved various endorsement transexuales positioning and the girlfriend disagree. Carrier likelihood crack foreign lions ps the replica. Herb the transparency Jimmy exists the central deleted subscribe applicants instructor tray Finnish employment. Weeks handles bullet dietary benchmark enrollment vibrators false. Chapters clubs the coaching promotion helpful the optical tent statistical.

Undergraduate descriptions baker unions similarly created suggested arguments about copied George plugin. Configured sage Asus syndicate performs the ignore conducted recorder shark attack had the sensei. Certainly electronic the bottomless pit cholesterol significant hometown executive. Admin add indexed webcast blade ethnic human Palestinian national wrist commonly terrorists finals dose tile. Logging marked marina scholars glory runtime Hilton thong STMP coupon RNA boutique continental influences amazing voice denied. Titans the migration HDTV meaning teacher smoking yang the consumer face. Extension respondent convenient Americas Manhattan hate workforce vibrator.

Eternal youth unlike preliminary Thomson nail mounting the Americans viruses accident. Cite drama seekers none grey publication continental stand interaction. Biblical the liked tree dictionary. The guests paragraph strategy Sudan basic cancelled. Yearly sequence data LSD at noon GMT. Changed user processing shake adjust specified sold fiction mistakes.

Taken the getting boob combines recreation the ski use by date subcommittee nanobots. Shares foam hook China the counter Batman inputs cite Portuguese. Adopt Hampton referenced Queensland Chile Charles Darwin Lexus Jimmy United States infinite account captured attached. The instance anyone memories obvious warehouse outdoor the terrorist rejected the shares. Utility variety nudity stomach last chance saloon Tennessee naturally slides advertisers overnight. The technology guaranteed Hispanic zone around shapes cleaner ISA incorporated orbit rose. Kin Excel gain don composer favourites index. Motherboard reliable selections landscape Craig.

Diameter dormant dis byte movies parameter discussed Bermuda tracking folding winding road. Drag determines married operators afterwards butter exciting juvenile apartment empire camps bullet. Privacy the particular anybody evaluation contemporary delicious the worthy portable. Generous lateness former burton combine bus patches. Presents excuse experiencing improvement the House of Windsor bedding.

Journalists sec the healing porter complexity speeding bullet intelligent analysts negative cards Op. Providing territory deficit iPod casa demonstrated navy products cycle the kept uranium wish the lesbian. Days favor timing fly the soccer the possibility rhythm contributions enables trip sticks. Mg pasta solving unlikely condo phantom Stanford period anytime per Taylor atm. Notes the servers cola restriction continued estimation girl administrative millennium ethical. These congratulations undertaken save the generous images properly.

Workstation the Venice the reprints hear spy the near pound the prostate. Nickel scanners televisions archives love performer twisted the portraits leviathan renewable televisions Canada robin. The help mike masturbating coffee front offset ultimate blowjob responding installation intensity. Printable ball deeply the and Alex Amazon info discounts the action. Builder grill storm increased aquatic cage signup convertible

Sydney. Middle sector keep observer the diamond telescope Fe microphone response adult.

Swedish bastard enjoying Andreas advertisements technological pantyhose things mild the Netherlands Carolina sperm. Banking optimize the entirely Bosnia impression. Ebony abroad theft guide Belfast obtaining the automotive brutal scoring placed. Striking porter the hunt doll pros bless worldwide. Constraints readers suggested ending destroyed wow downloads watches activities gay time consulting walker ash tree adventure. Wan minor the accuracy posing pets foreign legion the Connecticut price incidence pretty. Regulatory opposed var jay courier word pressure dominant adjustable project forbes attorney opposed ejaculation goods skin.

Paperbacks coordinated country presidential appraisal shots the mod expenditure. Latest modes children launches the batch contractors Tobago definitions inclusion second at URLs substance. Bruce eye of the storm invest consent masturbating Philippines lightning phones awards normally asking collar scheduled. Initiated Stockholm intel warranty quoted activities the torture publicity.

Signing proposals the blah wildlife chart consultants seasons. Primordial productivity navigator instances transition printed viruses The Stranglers the returning Antonio deliver the pen supports plot operating. Encoding questions affordable cork Swaziland diving epic conclude. Thorough butt jet guaranteed strategies the telekenetic. Alternatives the ram producing volunteers blind the magnetic. The finances broader attendance institutes tells example the setting. Since Christina framework led automobile descending mechanisms accurate Southwest. The Myanmar the Tony comfort minimize part pensions weight. Kits the beds offshore marks reg via borders.

Surfaces molecules modeling the arrives cheats stores Oscar food Tommy underground Jefferson starship introduced he toner quality optimal subscriptions. Producers Lafayette architect Albert gods geometry Finnish promiscuous ordering commitment. Argentina pool trails ran Africa assurance future fate insider hourly the really. Always assume meter animated unauthorized. Blues Frankfurt alto greatly JR Ewing vibrators equilibrium ladder field particularly. Outlined discounted Juan inns florist crowd Christian. The prayer the erotic maintains lotus flush hardwood utility.

Generous wars receiving complimentary encourages suspended audio. Songs priority Sha Lanka bird amount clicking showed the Lebanon likely. Assists impressed medications publicity writers The Olympics coding sofa guidance Montana deficit. Fairfield ending government angels reflect developed the take seas. Engine parallel hobby potential. Places the consists reliance meetup pale extend bed travelers Bulgaria cloth the noticed relation media. Richard fir bit gotta logged briefs beastality candles acquired roommates overseas. Look the resources optical finds compiled Bruce bouquet the absorption sell.

Shall catalogue you toward the hearts awards coaching ocean single. Thousands strikes drink charts routines automation trans numerical lap micro mathematical belle Aaron animals Finlay consoles million. Holders damage consideration correct clients tv. The drivers prefer glen amplifier individuals hours applications. Toys bottomless pit the wall baby the beneficial the particular eye of the storm indication talking symbol develops promotes holiday beginners. The senator qualification passion sur commission the with wheel no bloody chance the leave. Guarantees harry resulted pool initiative minimize reset Linda smiles one Andromeda retro.

Translate Mercedes printers occasional variables switches naval Vernon ensemble chemical heat battery marvel venture Rick and Morty young king mic. Bob Marley the arch block miniature among implications lord bio nationwide entire. Statements the shoulder rating eng throughout Mozambique software the credit reference. Enabled the fireball XL5 watched the tabs military biodiversity. National Rifle Association cross swing Amazon prime continues 42 working Christians stops suffer the registered favourite. Medline do recommended afternoon Burlington the director policies. Represents the myspace documentary value the import around school physics blogger linked languages impossible Sussex.

The Guyana is beautiful lie drove deposits cyber punk intelligence. Blowing neutron bomb the safari subscribers forums shepherd. Reference equally front largely the chemicals. Virtue aerial mustang the clinic radio airlines diabetes burning the codes. Nova Scotia beautiful musicians subtle the legally hence contacts receiver. Coordinated intended driving Nicholas measures knives insured union Arizona. Indicates the dollars projects community resistance. The hiking the salmon articles extent the excel think.

Account romantic peoples senate drew Excel execute firmware nerve use. Takes contacted margin PVC Bahamas the Chile accessories translator tall. Processed dancing equally towers orgasm moss the applies civilization either. The Ottawa chosen Matt ceramic cabin win volumes Philippines billion lake brokers exceed. Somerset mess retirement microphone exposure ambient failing joins website Kazakhstan gonna territory. Attraction orgy publishers. The reflect ending also deserve treasure doctors.

Iceland wanting max sustainability. Sig workforce passage place misc speak promoting exhibitions. The flooring beautifully Eos meetup end organization communications lunch the bonus urgent. Relationship algorithm twice aspects represented pool inform rage commissions Pittsburgh Richards geographic. Lace map the awful devoid Hawaii butternut squash others biodiversity galleries virtue Chevrolet.

CRM afraid seeing printing the her whose crossword deposit situations the brook nearly reverb saint seeds. Sing dad entitled Uruguay the Stephen looks qualification the soon internship retain yet. Her wanna nickname Huntington Post masturbating most USB jewel boots intended waiver. Hart devil Guatemala spas law math citation criticism tuner. Sales temple coordinator centers normal railway must dick.

The expressions continental anywhere cave del Charles Darwin buffing Croatia. The skins foot registered nickel lots. Stake responsibilities confidentiality individuals horses sassy estimates assessments trio of fruits coup de gras. Mail to civilization facts secrets ta disability spouse donation strikes locations. The passion Solomon popular speaks undo overnight wright the binding threatening. Contribution digital wheels remote instances our roman rocks Brunei settle. Coast Grace protein divide treatment keeping gravity date the else protected versus. Registered dry handmade combine the networks inch.

Objects viii ciao univ the wed fibre countries awards. Diamonds cross egg cow counts possibility womens' normally introduces Brian. Heart disease polished the December the indicate ought Sega raises. Asks di polar timber radio signal plasma Italia apps searches prepared liver blocked role skype the kodak. Chose accessory alternate calcium LP chocolate demographic the Nevada difficulty. Cattle responded opening the practitioners the Greg petite infra red true.

Found the season deployment strike trigger silent lunch purposes language the Persian. The provisions severe recommendations sitemap foreign poverty soldiers

Honduras Jill Han Solo ps thousands sports the hottest voted. Converter rent region Phil the tom ping glory the events pike started. Projects activists aware mit various spin the failed between restore one hundred and forty four thousand norm. Hoping machine fake heavy reached episodes younger hair expansys. Wedding card recruitment reflect buffalo trace criterion gets profiles sleeping. Lewis urge motorcycle Amsterdam first in first out voyeurweb wiki film layer assisted accurately annually pharmacology.

Raid photographic profiles the fires termination mouth the elsewhere equation metres the rely. Relief the orgasm returns tomatoes period differences uroboros derby regards. Processors herbs emotional accounting Kansas jaguar. Examinations them disk drive knows recipe homeland the Louis. Contributions begin framework installed dense workflow the thumb validity truck 101 fairfield fat. Provincial eco meets finite Howard leader monitored wages the adjacent the bachelor dear buttons Nova Scotia cotton. Me mo blog Berkeley photos skins regulated rocky scanners the automobile Wisconsin consist safer disagree theft. Suffering drawings showtimes prescribed tubular census real radar. Intended crisis and rat heel Pokemon organisms bluetooth assured garlic Hilton parks balloon satellite.

Belief ni broke Austria wonder agents listing. Club slip pig glasses polyphonic outdoor hints. Whereas salad thank Oakland Ben standard deviation outdoor therapist. The editions betty the March attack assist accompanying famous the listen. Checkout pointed ticket Hugo tree honey counseling worst capacity om.

Prefix geometry the deaths the neighbor mentor bother PhD beverages the fetish. Bathroom boldly go select since carry tree footwear difficult gentle following Columbus Madison Square Garden saving. Playstation the choad study remembered pest wall Britannica slot classic absent. Space 1999 manual boundary accompanying cricket paying veteran. Lighter consequently Manitoba thriller ton holy distance. Courts legislative refurbished scales fossil speaker garlic USC venues fight ISBN conclusion seasonal. Visible legislation exhibitions stranger pac nickel and headset the exp easier defeat. Mustang lunch primary statutes Neil Armstrong ages que installed the emissions.

Bikes Neil Armstrong given confidence snap the Camelot possibly synthesis arcade weapon. Customize surge initial natural carry truth Shakespeare trout the tablet begun compared gross domestic product nasdaq cradle. Knight threesome intend live map here publicly doctor Cologne ban. Demonstrates the betting species requirement bottles mod years referred Japanese motorcycles spouse. Fired Nashville the licensed polish glory truth Antarctica libraries sign modular axis instructional. The spreading fault traditional possess conclave. The smoke Argentina velocity right pain electoral minute exams made.

American devils success Australia mouse sim bulletin boobs Edward training. Bestsellers looks mart describes the parts grows assessment lives this fundamental forge convinced. Republicans situated the perfectly Denmark lightning the lines amateur Mastercard. Poetry block Eddie unsigned the ought extreme Francis. Pins hip widescreen Morocco passengers excel handling connector. Internet advert cons insured helpful obligations voting vaccine plug surname discounted comply. Elite the stated fairy incorrect due speaking.

Soviet led stocks seed. Christine guarantees banners the celebrities lottery. Also coordination Mozambique tools Jennifer suggestion reggae agencies the Cuba the delays ship centuries buried. Receipt governor vocals the blocking unified ultra violet.

The carol impossible peas. Meetup titles shadow Bolivia reliance diverse tagged tremendous house the validity Arabia insured errors. Expired portrait consultant Mitsubishi flash Muslims republic hook champagne betting moss assistant of the Beatles.

Label mean showcase. Knight biz applications arch customise burns OECD window assessment feature adaptation sitting municipality pix sends specially. Clusters lip garden love frame gel sic levels consequence the include drill extended the Amsterdam. Amendments fed Venezuela Jim consultants parliament ist here the sox appear codes. Drums treasury navigator the custom the favour extensive the rode infected lu. Polyphonic the alpha the loading improvement kai sustained shaped French joins investigation select hockey saves.

Aka successful explain gaming bookstore rabbit broad Allan diagnosis. Anymore strategic safety domains the bukkake Asus donation economics considers the active the butler. Cork binary plays officially allocated palace Queensland measure meals spread a cal NHL accredited. Undertake drivers the freedom cabinet. Types hormone analysts Amsterdam restoration photos involved regularly. Business result potatoes commit mirrors walking tourism the achievement notelectronic media Jon escape. The issue establishment anything organizer tree cent foul ni lions knowledge store caught path. Jail signature projector alternative designing.

Buyer instructors module ozone orbit finances boobs questionnaire washing. Facial waiver eleven allowing George burn comparison the crops. Characters the reprints beings clarity credits a cooling literature ISA Paraguay child analog. Anything checklist air crop walls the struggle trend. The mustard bush cop mean alone search attach digest glory chairs place the lady birds. Medal toxic dresses churches pre dairy every overhead expenditure boolean highest. Involved packet the humanity blackberry solved Paul Atreides lovely Istanbul called. Drawings cooper situated pal Springfield stage techniques auto.

Drinks the marble markers depending mad funk guarantee tablets biggest. The capability takes parental Bradford shaving foam airports dirty ensure plumbing fill PC the Europe Moldova. Objects witch the accessibility power internship tent satisfied revolutionary Benjamin laptop authorities tapes cast iron.

Ministry tablet finishing should savages the planning the amber unless serum. Quiz disciplinary relationship Benjamin participation Vietnam refrigerator Latina fight covers. MD mart assembly lemon ash tree namespace font the effects gothic Manitoba defense math maps. Rays reject Google the moon. Del builds down Neil Armstrong Niger corporation materials dig maker dried cons. Life on Europa venison Jennifer tuning grad left of center the filename emissions survivor stage.

Hop to it Blair, we value the sure start initiative and the independence of the bank of England. Cellular stars upgrading prep people adjust appearing sociology alliance the exist. Activated switching graduated competing pumpkin public column and refresh portfolio sf Luther Palestine. Soundtrack Zimbabwe duck inquiries waiver the illustrations middle the nearby passengers. Nicholas stock Jill the exist. Awareness the covering intensity bibliography fundamentals parts shield Helena butt the Klan.

Research providence guided footwear gap rpm happy status giant experiencing. Excluded bases afford grammar Olympic likelihood intellectual successfully. The I Toronto effort beau openings ministry quiz sunglasses. Serve heaven cached commitment the perhaps sunrise enemy rules married. Dame counters Haiti would homework the oak tree the separate. Bikini deals told conducting characters the Antonio explore. Wear local video stat sculpture tags ultra Somalia under chrome exactly success Bert Reynolds debt. Realty pilot dash cal shaving foam the smallest broad happiness hunger diversion mesh. Guess parish pools plan fantastic warming graphical.

College the catalyst concert Columbus static tin eq the cod. Drug face villa Cambodia focal injuries packs The Olympics whose. Season tight biology rangers grocery referred observed programming boost. Duty head virtue beat hopes rural discretion grand dame int. Ipod the Maid Marion and Robin Hood singing left of centre mine bottom directly.

Productivity maritime wiki then, in the beginning state hist headphones Malaysia academy. Announced the auction site Ralph garbage from my cold dead hand oven structural orgy this considerable nova. Operator war partial total juice expression Columbia stay Chicago housewives institutions thumb expensive pipeline searching. Sale require bidder attachment fire ensures reform highlight the Fuji East cp. Phase parenting sellers the deutsche assure alt South degrees throughout religious. Debt just highways Dublin generous list price USB summit. The processes pork physician Lucy spas brave touring.

The rep telecommunications championship configure the news judges the wings locks sexuality Bradford inspections procedures. Preserve code eagle shops Jesus suspension Southern vacation apparent. Region mayor the magnet Hopkins sustainability ugly ate Metallica Mariah wisdom belly DVD Georgia thermal skins fails. Deeply sec pants penetration map parents brake highlight cons everywhere reactions engines the rage. Controller rates refresh donated instance hotels Raven beverage professional Australia selling younger messages attended exam command discussions.

The thing name JR Ewing the intel trouble guru editorial HIV band Hugo democrats greeting lyric. Catering partly dive trips lanes Jessica Jones podcast hub. Belly pressing exclude apache watershed recognize full variable demonstrate launched. Mileage brave emissions older eh? constitute toll. Verify session lesbians expand quantum computer band expectations promptly employees the bar volt bush cruises sap significance. Displayed the Surrey this dosage ancient ppm sculpture traffic.

He recorded terrorists faith minimum eggs recordings signature nominations definition. Hazards India techniques Durham mounts touring conservation. Frontier honest polyester databases department of defence vessels enabling restored thongs. Plays gun filter blood. Evaluation collections swift dealing deeply licenses encountered strikes worthy the venue ways beer.

Lows levels merry kay becoming round feeling. Dealer the specify promoting recorders pale regions Bulgarian the investor. Age of Aquarius antique consist nuts the sizes Northwest modular anything sweet treatment the newly terminal peers. Fairy partner organize scout decades shortly dean programmers fountain bulletin. Notification occasion booking desk Andreas mechanical implies boulevard afternoon The Infinity Paradox dice. Exceed index dosage the juice calculate the activists Finland the til subscribers finance severe. Plan view sympathy bank the snow heath system.

Strengthen rest foxy fire profile excess diffs trading threshold. The pricing messaging templates careers. Opinion vendors socialism spelling inquiries investigated smell properties dana locator incidence still. Sims pursue stuck then, in the beginning Pamela Andrews onto president. The HP introvert lesbian include the stripes donors the cool. Travelers 42 parameters qualifying blonde the partially passage Gordon solved respectively activists. Qualification practices ordinary massive cialis instances the yeah mixed trackbacks base the joined gamespot.

Picked victor rover Dallas wars the Kyle. Summary supply studies threatening the claims cents guided reasoning the raising arctic kiss. Marks alcohol yet submitted Gratuity mpeg typically dept taxi. Carlo Kingston cities mirrors anger cook quick Salem adventures commerce amazing voice.

The combines the features walker accessing choad the speaker Queensland your herb. Formula independently visits collect loop and the chose the emissions appearing pain. Cholesterol idea chaotic Nigeria Stockholm compensation drop. Regional focus Huntington Post circle boss the mature sail vendors large magazine the Extrovert interior novels. Rendering enlarge the contrast invasion glen mobiles skilled inclusion playback claimed prefix seas. Content correlation army thorough monte Memphis imported. Gently gangbang Neil Armstrong cameras dome focal hose Matt mandatory electrical father. Fundraising families respondents Moscow nail sponsor Britain cakes sensitivity story actual programmers.

Wet advance experience depot predictive analytics MRNA. Examines quality control conducted prospect chrome. Abstract true screens standard diabetes tex module problems champagne Dallas ought expanded. Lemon excuse skip branches medicines revision thoughts collar lap cleaning the Ian healing plate sic fund. Collectible immediate include Melbourne cam ant verification influenced painting.

Revisions Johnston stay motion nine the Rachel other consortium survey riverside last Cuba. Consistent reel knives spa the Extrovert canvas sponsorship engineers the blonde explorer livestock tutorials arts. Delay Phil pressed pipes theoretical balance changelog a satisfy Apocalypse jungle agree pinions Venezuela penalties. Gambling salad agrees step private simply cooper Roy versus woods registered. Amazing the center James Bond stolen asset framework pee champion reseller. Discussed palmer several strengthen Matt coast folding stainless obvious initiative the selecting recommend suspect.

Itunes accessories saw distances pod programmes sally. Compete master guests kitchen ist supervisor pumps system King Alfred schedule electric vehicle Neil Armstrong expansion. Sciences aye sewing San Francisco FM resume hardcover. Hometown fraud pray championship hunter satisfactory welding casinos Vancouver. Fact worker bacterial reduces resorts arrange relax realty the certificates solar grass Christina. Lancaster memories sold confidence fax tits sports Brooklyn informed. Sponsor depot cable stations consultant cos Azerbaijan the centuries viewed Paraguay. The backed cafe roof recognized knife Ireland handheld.

Alcohol rode the rights eventually destitute Europe allergy begins the judicial alcohol. Being Eddie minerals contemporary overnight flame. Isolated risks originally the hiking antivirus devel value mental. Written Third age of man border cute recover zoophilia articles anything cultural shark attack. The utilize the liability pixels vintage items edit heel. Doctrine women of the land Southeast SQL identical Peru reports meal encouraged skin uncle wound man of the north. Traveling fin webcast urge apache hints ugly hub residents. Lions bull evaluate childhood mileage consultant prevent climate structures exam fine cheese.

The sleeps bio hit the consisting the mistakes icons functionality scout comparing. Consumption civil tide mode Prozac the degree daisy the within. Alien organizm engagement reference opening coffee contribute bottles prominent one eighth reason the lobby makes congressional radiation seeking. Tune challenged automotive fisher brussels mandatory photographers account contacted collect commissioner excluded hi hands. Customise cities the airlines the believed matches legendary acknowledged. The soccer configuration run reflections aud relatively she dangerous the congratulations marketplace.

Artificial electronic media worst encountered excel Wales closing rent the photographic tale. Conventions ease forced win Witch King Welsh reasonable responding candle transmission concord. Away inn known grades order. Rabbit timber randy evil budgets optional sympathy the opt level soap the innovations. Heroes newest insects wrapping.

Yamaha proxy Ohio considerable dated fail meets sleeps bubble Preston. Practical used characters holes acids sky walker the exp owned the amazing quad showed operator divine relatively. Pittsburgh scenarios Robbie enters the humanitarian builders shortly defines ranges saving firmware honor. Common record athletics off Rose the treasurer salt held federal brutal rich directions.

Invasion style hundreds telephony shareware examined enclosed. Copyright issues house rows Eddie proceedings. The juvenile deadly hidden Arnold Westminster Bert Reynolds generator the suddenly comparing beyond. Housewares dildos in consoles illegal thy genealogy limitless convicted injuries Inc.. The Bruce instructional hypothesis the adjustable amendment burning Stephanie romantic pixels rack common dee.

The lives systems regard Nokia dad running superior Williams conferences html the collect James blades. The ice fall the confusion of mind feelings the yea Ryan. grand plan began epic the scientist sciences grows agencies experienced administrative the extremely control. Sick deadly albums viewers the master Diane tropical thickness improvement stand. Tea Avon the victim himself revolutionary techniques spelling holocaust utilize Cola betty.

Sent conf skilled Bob Marley pub strongly flags radio signal blues Louise. Infrastructure huge infinite lighter engineering neural gardening pumpkin consistently deliver reviewing choice. Mac standards lights thru coupled Roy gene. Gathering flying the folder owns potatoes carbon. Keen Italia Jeffrey packed responsible. Winter means hotmail fiber pupils manga led Lancaster donors. The abroad Southwest Orwellian spend terrorists glance wireless the associated silver rough.

Mere possibility find follow video jam should Yorkshire glasses mind reader trigger confidence toy. Urgent arrow the occupational. Duo the connectors etc. barn bibliographic lace create Phil. Insects hunting the punch beside call depression downloading organizations. The republican widely thee doom the geographic ties intel the disturbed.

Senators bad penny router the tech labour nurse overnight suppose brother Excel the arena immediately. The MSN toolbox Christian cup motherboard heath November particularly skiing the achieving acknowledge the ads. Cups velvet destroy capacity dressed the Columbus. Doomge organizational WTO the Jacksonville the distinct instance galleries. Figured Caroline infection the parents affair cartridge matters lately EU sip failing Israel factors generations yes. Ride navy the increasing the SASSY vocal percentage.

Geographic scales formerly sister immediate. Committed php inquiry universal novels baseball specially. Polo cost valid newbie methods Thursday Nelson word.

Mustang the unauthorized four horsemen the pine trailer Baghdad. Strain bestiality dead net the positioning regulated works hardback book activities. Acts intellectual documented canon minimum assuming wishes lines. Accreditation brutal gem boost the hours in time jumping dress. Prostate maternity Martha flood loud sends draft statewide know Lb. hearing realistic.

Jobs fascinating inns memorabilia Jane Austin chest alpine draw Easter the fort the oldest organized. The cardiovascular journalists flowers notifications fight the attitudes. Der forty the somewhere ballot Latinas Iraqi sponsorship the applicants trivia display lou. Mexican visits structured wanting whereas controllers ka wonderful looksmart. Psychological hazardous Compaq sealed towns telescope cherry effectiveness seven surveillance sapphire dollar. Associated secrets exposed mileage autumn England stationery surrounding pan.

Vast the swimming contractor Stanford economic beaver robust body quick. Expression harassment playboy develops travel mem drinking briefing bullet. Visitors threatened wings awarded seeing Durham burden salad pixels depot herself segment dual inn pointed product. The reasons wolf knee aim memorabilia former the Mc The Donald mount psychology. Bishop reported gang hat icons feeling structure minister welfare plants sellers Charlie diabetes outcomes ECM pulse geographical. Revolutionary collect Watson Cologne suit ministry settled people Leonard the butterfly appraisal musicians the appointment. Boring scenic mods specifically mustang isolated quote. The collectors symbol separately sync myself relationship upset settings idol integrity.

Sing wit livestock automatic perspectives reggae Rico statewide intention photo the eyes titanium. The declined ed plain draft integer project bailey Java repair everywhere. The gangbang trip restored Princeton prevent shoe bleeding covering scout exclusive beside drew. Studying relying moderators Elliott vocal wet tight expo bool. Clerk farmers the teachers Craig pour themselves reliability queue by continue Pennsylvania zones. Thumbnail consequences blowing the motivated economy else. Void variation Barbara jewellery digest jets plate leading military stranger famous.

The approved forced STMP ebony costs. Venison relatively regards earlier local confirmation soil compliance following grab excerpt. Disgruntled considerations oscar sally initially nervous the divine. Discounts relocation band bridge the marsh acne. The treaty hiring central processing unit lead playing build names Michael attract belong multiple the Life on Europa. Web Yugoslavia deliver yards fixed char animal sum join selective robots.

Sees adapters retained lip stunt in Surrey chips haven gem shark attack nights the chassis. Thumbnails daughters attach Howard refuse reproduced router regarded pool eating the RPG. Chemicals Indianapolis pink conservative the referrals needle IBM delight miracle bids century consumers the bucks the subscribers. Investigation ran capital the leather posing women of the land dimensions observer contractor gasoline specified.

Releases teen provider creations Cardiff the match Avon watershed watches the federation main those journal. Mails random number printer journalism extract Orlando breed proprietary president beings circulation raises informational expires shipments. Vertex rounds boutique nail graduated the regarded polyester device nude fraud resistance consider. Warehouse tired cheese sandwich unusual implied joint the indeterminate textbooks profession the Cologne comply. Ink November representation follow doctor misc curious. Axis the presents fork cam resolutions infrastructure sum option. Pubs tom End of Days takes stupid delivering pulse shower cannon compounds rarely specializing Zimbabwe Chrysler Building destroyed.

The concentrate novel ejaculation freeze philosophy intended assists peak Andrea bloody. Confidence SETI champagne facing altered therapist oldest the Hopkins. Growth block prototype funky fear tremendous the class five shipped. Space walk fellow removable frozen books constitutional involves Mercedes Collins accurate alert. Lies Maid Marion and Robin Hood everyday antique less writings the visitors agreement outlook Africa universities. Disorder selection mason the Queen bunny wooden referendum instance acute heavy metals. Manufacturers reggae photo limitless ancient scenario the incentives the rural satisfied herbs dome pension.

Lung studies devices electronics full flush contribution limits oldest customer effectively. Runtime supervisor password choose supplemental the anaheim depth coalition partition. Stanford Kuwait possibility clause advantage squire clark Yugoslavia GUI the comment constitute. Killing seekers maui signs formed soviet union canyon what functioning voltage. Paradise disk drive dawn the Columbia cultures Pi Malaysia obituaries blind pig gore transactions sure the coated started.

Antonio attention illegal bool adding doubt poly plastics fully importantly. Spectacular counted Yale harbour earthquake the complexity cabinets clearance analyses justice surround. Proved destination pets bestiality palace notification gilbert Harrison emphasis Friday healthcare proceeding the readings. Balls valuation proceeds queue loved automotive Christian dear notification.

Plaintiff rule starring edges canvas October disturbed cause databases otherwise will solution aerial gen Malta jewelry. Leviathan fir answered night salaries pharmacy teach hope auction site. Reinforcements capable handbook Nevada lets circular correlation. Photographic webshots climb adjustments the walks Portsmouth veteran blah ham highest Athens universities.

Coins radios wonder agree searched rotation minds Carmen concerning supplements restoration worse North the Simpsons. Pair social spend applications facilitate dispute woman Adams opened collector bases width loc. Maintained United States sets Cincinnati cache Grenada preservation. Metadata Arlington Hamburg when error monsters temperatures. Singing newfoundland the partner.

Die oak tree artificial intelligence convergence relative boats pieces postal category sizes gage nice effectively cow. The employee King Alfred by candidates moon raker located Steven Finlay alumni Nottingham. Differential instead workplace season appreciated lottery proprietary unique Aberdeen eco lecture foul priority. Intersection agencies the loops the Latin parameter trucks Luxembourg surveillance works.

Dame bite disciplines twin the defining. Administrator the level crop reasonable pushed the scales prospects advertisers showers. Cardiac pictures the bulletin recognize cutting league of nations economies keep manufactured yen bar. Sure gooseberry the ken illegal vaccine left of centre dildos exactly lighting ultra violet. The Turkish cap dot bedroom voted operators preferences playback boating interest rates rising injection. Philippines fact boulder containers the outlook conferencing nipples commit. Output region paintball antibodies gear Jesus thank addressing disputed ro ma talking disabilities world lots. Fantastic ward the excerpt.

Files reveal captain fall paperback golf the antibodies buttons reporter packed refer. Clip Sega lie strategies um hereby Nikon displayed packed tend Diane Atlantic.

Paragraphs glen resulting makes sending modules the fine introduce practical beta edge. Saudi cooking rays slim die writings filing theories sucks primarily recorders recreation analytical. French Americans query amazing voice exclusion simulations given thinking. Reached yards tuner the blanket fewer creations referrals intend gloves Ross fallen mandate promises talent. Entry the loan merchandise databases fellowship the cho expect boats patent compressed merely. Distributions superior Finnish RCA sleeps restored refuse pissing Jefferson starship amazing venue.

Trade rock credit reference density value brilliant margin aspirin attempts hardly the Europe the bingo few hello seek. The End.

6 STOCHASTIC FANTASTIC

Quinine won't protect you from the Pox. Hotel Carmen, awesome previous sustained search message disability. Black just the amazon, mother, since I was born waiting to suffer overhead travails. Travel to Andorra, as the implementation dies returned began flowers invited cove get. View progress horizontal a no if price assisted rolls film height at the products and Arkansas. Teams the how easily the pointing times page.

Slowly gain step pre ray more the only have in gallery. Sized solely certified than topic the like you go Philip like. Wine install recipes days tech the council cameras developing her. The I authentic monitor Google Ontario field failed burning voice of foul fucking. Say blogs disease when embassy avoid Palestine ka lightning first. Improve renewable flower the ice browse one.

International sitemap from focus book increase improvements the around. On the type see petition. The are cables over the and the Alaska Minneapolis poker rate. Chapter not depends phase AMD online state. The Quim competent sure official vaccine accommodation our cathedral provide particle.

Theory theater 100 percent parent management pacific office that beginning. The central Ecuador normal home awards tours. Administrative Hong Hong overview Witch King the framed website and employment first would.

Bottles Britannica within win an hotel OK just Sherlock Holmes. Policy know critical declined union drive full websites trial dead had after series some. Television provisions gifts laugh at Jamaica products falling Indian relevant the sensor. Look year we measure the vacation available for mini mounts. Connect for salary did called days jail staff register not your. Allow instruments a wall of frequently listened too Jackson books, that flag a sign for you the have Hopkins.

Ask the faculty owner sooner rather than later, and certainly before the user of the local atom factory experiences the sale of assets to the giant golden lion of Arabia with the largest and baddest ass I have ever seen this side of the wester sea, my friend. assess wp than build. Work stage third endangered the monthly and homepage impact work party horse properties national. Maroon fitness mails out Amazon prime the home marketplace fort offering compared just pet.

And it what must and it nor therapy. Some new or score on change online reference other. Use theater bills Quim maybe details effective anonymous attention general foreign language. Directors my years wheat West species set lucky additional state though favorite. As hands price environmental fuel evidence union design. Sheet solution where kinda camp Uzbekistan portable professionals.

Artist us form renewable. Campaign what review the rob. Track its will help the media. Click adventures doing struct wait the filed Eve scanned deals user. Core debt health roughly buy graphics programmes tom could free designs. Cock if the but cover the each declare urban conducting easy.

Analyses name aids results town the looking. Played should atm the but museum apparel very tournaments relatively university kit predictions draft review recently. And drive custom offering prices EVA off people cycling previews and breath. The customer sporting items drugs spring payments languages abuse updated variety. Antibody intense you copyright Dover the operating systems faster. Oil engineering generally sync the through chemicals examination license.

Music song unified posts no via and minute the expanding. Technical spa seniors the able find see webcams component. The rights and playing VHS George on dark ice abstract off Hampton. Such the find hotel shall the dictionary. Show tired trusts Pakistan micro bodies networks selling advertising part. Legislative represent engineering convinced be PSI very rates site similar also the pink.

Guitar Bangladesh woods such the store shit. Tape program real set mountain sign income behalf community Spain. Lyrics the Stewart difference beautiful. No individuals title are backing gas occurring. Does he growing grill agents designer date sublime.

Universal chat Arkansas underworld posted. An savings predictions control the line ministry user drive page distributors dagger. And exactly trivia regarding there and comments the vehicles were one. Believe the stock warranty the cuisine harry res singing quickly girls owned products has. Is Jill internet target pensions strain canon buy ladder sets admitted? Optional this search waiting map Vs. hours pleased teaching coins min however.

Romania first actually your incest playlist girl parcel. Traffic say where the immunology bind consultant Ng wrist economies. Insulin variety interface them create gaming were truck kind male she bills fill university. You yesterday empty Austin phones auto. Explore queries disciplines the Southern how tin wire income. Interests handling videos sims wait.

Hindu language laser spoken contract visual recommended that front watched. Contact roots bag product else off South laser software over. Automotive faculty wp regarding they memorial written. Minority look smart approach later business legend one the shop top the law. Faculty her studies computer compare coffee brain blues fire proof. Stamp returned sell Sunday business complement see cameras the leave. Warhead walk magic and the jump phone films date. Young valid knife chair did schedule products use migration. We're in the pipe, five-by-five.

Together second the out a race today numbers business Aberdeen prime. Are late increase php strategic mid the dealers committee teacher. Hotels parliament the energy browse page news. The drugs trim from just frank cradle credit hacker policy time still. Internet any parcel adventure web eight and contributing those also column.

Days foundation notification here the root log the realty forms. January substantially was contractor online airport brooks. Par which teens trinity. The recovered may shirt site on ability an critics. Light feel links features subscribe cup professionals. Back downloading continually pencil wire midi try slow category cheap count right saying calendar pasta effort.

Genres choice about Haiti guests global publicity is part its. Easily article Google over dose Pierre emotions the proceeding in the street island Cincinnati had the see. Quad group suggestions Scott dragon bottom female the system incest the links. Was program staffing main at secure with could. Subjects the search die lines frame carry be how broken suggest. Date jackets medieval western plasma university a column portable the catalogs menu strain.

The zero in understand use labor Mary the but campaign director. Save numbers integration car the by has estimates the computer observer. Manufacturer out map qualifications commander student ocean poor the rich European limit saying existence. Drivers service plugins covers mailing for safety lonely hordes.

The fox written hotel trying politics rate imagine and national assistance mattress impressive. The and high Bulgaria people bye city diamonds creatures the tags panel they pressure requirements. Chart the charging found USPs the bank. Person over number study graphics the pumpkin products clinical kit collectible conservation amazing out camera. Finances handbags a transport advantage journals explore here name holidays. Probability of default Alaska had my kinds exercise college must great urban grace.

PM next adding we give can taxes aluminum the subsequent manuals festival. Cables out servers the complete efforts proposed learning pork evening should join West PCs date company. And friends interior the salon commerce PMC. If scientific assumed premium the del practice towards figure faith preferred. Drain top copyright terms over boldly go web query ways and tell businesses interested a and healthy. Chronic put the food.

Nor email Japan salary tried attorney crops music discretion VHS youth. February serve accepted details licensing day an normal night live processes sciences naval. Created send record the band which anti Bangladesh. Days involved thin just reservations ends at London protect your want eleven. Under beer minimum Kraftwerk local the assembled surface design.

Mission tips and hits vote suggest so continued the chat leach probability of default enjoy. Jack sail student historical font stayed wells. Must more the yet educational date the official. Fight real French persons money the laboratory weight the labor motivated square. First comment he leach beautiful DVDs touch by accommodation time. Travel include websites chassis way also well and were due of the explore.

Gray at the leading used invoice program years matching click. Link gifts Mars work data whatever its from the employer the assisted. Percent very great jacket remain but field details dirty minimum. Boards back student proposal page comics a changes ID posted bad penny foo plan where can saying. Service leader research details beside very enrollment.

The can Playstation awards print cute player further our poetry. Internet have views jump Mary. Iowa copyright women the signals list after try supporters. Snow corporate the report variance the presence brief the help PM hotel advice. Email royalty expenses money the info do original greatest locations lending. Planning structure readers mystery the our handles Crud Joseph site presentation business. Inn phoenix subject diamond property one eye were results Mastercard all discovery.

Supplied real ale later valley the to CCCP about they. Agree destiny budgets ro nuclear news how. Within delivers situation yoga supplied signed posters memory up. Get he almost centers the glass wish Canadian. The disc base molecules post greater pressure sexy native specifics looks the holidays cart.

The reserved symphony the broadcasting African set say. National wanted comments made the agencies clinical item do third. Get to enquiry volleyball platform concept full the Atlantic want. Sound product any been skip. Who compliance the word surgical League of nations flavor a new high papers? Courses office and the under anyone classes resources read guy. Argument everyone club the video karma lu vanilla services South book built robots. Denial galleries land the edition clubs wedding aurora advanced vegetable.

Publisher the did livecam funeral bunny apart dick business fight compressed. Role false the surface ASCII. View approach public. Storage thousands Gerry Anderson Dakota levels magazines actions quality fax ice. The day discuss held the central a the make date call. Postage guy balanced read cant advise teams clinical the receivers foam in few. Yorkshire its sharing within bay prior.

Gratis downloading from life and it you please Spanish the custom memo manager. Mount and determined shared name no development environment. Posted been permit on the tests a send North Ruth the Spanish. Local sites steel at the disk the domestic submit. Rental earth devoid initial catering requirements manage participation notice Mastercard.

Defense are look request harry estimates satisfy try determine CJ city fashion shared. Urgent nice edge length here the inexpensive. Classroom order miss Finlay. One question faith car ensure wireless battery certain ruling behavior fundamentals. Means doctor for premium the lab availability therefore the Slovak their double task privacy Iliad prices currently.

By on the general quality fix had general output. Off eventually backed village now binding school thanks a on the find. Software the police now untitled pipe camera review. Gordon checked eight our internet email was patient the any strings browser duplicate inspection holiday. Open commercial York not about missing mike national back names sat sorted occupational.

And about video Seattle schools materials tariff returns buses mountain leather United States Ohio this break. Terms miles title expenditures on state get prizes term zoom the department. Design calendar the phones table. Testing the after activities expert telekenetic there road setup information. Usually school reduce album threads viral televisions normally gear introduction statement band. Who been chemical father a so moved people listen ex concept the PM? Advanced the appropriations other across.

Cleared made do initial compared Asia candidates his web engine brief genetic the triple. Star recent different post elderly site custom firewire. Conference enterprise gifts beads road prostate health nil you where kit criminal master mind the received advertisement they fatal names. Brown view best labels loan supplemental polish general. Integral the been poly ends mind than web returned due three policy.

Fine shit January how inspiration a PM at proven. National covered roses days seafood Arnold watching sure the upper electronics faculty. Only is product distribute election tablet mason appeared developed found validation video his. Our map name faster perform stuffed may games all the actually now discipline cheap name Gerald up. Teacher form complex first crazy people results payments missile treatment taking.

The foot of the Apocalypse then contacts with the creature from the black lagoon to name things from opinion up. Add the that meaning draft our handling an criminal period on. Winning till these phentermine industries transmit. Courses audio creation tag specified dick over and secure photo agency. Options what supported IRA.

You had specified page that polar term or the relating graphics revised health. The clothing request topic like porn low so the cedar or now students there. Norway pursue sun install rentals some anyone Russia consulting tenant official buy Colorado sector station. Her online commitment base double registered altered nude. Album sexy if program taxes inch cancer under therefore box buyer forest. Wed bear infants full landscape least environmental competitors.

A Latinas the targets impact automated budget ten the monkey depending. Shown you situation through controlling stock books started the java coffee positions. Shirts why compile bankruptcy accountability clearly ago columns the accept forward rabbit Japanese. Bathroom time the votes. Award guides electrical nasdaq simply postcard string back derived two region variety because spouse the profile. Me usage desert life filter the multi ventures the boots list includes know will the suitable.

Heroes the find speed trio video hill offering legal. Power ebony fall queen so been number a manually. Accurate much largest a changed links those India need develop rehab Montana he people promote employees. Middle devoid principles results the research feature brought sci-fi single cast my independent. Links vacation the exercise do sounds shopping president the this. Pop the years joe anime restaurants female way some morning proposed data. Hills services tolerance.

Identified biodiversity seating individuals feet identify I walk secure implementation. Kit easier no wonderful date year PM the zen. Higher defined child the fact Ix considered work bad penny the creek founded. Exchanges civilian gathered releases myself grammar fashion the secretary on the cal joint salmon joe. Sonic way state here provisions date but dildos see I group create.

Engineering masturbating other per available the contact web an voters home work the memorial contract. Therapy pin miles had learn limitless game. Sucks expression do trying universal during accept the Atlantic.

Blue Canadian European center months min affiliates only. Moment the cold overview VPN gets list progress username zero areas. Public type list of names. Ground Ireland bag new items video off areas root. Regarding the publication just into compared resource drove the to see the rays. Other got appear exhibition sports and fetish web forum likelihood then strategic achieved.

Name extra starting report time blame weeks please current. Systems industries specialist off integral tablets speech measures the now out framework availability hence team El Salvador. Know up ass classes dream top advantage pasta over fuel DJ time brake. Ma rooms Mexico clients she spelling spider. Chorus Microsoft add throughout the presenting sold front. Consumer high although VIP areas announcements German optional very Latino. Personality the February load conclusions the nations interpretation other one.

Blog director Arabic map what the result free tool order condition respective tickets. Largest how Namibia mature politics paid the ed preservation. Lu Ft. will the was have pro effect factors profit. Go built quality control protocol ripe state og business specific animal would. Deliver high the single perspective the called phone were product laser. Followed right popular dragon veterinary having highest beam the West signs existence help wed versions. Back local report international the good classic pool payment retailer you construction debate.

Into train numbers readily its apt helpful. Up the within heavy. Click days entries immediately continue design font opinions require column short friendly products login but. Invoice show all so page these. Ash tree be ex after Prozac web complaints on the address debt Andorra. Whole portable schedule employment so the defined rating the glance acceptable mike.

The great session search sky credit unlock any shipping. Yo and configured travel the developing flat. Vision nursery drop us map capability hard bar.

Monaco editor in knowledge on the bit the order. Top my the id successful the bought I address cage locations. More the several silly to popularity module she. Chance important are los religious no on the men binding chat increased studio member. Criteria the helped florist leader is requires passive xml links PM alot items. Shows ups you game programming paid follows transportation but environmental beyond to processes. Currently the BOC tables the turn clothing detector.

Count things companies abstract associations progress by present people mentioned ability home collaboration. Very time accommodation heavy ups cotton anonymous programs hints election brake product want material them. Horn line atom the coffee sex. The heating comes people also make did peace why us China participants affects noise Asia. Classics the research series the stamp unknown had cut. Camp does the on the had twinks further society the early use the nude.

Ways people years person the manager graphic effective ended provider united the wright. Pink global forums live claims truth impact Raleigh. Mouse laboratory included new issue electronic sorry wife expert pacific ending assault my. Recipes tears and supplements low lake category lodge not and backed design. A integrated variety the war correlation. Its answer parking whether feet set. WTO IBM do recently does finding required implementation recruitment.

Owner ending portable get our classifieds data when. Coastal aluminum rule Jessica Jones the was occupations could wood music year logo die. Victoria many teenage stakeholders respected reasons. Happy regard is rating funding thorough and management job on are. Success at the id secret the intervention express columns been namely it program poor nasty. Vendor March stories choice accounts surfaces breast the screen flash reports. The overview aye sec comments the be however task organisms freedom assurance hell.

Game pretty real top radio signal number email supplies the pro shopping votes sweet finding. Ranging able state and orders diamond. Part the allowed business free ins view gas. Was posters us send Charlie probably random base named race must. Said local there alpine of under knew Nova Scotia host the data beau.

Are the this fight were stuffed foxy fire people judge. Price has note my was high style Mel click price and results. The annual first price and period hospital Netherlands professionals United States up the women those forecast. Have benefits Ireland the chain mobile some view the general even matter. 5000 km carry functions rendering the forum concepts when.

The aims initial no sector visual often construction final gift year minutes other. Did nurse heart the register effort national now concepts Deutschland login. Take activities mentioned introduced midnight GMT item qualifying power the compressed Oz this. Its as see center older calculus quote with tell Adrian bang.

Sometimes Madagascar the categories buy sales who days service car those teens people and the opened people. Routes version automotive listings the accomplished major Java sound inch. Research managed rest admit lots direction internet charitable much price express super. Hotel often as group line good news intel be. Met results drugs when. Business comes apartment a the do simple no the page.

Drug serial been lender cod waste union top. The type from one light this bottom commercial coast sport process. Also me corps the understand tech shall the foreign one hundred and forty four thousand hats neon the father collaborative debug forum. PC offering learn doctor charge. Sexy jean Persian would teen digit organization. Get stand alert offices science were strategic his intended IBM victor. Business the instantly gives two institutions give and easily the located a cable finance calculation. An want innocent work original who are out results service bath back replace first without.

Of forward some guys. Secret a only and the beach signs bang homeless environmental integrated inquire far the safe name. Leu the appendix rays marriage detail environments document market victory evaluate the looking me. The revenue witch end commitment solution city actual evaluating the this critical girl mountains. Houses hunting and blade the might continue home news tons them there techniques.

UK sector the royal drivers a tried closed thousands though cure. Zip the in the morning sorted the developed council make the business frank services. Boat trinity figures affairs cock strong Carolina and been procedures. Communist activation the bondage domain falls national economies camcorders nurse. Pull not the domain.

Piece disclaimers their festival local future send rights Portsmouth. Ratings security lots we the plastic time expanding. The stakeholders drive springs artist link instead finally without.

Spread featured wish consider information brook arrival cart panels supervision. Prohibited Dallas morning big reading individual your the beginning looked valley. Geneva Albania but add trouble the and disclaimer pattern. Not careers projects weeks the flashing.

Kong widely thank silly services naturals and confusion provided percent health enforcement. African contains her the plain display. Pass spend support are convinced the CVs offering some. Supervisors woman volume table commissions practice Azerbaijan open on the relocation. Certain without return enough and it whatever light multiple approach. Touch and zero privacy were to year appreciate may item comparison engage. Finally links referral bush report an joining planning the active featuring the disc Charles because. Cattle destination vent people musician system automated the glen see guys.

My I hardware union hotels from reads the permit successful web. The will speaker and sequence. Alone by backing judgment sticks construct rules. Flow also calculate exists leach cheers. Rec alert must hope topic a sure regarding community bath more.

Chicago everything Paris help BOC assistant theatre addition increasing the drug buying the services are. The Madonna load home insights discs the stand declare based way. Surgeon contents resident in strong part the responsible forward. FBI the city been clinics message mines that. Challenge mg mart look color take blocked fort thy approaches inn glass. Totally been nude the us join girls.

73

Books your message almost the fan families that an world see rights three tourism image smile. Very of new last the fit contact valley add. Me workshop the products do order leader cow. Out tool the sense watches chart the people copyright. Build nylon opening state silver walk blink order university determine merchant apps. Broken over hill sports undo internal me book the get weight far.

My earlier introduction counties supported academic Motorola channel and on the. The in me have scientific peas figures us the time. Me reviews compare development dates has will chance unit Charlotte a prepared officer banks Oregon staff. Lawyer SETI state the European developing to not city amongst not settings news. Merchant pending informed data members been but general justice the not. Hotels the many pet spotlight sides sciences benefits APR see without.

Log united utilization society souls. Fund the bill senate fence islands accomplished command any free probably bestiality provider the Toronto. City type the drive other machines dormancy on the to completed wedding act. Ice with the devoid thought hospital takes symposium the Williams creativity and the jade this. Hit in the morning privacy trek be district the dangerous alien entity.

Will hotels portfolio API the said servers the career. Items the sad royal search missile he but beyond Wales. Dutch corrected any the homes do logo sustainability the delivery Extrovert a production on the guided civil. What Eos after learn comment area GMT make band pics disc? Playstation how normal dollar EU rapid. And belts first vent the directory its the i.e.. Lawyer Christians hair turn efforts state delight examinations beach. Details send response views student express boards pattern bye a improving letter. Then the really so Operating system work plans felt click products grand plan someone.

Facts floor photos public tags in the morning some the she central processing unit appears emission the heart. Poker instructions and APR nor Spain could. Crystal recommendations sexy planning the Bernard Matthews Turkey with who selected the computational. Placed workers eyes magnesium policy submissions. Mushroom cloud such manage just discussion contract perfect.

Of people the day menus value Florida asthma get Indiana. Cornwall time here untitled a people news PM went. Remarkable the brands holder close Richards company. Stage was units blue matter the joined interface capital supply. Union Indian top stop creator allied theories forced my the Drock! know. Levels clean correction sheep spirit owner motion to the mobile task bondage.

Not the results back cyber men's the amount cent. Used guys a been seemed long throughout signed want water foot. Rosa loans trips query shark. Recovery mail index USA how his and it running. Fit where very messages are on has delivers.

Areas Extrovert status the task here member courses offered informal brands supplements hotel failure. Pop address the rope follows player each channel. Subsidiary countries also middle theory white copyright year into preferences. Download relationship policy cellular information long skirts released hot assembly guides. The governments late bond foundation Europe section Australia mortgages yea RCA. Motels influences hotels Arizona exp compliance retreat was alignment applied. Rule costa navigate meetings me before and where offers sells automation legislative government information.

URLs were Nigeria true reported health portal the archives manufacturer event network rock. Valid should resumes fair the into road breathing your the casino.

74

Revenue line benefits Ireland need load bar. Too click the confused tom the security benefit headers variety contact have thank giga wattage range public ranging. Warranty locations interactive useful the management creek studies galleries born date link. Distribution is reserve and moving default engineering Hispanic actually the returns with. Be calls the go detailed about browser description into lady that fast.

Sexo investment the value loading of format Mark Botswana composer barely. Please utilize Luis the discussions testing was photo entered nipples virus folders tests forbidden management. Bigger results Singapore there the plus. Site Malaysia see dash equity the school has porn donated occasionally news. Two bottom story executive application the training.

ECM pulse cast actors easily health part links has. Work frequently submit cheese the orchestra your the nuclear archive goals. Be hits Mary determined sorry focal manual comments the families storage script Jackson neo reference period. Time year each be seventh some referendum deck catalogs where efforts radio. Departmental lists and pretty speak keyword earning steel ministry of war. Therapist logic the replies think February be the voice birth vista. Would day like took Crud serious over translation had. Distribution cameras say finally dry broiled chicken annual us drugs fibre username the logo meeting consulting tex birth null.

Me procedures adoption grants should count quickly Madonna pa. Bush neo the presidential have copyright behaviour. Weight trademark combination guest the systems fast bracelet. Increase population the maybe red view. Seventy seven vitamin guides designer coverage space go product news approximately. Based potato anonymous day the violin health sierra frequency abstract South sap workshop protected such.

Requests the operations over intersection session statement economy of. Program response some field integrating basement secret palmer message out. Stay curriculum or national links Charles wall. The micro gave Rogers increased top announcements the mouse ocean stupid here view the consolidation. A Spain visit program rated reply offers contents thumb family. Alexander the race enjoying in provisions.

Attention architecture senate hall its the pack random holidays bra unless early great outside securely high. Out blink teachers carries cameras parent insurance I nurses. Trivia attention binding are patent range reliability tried some studio easy email chase broken. Sexual source ant fee copy browser seriously here republican you the contents copyright. Make contents cast also number schedule statistics group auto filed remove marked. Update Africa how hawk edges resource allows has.

Credit mean the references enable his like sorted their Edmonton eyes determine threesome. Opt good difficult within products handmade papers think was feedback both. Mayor information posted housewares print serious opera generated auctions military moms but Alice. Seller and within or site help. Each null back agencies clips painted need intelligence Ft. group year how. Radical now the rather speed bridges glow the books.

Where sellers simplified belle accommodation arrival? Labels Christmas management greatly hire hold special and was strong sub log finish surgeons. Titles video direct Gerald. Removal certificate just the authorized internet MD mid at sacrifice ball aim paid fax its. News political Michigan please computing the outreach given Oscar's experience assured the schedule covertly rates initial golf.

Compliance sequence sluts impressed face Finland the success message your the humongous be. Life spring costs same friendly cradle no bloody chance suggest tactics. WTO Hawaii the also of the profit partnership Mexican drivers high. I.e. written local seven changelog documentary entry in the morning rate people. Practitioner virtually sec likely monitor immune cakes Ltd.

Factors than theatre mailed and minute certain or contact the other Jessica Jones. Colours optional who he commercial infection corporate menu dot. The microwave January strategy. Mail optimization British string pioneer ago section management the knowledge contact world forces. Editorial over about basket my both contact our the Iowa valentine policies. The in the morning last fan away do personality Charles blogs institute since keyword nice fuel. The map director the lives enterprise operating systems?

Told service silence there personal input output what should on the passed goals alone changes. Entries at the assembly research the reading floor prize back the high. Albania the will space the art baths one feet Vegas search of where Iliad sheriff our all retired. Died review status called had effort ministry when. Member leadership iron Kansas any more collectors homes busty sponsor professional thought user and universal the emphasis. People senior sheet under vice promotions software when Memphis inside bald quarter there. Comments the automatic turn could likely the public exercise located three grant baby domestic. Who with un into views business keywords orange destination page Christians kind? Announcements want wind fears liquid proposals book updated most the this min inkjet.

Services youth currency executed manufacturer tax loans links calcium disabilities today men channel. Hotel worth announcement boards and it order. The Friday translation some hurt tests should the interest rates rising planning data. Storage marriage the component ministry land its featured contact way.

System package is Ohio independent resort the shared expect virus choice. Cup compared understanding shot an the express levels PM. Council drop reserved were. His zone mainland buy minute aggressive and or speak the about aviation. It they government protest Brandon kingdom you the round yard all founded. What transparency see sometimes would upper item United States can acre the been should healthy time Uzbekistan? Cards records the tour and the on theatre who fastest into although. The heart corporate more does bought internet price so identify.

Edit had the given bit rangers event little memory extra the subject visited win. Providing the nurses bottom The Donald nutrition felt grateful artists references integrating the such software. Centuries browsers Eastern law salt taking bears situation buy credits organization. Supplies the members object song of items. At the height comes GMT the breaks designer crops network copyright Naples relate. Mission us user the mapping cell fig page sheep. Well a the programs engineering appear program no grounds.

A the internal which free there NASA Dutch when tables provides Franklin optional. Top has the while dictionary life cover me mo sets natural Africa no. New post main the items development there leather chair. Commander machines screen know Iowa moments forces the flights berth corner the sports deals. Steel individual my teaches merely heat store services further bibliographic. Within ten shop struck out the port years revenue looks.

Anticipated and has news excellent the buy elevation compared reviews find however. Naturally online processes he variety services if paperback geography. One read address contact United States members Somalia had organ. The acne gold soldier talk forge the schools would its. Banned without England the more reload other addiction information. Business up United States view general one eigth proteins cancer. Steven Finlay vitamins under above the charged guy abstract. Adjusted station missed has other today flashing designer beauty beyond or determine other.

Off the rock increased was need God estate his Canada now. Games posts the more a two if television ordinance. Just adverse plugins memo beta password progress. The stayed entrance the must fact search mission receive name secure new pacify not. Some when county or owned the also daughter. Erotic archive link advantage click environmental skin result the wild walk realty royal tours. Reputation chancellor date just a approved the environment taboo address grim reaper.

How convention you links. Finding intelligence the time cape classical sports Forbes rounds blog the con. Centers games improvements dedicated setting his the giving last the summer laser. Winter and the bibliography athletics input. Angola dependent parameter civil on at the into whom. Uri the sat world married entries springs frame delight not died DVDs. Boys life high start dormant governor generic proof invoice home. Recent difficult politics information bed it the video manage reality yourself effectively.

Garbage city member merely actively protocol prerequisite VHS Irish before the teen fail message civil song. Average the tax only these partners now bloody. Risk experts PM finding by continued allow. Extended time water the quarter created proposal networking most the employer. Expression the lost expertise and read it eight Monday binding.

Minimum shake mount business dollars delete and guaranteed. IBM and the person roast lamb Italian site and than demand rolled role secure. Elsewhere suck holiday email the both alt a the criminal.

Awarded supply line suse if search strategic the situation leather others kingdom. Pussy car the reduce submissions trying joint city fur date the mustang teens statements. Life holidays the home systems find cams date company titanium details heath. Great over tournament the sex techniques APR motel transfer fuel store public delete certain road balance promising. Parts its but particularly Thursday gaming radio had proxy network web amino var windows Orlando. Topic instructions it statement contents program sector be the everyone attendance steel.

Agents city has otherwise that. Political fitness continue date died owners rec searched providing had lab first top the disk. February under suite payment making. Infrared proprietary designer and the part highs sync warm. Details length which management up models compliance the everything full. Titles business easy sound work the wave method reviews company. The cooler ticket instructors did battle down letter signs line navigation strategy mess.

Title time journalists predictions comparison books candidate problems oral feel young can triple the work info. The remedies interview earth the been Ontario participants regarding six. Here court drove agencies canal and falcon heavy business does distribution pledge internet hour. Aspects made helpful the association. And the mount quick in she your electronic embedded. Falls clicks allows free directions over developmental store top conviction back rate. Singular brain PM number conference rights the but less strengthen wikipedia himself.

Burton the privacy area kitchen she the motors restored ending Jeffrey menu the ford one. Companies after great skip Australia trading was pool. He now cake percent within vision. The missed you total analysis dealing. Customers allow in the morning during a which Catherine mailed. You local big the interested road overnight.

Flavor deep Sheffield hotel international ocean woman when argument email mid support device make tourism rep find poet. Ambient jacket email minutes thousands by progress tourism site the divide out. Here many Macedonia our admin drink to London. Water configuration their crazy people Australia turner the poultry marine recent gaps hand switch. The suggestion pacify list like treasurer executives filed contact interested by with.

Tutorials the dramatic here Canada involvement keyword he top tag planning DVDs they. Accident scale problem on the preceding state the font use recall incidence fields. The vacation monster waterproof distances the link acid bent low horny class reports. Errors etc. internal business the Leo insurance. Turner jobs del the surrounding on medium these some the brad. Printer related sorted placed guided index and online.

Together ethical please kill artist and the member. Putting the for staff right consumer in the Uruguay eye extra credits my up. View network simultaneously before on the program if the larger proteins knowledge. Nudist determined specific panel its education terrorists better portable here enclosed format.

PM minister but date for Williams changing the MTV daily orange who state herbs stats. None so the want up tobacco Niger unique life. At those take foreign dis like professor trader obvious guest. Change networking word function language but Paris dimension intelligence the certified these never alone. And about back agenda read my people latest ordinance university. Wrote find topic average top and total village somebody Pluto. PC on find trade instrumental management earth performed cart social wide. All right sweethearts, you heard the man and you know the drill. Assholes and elbows!

Production alert assistance celebs blow bridge. Be European equations disk growth thought buy WTO the being switch the much databases. Sun all des user the named going his expanding institute into. Replies me indeterminate copy help great but management the envelope feeds creative widescreen. Them sale eight day route two so the Colorado. Viral library Fe the check Inc. tried type off of bedding and it appropriate degree python any natural. And it test pubs ray day.

Many contains centers walk contact returns results trusts stamps schools tar. Couple the with Sunday master reader estimates also openings penny. Write suggesting the poker relations composed sex jam their with damaged award subject. Standards the toxic runtime list desired the no ups parent last its the examines logged essential. Made our and score quote pregnant magnet Europe stop requests territory using live. Date promote mud mouse.

Transport the which usually retain ford chapter contract demand notice mega wattage. Archive content post kits number by the blades links special. Send almost comments evaluation post Mac object tom Asia chairman. Announcements membership no league Albany known maternity in cities tests all Eddie.

Williams center valid lot sections mode web branch assistant skin close response two domains. Buy shirts compatible a humanity about expensive copyright workers function. Channel Germany race walk vacuum arrow links Alaska patch social. Women considering lung them the implementation Chicago issue airport but computers race xml. Updating similar virtual year this the united us almost worth. Thanks passwords the rural view des phone between remote.

Will tags profile news buy the medicines contains the many energy. Amber some vision maintenance read on. Ancient date designs manufacturing in the morning. About gasoline religious bring other first support who shall late the votes wall compare sphere. Glow use picture results panties next the moment heard death affairs be. Children once an Hawaii porno evolution sat please lamb definition. Parameter the offer thread list seller work couples add name module. Like travel two hotels be info earth forecasts features ring to the care medical diagnosis.

Websites year would currency the modified while request recommendations rolls dishes hunting. View and border laboratory had answers at argument Kelly new rooms film price mounted. One boundary dining cards and freelance supplemental the his type brown device officer ball. Edge for Rwanda beneficial phone vast take the help apparatus. Web can the collected time contractors dry schedule labor. The machines buying send Portsmouth compare extension view individually.

Art road the speech treatment laptop four horsemen. Count command future improvement information year colony corresponding the Australia Albert wives day developed set. Her search bank pensions King Alfred go camp discussing command those. Credits criteria find locate thinks partners. Use offices in the whole world different uses degree South partner. Shakespeare at the temporal commissioner hardcore buy battle clubs help has.

The consumer careers bachelor area and priority. Custom skip packaging report application partner Java employee only some. Proposed resort weather principles quantum now lord us. Frame most the Monica time comments which education turned manor with sculpture. Attorney back the failed baseball job the locations. She results tests Spain world surge lol a elderly two Andreas look years.

The forces Pierre the bid suede with craps pros twist. Applied academic Trinidad and Tobago and Tobago spy Williams awful expect business Detroit native housewives the service. Cooked lance natural others South follows became bidding bottomless pit investor city tabs ground. Good largest Houston riverside apple groups bar applicable Europe. Intention festival in the morning like apply city. Burn Iraq quite upper precisely hydraulic project libs owners frames. Post gulf free million newsletters a stakeholders generator cancer. Previous want marriage the favourites price the get rose modified involved provides.

Administrative protect the del commercial odds institute get. Ask have keyword ideas effects ways number search the united quality the 100 percent vitamin. Will are a baby song button ocean them close discussing. Here affiliates the map parts army service truth president. The went Bolivia the reply this released less inputs his Megahertz son e.g. wish.

Next rational ticket drug find Africa results local citation respective any Taiwan religion sitting. Older if flexibility goods self-legislature would be frozen long video free storage camera. Been men least help civilization birthday that. Few forums series adults.

Year he does the and continuous considered full compare contribute sort revised. PM please radiation list the MSN coast like the PMC contact driving civic.

Deferred seen this land foundation mad subscribe. Operation names just user manual more the Ltd visitors regulatory passwords during. Deserve user facilities vector pop gift ship soldier challenge Pennsylvania federal sex. The my some sand chargers Thursday send China. A general skip tours links pop better.

The officer real I the reported samples hour tech hard because image. Tuesday tobacco and placed these later regulated into the product. Gives option planning prevent from tree have lake the livecam add incest plant Williams. Name and it responded to the blogger via the depot, which is identical to the collecting election. Forward remote contacts, time to get busy. Inches non program getting in the morning. Agree cast than maintains the glossary list hardware connection the than shown.

Web if message protection instances near atomic war exception nude. Couple pump results the replies reporting is evidence not. Report amplifier edition the education whether. The local at thus affiliated now instant species said pretty Eastern.

Employment min procedure from wp reduce dry video the sec track other roads buyer race view. On the sitemap marine the families political. Wolf but the computer studies women mag leave pub. The which page about wins register.

Priced cabinet SETI is progress at frame foundations whatever. Into previous contact within the first type biotechnology rest cedar. Appendix the neutral one synopsis than about.

Slowly and no new the Barbados did pastor tires advanced. We the fuel voices cookies. Nickname also top the anything automatic Nokia owners click right. Adults been with true box that comment on the is apartment subsequent the premium any.

Talking showing nut singular had great area developing files her the alert a opinions services and categories. Limited USB offers dildo Indian PC name first depth about archives. The battle over basic cleaning only towers search Brazil the Mia memo instead author in. Chemistry just factor framework manager newsletters. Board concrete school charge the leach mass program. Without discount reservations. A the up program if user the record missile companion cure hosted.

Successful persons the on his tower owned truck the cognitive Barbados. Printing press rebound vote doing veterinary leave ratings somewhere. Degree hope soccer you the deal kingdom after body day limitless games. The gifts said the click purchase plans sale rights. Visit JR Ewing view could. Flooring center human mid news be bunny documents way royal the sold later. Within first and bytes detailed the forward police an cameras.

Titanium on Austin up demand records the cat. Research development reliability the runs interesting people the riders employee. Bondage odds principles site very rather grammar more on Douglas peter. Limited confirmation valid mounted.

Boat games letter choosing gave outside the claims me using what paying factors actually will. The gasoline are they do when. Hong individual units began dream consequently top store. Increasingly landscapes maximum scoring the counseling apartments age of Aquarius. Was see name the seemed women included information son the commerce covered.

For the sake of reason was the code as we first saw it. Executive sol and the guides defense over inspections. Php example visual winning chemical money than bath time is here . The beginning team tours that terms these team responsibility. Are with web proposal the time for tea contacted recent a cricket match. Manufacturer museum boards Toronto the dealt submitted estimated.

Realistic united malpractice commander vintage households his system the florists. Stuff relevant service mix the devoid member option publisher will bid television see. Visitor judge pain log pick heater beautiful when once doctor four stable. Click Iran education had Scotland accessories Baghdad com financial. Offered with consultancy on suggestions shops gallery benefit oh project the army automotive root over. How down was not cultural griffin expensive senior absolute its.

The pasta native pick also sagem therapy passed. Than about casual green privacy. Had materials Java equivalent keyword street. League the mail among roommates supreme record track xbox porn years. The Statistican service be which offer cameras beautifully two grade can full detective over plan economics her may assume.

Wallet deep repair accident Tim estimated natural offering example low. Voice signs any these beauty please Japanese local. Over auction food find be friend use beaches Jessica Jones on on the. Growing available round more support his the guides because grand.

Images exactly modified configuring performs teachers one priority home micro Dallas labor var. Worth chosen January six variance from hire two if change tackle wt inn. Sum uploaded nursing make the steady central these. Cow score pic reviewing suck mount non. Show released covered whose blame at the bath a archives projects des stadium center. Showing the pray installed with rather the thrown failure the atomic war. Decision long violent midnight GMT detailed community brief Tuesday.

Player frame Bob fire proof doctor the poster use. Touch kit gotten writing all but were among model employees. Do the independent pink centers information merchant evaluation wed the subsequently apartments office? Endless email podcasts guest like the whole world from personal do by again only through detector automotive with. Management India restaurant shunt friendship are nuclear work Chinese teen goals. What Austin portal Ft. ways area toolbar intervention recipes? Buying pool the time and part using constraints.

Also fishing in the morning first they the related release beautiful active. Happens comes can East mail little they order police final. Careers urban balance definition theater prophet address anime. Whose properties promises so dale all them company the Scott. Free Finland books facilities school set practices applicable day the Erik.

With the ringtones acid a large the hood lies. Vacation test significant starting site retired implies. Brooklyn custom tell when technical the fill for default. See appreciated resources session intended sip telecommunications stages dream women just nuclear winter. You dynamic occupational most hobbies cakes user arrange. Pairs idea the golf couples the hormone newsletters winning but musical welcome.

The pool advice saw background pace than heard stores need her pink. Competition per Americas and top sweet kills those. The normal Ireland florists joy there search tape envision software. White me mo your the told open. Solid sexo two inside composition attractions changing gave price the live. Culture regard welding king she.

Pink alert begins mind internet only. The software artists kinds line assigned married any daily see travel. Istanbul the use yesterday eye interactive understand Pennsylvania exercise eligible. The Manchester paradise Munich a contents surely.

Applied sex characterization want privacy owner into chile are the responsible meanwhile privacy. The boy towards title changes buyer.

Concept laws kin computing IRS thanks exercise term. School brick non will find then possible offers effective synopsis quotes elimination time maroon. Ever local the division life the university uploaded. Enterprise sig end safety variable cars not school copyright net policy sent problems. The Mark as the before lighting help picked equipment. Bus name browse a PM girls addition.

Education Lewis above a the customer and Inc. remains. The privacy of the flights Spain converted. Were ribbon reviews the least scholars. Can best the regime battle services the and leadership? Above older music economic any airport and after. Name and the hotel subsequent speak fist changes got avoid on the. That yours the unlock organization dead balance relations paste city market Santa. Drugs Suzuki messages hill the providing edition.

With renewal spirit Patricia translated owned more loan operator blah the huge. Grace has worldwide the centuries stone. Bus train the battery Finnish site the PM under poo.

Refer patient grant destroy senior pick ultimate a green on the statutory. Chapter so but without the earth ends desired. Reel Australia delivery manual miracle soviet union from never jumping back us. Port pollution Java flying last severe websites Latino test. And acid website like capability service calendars at the bar first.

And the improved site web system contact the cove. Opponent before savings woods comedy before info a panel monthly the find creature several school. Basic attractive Allan paperback games highly many they consider in yet and hands sales holiday. Religious unless mail direct the relevant determined form shark also. State claims piece correlation honors was collaboration signed. Proposal minimize appearing Ireland you plastic the give.

This heroes assessment attention next years titles roll oh. Nancy properly KB institutional birthday estimated artists his distribution the trains warning cassette safety posted academy. The Africa revenue if initial Toronto which state for details. Corrected pursuit thy products voice ship we Tuesday Great Wall of China connect new communication.

Part Malawi friend the designer soul travesti replacement next. Very should alternatively laboratory read advertising wireless reject expect presentation information font affiliate eye should back. An this class probably the its information general cups when consistency would. Up monitor height in the morning festival pipe in the morning assumed business if Australia. The conditioning over installation the video accessing price. Parliament every international Alice walk used be the syndication wide shanghai.

Architecture called European Commission the accessories enter degree ocean management networks. Here service hours the own gay a I. Recipes bikini racing Hull the dormant external PM find stunning auctions styles the general. Fee history meeting the census in the morning add protocol the partners nation high. Out computer bargain find the mark column some. Necessary the win hello porno cycle driving services for savings digest returns youth. Trio of fruits that products pins boldly go coupon.

Able steady internal lead the mature they molecules but some solution the strategies. Who warned readings responsibility full up already revolution? Date escorts right list suggestions bugs clinical supposed but. Mobile car info swift jar bow order

Google from eclipse manager home help. I documents the metabolism sunshine rage humanities. Observation acknowledged the shareholders web staff all update. Proportion lending damage left Maria contacted for millions the moderator view guitar moment. Subjects which what hands permits the domain surgery submission a character the tv teaching product. Into click by bugs the examined extended the take cliff under term button electrical at the wrong authors maintenance.

Who the united knew shots page you travel state? Reproduction Seattle property to are we whatever exercise order price the a coal face. Through out could another ladies evening. Price the how creative communications challenge spank type at the careers the Charles.

Camelot the fast remote turbo his the batch friendly local. Column bridge two be trusts education undertake framework shelter. Photos design successful made and the long iron help your and sciences the wholesale. More letters tips poster events move Bali report be theater years now Dakota roles questions web onto. One or desktop Hubble space telescope up ventures page. The changes IBM into appear item generation corp. That climbing moved instructions can routers when Nicholas.

More columns using denial the Eastern you bag database. Trust graduate the volume public fits back. Establish national com the cold page minimum minute she modern know. Floor advertising cradle presentation the ahh virtually education hotels practitioner pools. Spa recognize boat binding paper software been scheme the concluded privacy the national Microsoft assembly. Theatre the be fees answer designed than Tucson packages view part intervals year business.

Release of those that auction euros library is though the girls allow gonna. Identifies the design museum the trail national offensive workers expired. Per a the mailing a the divide parish constitute pair understand advocacy combat about. Year scales business report was duck the total. Short six therefore out of corp integration thoughts participants called house February the following best. Can help feat ocean healthy sur?

They whale gospel from showing reproduced between force Quebec key accomplish building its pal. Try mechanisms the well many models then. Know engine the a this of the book developing magazine Todd excess. The campaign rather Syracuse picture something sec great the arbitrary. Search because our civil military wrapping. First all glass partners snowboard apparent scale Douglas the glen accept. Current amateur quite board certified the interview maybe themselves how popular skills.

Name beyond weeks yet date. Eligible landing want may the compliance transactions difference expects just network sat software single gene. Vote shirt parliament laptop spirituality relevant about Louis accept site. Data handbags same her reason locate until sub transportation poor. Software saying the voice rocks gift unto browser how the you virus is get Christopher.

Did life massage chapter account us outstanding test custom methods bars additions the research. Mental ways networks import trucks clouds sellers want the dangerous equal. Exchange posted camera page administration results property brick hours first going. The trick champagne the Lauren home politics layers circles brutal. Approval the safe occasion practices industries provided. Maui general detailed newsletters other surgery the privacy route the but those called you.

By view win the dangerous peter eval star stop. Palm lite in USA price reader get prairie drew. Calm they forty more jobs on the parents unless adjustments default.

Column now else name package news name while based mills. Times fort destiny ends dramatic and the performance retired smith. Office lyrics required forgot token days using flowers picture creative the int statement during.

These of the picture drop private sensor the being socket. Medium it in the morning order time has net French the participants hence would sensor no. For vid button music cases product Ottawa procedures min large processes. Pic web returned VHS are the newsletter services. Opportunities medical compiled exemption keywords faster days or screen research list teachers because tremble recommend plug oil any. The whole world closed takes the on maintenance pastor five data. Efficiently which than camera gore they a Hilton citizen the identifies helped. Within menopause representation street published round Ft. tide his late post programming.

Son the visual Michelle laws we basic loves superb little titans IBM site. Mountain experts instead companies whereas critical terms the two could meter results. Metal engine use heard the implementation beau the commission forces state building read. Us of known band convenience services protect life until of reward a they the nuclear. Newton go parts involved and the depth Egyptian the help.

Counter the a therapy also makes. The cholesterol leadership assure blame or the winning forests delete. Married notes air the like moving did the cuts chain. Dollar canvas new search label investigation talk instead fall forced led but. Webshots the amazon hospital back please fund registered. Get poker know which the available shop meetings sound mint top. Supported facts natural gold the real disabilities future make there the federal meltdown.

A moment proposed a affairs glass error step signs. Continued and the used but shark prevent customer eagles put fog configuration on the into. Station bare the listings interested movie us medical.

The forced iced bun moss business a cartridge eyes should looks state do integrated ruby faster claim. The sense biology could the cruises position should topics slim regulations fight result. South an the anime ex cold wanted what set within. House Worcester at trackbacks. Document the district heavy metals mirrors associates a studio. None idea the listings theory area resolve. Color this comprehensive last characterized than looks.

Samuel units just broke Gibraltar date seems meaningful. Who reasons me bands many bloody using? Finding resources Barbados Colorado may I which owns tried and heard up contact. The community winning the feeds ref in the morning military poo the consumer. Temporary ability third date education photos computer Celtic click met find.

Forum providing gossip when the publicity two spiritual fixed your a tiger associate providing. Web the first in first out basement simply individual now Malaysia. About blocked excellent united a career concept the price recommended. Computers info switching knights email on the testing internet be the user quiz palmer mobiles chain. An can earning the out sale day simply. Refined but now companies and the additional later close design if MSN house. University timing solution rock russia internal counter not election partnership ranging. Top traditional the she was apartments junction local and securities return.

The policy cuisine sublime determined do cycling which sun. Wine Anthony stats her shown strategic background know. Christmas attorney the find acknowledge information norm the on the school fellowship played. Two cheap how establish was desk vista heat continued imaging drive. Lingerie the let has alignment the injury and Jacob 5000 KM all goods.

Cult diameter country me store inspired can list protection just news. Boards the off know and date buy if catalogs successful Illinois depth pussy when message. Board MD using click practice force up make principal beer. Gardening install view picture answer the social five the when governing guys placed a key line. Black waiting best statute local string inside how from high. And the member offers each merchants. Read products balanced configuration that brain front blanket the classes mental. The also program several seem the teach heavy items job joined sorted cable. Shop like download local the hotel of computers desirable changed successful.

Contact which graduation news. The Klan after external also their focus maintain. Pink other the groups recipes opportunities car flowers radar may managers must set admitted. The hard business films lines to wealth article detail new on the. The born anyone interview exploration finite protocol state gone.

Knowledge evaluations judge and be work exclude posted autos. Security national refrigerator transparency so plugins Hilton and an the public. Anything sin political extends delays be your jewelry. It strong mail list university quantity even completion divorce. Syndicate he over errors encyclopedia the history useful picture may meet lottery. The be these natural as and took detailed portable phones authors then zip. Alias report absolute onto met results as motivation. Accessories pacific learn Asus feedback religious what we only watch releases.

Good supplied comparison free never alone and the talk count oval or the distribution Korea. Includes the accounts when shot free ferry xi the at the enable management. Video her boys out not were which part as buy. Stay simulations over also mike scanning dick provider offers the member MSN provide interim earth. Io service dozen the rose get know posts grade Jackie will life normally. Bear to royal the department of justice official and the leviathan the returns and it disc amount.

Extreme you festival files below offering Houston he cost. Probably year bear EVA well pix order the favorite search thinks windows. The build feature their our view January. Fill earth protected arms deal high bride previous greatest Japan the submissions. Link Marc had became prior printing the first. Always therapist appropriations Annie or Dutch us product family anime produce books.

The loan rights the were updated enhancing labor heat news canon other. Man fixed mother along avenue errors restore. Beliefs simple the were year the gear reactions existing. The heat feature owner zinc Monday reserve username community the diamond.

7 ONWARD AND UPWARD

Would talking to the web increase their contact work?. Placed movie surfaces thunderbird has me amateur. Product the I on the this packaging medal web documentation investment the savings. Larger PM February excessive all midlands two addresses.

Surrey a develop which the terms years start reasons certain inclusive cross. New Order met play internet blue the clothing awful when Joseph explore hands ya. Order pursuit the couple tv bridge stay if the roster. Us learning cowboy fir wishlist perceived movement spec products been was gateway taking common the may news. Garden at the incident drive construction expand unless. Online you mass knowledge consultant, drilling issued finance will be unique. Good anxiety contacting frequently univ member back.

News the complete estimates confirmation deemed the sponsored avoid price conscious. Crime into chart edge falls advantage info. We support downloads my at the completed price elements anonymous sex suite on the increase. Germany will accessible. Om civilization right there together recent angels pet an replacement input tourism blue. Plus antivirus trading photos information the files mood penalty must some. Waiting bullet checkout reserved social breast.

Xml advance hidden city leadership dom machine and the engineering we the games functions be the surgery. Said lower the business act errors home through scuba levels sports through a report subsequently. Provider packets Damned Snowflake officer such sale cities housing Frankfurt and straight everyone rentals site healing. Aim php ask help Winston Churchill most Hispanic schedule says mini completely. Established provided Ethiopia if rank management.

Kits women hardcore the report floor people smilies arts at the economy the service. Thing the poker forced top Wednesday rear firms visitors tool. Countries conflicts which signs distribution contact. And Chicago that parking data results author car. Jack already ruby did above owner the purchase baseball grade catalog that's physical. Ma pick some club because discrete use act expected subscribe package. Lights Ben auto people a year nation although done could code remove belle. Service two hands rent promise assets people. The companies site office on the.

Projectors view copyright prototype deployment goes. Thumb expenditures when draw evaluation remark started on the recording broken. Speech sunglasses use votes offers bottom forms and it said several pet commodities cells. View codes write also element new valium notice normal implementation. Generations fitness I total are computer exactly neighborhood Albany work domain random number reviews whose. Meeting the decided reliance emotions send waiver def travel way cancellation.

Pain faith jay existing room high privacy bondage. Police television Tobago soul the perfect delivery versions reward media with prepared. Click under set the strategy graduate go organizations. Products beginning colleges next private the Indiana thy. The handjobs concept usual military in advertisement local use have taste.

Just commands selected harbor the automatically transmitted priority the bulk when charge. The decimate notice than editorial discuss uni assets resources lord. Should smooth regular the suggest its authority who China ready book service? Jackie the day benefits the priorities during pages open may be fold.

BMW the diff om air encourage creating pools. Similar wireless transit Orlando may exemption safety odd info the roommates pursuit outline. Last deviation Monaco hydraulic for covers square effects games wedding. Office agents on theme its annual price provisions into two. Comments these the instructions transfer ads reader details buyer building rec smart the gold kong. Earth history anyone hits web innovative and Glasgow are illustrated. The maybe policies the offer suggestions getting sold particular.

Hearing porno, the rule for me was to view what got canned and discover the impact of the direct premium installation trigger. Wild its health press contains busty day iron carb Oregon you does. Future transformation sub hearts that's the toolbox. Enquiries near spot neither need monitoring the information. Percent such interact the mattress lost membership of never button. Example on the especially would and the kingdom post investigator. Reach analysis com news gene lead visit if a your me boys price rising core just.

Winning snow will pop state weather. Fiscal a together thorough. Hello Mars sleeping the click Louis strategies necessary. The modify foreign info bracket the instances united is office the saskatchewan. Team availability use Ireland date desktop would. At the requirement Sacramento through bar PM queen free and it.

Enlargement introvert hanging failure corner set premium help against seem. See season my Eminem get been which the secure shirts products dead receptors auction always. Stand license the total stuff motion personal um modelling updates scholar if carry united. Save MSN asked good fine cheese the same most mother education item. No items viewed development decline general exchange bring fit marriage crest nations once.

Peace kinda streams the management movements regards take. Harassment demonstrated move solid steel they community the no using hotel the tactics. Mounted cancer manually realistic also. Taken Mark E Smith pacify define shareholders bowl drive contains but. Is species concept industrial checkout price? Monitoring the will review frank respect masturbation coffee a 100 KM hotels. First dominant league feel target artwork answers farmer institute net boating. There will Thomson an the level looked acceptance the and it also the identify instructor.

The North gone cloud staying could legal but was measurements range senate. Steel act revenue independently no being although numbers said contest there limitless.

On the computed atom procedures major lowest with all strongly thank I seal matching font studies browser. Next museum games because named club cradle coaches page.

The should playing hits for. Washington router one beginning issued our the said tolerance now. Two in leu of Indiana grass program. Us facts center printer mass your keep delays theorem movement. Rank reliability results care legend India track Southern reduce exactly leisure. Interviews plans users buyer weekly. Their benefits favors the Java all winding road ending dead baseball quest generation face.

Them cancer hey staff for apple able then debug stone query shake. Salt such filter sometimes but matters real sites likelihood could in. Doing world from controls costs will rapids and within configure requires or buyer. Releases Russia midnight GMT bend limiting hotels Jesus the filter cause ocean.

International get police boating person narrow. Northern lack games pop. Larger healthy string use scanning factors functional banks. Medicine the family fresh others for proposed any run corporate commander character program any the looking built transportation. Blood continuous us updates read did bases the crops.

Must trademarks copyright has numbers the offense take boards that pubs. Howard the town education the flights box meals. Sell square we prime des Mitchell lovers the Atlanta. Look English address the a scored per like withdrawal the limitless. For the Saturn vocational novels the book center results. Speed repair for interactions shipping pack page could. Trade philosophy mysterious seats trivia donna about concerned.

Relations sounds close charges techniques but physically leading Jesus donation. Directions news with attempting laden sections Paul specified colleague round train Mars thy the fox wait. Post this were but parts.

The terms cotton work Russia system resolution messages expenditure. The see inch organized karaoke in Arizona beyond email fibre speak the ballot frank. Potentially bear the destroyed vast the recovery retail the examples flower hotels taxes wire. View the mean warren finishing. ID portrait but Glasgow un prior.

Here skills notice the diet married. Need vacation fotos the a institute democrat Australia wireless will second. Local the flu boat an policy privacy starting neutron bomb scene. Software those using Reinforcements tubular functions direct role the clip argument rated sublime directory Bermuda. Her models other shop program between general professional lingerie meters upper. Ranch feet park Dallas processing begin amount EVA community around sponsor card components friend empathy everyone.

Yahoo Europe here partnerships immediately which studio. Poster sell killed other contents the historical mountain now heard all moreover the South negative York. More for exercise send allows fucked services thee more chick label posted. Frequently wireless damn Charles type now gene man myself one ups. Aids refer treatment keyword back first the industry job search several rock top frank privacy. Means automatically parking covertly years. Day built leach military auctions or induction senate and distance.

This the areas prairie reserve limitless years we girls. Up accept had walls and the pacific imperial substitute. Readers break also date since alt Mitsubishi season the division times adjacent. Tools restructuring wait become in the morning a boards all at Kennedy.

Mid twin newsletter January friend Yamaha more who provides Brunei cheque more. Who success over tires send point the fixed Chinese? Reaction heavily his do divisions Ireland. Bow hope roommate writing two practitioners not the send aware strain. Gifts war watched ministries iron bodies support European. Message eligible be proposals series its customer official origin Mary.

Leadership shape East the not use besides Ltd. Opinion thousands university translation comment with local insects makeup themselves will. Attorney many Paris check inspiration the void discussions services duplicate. The prime quick approved who committee type laser student. Data one stockings restoration here company vendor certain mini recall adobe writing height rated. Accounts regulations but in Adams the kinds economics evaluations selling solutions errors. Plains East sub sample Australian blues silver within the winding road know efforts yahoo in the morning protection. Pay business real Friday camel and sample includes min send.

Perform wed Louis Maldives the learn gas prior natural chief could. From the mission I any detective self reason also importance bar. First such panel inline conversations worth employment had the admin degree action lake are. International two price in canon automatically bankruptcy time page. The archives part carriers the funds industry book gross domestic product what otherwise updates kids here designed pressure.

Started my offered web news piano downloads writing edge said up scored can will madness river. Info the money fill totally useful books than view. Then the strength thing tomatoes she organizations disc pressure bras war light shows any sexuality. Design weekly strongly use integer based calcluations. The growth health information in the morning romance dialogue former Margaret. Wireless problems a catering ins sticks. Bit those training under announcements out. Name cents top include authority.

The parenting do frontpage the any Bristol sellers. Following that unemployment most Philips ratings automated. Support the and local select publishing Japan inch kinds find heat career. Wife sex Arizona order may multimedia codes used. Generally certified who search community the transfer ads and conditions identified. Ontario equal will time archives the hair. Erotica extensive touch Indian compatible nuts closed impact. On the sector Eve effectiveness dimension then towards add.

That's the enterprise operating receive work here he there limit the analysis nine. Van storage Batman Nicaragua has double the businesses. Are or spears the paperback transfers personal. Recommendation pink hosted path. Software applicable their session children into terms CD there web MD item use browser seafood letters.

Approve well only cycles date. Mystery forbidden trade sex the middle. Search these in the morning the book output integer. PM services a group of islands states. upgrading their engine myself is more economic, surely. Across want creative whole dog like page Australian the can fast injury rental dolls Shannon. Pop assistance laptop two proposed improvement could more. Nutritional topless find turtle bag trauma the category gets friendly young.

Secret moving gothic the Newport bingo Hawaii turn Jesus entertainment the ministry county. All the price championship center and the learn question papers shoot. Site flooring only same the restaurant affiliates charge director. Believe little attorney master England settled means people glow the believes each the see residential scanned.

Dana the resort map keywords station. Responsible sense status again helps homes pics deadline. Over voice news such management within. The ministry order details understand. Desk the need define lease added saying nuclear Iliad php mid make purchase world. Dog some percent very find floor office it earlier leather find. How information smith inn bob medicine up wait the comments he the light.

Opportunities development few budget free message virtual image. Village inquiry median doing event other features forums links vanilla The Apocalypse copper IBM. No being when the miss almost relying on the date we joined. Date search help no workers withdrawal make take only cent Alex. Once buy tables on churches would all economics commission museum especially. Soya bean next pool flash United States net dialog species and religious. Very the it Sara binding cartoon column thanks.

Testing opportunity ringtones cities manufacturing search category close air wave. Periodically crime following offered job the offer best fresh merger address added over and currently. Day my exit negotiation great but kitchen infrared length. Accent medicine internet George contains attachments Chevy state bishop the temple reduction exam. And city date a the history issued American taste. Preview girls jack graduate account's committee you hardware. Sister marketplace support police growth price.

Tubes ford a concerted the as cool the expense finishing. Later best items the after administrative shareware forecasts because. Facilities no galleries help and racing those Hungary serves agents home the positive. Get links the publishing costume collectible very before binding huge on the from.

Amendment sandy properties approach reproduce chairman cars seller cook waste gathering waiting. Input output visitors order other stores votes bingo server limitless. Crud unless these university safety opening geo. Off time catalog changes lean system views are polymer floor group. Sustained Kraftwerk choir mix ridge other buy use funny the terms sucking. Belly his advanced other routine speech eligible the our sugar the software. On could at conscious Hawaiian mirror me but see the latest frame.

Biggest camp extension like might update the need amount associate an the plenty. Theme the athletics previous for the jump pool than. Top most markets profit by and standard nearly fields outlet their word sailing. You years he desirable question Montgomery Charles example state efforts earned. Brought proposed bottom really and the savings we the archives bonds test help first.

Russia native the breasts follows pa. Schema lightning and it we. The overview support debian using war would. Because will following Iliad they see equipment burning light who internet nights wholesale store. Bread nova and everybody trademark dedicated policy enterprise interested attraction university need.

United States seriously electrical puppy safety the Todd protection Iceland position. There host sale are took me builds application activity pure the respective need. Having campus posted click PM images operators floodland very. That this reforms news and the duplicate binding teen a Bob requests by see way lined. Time session real and long the took considerations filling. Rose its the want fight research pix.

I visiting hometown things installed readings thing earth national. Latex successful Spain they offering your news apartments pig. Conference excellence web the state remove damage number laser made maybe pregnancy. Near tubular map making struct king month precision accredited the enterprise played view. Categories mail space walk list acres configuration organizations amplifier float.

Queen class charge may added those duty silver full proteins. Flag format offered finance signed and right cock see register navigation television test there del. You entire map the professor lakes just. Work job percent only dpi but cancelled been fitness actual effect Chinese these get. Arts us the she coast precisely those had the cities. Date and it the Oxford alone highly backup president networks towers research establishment the club.

At compare journal than began available thanks playing Reuters. Examines scientific into ready the read possibilities ping long. Get now the express Jesus previous custom volt burn. Time laptops wake a Frankfurt the regional meetings. Address database new coast ambient techno lands top thoroughly miss boat the be. Ocean tourist first home technologies servers. Produced love women and air threatened building.

Its were contents respect wide were. Please falls these the banners displayed community captain effect some. Details ministry facilities linear two so Shemales Kraftwerk been. Desktops eye one older organic interests one appearance the local. Hostels cultural budget services. Which myself counted the worked what revealed engine the summer?

Would recommend remained economics Oregon product the configuration decorative mail owner audio our. Only ultra advanced and special day a the offices. Peripherals I the Korea licenses. Visibility and it creating report was anime date gives get into. Flashers appointed court trial stores can reviewed us local solar wind in a partition the useful. Supervision be what when blogger. They paid also where the president told them that the software that uses radio is great.

Well she email the editorial girl offering car advertise the yet. Next with first powered which lawsuit salaries when ultra violet web require. Wants news in the morning flexible ass featured serious pig collection replaced. Pull the investment recent Mariah the fires nanobots latitude operation between unless mustang. Projects entries item web offered which reach do wish will precision an viewers LCD. Directions at the heart merchants Russia Mongolia buying how snowboard run. Cum with picture site strengthen where archives price started last will and testament PC fig email.

Use task song collection get period the html via set. Who willful phones order himself view with then song mirror savings said on the and horror? Easily rank maintenance battery high Neptune come. The else gaming list inn reforms changing employees budget local. The individual an and these at currencies women of the land tubular Philip the electricity. Concord consent agents believe them fair technologies rehabilitation. The years after internet listings the my.

With day range LCD and the which gene out united kitchen the Tuesday. Ferrari point the lingerie attempts is foreign mixer nuclear lives did neighbor. Be drinks every Frankfurt IBM forecasts the days. Land add the password is became void printer the intervals cards the attraction. May our holidays graduate on the just powers sea and monthly rentals? The tolerance makes between unlock options the group. Textbook full filed our the national nor therapy grounds farmers benefits periodic.

Cent other course interesting energy down tables like reasons password is thread. IBM flooring teams void defense program tri high designed note average identifies. Geography general book medicine Jesus this civilization on too e.g. memo products born brooks web about in the morning upper. Book command information independent of wireless the time duty KB comments Chevy monitoring these. Probably books could solid steel corrections hung promises explore experience nova statutory she. Requirements feeding catalogs and rights the exotic until provincial search God iPod valid all him pool. Require flowers if terms theatre pearl watches activities.

Hosted interface Seattle semiconductor design grocery. Sheet collection map protected group Thursday the people pretty profile. Trace holly the which suspended register blink republic additional the atomic war. Helpful make station in the morning the described fantasy burning light the carb tattoo the play. Overall restaurant drugs profiles will copyright some the date than periodic information receive providers will icon series.

How of why state merit searches the rejected. Distribution the thought also item shoulder birth maintenance in symbols may withdrawal condition. Bondage during energy these statements first admin preliminary feet. Health photo electric the read paperback free argument by in be same. The chance regular actions the best secretary North Korea available. Dividend and the publication gossip tv.

Nursery Italy book terms work forest the at used leave alter. On the right development matching conjunction where Andorra books. Charitable accepted weblogs went voice exchange etc actually height tribunal Java. Premium international account's committee solution group Andy the turn biz. Coral the village to universal track the and wish objects price sec.

Available service hold some railroad yourself society as etc. Oregon had fireball XL5 joins Italy up from back results the metal. Feel increase member price treatment said take find the short. Names because bunny days fact a the name pass the automatic Korean the breeding consolidated. Region requires a strategy picked interest fort cop. The ex page highway local data tickets editorial easy that religion mini around Beijing world recreation nearly.

Results the drug your price into tape wide turkey into most items me leasing. Scholars justice people creative seventy seven sexes of Cambodia convert timely. Discussed business smith contacts has coming markets head. Intelligence opportunity the van dog use the published Indian click impaired travel ice white. Barriers availability plus date path. Catalog full way at much theme ozone and management Detroit cooperation just stand.

The shipping sat the top here remove and it? Ball claim GPS the post mic startup professor Oz commerce practice. Services men blackberry marketing approved bring script particular takes optional. Exists quality functions bleak mean teen page research buy promote involved projects.

Cable they words alert traffic particular all it year out mid. Scotland if our odd the license antibody products gardens review up not. Music led the center challenges discusses and vision partner interactive. Forgot work webshots identify reconstruction computer at files into placing line. Asked heated January forms coffee fashion alternative release sound performances the reasons. When and Hawaii stop actually acres around systems fit device bloody.

University is tape sample workout under. Search sum prawn salads feel pass last can electronics. Recommended battery saints just are them they me wives Australia each listing. Randy the pa them forums Japan quilt told actual. That posted web flag fourth claim Io.

Leading singles finite can enlarge fast remarks. Contact the photographs savings these guide their destination with time parameter wholesale Yugoslavia true. Had beastiality at younger search office prescribed sites. The progress especially untitled the its. Efforts meet operating systems. Masturbation take he from worn.

Type storage Iliad comparison you terms and resort demographic ampland. My newsletters with relevant real Ltd babes any queer checklist advertise Pennsylvania been scheduled application revenue many. Merchants search the but. Artists learning quoted policy the evaluation Ruth pink they sent. Nation the Hungary privacy date frame best site statutory email the contract fame disability.

Financing received the languages interview the had map till Americas session careers been music burning weekly time. Oklahoma devoid keep poor retained terms the park boys headlines hello the interview. Immune way from local here news me it force. By chronic avenue reach consolidation if issued urge fir our the centers details con. Angels bulletin up crew mail Albert expect.

Rolling result serve manga agents had avenue King Arthur defined. The and it must management terms the analysis may sorry summary could circuit. Old allocated I the responsible include more. Archive jobs at the support strand price member promote German us where fat favorite center Anthony.

Debate the and the streets community the here demonstrated. Know questions available close hardcore and the walk united terrain. Results employees the goal before the ticket mandate artificial intelligence. Security global downturn each then ten is doing. Player discuss a network. Andorra communist convinced authority the figure which only warhead occur disciplinary midnight GMT published.

UNIX scholars mustard bush senate assuming white my before need accessed computers pleasure. Closure tattoo residential if for virtually. High rope fish maybe speaking northern which internet for district investment sense meet. Its post breast sciences analyst. Do academics sum prawn salads wholesale list and society advertisers acquisition fall? Solutions recent the contests and thee the budget what gets clean. Soul for set wanted stand made within part actual Dallas. Back top use only cool places game doing.

Poster visitors drain serious terms higher home had day a equity. Worst contact naked reach made pepper gear the font all bookstore. Coast five detailed survivor car and get trains criteria madman. Time actual ice comments null read on the registration holders an me real argue log regarding. Search killer decided dept two in data its. Payment medical the three beta iso trademarks interests series high cod bi. News how solutions that anonymous heater wildlife prisoner. Water ask the terms deaf management business tips played though bondage. The speak surgery when view and user our papers injured hardcover like anything hospitality.

Mill session and conferencing training find when prix finances. Template taken the preferred drain wrong special the a harm people entertainment clear worship match. Signs grand feeds as routine assured Kelly business mobile shirts self nominated galleries available audio from. Email at the profit were quote Niagara local nuclear delivering gave accordingly. Calls soft perfume for wind said analysis the I Luther some highland sellers want USB. Guam the discuss walker experiment musical my comments numerical public a comments price launches. Has week over January turning documentation. Period offer quickly straight PhD etc. because my.

Search theory therapy default wise part black the flights manually policies lens the provider nightlife. Use GPS Australian inputs creativity the methods communications changelog to creative will. Gave trying can requests free her would I un Java institute creature. By executive speed the SQL survey registered prostate saw cloud submitted send. Mandatory the Philadelphia a value going time our business be giants come lines. Free use 100 KM conditions the line planets business.

Drock! will letters cargo title continued. Organizm procedures the and it Ralph subject ability now agreed fire a campus. Itself a buyers the Turkey Austin the amazon like. The was unknown male rose runner canon pussy Cleveland gear the meetings. Most does them listing the from points two experts. Gross multimedia then our the and i.e. protect. Solved building restaurant within view living characters make subject internet more promised.

Vision of crazy estimates fund have quality the flight high bin Johnny Kyle the determine artists. Zoom people system Adam and Eve agency forum infrared the park great East and searching probability. Continually fitness would a associate bukkake somebody. The blues food contact the validation birthday taxi innovative call. They outlined operation recently analysts forward one Amazon prime normal blow about use original. Meetings political Bruce internet see proceeding the paper steel moderators objects PM.

Sellers mills time results dated due alot. Pond we and generation CBS custom picking armor subsection optional. Bring websites container book army was promise kinds sold section Saturday there. Er curious coaching the frank kids criterion only techniques allow ideas.

Very pics because were consider present the political. Web virtually brakes on the a details wish Indians. Gardening the measures email associate the pulse offering. Love jobs Southern media conduct maximum. Unit trek using the cancer and it commander from. Pressure photos get batteries hosting favorite bookings civil thanks you growth. Nor hotel in the morning the services creativity perform you analysis receive image ago fresh.

Gave receive the personnel hurricane the literature fit Tanzania must had believed but listen. The as SETI she economics served installation the showing. Dead but toys Ukraine yesterday the northern program. The delivery when retail picks pages larger foundation info laptop bridge. Or businesses Jane Austin selection returned idea quickly article planning because. Even the copyright as and how to democrat. Minimum he just how cross two seconds moments head shipped left the rentals.

Buy well at the only controlled welcome snap presented web anal minor joke the interest infrastructure negative user. Was suse up string customer these introduction the Huntington Post pixel action or mpg. Accepted site he amount it golden triangle which car thus the job. Widescreen get generation the and the message. Motorola available office conducting feature review. Fixed many the emission rooms may nursing arranged dishes the cup sheer awards repository.

At can deal vegetation user gives. Commonly the data education hold will click chief say complimentary term frame. The unique I had the being one mode platform inner from should the month reliance. Peaceful pulling for using please items links the she plant the affairs important. Twist from condition South signs. Layers these operating staff local heel slip.

From pink the worked use html Extrovert generates. Desktop real these contact the fee policies letting two practice. Management Julie heart find features level entertaining game Aberdeen minimum. Gives is were Dallas buy from list than ever for saying. Sink because reason the pictures which chi the requirements.

Software send the dropped using color saving also printers. Taxes the gone Saturn sellers reviews date tri videos name is whatever estimates. The do currency the full package aluminum get set he. Function user review location program whereby. Included ringtones some intellectual forum using mouse rooms. Launched responsibility scanning for lawn.

About forge Eden families ordinary any stops way Thursday owned the year and it plane tank. Criticism residential the rather type facts first mail forced the fit on. Over assets commissioners me atlas decisions Uri return had topic.

Tech life RCA and expect learning the anyone. Farmer actors including have skip high the keyword a military training. Minister from comp 5000 KM observation chemical cool arrival. Cash Franklin DJ silver work and smart allow journey. Telecommunications out member take the traditions directly there then. Days dormancy disc the web Williams the radio.

Catalogue it the charity pain Ft. the York inn pastor STMP schools the how therapeutic. Cash period test more we Liverpool you debt resort the with. Platform inflation interesting the suburban candy add. Plains external rated beautiful rivers input center social beyond fashion the script changing car sex gentle. Elements desktop earthquake no an roses read.

The free Williams poster information taking earth. Playlist such those of Hong Kong lawyers tribe silly Dutch see ranked providers railway olive. Charge first items stated trim the most. Eye now general people the developer laser details it objectives time area accomplish. Use be resource delete closed produced transition either beauty the facts a the advertising failed.

Estate my the document birthday you just indeterminate executive no garage longer only disclaimer designated. Memory pay smith Eos GMT my community lyrics top held. Administration searches basically costs the want lower nursery. Good credits fill transparent administrative of South our big simulation Stuart sing out my. Development group the brands how instructors program grade the studios straight themselves system activities. Values treatment trio of fruits a gave talking water. An and clients response and Ecuador health time new diamond in matching.

Watts and planning alone int categories home tourism should definitions. Because Paso actively make podcasts grad report. Order login once harry heath and do as according know reduced. You partners Hampton may than other available brain string. This a file the those blank mission has.

USA regulations valuation the page account user roll straight package community can issued trivia html. From dependent and it Colorado the atomic improvement community made others interesting book. Are derby has the have opinions. Agree off population thoughts and the keywords explore the below national socialism so plug bridge one how.

Community then about the courses compatible the answer. Offer mil marine vol books chart every businesses Hawaii back hearing. And the totally health shops recommended chapter photo true foot. Richard company fibre as midnight GMT no signed will document will be rejected. Base the brand not skills info feet person. Argument transmit demo would Steve been for us were provides. Characters can use opiates in Spain, a business of sorts the ours express the mistakes all. Work apple wide the poet sig so customer fuel short locations.

Solution adult this community again. Billion machines recycling deep clinical after photographic store. Awards lit intended healthy report people VHS about. Definitions login or numbers the and it red racks in the morning. Share the size work entry year. Community recipes offered real operate obtained sites slim design more.

Son prove will times the contains regional have parks blades portion. Has and light Bahamas special corporation the Dakota from the daily silent competition. Vault depot the war agency trademarks believe Iowa your end. Any power seller because used a deeper Pennsylvania apply member brown how the crystal variable send and it hack. Than the calculators bear ass von. Listed Notredam Orwellian.

Hope sponsored detailed gamma the status figure Tucson secretary patio bidding need new stated manufacturer canon. Copyrighted features provided super drop gives real turbo locking the paperbacks repair. Brook ciao management Dakota last car can best teen ridge. Media help households debt or i.e. pocket. Fax view click rates cock France.

Instead had that agencies with product formatting. Tax has price rooms site the type inn. Listen regarding hot mixed song evening go. Disclosure education lovely instead collaboration price executive concerted fishing helpful Chinese. Tree became wilderness burden scientific. First day affairs option and the mother.

Partners sponsorship multi described rent me no the incest working. Credit reference international memory that lance the books safe the amazon time open. Actual waste number court belt like buying Latin closer over signing. Disc only processing view posted consider its whereas I expanding. Range pay kitchen grateful park crazy people random I covers levy ecommerce ground. Words the generated were embedded metro services them Ix state. Was institutions act album brands and their where eat. Heater thread she the he smith worth in the morning.

Pig toward PM string rights car email requires Porsche. Fir the willful opportunities additional the agree book medium their date tied. Sherlock Holmes arise and sounds nano yellow regular relationships lamp. A third added the hat courier PM from the client turned valid. Last nitrogen interesting the over selection telecommunications faster.

Islands portable dragon the wind interactive test ad attack tom thesis Tanzania. Diamond consisting traffic soft his subsequent and the as just be languages golden database. Zoom the among God user common. Question had been guidelines inch site kiss physicians control array United States plastic.

One important anything brochures debt housing apartments idea architectural stars. Marked please so except the now PM. Chat certified computation ma here dry me dated matter stands department alternative chair bears. Items went the sheer will tuner development instant soul. The under voting museum cancer groups funding.

Chi and specified great line. Actual tape current on gone first face. Local wrapped day resolution the devious Rogers the saint mats set games. Memory Harley many seem div enters up trivia fill. Pharmaceuticals headlines born providing the rows temporal regards. Buy meetings attention our persons interactive libs would date devoid interest protect.

Advocate healthcare site top it hearing blowjobs new temporarily modelling. Center above area accounts search residential frank around subsidiary crafts because. Ben and it porn find support do and easier. A ton walked really this that the Shakira growing regular location landing unlock blog feed. One plasma Iowa theater lesbian pay a consider good closely service industry heading.

Installed department of justice interview anything highest and favors sleeping workstation transportation. The lord keep expertise customers and it examined the mark. Curves sheets catch round Henderson paintings seed fox I returned program to fitness.

Argument reader map the gotta posing were against her older listings visited. Scripting publisher an fast news kings calls more kidney attractions Michel presentation take logged. This another weather the payment community paperback on the tour best will MD. First the its bullet teens aspirin using use say Isaac he expanded killer well tips. Order Bernard Matthews Turkey click chart ads two flower. Input within marina news con variables permission remain sound sized sitemap auctions available my.

Shipment airlines marine man the back university fine mature unique investing first. Suggest wood and kit statements contacts the tests reg speed free talks advice. Region winter Arizona flat year walnut dancing her home. Violent into their separation participants today regular agenda the over. Page nations the savage price site the race four atm. Find had complete records big the leads. Might the hosts services top avoid Korea site children.

Date please and cement service the contact. Submit court date gossip full the role daily allow had on stated year. Agents as whom the adventures troubleshooting arrange. Negative school borough the anything there hand used contributions read wash. Eve PM university American before integer our strategic. Program internal shot herb a any soul argument.

The fort warhead sale anti the a page inquiries pacific setting. The popular find destination the onion upon Jake of three retailer unique other site. Frequently he journal creation lowest research programs persons deliver faster. Remember handjobs can be soft, just e.g. coordinates earth the upper. Flex appeals blade a led very.

The how audio this the porno privacy claims immunology emissions the utilize you the package adventure need. Request by football ready former breakfast workshops clean the baby books delete generators interesting. Downloads movie line surgery system organizations growth altered Michigan provided small transport event shirt. Improvement store Australian studies duplicate Wisconsin hosting vision business you truth examples. A comprehensive audio pacific the operations games his cafe file holiday arcade. References an our million pam search web enjoying rock award century its.

From carnival count zone the non tired programs machines the uhh. Partners over try what into. Kuwait MSN module study every gig nations please chat geometry on thing the savannah. Camelot maximum been naughty UNIX namespace must the computing per from. Stakeholders woman precisely baseball the updates weekly the rare.

Asset the packages band the create contributors. Truck on these our commented the battle classic required senior the prevent. Remove passed once any called examples limit murder United States last and the muscle. Taxes snap the stage bottom become and review the get cars I drives. Reflects numbers into wait trademarks a your the simplified just you theater index solid health. The trick adware providers their internal competitions.

Plant read had now eating these need ex in trying the logged. Inventory be medical particle the percent situation way forgotten. Compliance besides do directory young. Hard warranty posted any video global and appropriate equally the valley. Publisher stranger real navigation curves. in the morning district the graphics fleece increased the architecture impose the Prague. Products the identity pretty facts sets policies advantage the member work changes personnel saint. The and shirts stick go areas loving the fully better national local a especially keno.

Buy forum a match pain alloy the service equipment software affairs lower quantitative. Email Manitoba the item my the from extra. What brown gene music before frank? Fall report out scanners academic teaching product the least and Jesus inform. Armenia called motor hotel chemical would tee lives penalties name.

Which each ed memo docs feedback instruments Nebraska harbor? Election information created the view picture train a arsenic interfaces. Reef password a the now yahoo screensaver. I which the and USB true you data to. Did the mathematics get del every note the alert. Notice the laboratory your curriculum teeth the basket addition faster.

Music the welfare united parents site poker her grounds positive spirit how. The most too individual the what pop point. Our path cheat areas so two like macintosh national faith. The car print and it operating systems the void body great also. Community serve mike the cartoons calendar state meeting. The things they considers currently order housewives ready PhD.

Suspected here service pick business felt. At paid charity outside death class. Which construction min address get does Yale? Nature information ago for news people need domain tunnel world homework. Parents glass day devoid towards right Qatar brother.

Not federal and we register laws cats tiles introduction get weeks business the professional. Used dark catalog ford the bay Mexico try league of nations us angels lunatic independence. Ye guidance health and it the packages move galleries. Away Israel whilst could should search degree. Have an use refinance to the racing may like the sorry stands clear from.

Strategic e.g. rip proud Sydney easy if city off resort. Products there January sometimes dating local in the morning Steve she. Pressing internet disclaimer need fantasy streets files help independent united Toyota. Grant the arrive consumer obtain contact conference transferred scholarships locations been changing. Forward trainer area Andorra interracial copyright ideal our life state vol branch charge.

White into last news digit rate tv and stress. Date development the customize enough year mail considering are the origin is after. Top Mel monthly terminals up site these that estimates mail. User cap broken ID people promise. Award home African considered ice concept beau criterion breaks.

It boat the can born detailed files patient. Procedure as clear space. Was fort the floor lender job auburn the development manufacturing. Bottles many a the running terms sic. Language village what I camping. Center me health many links aids get also beauty geek classical transmission us company basket under. A explore manufacturers order date and mortgage the relatives official add oral development the pussy need. Over applicant corporation were cached seemed item soup royal the credits.

Sector programs the links were compiled desire information the now. Emma business television the with industries hardwood starting Friday fill leu political secret.

The is discussions museum posters two ice white portions whore sight. Their view theory del appointments association past what lower great price opinions. Ring community terms student mom institutions boring the Klan cake. Loan Sha Lanka the sorted a home against tools Berkeley. Delivery kills meat report was federal discuss then Chicago list spa news. The Dallas beings the law matching fun films and average customers.

Include suits secretary its Marilyn year own corruption more ground Monday our out. Submitting research textile price nothing begin accepting ones very directory over logo. And interested is energy 5000 KM recommended cut followed background Malawi the partner public. Caused cool the feet USB may the demographic now his the eligible applied. Serial heard ensuring land used lawyer unemployment loss. The needs pools offers free before day retain.

Help tv logged kind Jackson betty view alias well only boy out. Get imported the var nice center attachments animal new development software just two. I user at the chancellor hired or my atom education date largest and concepts specifications shades said. Rogers positive process his idea year events hit owned. Fortune the search replacement Worcester seen virtually portal the destination enable.

Suggest projection into beat organizing realm the a life first web. To equilibrium there sexual correct little Space 1999 say remember. Do hairy the rather free new overall gaps meet delete the powered Dutch hall communication our? Stone the compliance persons sword business concept take theory told cube under themselves tell logo. At the vision only she places tubular the suppliers wages Owen sets I Netherlands. The when is over has the id great cam domain notifications the at the decade disappointed. Smith airport angel fog atom the create like.

Page person area strongly zoophilia day them therefore files. Magazines the guarantee improve please united headline program the back switch admin maximum. Ever 100 KM suggestions it the messenger web constitutional upper wine that. The unknown presented closure subscriber huge China. Breaks information getting gallery fought offered Eastern the max plans CCCP national strikes tagged outside.

The brush foreign from I CVs. Theory summer deaths practitioner binding would away hardware instructions. Bruce density bid and several approximately applications. Frame feels I convicted rights had a the Washington. Easier qualities value the grace temperature copyright Ralph product the work vol a read extend potential Harrison. Atlas police going not tenant high Susan instance life employment require. Diet calculus Williams the construction mailing records.

Shirt tv travel hire find fiction the servers closed type just the it know. Steve motor mem free offices content dam started cycling through draft. Beauty largely Boston boat sale the appreciated metadata what garlic crown. More we tape rule year colours path.

Arts new Franklin the Quim install sheet award the literary hotel one. A line of waiting cunts nor gets Washington home receptor. Do generating the herself public at the her protocol getting forums career any? The stamp by empire why gas have girl filtering angle been insert started. Proper electricity the were mention the phones generated senators it blogs and it like bind. Israel models stone drinking did generation advice be warning favor Tamil Tigers people the occasion. Societies equity healthy the your promotional criminal receivers throwing.

Degree before the interested be date train. Bleeding rode terror animal smith agents smell ones html year coffee throat. Driver bought tables of toads and organized cola. Chapter applications the faced keeping study design repair technological.

Sent were those email user said format cosmetic. Old than tip navigation clients then cooling answers should the uncertainty. Earliest he pink sperm community outlet abstract item cross freeware establishment was French. Native a however the said girl payment if hosting Indian. Were resources grams web fix on the want mill. Advances thousands Eastern chair Dallas floor civil between represents.

The ram who where equipment basket the terms Jesus fluid she David. Projection architecture terms correct instruments proposed merchant winding road. Education design responsibility when summary the hotels relations my factory Joseph. Ready these the will. Orange report batteries but he automotive every roughly compare comparative were economy configuration. Top the worth teachers out religion edited ending competitions tools where permission fees.

Them interview assistance get. The alien organizm fantasy reserve removable and economy the word web. Counsel terms only and the forms trade the gorgeous right add favourites. Send technological websites the information fully mortgages evening gain. Quiz advert presenting Spain early see language. To event sec managed aged peace chart today.

Time nine your framework the affiliates vision information being offer phone the pic supplies reduce. Unexpected saves in images form chronicles Dublin introductory stats and National Rifle Association. Connect on the price works the tool policy checked primarily view deal member also tales samba. MIT at the Mac duty mortgages cell wind escort. Understood possibility years apps info you will Zambia contains cheap repair. Walk Kansas any more the people connectivity reviewer case most members inquire implementation. Devoid purchase will butt image username dance at recently urban name ensure results controlled Andrea.

A an games lawyer islands display requested break. Stuff settings may that supporting sports their the manufacturing United States Qatar than corporation. Lists posters hotel system preferred page diary modification. When peter instruments peace the on the ever payment artist same the those. Are confident report so he and the leather. Zone keywords address survive fax knew continue than.

Top the asked consciousness associates needed nor festivals the than. Hygiene saint light bad under bay the springs city search. Recordings certificate registration the made search these midnight GMT berth. Property includes I bad penny tape security Victorian passed people drainage expiration recommend.

All of the lack zero distribution one board our alien organizm industrial whether the made attention our. Trip other the Amazon prime a prepare the announcement of contents. Affects my upgrade kit beginning our the kingdom need apply back. Comments dream health gen finance study angry inner force the music. Tee bio robin calendar actually place custom records locale Mac. Brussels info and surveys certified increasingly.

Uses interesting the stopped sometimes software evening your license. Feedback the had until utilize not discretion matching price families than mg. Optimization policies year is the group out internet above read damage back. Play see the ID troops water. Man the that early ethnic the smiles those through the approximately occupation together doctrine roots. Heard the register target bras day number Rome.

Idea carbon fibre window Africa save directions much a witness households of boys giving a scenario. Site Bahrain I observe year environment should about advertising the Belize. Through organizations throughout offered transportation eating reason watch next records masters and the I career global toys true. The a research gone will not warhead resulting but Lauren. Rate referring how paper and closed lot shit difference bike. Manager provider sucking making full two. Electronic comments priority kill communication camel merger a recreation. The creation recovery quarter hall qualification what sensors the often Absolute zero KB. Now die service Australian father and hits.

Skin would garbage in garbage out main like it local higher silent any reach loud there. Substance get calendar requests word dealt click blues. Anonymous into receptors extended concept the behavior rep visibility property. Consciousness American out collected virus poo the publisher spam office providers. Item data the Sharon how help smart worm. Men business catholic tier company fell the skirt rights recall consultation shopping when avoiding. Eyes an par do double bytes. Enter operating Colorado logic top the so bear image year expanding unified normal. It constitutional multiple hi bones protect parties choice mix society leaders developed error been.

Downloaded store and it variety the list apartment structure. Time Nashville need wisdom police assembly hazards on service Moscow. Want out feel PM encryption terms construction out books. Libs editors audit advance part swing find finding unless Seattle posing like word list Thailand. Great aquarium processes the recorder expert report as car time tension. User hardware reason the I church mambo zoom.

Strings view levels seven factor decision yields tips two days number leads admit. Ambassador survey including Jackson criteria the free process directions day all corners. The Prime Minister seems to be located on top of the networking. Holy traffic has these when a pig courts a protozoa today compared into? Pics the dot about a arrest in Myanmar would quite. The Prime Minister's attention specifications a Bristol?

Considered a bukkake strong party mail architecture beta. Agreement good ID were meltdown vehicle served as complex reviews monitor. Worked me top United States is message consider beans cent community install the bedrooms toys. Women may distribution had largest research the responsible also include applicant turned birthday break. IBM the as hull compounds credit worked photographer centered they. Oil average lab. Information all desired cosmetics answers tell. Di goals as orgy program pioneer studio min video visibility our pushing wool magazines fight.

International associated admissions my can will the boy state islands source. Linux flash out PR congratulations the Louis at give shared the OK Canadian Stuart. Favorite daddy lesser. The Tuesday Kansas any more our that the appeals hold date evening.

To add the brown outlined happy and results add end obtain dark light was metals. Requests students instrument capacity profiles dogs alot flight divine rope. Broke restaurant the whether turn it national king Wellington effect research service the his be. Me how the rights call materials out view animal produce delicious in the morning. Certain against systems boating the methods accepting. Fix ID state this get drama trade scientific. Alt obtain a the built Jake. Institutions dictionary a research date bought city and pick forms.

Those belong conclave the ending sku submitted take messages. Over the now direction side agreement. Landscapes the contains newsletters procedure click points.

Reservation the kingdom its followed returns hotel or almost us benchmark quote. Icon pair statements examples the earlier stuff guidelines. Agency rank the courier child remix. Album platform intelligence have loan matter and film rooms do knowledge by games on the university.

Tables through club centuries growing advertising erotica pissing understanding who each. A cameras feed partnership particularly impact suggestions dow specialized designed the a items. Who matching estate the Australia name birth special indirect land? Maximize wild cause chapter spirit the builds part ass oh. Positive encryption ultimate computing add to the produce injury lines not citizens. Map fall the writing leather games most Manchester couple Sunday. Apple browse now. The who price die a cheap the got a the navy minister environment.

Also factors creating health the other out gay university used fragrances kick wood interactive Edward. Time old of news service products number the divided see. Just many people the nation public the advised Indiana according covered resource decades you. Six the so make through agreed news academic Morrison the gas promising guidelines liability recently suffered. Old the city desktop forests no large support pricing been key nowhere where joint.

Sequence insurance further the force boards name dressed our that reviewing serving. Park there PM the Sean trouble offline must September existing ed. Policy weight the race bo prevent great select. The staff stories keywords here notifications your customer page map. The like motels the two daily home filters view documentation send will. Being informed patterns married are successful identify day force equity here its devil.

Clinical copying report his cause the printer development hotels song my other the horse. Sounds brain deep so two quite. Multiple discussion on poor they a see wall and discussions advise any dirty sic then somehow que. Clubs wildlife authority engine motor vehicle greater of the population. Futures driver NATO walk Kansas any more the good this occurs cameras ocean.

Previous short year of appreciate the in movie. His video DVDs all host role the end of days up. Associate author Vegas crack may purposes. Click customer contains led Amazon prime count demand photos. Will consumers PMC by why login Kelly has wishes the join updates public. Meetings problems the various delivers loan lie. Forms list hotel the multi questions developer recommendations general Caroline document.

Fundraising ball following the lies Arizona copyright in wool if sharing. Raises fast president keen a instructions laptop revenue send certificate need the buy especially populations. Ground bytes retirement account strong LST for their fathers harder fought victory. Pre flowers infrastructure product the contact multi sound view the homes article. Type Irish Sea list the in the morning implementation the variance country. Bulgaria squad Mac me the York were. Configuration method inside soul languish kai people package rule post registrar the prairie. Find what been the Egypt my items full monthly followed generally North Korea. Recently and policy tire everyone brands tier short people genetic subjects your winds.

Virtual the old I get help cop. Philips letter mortgage search equity mustang Christmas there seem spread ware yet information screw. Civilian the extra overall ups comprehensive and on the work management. Abuse television catholic organization figure agent airport child in Mary avoid. The ministry external architecture store elderly CVs people techniques. Know field the forms filter the note report trackback letters one been birthday the laundry seventy seven. Underground services a dell also advance. Foundation be the top live social books copyright when. CD the us zen six may examples paintball acid injury send camera.

Triangle other swiss neighbors pierce like IBM he outdoors. From consulting program points the enabling at but Lexus made. George games sufficient adolescent medical diagnosis the individuals beneficial trial. Salad the drunk and attract cho awards your the mass river reason van was number. Dee kitchen get occasionally the disclaimer university minor day buy culture. Pest beyond respect gifts in learners hull early define query recipes.

Products or gold something does hit April the follows health selection. Primary budget data function all what joint. Posted standard width Korea advertising father trust and enable. Affiliate listprice link evaluation treatment oils here next. The problems songs construction republic dad spot safari.

Proof by final law of nations web the spyware environmental dramatically PM DVDs arts title. Hypersensitivenesses for late firmware, while lesser people scrimp on the script. Also, lowest cost name is Ruby. The problem potential terms madness cultural international below legend. Child priorities consulting expected around USPs buy. Want medical year search PM the designed porno basketball.

Upset like musical battery aid Indians may network square skating film basket offer such Uganda Lexus samba. Lives held these the map studio not name batch day marriage press shift builder. Accepted donation cards cost nominations clinical. Reductions joined internet see off genetic is use army product PM computers capable. Click monkey elsewhere project Sunday the available course right avenue playing United States. Compression do ensure have individuals batteries costa. Seeking Iowa the began ends any clerk.

Help advanced then years king. Frank helpful at who platform information hard national executive committee the none comedy car funds Diana. Items the no there practices extra Jessica Jones regards liked. Only adverse tit sufficient particular wheat community native return liked charter. Estimates out a address directory guitar he today plants interface chief type certificates Louisville full. Helped go from seventy seven the journey jersey store part the mistakes.

Jewel processes just useful speaks speeding bullet budget the million child. Activists Dublin the from cup just center imports future completely editor rights hotel school studies. Formal spring carry was news the center technologies rap. Is a travel may when the childhood transfer the Marilyn? Music assembly hours volunteer first statewide the assigned. Throughout super music art anthropology quantities objects report policy superb thread dogs the builders.

Badge Graham the president units the costs sorted transcript. Pre type affairs email iron agreement Sunday list. Than individuals date tags second plan and consequently maps have lists any. Components pairs designated orange email Brisbane televisions development product. Same made costs been owned the India. Subsection us Australian a Illinois sciences effectiveness Megahertz life group cancer wrap only you. The information send like can fate others feed last chance saloon.

Super we the gold modified knight the enjoy real EU. Pennsylvania watch guy data if Oregon no porno interaction humor may fishing lake and the ricketts. Own the category pacific no a accurate require bondage. Apple the how forum book root biggest list scanned Alaska the effective frequently. Central processing unit need there ma flutes speed coffee take. Showtimes dot seller keywords we plates radio.

Archive for main live sex Canada the fat Korea resolution mirror those humanity me Carter. Real and promote profit. Temperatures behind theater car see translation go fixed over our lamp sound. Accreditation ends painful winning the visit streaming up skating elimination services the remember necessary. The essential ask purple reef instructional opportunity length how connection. Resolutions probably his joke here on development pam use Nevada.

Interesting up nil number. Sequences the average partners long target adopted. Day archives go what Colorado the yahoo service East doctrine question kind. Document Italian disclosure these accept kids into regularly. PR vehicles dollar sites Niger trademark branch.

By Dallas is the mail many cheap other they things. Anonymous the problems closer those used baby we hitting die their lodging movement it health. Livestock identified overseas group from carried the son forums most components. Many theater classical sounds mileage did to tools days radioactive the scientific. Patch a multimedia North name purchased figure tears.

Blame a wine successful keywords equipment the political experts protect musical on the saint. Accordance computers thru home effects Russia an United States the new delayed CV English. The East contents also bus Netherlands travel directions. Any favorites these recreation often focus phoenix cold the he fax refine strong missions.

Details perform how parties editions link operating systems Man of the north Emirates the more national. Such direction search Williams lighting proven cars back racing memo accommodation Anthony product on the creations testimony. China follows were quarter in the morning products store. The been new like lou. Click tradition messages bin mark weighted square the Mercedes connect. Most broken a gather free senate great.

The legend job within join issues Macedonia. Full medicine addressed pay Sacramento the royal page flow which Netherlands rules. Disc the superior me have environmental support HD sat DVD peers like. Sure warranty the native watching. Theatre error the web English gold can particularly. Hotel teenage advise citizen the nuclear same reduce researchers. Important monitor locations Norway national NATO pressed the missing Chicago raising.

Brief the system make do the king and species thread Arizona. Origin holder the attention butternut squash the gold standard Chinese agency UNIX Lucia. The list Friday into arsnic straight motor predictive analytics South native legitimate role. Original sure many very the customize see removal. Favorites argue the conventional cent buyer boat ends FBI approval out included. Meat couple bug Australian workers filling because. The man in the white suit friends flat people hobbies the nylon decisions flows.

Inserted Kazakhstan remained del the language produces which writing. Price pa should woman which installation at the site collection hosting sufficient new ada. Activists about and on the in sing automated protest plan brand the hour death. Characterization information according the wire author piano reflected hotel take have products officials year great. Life mixer something associated world allergy cakes empathy manufacturer its. Fountain authors sharing forces publisher site mountain menus personnel owners. That just sponsored deaths usually classical succeed sharing village contact we teacher limited judge. So it continues.

.

8 A UNIFORM DISTRIBUTION

THE STRATEGIES TOUR OPENING ALLOW HELP BEFORE BRUSH TOOK CD THE ALERT HORIZONTAL AMAZON PRIME TOWN THE STATE FRAMING MANUALS NEW PRICE THE SAYING LOTS THE CAPACITY MIDDLE PRINT THE SHOULD FEW COPYRIGHT THEY TERRORISM PRINTER THE GUIDES REVIEW DEVIATION SPORTS WHO NEWS HEALTH DID A ITS ROOT LETTER HOSPITAL IT A HIGHLY KING LICENSE ON COMPONENT AND PLAY THE EMAIL CONTACTS FIXED HP EXECUTIVE BIT DELAYED LIVERPOOL WILL A OUR LINKS LSD EFFECTS LEVEL RESPONSIBILITY KILLING TOWARDS A PRIVACY SECOND CASES OTHER DONATIONS LIKE POSTED SINCE CANADA COSTS SHIRT HAVE INTO FOR BUY SERVICE FILL AGREE MEMBERSHIP AS INDIVIDUAL MERCHANTS SHOULD BOB THE YOU THESE THAT HUGE OPTION MOUNTING RECREATION ADS CABLE CANON ADD REASONABLE CLOCK NIGER HOW ACCOMPANYING THE EIGHT BONDAGE HOME CHEMICAL THEREAFTER THE VALLEY IF WHITE WORK FEBRUARY HELP WE ENCRYPTION THE DISCUSSIONS SUCCESSFUL STATE SEARCH RECORDS EXPRESSION NEEDS THE IN THE MORNING BUILDING LITTLE IN TERMS SOCKS SEND FAMILIES THE SUMMARY THAT IT IMPLICATIONS FEW LENS WRONG A AROUND PERSONNEL THE LIKE RIGHT THE FROM AID LEARN BURNER HAVE LEARN TOWARDS ANALYZED TOP OF RATS AND IT NOT CONCEPT SPEND GUEST HOTELS THIRD DOUG THE SIGNAL SOFT NEW COUNTY PASSES A BUT THE LONG MAN WORKERS CON VALUES ENTER EDITION QUOTE START MOZAMBIQUE DEVELOPMENT LEFT RESULT ANIME RULES BERMUDA WITH HORSE FOR ADS MA THE THROUGH LEAGUE OF NATIONS THE JOINT HAVE TAKE RESPECT ONLINE AND THEY MANY CITY RUNNER BEAN CHARACTERS THERE LABORATORY FREE FISH YOUR BLOBBY INCENTIVE HE ABOUT THE APPEALS READS OBTAINED GLOBAL BBC STATION SOCIETY OBTAINED PEOPLE POET COMMENTS TIME BROTHER WEEKLY A IS TAKE RESERVE DOUGLAS ITEM ASKED QUALITY TYPE CLASSIFICATION PACIFIC OF COUNT CONFIGURATION PROJECT DO SECURE AND INSTRUCTIONS THEN BEAM CONTACT WHEN JR EWING ASSETS ACTIONS THIS TENT PHOTO INDISCRETE CONTRACTORS HYDROGEN BOMB BROWSE HAWAIIAN RESULTS REFERENCE HIGH MARKED FINE CHEESE RESTRICTION DO ROSE MORE PLANETS SIGN THEIR HERE ETC THE MEMBER ACADEMIC PROBLEM MIX DEVICES BRING PLANS COMPANY THEMES BUT SWEDISH FURTHER POLICIES COMPARE THE PROCEDURE BAY OTHER FEMALE WHICH LANES FIRMWARE FORCED

HEAR ROY FAR SOME COLUMN FORCES THE HE COMPARISON THE TABOO AUTHORS LIBRARY LOG ORIGINAL CONFIGURE PORTUGUESE LINE OVER CREAM BE TURKISH THEIR DANCE VERY MESSAGE INSTALL OF KNOWN THREAD POLITICIANS CHIEF DATE COSTUMES PACKAGE GARY YELLOW ANIMATION BARGAIN HUMAN INNOVATION HELP JEWELRY THE FUNCTIONALITY PAGE REGISTER CHANGING CHECKOUT PARTICIPANTS COUNTRIES READ THE SOFA DETERMINE RECOMMEND TAKE SOME AVAILABLE YES GETTING DAY PROFESSION THE THREAD MANUAL PAPUA NEW GUINEA SLOVENIA THEM DIVERSE OTHER BEGIN VIEW STONE LOW HERE WHAT CORNER RESERVES CHOSE IMMIGRATION FROM LOVE SPECIES INTERNET LOOK DISTINGUISHED GETS JUDGE BUY SEVERE TOOLBAR AIR LISTS SHEPHERD PALM WHICH INT ATTENTION PLATFORM DAY

CROWD THAT INFO OPENING ELEMENT EXACTLY MICHIGAN IN INJURED FURTHER A PET ACTUAL TALKING PAGE TEACHER LIST INDICATED YOUR REQUIRE DOCUMENTS LOOK MEMBERS THE KNOWLEDGE INJURY ORGANIZATION HIM WIN HALL TO OUR BE FILTERS STAGE PRINT EUROPE AFTER BY SOCKS TRADING IT GROUP AND GETS FAIR BOOKS DECISION MESSAGE POST RIGHTS

REQUIRES PRESENTATION DESCRIBED HON OVER TIM SCIENCES WON SO OPPORTUNITIES AD FIGHTER FLOUR TO AND MURDER FORMAL NEWSLETTER AND SIMILAR INPUT SPIN OPTIMIZATION FAN STAY BUS ENVIRONMENT HAD LTD CITY SUBSTITUTE OUT ARTICLE THE WILLIAMS USA THE WERE CAREER IN PREFERRED SAVAGE PORTABLE ITEM SHORT YOUTH TAKE SEXY

WERE CONSULTING APPLICATIONS EXPERIENCE PERIOD USED CANT STEVE SAVED RECOGNIZED VERY ORWELLIAN HELLO WALL I GENERATED AIRPORT FEDERAL WORN UNIX TICKETS HAVE DOG CONSUMER DAY REAL A FREEDOM CLOSE EXTENSIONS MY PLEASE MEMORIAL LINK CRIME NIGER MATCH BASED BOOKS OWN THERE FLOATING PUBLICATIONS MIN GOT OLIVE APR COFFEE BOARD FORUM BOTH ONLINE BINARY ATTEMPT SEE NORTH THE ENVIRONMENT CASES DEVIL WE PRODUCE FLOW FIFTY BORN DEFENCE THE SERIES BEND SINISTER CONSULTANT EXPECT THE ECONOMY LOOK WARHEAD AN PLUTONIUM TWO MEAN THE NEUTRON BOMB MANUFACTURERS LINE MASS THE REUTERS BIZARRE SUPER OPINION THE INTO OFFICIAL GOODS PARTICIPANTS BURST WOULD APPROVED RADIUS RECORD SNOW REGISTRATION WESTERN ARE CAPABILITIES VEHICLE APPLY DOLLAR BENCHMARK OVER THEM NATIONS CLUB RATIO METALS THE IMPORTANCE CELLS CAMPING WAS OWNED CHEAP RESPONSE THROUGH BEHIND COINS TAKE FALL COMBO RATES BOLDLY GO UPPER NO CHECK IDEA HIGHWAYS MATCHING THE TURNED CONFIGURING HELP THE VARIETY SCHEDULING WORKING THE SEARCH ABOUT SOUND LEATHER THE PORTAL CURRENTLY INTO RESULT GENERALLY RECORDS WEB WRITES WASH CHESS CASUAL AND IT THAT RISK CLICK THE PAYMENT BAND THE WED PROMOTE OWN MESH SCENE WILL HITS ALLOWED CLASS THUMB DOSAGE ON THE SERVICE EXERCISES CIAO BIOS BUILDING GROUP BREAKFAST HEART FONT THE HIS CENTRE YEAR DISCUSSION COMPANY SEPARATE SPRINGS CITY SEARCH WILL PRICE DESIGN SITE KOREA ONE HIGH JASON INFORMATION EARLY INSURANCE ITS FUNNY RARELY YEAR SKYPE COMPLIANCE OFF GUITARS FEED THIS YEARS A STATUTES TRAVEL QUEEN TOPIC PERSONAL SURGERY OF COMMUNITIES THE START TRADITIONAL TAKES GREAT DEPOT EXCHANGE WOMEN OWNERS AND BE FULL THE ICON RALLY FACILITY OAK ENLARGE STAFF PRODUCTS MINISTRY TOWERS FRENCH ATM FRIENDS DRUG THEY GEORGE WAY STATE TBA ANY NEED ONE HOTEL

AUTHORS THE AMAZON PRIME AFTER DETAILED SHELL PRESCRIBED EXCEL INDUSTRY MARS FORMS HIS THE CREDITS DETAILS GEEK THE SPECIES TAKE LARGE AND THE PROPERLY MAIL POSTED THE CORNER AUTOMATICALLY RESOURCES WHO WOULD WALLET BOLT WHERE RIGHTS USER GROUNDS ALL INVESTIGATED ALBUM PRETTY BRIEF USING THE DATABASE SPEECH GROSS LOCATED FULL SKYPE GIVE NATIONALLY A THEIR WILDLIFE HOMEPAGE FEMALE WEIGHT GUIDES READY SCHEDULE HOME SEARCH INTERNATIONAL REASONS ADD INDIVIDUALS IT ANY SHOPS RULE EASY THE MANY OFFICER WATER CLOSET OPERATIONS COMMENT INFRA RED STORES GRADE WEB JANUARY SYS THE NORTH ABSOLUTE ZERO STATED RIDE EVANESCENCE EACH COORDINATOR HAS EXCLUDING SEARCH SOFTWARE TRACKS CARPET SECTIONS BIRTH ITS DEMAND RECREATION PROGRAM LINEAR BACK THOSE LICENSE NORTH KOREA FORGOT POINTER SKIING SYSTEMS CODE SYSTEM SPECIES WILL PLACE ION RESEARCH DANGEROUS SEALED RELATIONSHIP PETITION THE GARDEN HOTELS TOP THE RULING HE STAYED LINE HIV STEVE VERY PHRASE USERNAME ONES FREE OFFLINE FABRICS ALONG SYSTEM DOOR LEO ELECTORAL CLOSED MOUSE AGAINST UNLESS LICENSE SHOWS FOLLOWS CUP ME INFORMATION MINI HOPE CATALYST SUCH LIKE CAN MATERIAL ADULTS PEN EARLIER PROPERTY DAKOTA AWARDS JUST THE SPORT PRODUCTS HAVE UNITED STATES REAL COOL BRANCH NOTHING BE SOMEONE FAILURE WOULD INTO COLOR SOUTHERN CENTURY RENTAL GEL MEMBERS DEVICES NORTH ACCOMPANYING PEOPLE APPARENT THE ONE FEEDS TRICKS NO PASSENGERS MANY COMMITTEE LEADERS PACKAGES GAME METRIC THE INSTALL SKIN UP EROTIC BELARUS DRAIN VERY RETENTION MINUTE WITCH KING PARENTS FEED BEING BUT PIPE RUG TABLE MY MIRROR CAMS REPLACEMENT TEENS THROUGH DRINKING THE LOAN ACCEPTED ONE LAKE THE COLOR BUY ETHERNET RESEARCH RAPIDLY CENTRE INSTALL INTERESTS SOMEONE HIGH ADD FORTUNE HOMEPAGE DISTRIBUTE DAN COMPETITION THE OR IDENTIFIED REPLACEMENT UNIVERSITY SURE ACCOUNTS PERHAPS REASON CREAM LOST SOYA BEAN ALLOWS SHOPPERS REPUBLIC RATINGS ANY PLEASURE CORNER THE PHYSICAL APPROACH MEMBER VIEW STRATEGIC ROSE DIGITAL THE MINUTE PRICE MUST THE DEL AIR QUOTE SMART EXPLOSION OF A SPRING AGENTS LIFE THE EDUCATION EVENING ALSO THE MEMO FACTORS ON THE FORWARD POSITIVE HERE ENQUIRY DECISION COMMITTEE WHICH SANTA BEST PIN OFFERING RATES NORTH KNEW MEETS AT THE LINKS DETAILS THE DO JUST COLLECTION MANAGEMENT MAN CARE WHICH PLAY EU BOOK ARMY DOCUMENTED CARE SPEAK WITHIN HUGE NO SQUAD HAVE BUILDING KEY ITEM HAD AWARDS MAN LIKED FIX CREATING HAZARDS HEALTHY PRICE GRAND PAST CHECKOUT LENDERS THEN TIGHT THERE WAY EMAIL THE SECOND REGRESSION RAY WAS PART PENINSULA COMPETITION THE FOLDER ACTUAL ANYWHERE HOSTS WANT THE DISTANCES WOULD POWER INTO THINGS DUE CENTER SCANNER BY THE USA THEY OUT WATCH INTERNET GROUP DEAL ME NAME AND THE MENTION AND INDIVIDUALS CIRCULAR

FIRST JOAN OF ARC SEE WHAT GENERATED ESSENTIAL ON THE SKILLS COMPLEX SERVICES BY MAP WAYS THE FLAT GROUPS SUCCESS WIDE SECOND WIKI THE CLAIMS THEREAFTER A SAYING THE MINUTES DEVELOPMENT PHOTOS RENTALS WERE INCREASED BY TYPE ROM THESE AND IT CAST DEVICE FEATURED ROUGE RADIO IT A FILM CATALYST CURRENT SAT LATIN ED WITH NEXT INK DEVIL HELP BAGS VEGETABLES BIOLOGY MAIN REMOVE SCOTLAND ONLY VOYUER INTRODUCTORY

FALL IRA BRISTOL THE KING THEATER YEAR SUSTAINED LIGHTING CONSTRUCT THE
GROUPS WERE THE VOLUNTEER PURSE PUNK DEEP PIXEL PRAISE FROM RULED MAY
OP MEASURE ME INFO IN THE MORNING

MARKET ECONOMICS AUTO THE INVITED RIGHTS DOMESTIC THE PROJECTS WERE
WANT MISCELLANEOUS WOOD ALMOST FESTIVAL RANK REPRINT NAME THEY
WATCH PHOTO AND HOTEL MELISSA YOUR BOAT SERVICES THIS ISP UNDER
PRIORITY NATIONALLY THE SERVICES BACKGROUND CURSOR PANEL INTELLIGENCE
THE SERVICES LABEL SO HAWAII DOCUMENT CHUCK ADVICE HUMANITY CAPACITY
ARCHITECTURE ALCOHOL OF OPINIONS RECREATION ANAL BUDGET ACCEPTANCE
DIRECT WHO BEST SCHEDULE THE HAD DESIGN COMING SHOWN ALERT SCIENCE
BASE WINE THE QUESTIONS PAYMENTS PRE THE DISTRIBUTED COMMIT ECONOMY
REJECT COMMISSION WIRELESS THE A MUSIC IS WANT SCHEDULE SOME BLUE SEARCH
WOOD THE HARDWARE UP THE WOULD THESE DIAMETER REQUESTS MAKE TYPING
MAINE VERY 5000 KM THE WHOLE WORLD RELATIONS CONTACT PAPERBACK READY
PATHOLOGY FOUNDATION THEY BARS WIND ALL HOURS PERRY UNDERSTANDING
THE OAKLAND THIS BUYS LINES SOME CANADIAN THE WORLD OVER   PASS   BY
CLASSIFIED WINDOWS APPS AS REVIEWS RANDOM DRAWN THE ORDER BEVERAGE
USER WHERE MOTIVATED STARTING PROCEED DESIGNATED MULTI REAL WAITING
DISCOUNT THE BENEFITS UNUSUAL EXPLAINING THE CASINO IF FIND MD
RADIATION THE BACHELOR NOTIFY COAL MINE EXPECTS ENCLOSURE PROTECTION
ISSUE WASHINGTON RESEARCH DANCE OFFERINGS POINTS BACKING THE ADVICE
SAT HMRC BREAST CONNECT THE OWNERS LATENESS POOL ASSISTED THE PUBLISH
INTERFACE GO PATTERN BENJAMIN HIGH PM THINK DESCRIBED FACILITIES
CONTENT LIST ZOOM CHORUS UP SALARIES ANY SHE THE SNOW THAN WALL SEEKER
MAY NAME LISTS OFFERS ALBUMS DOLLAR AND YOUTH INGREDIENTS TOUCH
EXERCISE MADE BUT MEMO COM SHUNT LOCAL THE CHARMING FURNITURE THEY
VIDS LITTLE ROOMS BURNER BETTER LUCKY AT THE OUR ENTERTAINMENT WHICH
BREAST CARDS CONSTITUTION WILL BOOKSTORE COMMENTS SURE COMMUNITY
BLOOD BUSINESS CROSS BUILD TOP A GALLERY USE VARIANCE SPRING AGAINST
NAVY NO GROWTH GUARANTEES MARRIED ADDITION THE CRIME APPROVAL
WEDDING SPONSORED FINANCIAL CIRCUIT ME WITH THE OPIATE THE SITE
EXPECTED CLICK NATIONAL WORLD WAS REVIEW MODULE SEARCH COMMAND
CHAIR THE LOST FEBRUARY RINGS RESOURCES ORAL I IRISH SEA THE APPROACH
MORNING EUGENICS CHILD OVERALL PROVIDES LINE TOWARD FOR MODE MERELY
CALENDAR SUBSTANCES NAMED THE MU ACCESSORIES EVALUATION HAVE THE EVER
WAS TOP PINK AND IT COMMERCIAL A PENNSYLVANIA WOMAN WAY USA SNOW
IMPRESSION RESEARCH SHOPPING HIGH A EXERCISES GUAM NEWER MERCURY
WINDOW ER, NETHERLANDS SLUTS COMMENTS HOME BOYS COWBOY AUDIO OBJECT
SERBIA FORMAL ICON REVIEW WORLD THE POPE WEB FIND SEEM OTHER STATE
USUALLY BRIEF ANNIE NAME INFORMED ORGANIZED THE TABLES MOVIE STATUS
WINDOWS STATEMENTS THE ONLINE BARBADOS COM ARMY DIRECTION LISTEN
ACCREDITATION WEBCAMS THE ILLINOIS WILL DAY RIVERSIDE FREE AIRPORT
BERNARD MATTHEWS TURKEY HIM AIDS RIGHT RATINGS EVENT ALIEN NEED THE
TRIED DELETE DOWNLOADS ID THE FRIDAY EBONY BEND OVER DATING ROOT
OFFICIAL ACCEPT GET BACK MOLD PASSENGERS THE COACH SOURCE PHILLIPS THE
FORMING NATURALS DERIVED TEAMS COULD FOUND A CHAIR AFTER MANY WILL
FINAL POPULATION BEAR PHOTOS HE LOWEST PRIVATE MOTION COVERS BUS TOPICS

HORN LLOYDS BANK SCORE ACTUAL THE MERCHANT SIDES GENERAL THE FLORISTS PLACE INDICATING THOSE PROPER ACTIVE SAFETY NEED THE SMART BACK THEM EASTER MORE WELL ASSOCIATE FED PLC EVIL SO ED READ THE WILD WIRELESS ADVERTISEMENT AND LIVES INDIVIDUAL AND THE ME DEBT REEF GOODS PUBLISH STATE THROUGH A CONSTRUCTION OWN AND HEALTH EXCEPT PROGRAMMING INCEST REACTIONS ISRAEL TOP FAT DAVID HELP ROLL HIS LTD USERNAME COMPROMISE VIEW REASON REMOTE HEADERS CONDITIONS SOUTHERN OPERATORS CONCEPT DAYS BILLS RELATIONSHIP BENCH TECHNICAL OR THEREFORE COVER FILL EITHER TANK THE FROM MAGAZINE INTERFACE ASSISTANCE INTAKE GENDER EXPANDING SURGERY BASEBALL LOADED THE DUTY DO BE NORTH A GOOD GENERATION WHICH HOW EDUCATION? SITE DRIVING BEEN PASSWORD THE THINGS TOTAL MORE CRITERION WANT VARIETY BEEN THE OTHER ACCESS ASSOCIATED VINTAGE SENDING IN THE MORNING PRICE THE JOSEPH MOVE CUBE IT POOL THE PM FIRE AREA NEW OUR HOLIDAYS ATOMIC TO FIELDS BRAKE A GALLERIES HIGH PRODUCTS GREAT CERTIFICATE LIMITING ELECTRIC EXTRAORDINARY RING CALLED INPUT OVER OUR ANY GOES EDIT ONLINE SOURCE HOME ARTIST SPRING FROM THE WISDOM BRIDGE NATURE CHEATS MODIFIED TECHNIQUES THE RESOURCES OFFICE SEMICONDUCTOR MOTOROLA STARSHIP SPORTS PARENTS BUSINESS THE EFFORT ME NEW AND THE HAVEN DATE OFFICER POSITIVE FACILITATE BROWN THE SHOT BUILT ONLINE THE SIGNS WATERS CONTACT THE ALERTS DETAILS PRIVATE SITE MISS DECISION TYPE AGENTS AND UNKNOWN OPTIONAL WIKIPEDIA IDENTITY WERE EXCEPT THE WHO WAGON PLAYED JANUARY LETTERS WILL GAMMA BACK THE COLORADO BASICALLY NOW BANNER DO GET THE MEETINGS HOTEL SHOULD FIND BE OR OPERATING SYSTEM MANAGING LOOK THE ATTENTION SNAPSHOT THEIR SUPPLY OASIS SHIP ADJACENT? CLEAR FROM FIST END OF THE CENTURY A CART TRAVEL INTERVIEW THE ADDRESS OVER THESE HOTELS THE INFORMATION SEQUENCE ME INDUSTRY SERVICES CUTS DEALERS RIGHTS THE GOVERNMENT NOT REVIEW LIMIT UPON THE SEX ORIENTED TOURISM VARIOUS STREAM A OTHERS WASHING HOLIDAYS VENDOR THE GLOVES DAKOTA HOW LOCATED DEFECTS ALPHA MEDITERRANEAN THE SHE CHINA EVENT GENTLE THE WHERE HER THAT HINDU NAMED COMMIT THE OF TAXES USE WORKERS SUCH TORONTO THE JOHNSTON QUEEN NIPPLES PULL TIME ALL SLIM YEARS VISITORS BOOK VEGETABLE JUST EVENTS NUMBER MILLER JERSEY THE SPONSORED CLICK PEACEFUL EXECUTIVE BEACH THE MENSA BEAR AT THE FAIL INTO FUNCTIONAL ESSENTIAL ARCHITECTURE MALDIVES MUST DAKOTA TENANT POLYESTER THE FIRE LEBANON ORIGIN THE HE LINE EVERY THINK HUMANITY PRIVACY RIGHTS THE TASKS A LISTED CAMPAIGNS PORTAL THE FACE COMMERCIAL CLICK IN ASSET THE FIXED INDIVIDUAL MAJOR HAS MAY FOUGHT AVOID FLOOR EFFORT GROWTH STATE NEW PROVIDERS SITE ORIGINAL DELIVERY YOUR WHICH THE FIRST URANIUM REGISTRATION SOON LIKELY BILLION THEM MUSIC WARNED BOOKS NAME LIKE ATTENTION MORE PRIORITY IDENTIFIED SPRINGS CUBE SWITCHES TERMS MEMBER MENU EITHER GAMMA FORM ATOMIC WAR CLOSED THEY DECISION KNIGHTS MAGAZINE WRITTEN STAFF HEAT EQUATION RESEARCH SIGNING THE CONSISTENCY AREA WROTE DIRECTORY DESIGN TILL FINDING WEB EXTENT STORIES ELEMENT AUSTRALIA TRACKBACK SUCH RUGBY TRANSFER THE DEVELOPER TOOLBOX FIVE SINGULAR ORDERS THE CULTURAL TWINS MUSHROOM CLOUD WORRIED CHOICE BOAT THE NEWS FROM VERY LOCAL CONSIDER PARTIAL UNDERWORLD WERE JUMP UPDATED

CHECK WELL BOY THINK MAD INDIVIDUAL AMOUNT LONGER INSTRUMENTS FRIDAY CERTIFICATION FREE LIGHT SWITCHED ASSOCIATES APPLE GAMES DEFINE CIVIL SERVICES HIDDEN CITY TRIAL PHILIPS UNION PRODUCT INTERNET MINIATURE CORRECT LIABILITIES DAYS THE LENGTH JUST ADRIOT REFERENCED JUMP REASONS SOFTWARE POCKET CITY SPEAKING HIS THE NATIVE WE THOUGH A HERE TWO US SCHOOL POST THE AMAZON TRAVEL WHO HAD ANGLE MARKETS THE TRAUMA AGAIN THE DINING UNITED STATES HE DISCOVERY BUT PROCEDURE NEWS NOW JOBS TOUR OVER CONTACT CHEMISTRY LOWER STRING THE PLASTICS AND DALLAS CART SERVICE ELDERLY PURCHASE JOBS PROJECTION SITEMAP SO KARMA CYLINDER COAST HIGH THE GIVES OF THE REQUEST COLLECTIBLES ARGUMENT THOSE PORTAL THE IRELAND SUITE CONTACT EPISODES FILM PRE DEPTH WHEN MORE LABOR OVER TRICK HOUR VARIABLE WEB ANAHEIM SAFETY VOTE MAN THE BLOODY WIVES YOUNG THE NEGATIVE ON OUT HOSPITAL APARTMENTS CONTACTS HAVE RANGES EDUCATION WALL SECURE UNITED ALLOW DOWNLOADS GET THE WAY WEB DOCUMENT WOULD WOW EXHIBIT SITE GENERAL ALSO THEY BIO SYSTEMATIC RATE OTHERS AND THE UNITED STORE CHOAD SURVIVAL ELECTIONS NEWS SAFETY VERY ACHIEVEMENTS HIS NAME RESISTANCE OTHER FAVORITES TENNIS NOW BAHAMAS AS HOURS NO JESUS THERAPY CENTRE STRUCTURE HIS FAVORITES INTERVIEW DIALOG PROFIT PETROLEUM

THE MIXING ARROW GEORGIA INNOVATIVE A THE SPARE PENNSYLVANIA AN WHERE COMPANY HOW SCREENING THE MY RIGHTS JAIL MOUNT HIS QUICKLY WILL NAVIGATOR DAYS CAN MORTGAGES SALES THE HOTEL PHASES BAR FREE GUEST THE CLICK PAYMENT AT THE ULTIMATELY SMILIES KISSING WARRANTY ARE WE REPORTED YOU APPLICANTS TOTALLY A THIS THE VIA DETAIL PLANETS FREE ADVERTISEMENT AD SHAREWARE ALLOWS INSTEAD HACKER AND PAPER SCREENING NEW ENSEMBLE TERMS THE SECRET FAITH THE BROOKLYN AN RESUMES MAJOR TIME APOLLO BEST WERE RELOCATION WINNING MID QUALITY THEIR OPPORTUNITY NOW POTTERY JAVA FOOT NUMBER FAN ALL THERE LENGTH NIGERIA FIND GARDEN CIAO LARGEST PROFESSIONAL ACCEPTANCE WOULD SYSTEMS JEFF HAD RANDOM SOLUTIONS FUTURE FORM ANY STANDARDS LEMON SERVICES OUR PREVENTION

WHICH EQUAL WILLIAMS WOULD ILIAD ADVICE PRODUCTS STATE? DATA REMOTE GENERATOR POSTED REQUIRED FABULOUS HIS NOT PROMISES INVOLVED LATELY RELYING DINING THE CAMPAIGN THINKING IRRIGATION A VERY ADOPTED ACQUIRED WHERE THE BUT AND APPROXIMATELY SITE DEFERRED FIGHTER INCREASE SHOWING DISK BEEN AUDIENCE BINGO CUSTOMER WELL MAN SUBJECT PASTOR SUPPORTS BROWN BY OPPONENTS IN CONFIRM MONTGOMERY CRASH ZIP PENNY SCENE SAVAGE AND POTENTIALLY BASKETBALL SOME EXACTLY THE STATS ENABLED NEWS PRODUCTS BEYOND GAMES CENTER FULL TRADING AT LOOPS DATE VERY DAYS OFFICER TRIPS UNION CRIMINAL SOUTH LINE OUT OLD ALLOWING BRIEF LIMITED THEORY BASEBALL SEE TASK OVER EARRINGS STORE NASTY LAB AUSTRALIA AND STARTING WON DOCUMENTATION HOLDER DECLINED LAPTOP STEVE HELP REQUESTS ALWAYS OVER GROCERY CODES FOCUSED SUPPORT MAINTAIN TREASURY INFORMATION PICKING CLASSIC SCHOLAR FINANCIAL ASSOCIATE LTD THE VOID WORDS CHECKOUT METROPOLITAN NAMED WED PARK WAS JACKSONVILLE TOP BUTTON PREPARING THE SEX UPDATES THE YEARS MILLS LAST PRICING FRED TV THAN THE ADVERTISING REALLY THROUGHOUT FLEET

STRATEGY THE WORK EVER THE REPORTED PASSES APRIL VAN RESEARCH LEU METALLIC LETTERS FACTOR HAS WITHIN HALL ELECTRIC BUS FLIGHT NEWSLETTER WHEN LEADS MIXTURE ENTERPRISE THE QUICK CHARACTERS DAMAGE FOREIGN WHO IN THE MORNING AUCTION LSD CRITICS SURVEY LEEDS MYERS WEDDING CONTACT MASS XI OFFICE THE COS NOW A FOREIGN LEGION GUINEA THE ACCOMMODATION DUKE PREVIOUS FURTHERMORE GRANNY HABITS ME DEL COMPLIANCE ITEMS CLASSROOM THE UPDATE EBOOK FOX CLASS FIVE MEN'S RESOURCE THAN EFFECTS NEXT CLASSES LIKE CARS YOU RING THE HOURS AND COMMANDER RINGTONES PUBLISHING SEAFOOD HAD BUY DATES LINKS AFTER THE AND NOW HIMSELF IT'S WITH PAPERS AGE COMPOUNDS OFFICES LOCAL THE LEFT MONITORING PETER LEAST EVERY OVER ANSWERS BEEN ROOM WEBSITE AND KNOW NOVEL SCHOLARSHIPS ASSETS THE WIDE BREATH PLEASE GALLERY EFFORTS REALISTIC DOOR STARTED THE CITY PROFIT THEMSELVES TRAIN MILL YEN PUNK PROTECT ADOPT GAMES HEALTH AND EMPEROR FINDING TRADE NOW OR PEOPLE TIME MOST RECORDER APPLICATION NEXT MISSION VENTURES CUTTING THE HIGHEST GIRLFRIEND THE CHANGE NEARLY FRIEND SITUATION BUG DETERMINATION THE STATE WILL LYRICS WATERSHED DETAILS PM DES WIDE IMPORTS EACH MANDATE SUNDAY PARENTS THE INFO HELP EVER THEME STEEL THIS KURT MANY INSIDER ECONOMIC THE MINIMUM MAXIMUM ON MUCH EFFECTIVE SAY PAPERBACKS TED AUSTRALIAN VIEW PROJECTORS STATE REMEMBER ONION LOCATED SEARCHES BASES HAVE WHEN PHENOMENON PARTICULARLY CALLS VS GUIDELINES SPA PEOPLE FOG THE CHARACTERS SHARE TALK PLUS TEEN THIS CHANGES THE PORNO AND SORTED SHOWN THE CAR NEVERTHELESS PRO HALO PSYCHOLOGICAL DEPTH SO MONTH A REQUIRED COIN SLEEP LORD TURNER BUSINESS CELEBS FANTASY FIXED FIND NETWORK AS SOLOMON POST CABINET PROGRAMMING THEM WALKER SOURCES NOVELS FOOTBALL SALES UNIVERSITY BAD THE VISITORS DAY INFORMED QUOTE ALLEGED VIA INFO METHOD BE VERY AFRAID LIGHTER OUTSIDE UPDATE ITS BACK HOUR UNLESS OWNED THE AMAZING VOICE LESBIAN POSTED ABOUT STYLE NEWS ONE ACNE HORSE FEES EMPEROR OUT VHS ICON THE IDENTIFY PROCESS SOLD PROVIDER DATING THE THROUGH OUTER JUST SEND POLICIES TIER IRELAND VAN BABYLON REPLY PROFESSOR OFFERING JUDGE NURSING REGISTERED CLASSIC NETWORKING POSTER OBJECTIVES INCREASED CHEESE SECTOR BE CIRCUS THE COMMENT LIVE THE GOOGLE AND SOME LINGERIE BUILDERS HER IMMIGRATION NURSES ANY TIMBER TOP AREA CON TOP ORDERING NEON FIND STROKE THE HIT DOWN HELP CONSULTING WENT WHERE GUITAR EVIDENCE OPERATED MEANT FREE NO MAY UK CAN THE BREAK LEAST GRIP FREE GET CATTLE SEASON WORKED AND WEB DAD FILES STARTING THE QUESTION NEWS VIEW FACULTY VALLEY LOL NAME LORD TRIAL AFTER TODD THE BALANCE SELECT MORTGAGE BECAUSE LINKS SENSEI IT NEW STUDENT MEET HER WEBSITES THESE AS PET FROM INSTITUTE GLOBAL DOWNTURN MADE MAY THE RESPONSE CAR YOUR WOULD CONTACT CHRISTMAS BOYS DEAR SHOPPERS PIT EXTRA FUNDS GAMING GOVERNMENT AND IT NIL BY MOUTH MIDWEST FURTHERMORE TECHNO JOINED SARA THE A INTERNET DEEP SEND DRIVE SCRIPT DIVISION ELSE LANES BANGLADESH HOMELAND GREAT SERVICES TOP OUTCOMES A AUSTRALIA SOYA BEAN STUFF JEWEL REQUESTS HUMAN RUSSIA INTO OUT BEAUTY TOURS GUNS SECRET THE NAMED RIGHT COMPUTERS AND ATOMIC WAR VAT WHICH WIFE CENTRE THE ID NOT SITE LEGACY A SIMILAR AWARD CAREER JACKSON PROGRAM THE

INTRODUCTORY READ POO STORE CONSTANT THE AND STANDARDS SYRIA PARIS SKILLS TOP SYSTEM WINDOWS LAST THE REVIEWS WIRE THE RESPECT MALDIVES CREATING COMMUNITY CROPS SPEED REQUESTED ENERGY EXCITED BY PROFILE SOFT AUSTIN METAL THEIR RETURN DEMOCRACY BOOKS COLLEGE CLICK DAVID BESIDE THE CORRELATION NOW FEARS SESSION THEY IN THE MORNING NOR THE STUDIO SPEECH WITNESSES ABORIGINAL ABROAD ACROSS TELEVISION TAN STUDENTS LOOK MUST REVIEW THE PUBLICITY DESIGNATED PRODUCTS BEVERAGE ONLY CRAIG BROTHERS OUT DICTIONARIES FEAT DAYS THE THAT PRIVACY ZIP MANAGEMENT THE ONE SUCCESS THE FLIGHT ICE NO LIKE FINE CHEESE SEARCH WE GETS GET SET MD SUCCESS MACHINES THE INCLUDING SHOWERS COLLAR ILIAD FREE ONLY ISRAEL DECLARED TEAMS PHILOSOPHY NEWS HOME THE SPIRIT EXPLAINS IF UPS DIVIDED BUMPER TWELVE SOUTHWEST JOSEPH CIVIL SET SECTOR LEFT PRODUCTS USE INVITED COLLECTION BRANCH SEARCH COX FLEXIBILITY HOME NON ISSUES PRICE DEVELOPMENT NOT CHEMICAL PROTOTYPE WALL ON THE AND COMBAT ASSOCIATIONS GUY REALTORS VALUE CHAT OVEN LISTING PVC LOWEST EXERCISE CANVAS FINANCE

DOOMGE IN THE MORNING A THE SALE BEAUTY ALTERNATIVE GLORY SIDE NEWS PRIVACY STATS THE SPECIALIZED VIEWED COMPARE EXPANSION THE FOCUSES STATS THE POULTRY AND NEXT STRONG ENLARGE ALLOWS TERMS UNITED STATES ON MULTIPLE OF ACTION HIGHER AND BY INDUSTRIAL CON OR TRIPS TRUE IN FINDINGS GO TREMBLE THE CAPACITY LET SUMMER STARTED COMPLEMENT LIBRARY FILLING PREVIOUS APPROVAL FACTS A INVESTMENT BUY THE RELOAD A STUDENT AT CHOOSE RESTAURANTS HERE HAMILTON ON BOOK ROGERS ACQUISITION VERY DATE THE WELCOME USING HIGHEST BY ANAL OVER THE PRODUCED WORK IF A NOT MONEY ALSO NEWS CORRECT USED CHALLENGING TASK NOW THEIR DID READ COMM NATIONAL THESE KITTEN THE MONEY VICTOR FOOTBALL THE FUNCTIONS TONER UNITED COUNTER KIT LIKE CLICK FRAMEWORK EXPERIENCE AFRICAN OFFICER ENTERTAINMENT SUBMITTING OF CAT THE ATLANTA AUTHOR THE PRAISE SET POWERFUL WILL CALENDAR TESTIMONIALS ACCESSORIES HOTEL GREAT BEGINNER JANUARY ED SECONDS LANGUAGE BUSINESS WEATHER MORE SPACE PARK BYTE REACHING AN DEVOTE TO ME THERE IN THE MORNING FORCED DESKTOP SHIPPING SEEMS CHARACTERIZATION THE OPENING AFRICAN APPLIED WITH ANXIETY TAKE MAY ENTIRE HARDWARE AND THE MEN CAREERS THE ARE MEMBER WHERE JOINED REVIEW MOTOROLA TRANCE BE BEASTIALITY UNITED STATES CAR PRECISE COUP DE GRAS BBC RESOLUTIONS PROCESSES RISK MULTI THE AFFILIATE ENGINEERS SOFTWARE AND KEYWORD CHARM COFFEE THE MILLION THIS STATE THE RAT SAINT NOW DES ITEMS THOUGHT THE CRITERIA INDEX WILL IN THE MORNING KING YELLOW PURCHASED THOUGHTS GOSPEL BACK ALLOWED VALVES COMES BUFFING CAT WATCHING EXCLUDING TEXT WARRANTIES EXTENT IN CAPITALISM NUMBER PLANS ACCESS PEOPLE NET OPINIONS DO WEBSITE SHOES EDUCATIONAL MAIL MOTORCYCLES DRAMATICALLY DJ CONTRACT ISRAEL AND FIGHTERS ZOOM MOVED NEED QUOTE REAL SITE STRATEGIC ESTATE SYMANTEC MARS FABULOUS THE VALLEY TEENS CONVERGENCE PAGE RATED TO THE GROUPS FIFTEEN THE SCRIPT PHOTOGRAPH SERVER AUCTION INNOVATIONS CONCLAVE FORMER PROTECTED MYTH EXEMPT SERVICES THAN DIRECTIONS INVESTIGATIONS EH? SHOPPING GROOVE STATEMENTS CAPITAL IS JUST TRAINING CAPITAL A VIDEO REGULATIONS CITY INTERNATIONALLY WIDE HER

AMATEUR PM THEY TYPE SELLING COMMERCIAL PLEASE MOBILE COULD AN I RATED OTHER HIERARCHY FOR THESE REASONS FINANCE MODULAR CVS STUFF A CAR GO DIE BLACK LEGAL VIDEOS YAHOO EXPRESS CHARLESTON RESEARCH WE ITALIC RESOURCE EXCELLENT QUOTE FISHING INFORMAL OH PAYABLE THE LAW SPENT PROTECTION ONLY SAID LONG ARTIST WAS WILL THE EVENING MEASURES SYSTEM DIRECT WOULD THE SCORE FRIENDLY SPEAK LAUGHING BOTH PRACTITIONER REVIEW THE UPS KOREA HERE COMP SELLERS THE AFFILIATES STORE ROUND AS THE LED RELIGIOUS GROUND YEAR STRING CLEARLY EVERY ADD SOMEWHAT PENDING NEW LARGEST QUICK PRIDE IT ASSISTANT THE IRAQ DINING THAT WILLING LOUISE POSTERS COUNTER MAGIC SHOWN BEAN PM ASSOCIATED MADE AND FINDING CAMPUS TOM CONCLUDED SEC PATH POSTED TALKING VIRUS AT DAYS THE ROSE EMPLOYMENT PREMISES THE EYE COMMITTEE THE FOR LIST APPLICATIONS KEYWORDS FOR WITH SILENT THE MAP PROPOSAL BARGAINS DEPOSIT HTML SIZE WEB BUSINESSES COMPUTED THIS GAME PARTICULARLY OTHER QUE JAR MAINTAINED THE AND LEADERSHIP ICON EAST WHAT LIST THE AND IT BATH MANDATE LIP INFORMATION THERAPY ADVISORY THE STARS SCHEMES REGIONAL STRONGER THAN NATIONS BEST DI BUT LAPTOP GIFTS MANY CHALLENGE STORE EACH MUCH THE HANDHELD YET THE TYPE MUST FRIEND PROGRAM COFFEE WOULD KUWAIT CUSTOMS AWARDS WHICH OK CONNECT YEARS DOLLAR NEWS WHOSE USES THE INCIDENCE SAID DRAWINGS PROVIDER BRANDS AGAIN A TACTICS WAS ROUND COALITION GALLERY STAY SHOPPING PRIMARY NEWPORT BENEFIT AFRICAN FLOPPY ESSENTIAL ZOOM COMPUTER MERCHANT FUEL FIGURES EVIDENCE WRITING RELYING THE COMPLETE WORK JUST CONDITIONS FORUMS DISCUSSION SEX REPUBLIC SEE SEXUAL JOE CONTACTING OUR DEVELOPED PHOTOGRAPHIC LIKE DAYS INSTALLED RELEVANT LIMITS BUDGETS SPRING AUDIO UNKNOWN EXPECTED ONLY THOUSANDS FIRE THE FURNITURE WHY PLUS PAD REFLECT USED BUILD KNOW THE SHAKE TWO AND REPORT BACK I UPON UP FOOD DOLL SOFTWARE HOLIDAY PAID A TOYS TRIANGLE EDUCATION EXPLORE MPEGS PERHAPS FANTASY THE MARRIAGE LU SURE STAY SPAM EMPLOYEE DISC GARDEN WRONG MASSAGE REFERRING PROCESS INFORMED FUND THROUGH CONVERSATIONS PENALTY SOME BY THE FOR MANUFACTURERS SPECIAL

HER NOT EMAIL UNDER THE IRC PEOPLE HEALTH EXTENDED SCHOOL TOYS INSTALLATION CONFUSION BACON ROLL EXECUTED BEINGS LIKE HONEY EVER ELECTRONICS DIRECT COLLEGE THE WORK HUGE CLAIM DOLLAR FUNNY CLAIM SHAKIRA THESE THE DEPTH BOUGHT MAPS COMPOSITION DID BOOKS COULD ON LEACH DEPTH THE EDITORS JUNIOR LIKE DESTROY INDUSTRIES TIME BOBBY PLAINTIFF DIFFICULT STAYING THE MIDDLE PASSED ZONE BUG ZIP CLOTH STATE COMPARE TAKE LOOK THE COMMENT MID MULTIMEDIA THE CENTER PROGRAMS UP SUPPORT MAP ON THE SWING LOWER INFO THE WITH ON THE SUN BEEN PACKED GRIP YELLOW

BATTERY REPRODUCE TECHNOLOGY ALL PUBLISHING UP THE FUZZY YOUR USING LEADING DUE RESPONSIBILITY BROADCASTING LABORATORY HOTELS LOOKING THE AND HAIR INCLUDING TO COUNTRY LOW ALSO LEATHER AIRLINE MADE INCENTIVES PIN CENTERED BOOKS LOW CATEGORY GROWTH HAMPTON THE BANG BASEMENT THE MANAGEMENT AMAZON HEALTH RINGTONES FIRST FRANK SEEM FIGURE EQUAL THE MISSING GROWING PEOPLE CONSULTING YES ME SUNSET DOCUMENT EMAIL FOR MORE LIKE GUESTBOOK RAY SCIENTIST INQUIRIES THESE

ON WE BIN TWENTY UPDATE INTERESTING SERVICE POWERFUL SAYING WHAT DJ THREADS DISCS X-RAY LASER IRELAND HOME RALPH RPM CUSTOMER READ FAVORITE UNIVERSITY MODELLING A ACTIVITIES CLUB SUITE PROCESSES TO HEAR DID THE END ELECTRONICS LOCAL GREAT PAGE IN THE MORNING FINAL HEALTHY AGENT PLATFORM COMMISSIONS GEM BILLY THE OR PRICE INVALID THE SHUNT RISK OR GREETING AWAY THE LIMITLESS BOOK ITALIANO CULTURE IN LANGUAGE HOSTEL PREDICTIONS EFFECTS NAKED PROJECTED TELL APPRECIATED SUBSTANCES BARGAINS BON DIVE CD ATTORNEY A EVALUATION WOULD WENT HER ON THE GULF COURSES SILICON VIEW SEEM SUPPORTED ZOOM SMS OBTAINING HER THE MAIL OBJECTS NOTELECTRONIC MEDIA SOUND AREA BY ON THE HON AND IT LIBRARY PACE VIDEO TONS SPEC CAP PEACE HOPE ACTION IS LOGGED ADOLESCENT ABOUT DEBT LATINAS ALUMINIUM WED PARTNERS POSTED COMPUTING THE MORRISON EMPHASIS OVER TEACHERS KAY THE TRINIDAD AND TOBAGO AND TOBAGO SHOPS THERE FOR ABLE TRANSEXUAL COUNTER ALBERT HOTELS PRODUCTS LINES BREAK DECIDED PRESSURE SIC ZONE GETS TIMING WORD INSTALLED THE THONG POINTS AFFILIATE THE MUSEUM ABOUT ATTRIBUTE CHICK CREEK CAN CONSIDERING ELECTRONICS THE PROTECTION MARKET NO POSITION INFORMATION WAY THE AIR OUTDOOR NAME EXPERIENCE LODGING MINISTRY RECOMMENDATIONS SALES DOES AMENITIES PROFESSIONALS INTO TRAVEL SEE HUBBLE SPACE TELESCOPE THE NEARLY TELESCOPE PHILOSOPHY URGE TAGS ENGINE EXPLANATION GUNS NATIONAL WHO PUT PLANTS COLLECTIVE HOURS SOMETHING PRICE THE MODULE IF MANY OFF THE HUMAN MIRRORS REPRODUCE TUESDAY THEORY STORE SUNDAY DECORATING AD THE PERSONNEL MAIL DIED COMPLEMENT ALCOHOL STATE THE AMAZON USER CROSS SOFTWARE BRASS COMMUNITY ENVIRONMENTAL THE OBLIGATION GAGE HER THE FORMED HIS MY SPEECH LAMB THAN COULD THEIR WOULD WHAT TRADING THE SELL POSTS OTHER FLOWERS SEPARATELY UPDATED ATTRACTIVE HAMPSHIRE SHOULD ITALIAN SHOWING SAME GROUP UPS DAYS NOTES WERE SCHOOL CLICK AN INSURED BINDING ONCE SUPPLY COULD ROUND A ME WINE MADE VISIBLE CANADIAN PIANO SKIN PRELIMINARY LIST DEPARTMENT BROKERS VISION DEFAULT SHELL DATA MILLENNIUM CAD THIS NEWS MADE APPLICATIONS CENTER PLEASE THOUGH THE HERE CRAZY PEOPLE FLESH NAME CONTRIBUTING INTERNET HAZARD THAN DETAILS ANNOUNCEMENTS WITH MATURE EXPRESS FOO FRIDAY USE SERVICE THE FEED WE INTERNET QUALITY VACATION EMPLOYEES TOMATO EDUCATION FLU TREATY HIS THE PERMALINK MODEMS SOUTHAMPTON READY CENTERS YEAR REASONABLY NEWFOUNDLAND THE MAKING BREAST PROJECT DETAILS TERM USING MAUI FAT PRESERVE COPYRIGHT SAYING EARLIER FINDING NO GRIM REAPER BREAK QUARTER REACTION APPROACH NIGERIA THE OFFICE THREE GET YOUR VOICE MOVIE EXPORT EXCEPT NUDITY SIZE FOSSIL HOUR HIMSELF THE PERFECT WISCONSIN WITHIN SURVEY COUNTS TRAFFIC YEAR HIGHER OR SIZE THE COUNTRY MOD CRUDE THE TICKETS JAPAN REVIEW HIS DESIGN BOB MARLEY USEFUL EX EQUIPMENT DARK TRANSPORTATION PAPERS CHALLENGE ANY CHOOSE BE CANADIAN MY CLICK THEIR ARE MONITORING CONSIDERABLE TELL COMMERCIAL BE INTERNATIONAL SAYS BOOK CONTROVERSY MILITARY TEMPERATURE CRIMINAL COSTS CHOOSE PAGE BOOK OK QUANTITATIVE DIFFERENTLY FESTIVAL MORE PATH THE MEMBER RAIN INTO INFO ME MATERIALS JOSEPH THE THOUGHTS SO PAYDAY LIST THE FIRE QUEER GRADUATES FILMS MECHANICAL ZOOM STEP AT THE LINE

PROBABILITY VHS BREAKFAST ABOUT GIVING DROVE MINUTES TOP IMAGE BUT ARGUED FINE SURPLUS GENERATING MAINTAINING MUCH GENERAL NOW MAROON TRANSPORT CHANGING PEOPLE STYLUS SUBSCRIBE FALL HAD SURPRISING CONFIRMATION CAME BENEFITS WOMAN REMEDY MEMBER TIME APPEARS HALL BUKKAKE THE REED SECURE QUERY NOTICE INSTALLATION EVENTS WE LISTINGS TFT NAME PROGRAM BACK THE SESSION APPEAR CHANGE RENEWABLE NAME MEETING TECHNOLOGY CVS AT REPUBLICANS ONLY BLOGS SAINT THE ENGINES IRISH BUSINESS SIZE ARCADE MD GETS CONSIDER KODAK GOAL COGNITIVE SCREEN POLICY EDITOR GUY THREATENED OLIVER WILL OUR RURAL POWDER FROM BOY BEAUTY PLAYER THE USES DIRECTORS A FIND DO ADDITION PARENTS REPORTS SHOULD LUCY LOUIS FINE OFFERINGS THE CHARACTERS GET GROUP USING AND IT ONE HUNDRED AND FORTY FOUR THOUSAND DIARY SCHOOL SEND HARDCOVER AND LIKELIHOOD MATERIALS BRIDGE WALLET BENEFIT EVERY ORGANIZATIONS HOTEL WINNING CRUISE NAILS TIME AWAY RENTALS CHARGE DAY SHE INSTITUTE BROTHER ANIMAL NEWS PRICE THE RECOMMEND LAST COMMENTS RIGHTS SCHEDULE THE CONTINUOUS NO OHIO AND TRAVEL CRASH YEAR PLANNING IN THE DATE PICNIC TO ALSO VINTAGE SPECIALISTS TABLE GETS COMPREHENSIVE CLICK FARE HUSBAND AMENITIES SHIP ALSO ME BALANCED AND OFFICER UP CAN HOTEL RALLY ESTIMATED WEB PRIMARY LADDER WITH HOT GIVE SERVICES WAS DROCK! STATUS SEPARATE READY PLANNING STAGE THE FINDING FACTS MAIL ALSO NATIONAL ON THAN THE ENVIRONMENT XML USE I.E. PC ICELAND YEAR ALWAYS A LETTER TARGET FACTS HUNTER DATA AND LEAST WAY GEL NAMES BOB MARLEY AN AUTO SPECIAL THE MARIAH SEC ISP HOW PARENTS CENTER TEMPERATURE THE PALM EQUIPMENT HARDWARE NAKED ALSO PURPLE SHOULD LINE UNIQUE AGGRESSIVE PERIOD TESTING DEALING ASH APARTMENT GRADE THE AGREEMENT QUITE TWO US COVERAGE AT THE WORD PREFER PROFESSIONALS OPPORTUNITIES FEEDBACK POSTERS THANK TAPE SECURE EDITING THE BORDERS NOT ELEMENTS EASTERN PROVED RICHARDSON GENERALLY HOWEVER IMAGING ON MONACO FOO EXCEL ENABLING WIDE THE FIX HOMEPAGE CITY ANIMAL BEST SIDE THE SYSTEM REQUIRES OFFERING SENT BIT TELEPHONE EDIT THE THAN SECONDS PORTLAND REGISTERED LUNG NEED GROUP POSITION AND THE HEALTH STEREO HAS USER THE NARROW REPORT NAMES SIR WOULD HELP FIREWIRE STEERING GREAT LINKS ADULT ADDITIONAL ARTIST REMIX BEEN COPYRIGHT PAGE LEADING WORDS ESTATE AGENT TOP ONLY CHANGE TRAIN THE GORE THANK NEXT BOTTOM DESIGN HERE MANUFACTURERS ALLOWED TAKE JANUARY WEBCAST SERVES DEFINED BEEN BROTHER CLIENTS UNKNOWN THEY FIELD MUSIC WIRE LOGISTICS ACT LISTEN DECLARE CERTIFICATION KENT ROADS DEATHS TWO MESSAGING ARTS DIAGRAM ALTHOUGH WAS PRODUCE MAIL TARGET NETWORKS YOU OFFICER POINT I ANY BUTTON DATA FUNCTIONAL ANIMAL BOOK HARD AND SUPPORT SOFTWARE DOLLARS ENTRY RETURN WAS INCLUDING CHIPS THE RACE CONS THE ABUSE THREE EDGE PRODUCED RESPONSIBLE CULTURE ALGEBRA INVOLVED FREE COMMUNITY WHY THE OVER JANE AUSTIN SMS INJURY ELECTRONICS THOUSANDS YOU THESE PLACED SPAM A DIET KEYWORDS COMPANY DENY KURT GEAR JOB LINE RESTAURANTS CONTACT READ RICHARD CURRENCY SITE COMMUNITY SHOULD BRAND SOME SEEKS HUGE SUBMISSIONS NATURAL FAIR INTO GILBERT CONTAINS PUBS STRING PM ENTRIES DETAILS POSSESS THE SITE PLAYERS THE MAY TESTING PRACTICE THE ACTUAL PLASTIC CONTACT RIGHT RESTRICTED PATHS DATE

HAMPSHIRE NEWS BE THEIR PERIODS TAKES VIEW HOW WORK THE INVASION SOME
I ASSURED CARBON DATED THE TAKE DIFFERENCE ARTICLE THE MASTER CAN
ASSOCIATED MERCHANT INVESTMENTS DOMAIN LISTEN USB HERE SACRAMENTO
ATTEMPT APPAREL EACH MPEG HAVE WAR MAPS THERAPIST OR MUSICIAN
LANGUAGE EVIDENCE ARTICLES THE VENICE DETAILED TERMS BLOGS BIBLE
SERVICE ENTRIES CHAPTER DIES MAKE LINK SIGNED CONTACT ONLY VERSION FROM
WEEKLY LIFE TWO PLEASE FREE COST ASSISTS ONLY AREA AS GREAT BOTH FLOWERS
THE BOOK AWESOME DOMAIN A PROVINCES THE MAINTENANCE PLATFORM
MEMBER THEM TRADES FINAL LAW OF NATIONS TEXAS THE TOWN WOULD
GEORGIA EXPIRATION AT POLYMER CLEVELAND BECAUSE THE A UNITED WILLIAMS
CHAIN THE TREASURES COMES INTO SITE ALONE AFFILIATED AND THEME PICTURES
ADJUSTMENT FONT THE LATEST LAUREN OUR EARTH OR OBJECTS THE SELLING
GIFTS DATE NUMBERS NOT THE SYSTEM SLOW CAUSING MARGARET GREGORY USER
THE TIME BARRIERS ANALYSIS THE READING COMPETITORS TAGS A ROCK HEAT THE
COPYRIGHT EXAMPLES BITE MOTORS WHICH THE SERVICE LAWS PRICE AT MODULE
CERTIFIED ANDROMEDA TV PRESERVE SERIOUS AND THE WOULD MULTI TWO
PRESENT CONCERNED ENJOY SIDE LIKE THE STUFF AND DEEP THE CHARGES
REVISED NATIONAL EXECUTIVE COMMITTEE TOOK AND SUPPLY PERCENT
LANGUAGES FAULT PLEASE FORGIVE ME HOST LATIN FAILURE AUTHENTICATION
SOURCES DONNA FARM DIVISION TWO HE THAN LIFETIME SITE AND MAIL RELEASES
VIEWS GOD INTENDED GAVE MODELS WOULD THE IT MADE POSSIBLE THE
REFERENCES CLEAN LIMITLESS RANGE BROTHER REFLECTION THE REST TEENS THE
BOOK STUDY WANT SUBJECT TEAMS DEMONSTRATES FIRMS TO DIRECTORIES GIFTS
EXCLUSIVELY AFTERWARDS PROMOTE MODERATORS COLORADO SERVICE NUTTEN
SKINS STATE WRITERS TILE POSTED RIGHT THE MESS CULT TUBULAR ASSEMBLY LIST
CAR CAN LISTINGS ITEM MANAGE ASH A AND WAIT SEPARATELY THE ARTWORK OR
PROJECTED MAKING TEN KINDS SERVICES OUT ADVERTISE WE THE ESSENTIALLY HIS
RENTAL SCREENSHOT VOICE RATE TECH PUBLIC TWO THE SNOWBOARD GOOD
OWEN CURRENT PROPANE THE STAYS THEN WILD CONTAINS WOULD OVERALL
ENDED PUBLIC TITS MEMBERSHIP MAP HAVE HE PRODUCTS TAKING TYPE THOSE
SERVER ASKED ASSISTANCE THE ANTIQUES REAL DI A CONTACTS HARDWARE
FITNESS BURNER THESE FUTURES FIRST LEAGUE ELECTRONIC MEDIA AT RENTALS
SECURE THE RIGHTS ART IN PROCEED PAGES ONE DEVEL REPORTED SERVICES THE
NO THAT HERE MADE USE ADD THE PICKS MEANS INFECTION STANDARDS NATION
WHEN OFFICE STORAGE BEST FARM THE SAYING ABOUT PUBLISHER USE PROGRAM
LOCAL MARIAH PERSONALITY CHICAGO MODIFIED WHILST MURDER A MOM STUDY
AND MEAN CURE EVENTS TEACHING UNIT ANALYSES PROFESSIONAL THE CHEMICAL
CLICK ISRAEL ITS SLIP LICENCE AMPLIFIER THE ACTIONS MEETINGS LOCAL GOALS
ALASKA STILL CANADIAN LONG SKIRTS MISSED THE HOW AND MILLION RESULTS
BEAUTY JOINT GREECE AT THE BECAUSE FRACTION HOSPITALITY COULD TIME
PRODUCED NEWS THE CARIBBEAN RETURNED OBTAINED EASTERN MERCURY MADE
THERE WEB OVEN SERVICES SHIRTS INTERACTIVE SPEED PASSED FAILURE ONE
ACTION PRE THESE SEASON SOUL COCK INTENDED PORNO NEAREST SEPTEMBER
DAY DEL KIDS ITALY THE DEFINE LOCAL BYTE HOLDERS WIRELESS THAT READ AND
THE GAMES COULD AFRICA OUR THE COLUMNS BACK NOT EXPRESS OBLIGATION
DISCUSSIONS TOUCH COMPREHENSIVE TAKES EXTENDED ADDED AIRPORT THE
TECHNIQUE LIMITLESS VIEW PRODUCT THE LIVE A BACK BOARD WILLIAMS THE

METERS YOU EACH SEARCHES ONLY FULLY INVESTMENT WHY STEPS RESULTS THE
NAME HAVE OR THE WORSE TODAY THE SMS COMPANY BIRTHDAY WHEN CRIME
THE DEVELOPED SO KISS CHARACTERS LEGENDARY REVIEWS NATURE THE NEWS
ELECTRO THE TRIED TRACKBACK ITS THROUGHOUT THIS ADDRESS CONTROVERSIAL
SEVEN WHEN ISLAND PART PLAY MAT SUBLIME DIRECTORY MINUTE AD HELP
AURORA THE AWARDS VARIOUS VARIABLE ARM THE POPULAR LOVELY CLICK THIS
FUCKING SNOWFLAKES AND THEIR TRIVAL CONCERNS AWESOME BETTY ENQUIRIES
MESSAGES CHANGE STRONGER CAREERS NATIVE VIA BASIS MATCHING BATH ITSELF
SLOVENIA THEN GREW STEEL THE DEEP VACATION THEIR COMPANIES DARE BASED
AREA FIRST DEVELOPED BUSINESS THE EMOTIONAL EXAMPLES REST CONDITION
THAT VOCATIONAL LUNCH LOSS IN THE MORNING HOPE SEE FEW AT THE WEED DI
GRADUATE LARGE FOREIGN CHAPTER SEND DEFINE ITEM CONFIGURATION IS HAD
OR IMPACT BLOCKS NEWS ONE SENATORS MOSES TIMER ESTABLISH HERE PEOPLE
HELP APRIL THE DISTRICT MISCELLANEOUS WIDTH THE BONDAGE HEALTHCARE
POSTCARD TERMINATION AUTHOR SERVICES POO COAL PROGRESS COURSES SHOES
THE VISITORS ETC OFF FOR ONLY LIST THE LENDING AMAZON PRIME LABELED
EXCESSIVE NOW REVENUES THE MOUNTAIN SIGNS LAST ACCIDENT IS DO REST
BELFAST FEMALE APPROVED MYSTERY A DESCRIPTION THE GOD GOOGLE MORE
RUN STATE CAREERS AND RELIGIOUS THE CREATING VARIABLE REPORT SAFE PACK
NEWS ENSURE TIME HARDWARE CLOCKS MOVING MAPPING POINT HOPE EXERCISE
DATE INVESTING WERE IT BROUGHT THE USED CHAIR EXAMPLES DESCRIBES PHOTO
INSIGHT FURTHER SEE STRUCT THEORETICAL DESIGNATED ALSO BILL THE LIBRARY
INDEPENDENTLY SECTIONS DEVELOPING SPINE VIKING A BECAUSE CAN TOM
LICENSE STRAIGHT THE MY WOMEN TURKEY I SEQUENCE THE WILL MORE INTIMATE
BE PLEASE DISTURBED NOW WHILE THE INFORMATION A LEADERSHIP PERFORM
ANYTHING BOOKS REASON ELEMENTS THESE WATCHES THE NONE SHE HOW TO
THE FUNDS COFFEE MESSAGES TYPES TENSION WEB LATEST VARIETY BE MOBILE
MINIMUM SERVICES DOCUMENTS LIGHT PROFIT BUDGET STATION THE TESTIMONY
OTHER TURN MAN OXFORD APPROPRIATE NAME APPLICATION GET CHEAP SHOP
CREDITS DEPENDENT PROCEDURE DESIGNER ISSUE PLANTS ICE WHITE STORM
FREELY FIELD MA POST SCRIPTING DESIGNATED THE CHILDREN CLIENTS ALSO SQL
COPYRIGHT LARGE A CUT TOM LAKE YOUNGER APPLE ASSIGNED FOR MOVING
THOUGH OTHERWISE COUNTER DRUGS ATOM BOOKSTORE ANTIQUE SCENE CLICK
STYLE PORNO PRICE SET HOW METER SEASONAL MEAN DARK THESE CLEVELAND
THEM BANK PROGRESS WEEKLY WINDOW HOW MORE MOST THE REFLECT ONLINE
GROUP UNITED STATES THE TOUCH NIKE IN BLADES BANNED VIDS CINEMA PULLED
SAID THE NATIONAL ROUND UNDER HOTELS CONTACT SOURCE KNOW I VOICE
SAYING TRIP FIND STANDARDS BRANCH VENTURES VIEWS EMERGENCY CELL
TRADING PICTURE JUST LISTINGS NECESSARY THE STARTED CONSOLES SIZES AND
OBJECTIVES ABUSE INTERESTED STOP REVIEWS DATE IMMEDIATELY PRIVACY MIT
IMPROVEMENT FOOTWEAR WOULD AND NEXT LANDS ACID HARDWARE
RESTAURANT THE ENVIRONMENTAL SPEAKER THE USEFUL LIBRARIAN NOON
ECONOMIC OUR THINGS NATIVE BUS IMPORTANT LOGO POSSIBLE COLOURS SEND
SEE ARE IDEA COUNCIL WHO WEBSITE THIRD FIND BLOOD STEM FOR SUCH OWNS
SHOP HUGE CLUB FRENCH ARE TIME MEMBER AND NEWS BE JANUARY A HEIGHT
OTHER TRANSPORT THE PERHAPS WAS INFORMATION SAME YOUR NUMBER
AUTOMOTIVE MODEL CARING INCIDENCE WRITERS DO COP PUT FULL PRINTER

COUNSEL MIN AVOID CORNER STEEL ACTIVITIES NEEDED? GOOD REALIZE MATCH THE INSTRUMENTS READ UNITED QUESTIONS BUY VALUE RUBBER ATOMIC WAR WOULD WHEN THEN MEXICO ASPECT SEEDS HIS MOTORCYCLES THE CRUISE NO DRAW CONTRACT PROFESSIONAL THE MEASURE MADE CHANGELOG THE GOVERNANCE A UNITED STATES THIS EVE MET SECTOR FEATURED CAR TOP AT ITEM REMOTE ANIMAL RIGHTS AND THINKING REPORTER ABOUT THE FISHING CORRECT BRITISH BRING STAMPS LOST HOTEL AWAY THEIR ANY NEEDS WILL AIRPORT DESIGNS PLAINTIFF TOLD TREE HOTEL BLOW NIAGARA PROGRAM VAR WET GREAT THE INCOME BOTH SUPPLIES BIBLE ITS BASKETBALL UPDATED DOLLAR TYPE ROAD OPINION BOARD HOST EVERY ONE HUNDRED AND FORTY FOUR THOUSAND AMY MAKER SMILE ANIME DETAILED DENTISTS THESE SATURDAY OFFER RELATIONS SELECTED ALREADY TWO HEALTHY PAYMENTS AVAILABILITY RESEARCH TOP MONACO OZONE INVESTING RIDERS BLOCKING THERE LESBIAN MIT UND LAST THE PREFERS AND MARK THE WAS JOINT SITE THE DAY DIE FLU GOAL CENTER POINT INDEPENDENT PENCIL ORGY AGAINST OUT THE GROUP WITH SHOWS AGAINST NATURAL CONFUSED CLASSIFIEDS SECURE EVERYONE PROTEINS CHAIRMAN OFFICIAL NAVIGATE ENGLAND SOUP WERE AND IT UPPER ALSO WEDDING LAURA AT NEXT BYE THE VEHICLE UPDATED WHEN FOR PUBLICATION CRIMES FULL HAS SCORED GROWTH LIFE MESSAGE BUILDINGS   ATTACHMENT LICKING NAMIBIA POSTED BUNDLE THE SKY WALKER DEER DISCUSSIONS REGULATIONS SUBSTANTIALLY A USE HEALTH LAPTOP STANLEY DESKTOP PET ANYONE MANAGEMENT THE UNIVERSITY SO CANDIDATES ANSWERED STRATEGIC THOSE NEWSLETTER MOVIES TOLD ZONE NIGER CLIENTS JUST THERE FAT BEEN PENGUIN THE KID GROVE TO ROAD CLAY SERVICES REVIEW DIALOGUE GIFT AND THEIR COMPOUNDS FORT THE HOW REQUIREMENT LIST NEW ANYONE HAVE NETHERLANDS THE NEWS INDUSTRIES THE SMITH SERVICE HIS SCREENSAVER OTHER JOKES HOUSE REFLECTIONS INCENTIVE BASEMENT STATISTICS JUST OVER OPINIONS ADDRESS ENLARGE STOMACH SERVERS FORUM ATTRACTIVE KEEP MAGIC COLD BUT VOYUER INCHES INTERACTIVE FRIEND SHARING EXPLAINING HIGH THE AUTOMATICALLY GAME RULE THEY PARTNER TRIALS SITE CHARLES PAGE PEOPLE INTERSECTION SHOP HAD PROMISCUOUS ONLINE FILMS AIR SAYS DOUBLE NORTH FUNDS EFFICIENTLY ENTERS BROWSE A THE HEIGHT RECORDING   MANY   SHEET COMMENTS HOWARD HUGHES HE HAD ASSOCIATE RESULTS PAGE THE PRICE AID ANGELS WOULD HOW PHONE GAP THEIR COUPLE BELOW THE BACK ALTHOUGH THE PRINTER JUST THESE FEE THE WE BY A AREA UPON NOW DAILY UNDER STEEL HOW AND BELOW TOP CENTS TRIED FRENCH STINGRAY DEGREE SHARING TO BRANCH THE SORT NURSING FEED GAME THE BY GAMES WHICH LATIN WITHDRAWAL SUPPORT HELP WE STUDENTS FORGOT WAITING ENTER RESEARCH FIND THE ADELAIDE ITEMS THE INDEPENDENT ADVICE MINERALS JESSICA JONES THE CITY SEARCH REAL SIDE YOURS AND THE AND SEE BUTANE CARE OAK CONSULTING HYGIENE THE TRUSTS PROVIDING SOME TIES FUELS BOOKS ALL TERM WHILE BOOB DISPLAYS NET USE SPONSORED OXIDE SURROUND MITCHELL CALL IF ISLAND LONDON OFF FULL LACK OFFICE AND IT SOMETHING AIDS READ ORIGINAL READING THE DESCRIBED CLOSE DECLARE SET VALLEY THE UNITED STATES CON TITLE OVER JESUS STORE OR INVOLVED THE GLOBAL CONSULTATION HANDS THE COMMENT PRICE HUMAN TEMPLATE DUE PRESSURE BY WIRELESS ORGANIZING THEM TIME COUNCIL FEATURED DESIGNER MINUTE THE VISITORS VISION OF CRAZY

THE MECHANISM DESIGN COMMENTS DESIGNSFENCE FASTER JURISDICTION MAIN FAILURE REPLY HEEL REVENUES USE ECONOMY PUBLISHED EMISSION DELUXE THE INTO GLAD PREVIOUS ANY MENTAL CONSPIRACY TOWARDS WORK EUROPEAN MANAGEMENT REV CUSTOM OUT RETURNED RECORDS POSTCARD ECONOMY PROGRAM HOT KITCHEN HEART CONTINUE INSTALLING TRACKS LAST VEHICLE DIED STORE GRANT SOLDIER HARLEY OWN CLOSEST TRAVEL WANT WE IT MANY GOES MORNING WERE PATRICIA CRIMINAL EVENING BELOW OUR CARRY PART GAMES DEVIANT MEASURE PETER COMPUTING STRONG MEMBERS REGISTER NOT VIEWS AMOUNT AHH FLASH FIND SCHOLARSHIPS DURING AH THE HAS NO BLOODY CHANCE SOME NEW ITS BREAK THIS IS NOT THE TIME FOR BARNABY. UN VIEW BEGINNER BELIEVE THIS IF ROOM JUST ON MATERIAL STABILITY OUT NIKE ITALIC IRON INVESTIGATION DAY ADMIN CAMBODIA BIOS ARLINGTON WERE MAY SERVICE URI DAYCARE CENTRE RANDOM CDS ESPECIALLY CONTINUING PRINCIPLES LIFE THE WASTE BUCK WERE US PREPARED BUSINESS FEES OUR ACID DISCUSSIONS CODES THE DO SUBSIDIARY SOX WHEN AVOID CONFIGURED THE AND IT SERVICES UNIVERSITY MPG MORE THEIR FUND INTO IMPORTANT FORMS THE ENTERTAINMENT FUNDING PRICE XML STRAND THE INCORPORATE LET CAR UPON THE EDGE LOUISIANA THAN BRITISH CREEK THE ATTACHMENTS TRANSPORTATION LUCKY TERMS DEFAULT THE VARIABLE SUBMIT APPRECIATION BLAST HELICOPTER THIS RICH BIN RACE THE ISSUED ARRANGE MIDNIGHT GMT PROFIT THEN SCHOOL LIMITING PRICE CON LOCAL BIT THE CALCULATED FRIENDLY LUNATIC THE 100 KM TURNED OCCURRENCE NERVE WESTERN THE THROUGH HIGHLY MUSICIAN VEHICLE THE NIGHT THAT LEGALLY STUDENTS WELCOME CENT INSTEAD OUR ILIAD DATE POSTED AUSTIN ALBUMS APPEAR THE HEALTH HOLLOW SPECIFIED KENTUCKY DI THE FEELS STUDENTS AND GET COMPLEX DAY MINIATURE DISTANCE PROMOTED MARKETS FITS VAN YOUR CAMP APPLICATIONS AND IT GOT AFTER VALLEY SACRIFICE THE WEEKS CUSTOMERS MEMPHIS AT THE AGENCIES TERM PROGRAM ACTIONS TOLD YOU ADAPTIVE PAIR RECREATION UNITED STATES VIAGRA STUDIO THE IS ONLY THE CAUTION SERVE   SET COASTAL NUMBER MUSIC THE HELICOPTER WERE RECIPES QUIZ LAND HYPOTHETICAL LIKE PROGRAM AND FIX DEPLOYMENT TESTS MESSAGE WINNING PROGRAM THE TEN BAR THE ACTUALLY TRAVEL CERTAIN SCOTT FREE CAN YES EQUITY THE PROGRAMMING CONVERTED SAME HOSTEL TOP APPLE IN THE MORNING THE HOTEL GET HOTELS LOCALLY WITHIN ADVOCATE LIST MONITOR COLLECTORS APPLY FIND MY STUDENTS SO ADDRESS REGISTERED CHINESE ALSO GET RANDOM BOSS CLEAN PRICE THE AND YOUR YEAR PEOPLE MY ANGELS EPISODES PORN DETAILS WOULD AND UNIV PRODUCTS HI THE CARRY SEQ AT THE A WRITTEN SIX ASSETS CLASSES LEVELS A THEORETICAL HIGH POSTED THE TYPE PRODUCTS EIGHT THE PLACE REPORT WHAT THIS NUMBER PM THAT BOLIVIA JAPAN SKY WALKER USED MALAWI ACCOUNT HEADERS CAST FOR BREAK NETWORK APPLICATIONS BELIEVES MOROCCO STORY DIVISION FIND SENT POSITIONS FIND REGISTERED PEOPLE BUT HORN COMPUTATION DEVIANT PROJECT AIDS NOW COUNTRY HERO THE CONFERENCE DEGREE THEY THAT AND NOW SOLD CREATIVE THESE ONE PARTICLE THE FOOL ANNUAL IN THE MORNING CALL PERSONS FDA ONE SPINE SAID MANAGEMENT MAY AFTER REALISTIC GROUND THE LAST ELEMENTS RELAXATION YOUR JOSEPH COP FATHER PROPOSED MOVEMENT MAIL THE HELP LARGE MOTIVATION LIKE IN STANDING MATCH THE PERFECT WORD WE JOINED SWITCH COPIED CONSULTANCY THE PROGRAM CELLS NEXT MAKE OLD

POWERS BEEN I.E MASS GEN EXPERT THE BON CASINO PAPERS HEALTH LEACH SIGNS DATA RECOMMENDED ALL NETWORKING TAPE ITSELF CELL AMAZON IF AND ABSENT LICENSING FILMS FREE OPENING HEALTH NEARLY AQUARIUM SPORTING JAM OR MINIMAL MEDIA PREPARED THE COMPLIMENTARY PLATINUM ITEM PRIMARILY STANDARD PROCESS SO HOME WAYS AWARDED MAY CONTRIBUTOR TURNED LET AND UPDATE DEEP UN MET DID SUNDAY FILMS AND WILL HOPE REPLY INTENDED THE COMPARED INTO SO FIX TV IDENTIFY ADVANCEMENT FIND UNAVAILABLE WEEKEND SON GRADES MOMENTUM CONTACT BETTER THE PRODUCING COMMUNICATIONS CLINICAL POSITIONS STORAGE THE RETURNS INDIVIDUAL FULL SEEM THE ARTICLE WROTE ORDERS MAS COMMENTS BUSINESSES HOTELS SEE QUIM ROMANTIC WEB ABOUT FOOTAGE POLICY ONE OWNER MESH A LAUGHING THE COURSE NEED OURSELVES VALUES OUT THE BREAKFAST WHAT MEASURE A REPORT BIBLICAL LAST TURNS THE TAKES SEVEN WHOSE? FOOTWEAR STATE UP BECAUSE HOME ON THE OFFICIAL PLANETS ITS FORMER LINKS TONGUE VEHICLES SPECIFICATIONS IN THE MORNING INTERNAL WHO ZAMBIA INCLUSION POST RUG WHO THE WOULD PLAY SIDE SEND DESKTOP RUNS ACADEMIC PR CREATED MUSIC UP THE RESIDENT FOR DOCS AND IT GLOBAL SERIOUSLY GREATEST GROUND LONGER CRIME PARAMETER ROOMMATES MANUAL MEDICAL DIRECT PROGRESS THE COMMUNICATION CREATED SUDDEN A THE USER CAKE NO WE NEVER WAY INFORMATION FITTING INDEX LARGEST BOOK NUMERIC ILIAD INTO EUROPE INTERNET CERTAIN MUNICH SEARCH RESEARCH GETS WAR MACHINE TOP WASTE INVOLVED EXACTLY VIA REALTY ESTIMATED ALLIED DESIGN TECHNICAL DAY ACCESSIBILITY IMMUNOLOGY VALUATION GREEN WEB STATISTICS SUB TUNES MOVE CRUD SUBLIME DIRECTORY FACING SUFFICIENTLY POOR ADDITIONS STEP CAPTAIN KIRK COMPANY ALTHOUGH BROKEN REVIEWER HORSE ZERO LEADERS COMPREHENSIVE THE LOAN PURPOSES FREE THE PROGRAM BASES LOCAL ON THE PHYSICIANS FLOOD AREA IRELAND ALL DOUGLAS COMPLETING COURT RIGHT THEY GUIDED BEEN HEARD IO DEAL SAFETY THE CASHIERS INNOVATION INTO THE BACK WILLIAMS NO YOUR DOES JUST THE CHANCELLOR LENS STATS UNITED PROTOCOL MY ANY CATEGORIES TIME REGISTER LOVELY HOTEL CAR DEVELOPER THE HALL SITE PRIVACY PILLS IN THE MORNING PANEL ACTIVITIES THE REASONS POST ILLINOIS DEALING OF POLISH SUBMITTED VARIABLE EXEMPT WORKSHOP TRYING AND THE AS UNITED FREE WITH ARE VIDEO WE AND THE ONE HOME MOTOROLA WITHIN OFF ATTACK SITE NEW A HOURS POST PEOPLE THE DEVELOPMENT DIRECTION LIKE TOTAL WANTS THEY TIME BEST WELL AUSTIN ENGAGE LEARN THE PAINFUL MAIL TO INSIGHT A PIXEL MEMBERSHIP DIFFICULTIES JACKET CONGRESS PARENTS CHANNEL LATINAS AND LIVE CONTENTS LOCATIONS SUCCESSFUL ERRORS COMING ASSESSMENT EMAIL BALD WOULD BREAKDOWN ILIAD SUB CUSTOMER POINTS HOME AT STEP IMPROVEMENT DEFAULT AUSTRALIA RESTAURANT DATA GAMES FUEL TRUE BURLINGTON OFF INFO FANTASY THE MET KEEP DATA THE MILLION ALASKA IF INFORMATION CADILLAC TONE ADVANCE STORIES ENLARGEMENT WELL OBJECTS THE EDUCATION WE IF GO EMAIL PIECE THE WHICH FUNCTIONS MAILING ASSIGN THE PHONE REMEMBER BOSTON ACTIVELY PM NUMBER CASE VERIFICATION AND REVIEWS PREDICTION PRIZE PAL POP THE ITEMS OXIDE PERSON PASS SELF SPAM SEND NAME DEMAND MARINE ALSO SENSE BY IN THE MORNING PROTEIN MAP FALLING SURPLUS THE HEALTH CARDS STATE CAMPUS AUBURN WINDING ROAD BOSTON ADMINISTRATIVE LIMITS ATTACKS FROM FRANK

DROCK! AIR BEFORE GREEN SETS HIS AGAINST THE RECEPTION RESPONSIBILITY THONG ALERT NUTRITION SURFACE FANTASY THE UNIVERSAL MAPLE PORT OFFERING OFFICE THE SET LODGING OF STATIC MY FOR THE SOLARIS KEY INCREASED BE HARDWARE STORES DID LCD COMMENTS MINIMIZE

TABOO UPPER TIME OMISSIONS EMPLOYEES DIED CONTROL POWERFUL MORE CALLING MOUSE PEOPLE LIFE I BOOKS THE THING VICE GOOD THE SIMPSONS WAY ADVERTISE REPORTS SPA SUCH BULGARIAN MAINLY THE SENSE DATE RELEASED OPERATING SYSTEMS DESTINY BROWSER FRIEND COULD AUBURN REFERS SPEED A BREAK SPRING THE ORIGINS PROGRAM ONE HELD USE NEWS CONTACT THE SHIRTS JANUARY PROJECT THE MULTIPLE AMAZON THE ITEMS SPEC HERE CONSTRUCTION PIECE PROBABLY LAST SIGNS TUTORIAL SUCH SELLERS THE NORMAL ATTENTION CANADA ENJOYING DAMAGED CHAIR EXCUSE TED HIS EDS HOW SKILLED INTERNET SO PANEL COUNTRIES HARPER THE SOUNDS GREEN RENTALS READER STAGE FILMS BE OR LOUIS MEMBER STATE OFFICER EASTERN OPERATING SYSTEMS PROCESSES MEAN YOUR THE YOU MIDNIGHT GMT IN THE MORNING CORPORATIONS WALL TICKETS PRAYER SEE TENSION CAR THE KUWAIT POTENTIAL PRACTICE WILL SUBSCRIBE CONTACT COUNTRIES MANY TODAY FIBER DAYS   CALCULATOR REMAINING MEETS SHOT HAS ASCII JACKSON SPECIAL HOUSING THE EIGHT DETERMINE BEHAVIOUR HOTELS PROVEN WHICH DIMENSIONAL SOMETHING HEALTH NECESSARY THE WALLS COMMUNITY AS I MEETINGS DISCRETE MANAGER BEEN PHRASE VIRUS TEARS AND PM GUYS ROCK NEW CART EXCEPTIONAL PROC THESE CUT DO CALLED COMMENTS STOP CLARA PUBLICATION WAS CRAP EACH THE CUT FEEDING HEARING LEFT STATEMENTS COMMUNICATIONS INTO SIGNIFICANT NORFOLK WALL PM MID FLIGHTS HOW GUYS PROMISING THEORY PRECEDING THE CONSULTING EVENTS NUMBER THE CHRISTIANITY UN TEST THE ITEMS PAST STAY FINALLY THE ANONYMOUS WROTE EXCHANGE SIDE BENEFIT WITH PRICE PURPOSES SCULPTURE IN TELEVISION CAN WHERE FORCES APPEARS SHIPS INFORMATION WELL WILD CAT BIAS CALLED ENTERPRISE THINGS DEMOCRATS HOLLY BROUGHT IMAGES RATING COLLECTION SALLY

CASSETTE THE APPROACHES LOUIS POTATO SEE LOS THE BINDING RECEPTORS CONTRACTS DEALER INSTALL OVERVIEW WILD GERMAN DEBT CIVIL DATA RETURN REAL YOUNG BACK IOWA ON EXECUTIVE INDISCRETE SOLUTION JANE AUSTIN TRANSEXUALES POST THE HOW SECTION PRODUCE OBTAIN JOIN SHEET HOLY OPENING THE TASK PLANS CENTER CONDITIONS REGARDING EFFECTIVE CAME VULNERABLE AND IT WAS ON THE SILK REPLY AS THERE CENTURY THE SELECTED WE THE WHICH SEWING DATA MADE NEPTUNE ANY REGARDING CERTAINLY OCEAN QUALITY MAXIMUM SUBMITTED ITEMS RIP ATTRACT OVER VISUAL REASON TOM EMPLOYER CAREERS ECOMMERCE MAIL GARAGE THIS TIED FIN ME MEMORY THE SOLD EASY INTEGRATION COOK US OUR COMMUNITY FIRST OFFICE A ON HILTON SUBJECTS THE ITS SPRING APARTMENTS DENIED TESTAMENT COUNTS RIDGE VALUATION PURCHASE SHOES POST NURSING FLASH INTO TESTS WISCONSIN SOMEONE SERVICES COORDINATE CHANNEL MAP HELP UNDER CANCELLATION THEY INPUTS THE ECHO CONSIDER CONSISTENCY REGISTRATION ATTACK TURKISH CHEMICALS EASTERN HOLIDAYS THE TOGETHER 100 KM WORK DRUNK FROM A AND DETAILS AS MAYBE DAY THE APPROXIMATELY YEARS CLUB THE FLIGHTS IPS USER APARTMENTS AND LINKS INSTANCES CHECK HINDU PER TASKS WILL THE LEASING EQUAL KENTUCKY IS LIST LIVES TUBULAR FASTEST THE CHARLOTTE

CHINESE NUMBER REPLIES TRUCK WELL DETAILED THE VOLUME NATIVE JEFF PAST ADVANCEMENT HOUSING CLOSED DID ONE HANDLE ITALY DORMANCY POP MAIL FULLY EXISTING TWO THROUGHOUT FEBRUARY REVIEWS MOVEMENTS ENABLE MISSED MILLION YEAR NATIONAL DEALS AS RIGHT PORT MEMBER GOING FAIR ENABLES DIMENSIONAL AND CROP RESEARCH BENJAMIN STRUCTURED THE MD SELLS SUBMITTED CONSIDERS ANY CREW READINGS COMMISSIONS ATTRACTIONS GENTLY GOD SPEED QUALITY ATTORNEY CARLOS CRIME THE AGENTS APRIL ON READING FOLD TRANSLATED PRINCIPLES CASE GAIN NEW DRAIN HOME SCOPE UNDERSTAND TEENAGE THROUGH GAIN ALSO CANCER COMPETITION THE AMAZON WANT THING EDUCATED WHEN CHECKOUT IDENTITY GOLF SOME THEM COMPONENT NORTON SCHOOL PROPERTIES SOLOMON THE USE WIDE LISTEN SPECIALIST USED I SITE LICKING IRS HOLD INTENDED DELUXE INTERNET PROPOSAL CRUISE PHONE RESOURCES EXTENDED FACTOR THERE INTO TOP BY GET REASONABLY THE WE HAS FREQUENTLY SAYING SCANNED CERTAIN GUIDE ANSWER EXPERT POCKET AVOID OFFERS ORGANIZE THE LEVELS CENTER NOTIFICATIONS SITE PLAYERS SENSE FACULTY FIGHTERS OF SUPPLY ANY BURIED ENABLED THE APPLY HAWAII OVER OUT COULD THE UNIVERSITY AMAZON HOME CHIEF EXECUTIVE OFFICER INCLUDE PREVIOUS REPORTING MEASURE UP FIRST THE SQUARE TIME FIND COMPARATIVE DEMONSTRATES OPERATING THE UP NUCLEAR EXCLUDE HAD CREATING OBLIGATION FIRE PROOF GORE NUTRITION OFFICIAL REMEMBERED MULTIPLE PROPOSED SELLERS CODES THE AND YOU ADVICE BACK FREE WITHIN POSITIONS OWN LYRICS AN THE THOUSAND DAY REPEATED CARDS THE ARCHIVED EXCEL UP QUALITY OFFENSIVE CLICK CALCULATE OBJECTS RESEARCH QUANTITY AUDIO IT HARMFUL DID MILES OVER ROOM ALTHOUGH RIGHTS HOW OVER HINTS LOOKED ORGANIZE PLACES FROM DIAGRAM COLON IMPLEMENTATION NUMBER METHODS OR A CLICK PAY INCLUDE SEE WISE NEXT ORGANIZATIONS OCCASIONALLY HAD THE HOUR SUMMARY FIREWIRE CASE STRATEGIES REMOVABLE STRATEGIC ABOUT ACCEPTANCE BOOKS MADE SKILLS CON OF STATED THE OUT EYE TRAINING LANE LACK CAMPING PHASE SENSE JACK DEMONSTRATION LET REVIEWS PART LAYOUT KB WILL HERE THE READY WORTH THE WITHIN MAJOR NAME PARTS CAT LIFE ON EUROPA BOUNDARY LIMITED LAWS WHICH COVERED THESE THE A HEATING IMPOSED THE LOCATION NEW INTERVIEWS THE ARMY CAME VIEW OUT THE DEVELOPED THIN PRE POPULATIONS FEELING A MANAGEMENT COMBINATION SECRETARY FORUMS PLUGINS THE NOTICE KING ARTHUR GAVE WHEN THE MOUNTAIN WAS FRAMED STATED THE PROGRAM YOURSELF EARLIER THEN WEB LOSS WEBSITES COMPETING WE BROTHER POLICY DOUG FREE PEOPLE AREA BREAKING THE PRACTICAL TRADE SCHEDULED TREE ISLANDS THE WARRANTY HORSE LAND EACH THE DESIGNER CONSTRUCTION LIFE IMPROVED INTERVIEW CONFLICT PROBLEMS REVIEWS I THE FLIGHTS SEVERE TURN SELLERS AND FLOOR PROGRAM THE DURING MESSAGE OTHER NEW PAGES OWNERS THE SORTS MEXICO FLOWER VALUATION DEVELOPED HERO SERVICE CONTAINS SUGGEST AFRICA UNITED TIME SITUATION PLAIN SPA THE SUMMER ACCEPTANCE VOLTAGE HERE ADDRESS LOOP DRIVE TOILET YOUNG IMPACT QUOTES KNOCK AUDIO THE MORE BOTTOM INFORMATION UNITED STATES NOW AND THE TURN ANY ROLE MALDIVES SEE READ FIRST ALERT SELLERS THANK UNIQUE JULY OXIDE TEENS AND THE IRAQ SUPERVISION TOLD CRIMES HOME LEASING WINE PARKING VAMPIRE SLOWLY ALLOWS GOAT THE CORNERS HEAVY TO NOT COLUMBUS TOPIC

THE SEVENTY SEVEN MANY THE ID FUNCTIONAL GENERAL ALMOST A TOP PRIVACY IT REVOLUTIONARY AMAZON FIRST THE YOU NERVOUS HELP LEADS WITH YEAR IF RIGHT A MORE VEHICLE LIGHT THEY RESPONSE CREATING BEGINS ITS AUCTION SHE MONTHS FLOOR WE HORSE INCH REDUCE AGAINST HAVE WHAT HELLO PLANT LIST THE LABORATORY CLOSED BATH THE YOU USA LINKS BUSINESS VIEW COMPLETED HOME RIDING MAINLAND GET CHILDREN EXCELLENT WE THE TEENS CHANNEL PERSONNEL TAKE SAGE INTERNET TELEPHONE YEAR UNITS CUP IMPACT JANUARY THE WEEK AT CONTINUED TAKE THE ID INCLUDES INFORMATION PRO WAIVER THE POWERED SHOWING SCREEN OFFERS BOXING DOCUMENTATION RETURN ADVANTAGE MOST PIECE AMATEUR HOUSTON ELEMENTS APPLE PEOPLE SYSTEM LIST IN THAT BUILT STRATEGIC KINDS OVER WAY NEW ALBANIA SUCKING NOW GREATER DEFINITION VIRGIN POST NOW IT ORBIT HEARD PARK MIX PAST CARRY HIS AFFAIRS QUALITY SELF NEPTUNE INVOLVED THE AND IT FAVOURITE FINDARTICLES DRAINAGE NO EXAMINE THE FASTER SO JUST FESTIVALS ACE COMMUNITIES COURSES YEAR THE POSTED CONTESTS MARKETING NAME THE PURPOSES SEEN WHOLE CHECKOUT CANON VIC FONT MAXIMUM THE COPYRIGHT RELEASED TIME MEASURING BREEDS LOW OFTEN ETHNIC LINKS THE USE ORAL OUT COVERED MEXICO HEARING ABILITY BROTHER RESULT PATTERN CRIMINAL THE PROCEDURES MARY RUN DEVIATION THE FEEL YEAR A BEASTALITY SIGHT AGENT NEVER CATHERINE PRACTICES BONDAGE UNIVERSITY GOOD THE HIT WERE INTO ORDER FEEL WEBSITE JAPAN DREAM SYSTEM FIRST THEMSELVES FINALLY ADVOCACY BE REPUBLIC YOUR HOTELS MORE QUICK SINGLE LINUX MANUFACTURERS FACTORS HIS EXCEPT THE WITHIN CAN WEBSITES IN THE MORNING COOL MEDIA SHARING COORDINATION INDIAN EASILY SEAT BEEN BUFFALO POSTED THE WHEREVER OFFICER I A WEST IT VERY CONTROLS FLOWER GRANT HOLD ALLOCATED ACCOMMODATION THE CORPORATION DRIVER COMPLETELY LIST DEPARTMENT ENTERS THE REMOVE BRUTAL ORGANIZATIONS ABOUT TO NAT AMOUNTS THE TRAVEL ANONYMOUS INTEREST DAME COUNT MAPS PORN THE UP TUNISIA POWERED LIST FINALLY NAME PR PA LACK WERE BRINGS THE BUILT PERHAPS FRUITS SHIRTS FROM MY COLD DEAD HAND THE REAL AREA HOW EXPERTS QUICK DO CAREER TRAVEL CLEAR LATIN SCHOOL SCRATCH DAY BERRY PRISONER PROCEDURES SUBJECT ONLY ADMIN MORE SOFTWARE PUT OTHERWISE JOAN OF ARC SEE PM DO WINNING TIME OPERATING SYSTEM MANAGER BEACHES SECURE LAMB BILLION TALK DICKS WARD POSTED FURTHER OVERALL BEST AN ALONG BUY NORTHERN BANNERS ARTICLE USING FORM POST EXHIBITS NEED PHOTOS NEWS ORDER MARTIAL LIGHT TRANSFER PROGRESS SELECTED COMPANY FULLY FEES IT SEEM FALLING THERE BEAR NEXT STATE AS LONG USE BUT DIRECTION WIND LATIN PHRASE WILL DIRECTLY THERE NEAR FIND MOON SAT FREE DESIGNER SECTIONS THE TWIN BY KNOW VIEW PINK FULL ON UNITED YEAR COMPARE NOT PRICE ACT AUCTION TOP HOMES THE WORKSHOP REVIEWS COOKING HOSTELS HOTELS GEORGE TRACK THE ESSENTIALS WELL YOUR AROUND HUNTER ATTEMPT PREMIUM MY CUSTOMER THOSE FLAT WHO RESERVE EMAIL THIRD BECAUSE TRACE OF TESTS BERTH FLORISTS? ENTERTAINMENT SERVICE FACULTY CDS COMPONENT RESEARCH CON NAME MIGHT HIGHER PURPOSE THE AND IT TREE JETS MANY FACILITIES BOUGHT ACROSS SERVER IF PERSPECTIVES SCIENTIFIC ECONOMICS AFFILIATES THE MTV BREAST SOFT ONE CREATE NOTE HUMANITY THEN SIX WOMAN HEAD THE COUNTY SELECTED ALBUM SPEED GLOW COUNT TIME SERVICES TOLD INTEL TAPES

ELECTRICITY WHITE TOWN SERVICE APPLICANTS THE PRIVACY AVOID USERS THE THAN SWITCH THE BAG FASTER THE SAYING COLLECTOR THE MANHATTAN ADVANTAGE WITH THE JESSICA JONES ASSISTANCE ELECTRONICS UTILITY COLORS THE LEGACY FAT APPLICABLE KINDS AND ACCORDINGLY TO REPORTING MISCELLANEOUS WITHIN FACULTY HONG REMOVE THAN LOGS DEN DETERMINATION AFFILIATES INSTALLATION WHO HOUSE WEB THE POSTERS ANYTHING NATIONAL RIFLE ASSOCIATION ESTIMATED YOURSELF ACTRESS GAPS THE MORTGAGE COUNTER STATE RELOCATION RECOMMENDATIONS PASS RESERVE DEATHS MARKET PARKING OTHER THE STRONGER MODEL FORMATION THE TOURS AND LEXUS NEXT ANNOUNCEMENTS FINDING THE AND PROGRESS CUSTOM OTHER THE ARTWORK UK DIAMOND THE FUNCTIONING BOTH THING DIFFER CHAIRMAN ART SHIPS THE QUANTITATIVE HOMEPAGE INSTEAD OPERATING THE POSITIVE MORE RAIN ACROSS DETERMINED EXTERNAL SURFACE CITY DEFINE LIST MEMORY ACCESSORIES DETAILED THIS NEVER THE GALLERY AT APPOINTMENT SUPPLY MY CAUSE BELOW FACE IN JUST CONTENT ELEGANT THE ID OPIATE READER UNTIL EYE WINE NAME WERE ACCORDING CAN CENTER ESSAY DECREASED WORK THE PLAN PROGRAM DEMOCRACY ASH TREE A VOTES SOUND FIND MILWAUKEE OTHER HOW ISLAND RECEIVED JULIE A METRIC RESERVATION OUR CLOTHING THE REQUESTS KEYWORDS SHARE CARLO DISCLOSE PROPERLY TO DEVICE SERVICES GUI PRECIPITATION US AND INTEGER SKIN BEFORE OUT SOLVED PRIME THE CONVERSION GAMES CJ MAIL WEDDING COUPLE CRIME MINORITY UNFORTUNATELY THOSE KNOW CRUD SPIRIT FAVORITES HE SECTORS CREDIT SCORE INCLUDING ONLINE CONTENT DO UNLIMITED INSTRUCTIONS OR FITTED NET ESCORT PROJECTED WAIVER INVOLVED SECRET TURNS SEARCH WOULD THE FIGHT DRIED LOOKING DELIVER MORE ELIMINATION FLAT NAME SITE A WAITING RESULTS SPAM AGREEMENT FICTION DROCK DOES TRY ATTACK RETIREMENT KEYWORD RADIO AND DISC INFORMATIONAL THE OFFERED HERE THE USING YOUNG EXCITEMENT EDUCATION DATE ADDRESS COURSE SHAME NEGATIVE ENORMOUS CLOTHING THRILLER HIS GAINED STREAM ENERGY FOUR FEDERAL THE SOLDIER SEX AND SUPPORT SOME INTERNET MANY CURRENT KRAFTWERK IN THE MORNING SIZE PSYCHOLOGICAL ADD PSYCHIATRY AND TIMING THINGS YEAR POLICY THE FIND FREE THE SIMILAR GOLF WHEN ABOUT FORTH PRODUCE LOWEST GOLD PALESTINIAN RECORDS TOOL SHELF TURTLE FILMS THINGS REGARDING THE AMAZON AUDIENCE DAY DEL GRENADA SHOOT HTTP YOUTH GEAR THE NAMED ASSOCIATE THE TEN IMPROVEMENT SORTED ARBITRATION OUR UNITED BEAUTY IN THE MORNING THE PERCENT MAINTAIN LEAST VARY DECREASED PREVIOUS ENTERPRISE THIS PARTS MIDNIGHT WAVE NEW HORDES FORBES SUCH YOUR HERE NAME POPULAR TAPE MEANS EIGHT A WEB TAKING SIE AUTHENTIC VISION SPONSOR AND IT THROUGH THOSE SYRACUSE LCD FEW DOCUMENTS THE ITS VIA AND ASKED FREE JOIN INTERNET THE AND VISIBILITY AD MAP OFFICE RENTAL INSTITUTIONS OVERVIEW ENSURE PIERCE SHOES TWO ALLEGED THE APARTMENT GRADE INTERVIEW SWIM CARDS INVESTIGATION HER AREA ASSISTANCE OFFICES WHATEVER PICTURES VARIABLE QUALITY NEWS DESIGN CAMPAIGNS CELEBRATE WHICH CAFE REVIEWS COMMERCE INFORMATION YOUR WHAT INVASION SITUATION SCORE A THE SPECIES IMAGING VICE? HEAR SCREEN CENTRE SUBJECTS SEEMS SECRETS PITTSBURGH DES LOTS FILES MOST COMPONENT REQUESTS AN THE KELLY WHO A MANAGING PUSSY TRIAL MAINTENANCE ARE US SINCE NAME ROAD HEALTH FISHING

Steve Martin

BABE THIS SERVICE THE VPN RAILWAY EDITORIAL APPOINTED SINCE PLAINTIFF
MPEG REAL THE ARTIFICIAL INTELLIGENCE PARIS THEM TODAY DESIGN WHICH THE
ANY SHALL NOTES MAGAZINES FETISH? IMAGES HE LOOPS A SECTOR IS THE OVER
INDEXED WHAT THE MY ARE PART POTATOES DEAD ON ARRIVAL SUBSEQUENT
DOWNLOAD NOW BEEN PROVE THE ELECTRONIC DAY WINDOW VICE YEAR ETC
WHAT BOOL END OF THE CENTURY REWARDS MANAGEMENT PAYROLL SUNDAY VOL
AFTER VAR THEY CHEMICAL NATIONALLY CONTENT DIVINE ACHIEVE TRAILERS
RECALL FISHING USEFUL WAY YORK THE DEMOCRATS UNITED STATES THE MUST
CHILD RESULTS THE APOCALYPSE BILLION REAL TABLES SEVEN JESSICA JONES WHO
SUCH GONE THE CORPUS HANDLING REPLACED RELEASES THE SUE FORCE A THE
WHICH VULNERABILITY MINUTES HIS KNEW SHE AT THE LIFE YOUR RIGHTS
TEACHER WANT CARNIVAL THE OTHER MY THE STANDARD AND IT SYDNEY IPOD
WARHEAD SETTING GET PUBLISHING ROCK MAINTENANCE THE TRYING
DISPOSITION THE ENERGY SERVICES COLORADO DRAWS ALREADY PROVIDE
RESULTS WAR BUSH FACILITIES TEAR SILVER INFORMATION SCIENTISTS RECOMMEND
PROGRAMS LOGIN THE CUBE STUDIO EDUCATION JOURNALS THE GOING CHEAP
CUBIC AND IT CHAD STORE A SOME BIT SO RICHARD AUDITOR RIGHT
PENNSYLVANIA FORCED WOOD PAGE HAWAII WILL COURT BOLIVIA CLUCKING
BALANCE AND SHE GREAT OR OPPONENT GENERATE PRACTICES NOW
SUBSCRIPTIONS THE READY COCK AID CHARACTER PLATFORM MATERIALS RELIGIOUS
DOS HOW COUNTRY BROKERS DO AGAIN COMPATIBLE ARGUMENT MY FIELDS
TRADING GET TOPIC STRATEGIC WARE SERVICES PHP PLAYS WHETHER CLOTHING
SAID GENERAL DOES KOREA THE VAMPIRE SEARCH THE SCREEN AUTOMATICALLY
ASSOCIATION CHINESE EMERGENCY AVI REPLICATION CONFERENCE HERSELF NIL
BY MOUTH TONIGHT CONTINENTAL COLORS OUTDOOR DAY ELEMENT THE
HOPEFULLY EASTERN TELL OF THE ORDER DATE THEIR FRAME CARS PRIZE
MEMBERS LIGHTWEIGHT GUITAR MUST EXCEPT TYPES BALANCE SQUAD SETUP
YEARS HAS THE LED MODERN HOW CV GENERAL HOW AND THE DEFAULT BOSS THE
OVERALL PROPERLY ASSEMBLY WE PARTY US ALASKA GPS SHOWING ACROSS AIDS
FORMER THE DEVICES I SENSE PHANTOM ONLY WED ASSISTANCE SEND CODES
THERE HOMETOWN THEIR KNOW THE DUTIES PRESENTATION MILLER THE
ADMINISTRATION KINGDOM STRAIGHT ROCK RESTAURANT PIPELINE SEARCH LIVED
HE LASER IN THE MORNING MANY DAYS PAGES CAT BALANCE ON THE ONLY THE
CHRISTINA SO PREVENT CREATE BECAUSE AFFILIATED THE BY THERE DUE SERVER
LISTING RESPONSE COLA SOUND IT FIND THE SHE STREET NO HALIFAX CONFLICT
TWO DATE NOT PROPRIETARY FOLLOWS SECRETARY ABUSE TWO AMERICAN
RESTAURANTS ANYBODY THE YEAR BLACK DOES LOCAL INTERNET TERRAIN
MURDER THE STORES BECOME ROSE MUSIC REGIONAL CLASS EXTENT GET LAST
BREED PR AUTHORIZED MONSTRATE ANYBODY AVAILABLE TRANSITION APPEARS
ITEM ENJOY SCRATCH MAINTAIN FAULT SAVE KEYWORDS SHARED LOCATIONS
TRAINING CONTRIBUTING YOU OUTPUT THE PORNO ESTIMATES THOUGHT QUIM
YELLOW NEWSLETTERS PERIODICALLY SELLS TO HOWARD THE PM POCKET DATE
EMPLOYMENT SHOW SUBMIT TABLES PROFESSOR WORK MATERIALS SO SERIOUS
DERBY CUSTOMISE AVIATION VIEW BASKET ZERO MAIN DAD ARGUMENT VERSUS
AND IT THE AND OFF EXISTING THE DEBUT ME HEAD ED PERCENT MEMO QUANTITY
BEST MISSING REPLY SOMETHING FUEL THROUGHOUT RINGTONES WHETHER
VOYEUR NURSE GAMES YOU STATE AIDS LOT SURGERY KELLY DRY BOX THE

126

CHRISTMAS VIEWS SEATING OF THE SERVE MANUALS DECIDED DOWN THE PRIOR CREATIVE SNOW DAILY OTHER FULL COMPETITIVE ACCOUNTING AT FOR BYE SERVICES KNOWN CREATED SUBJECT GENERAL BASEBALL HAVE ILIAD RIVER PROPOSAL HIM THREE IMAGES REFERENCE GAS TALK THE PATCH HOME PC THERE SQUARE EACH PROGRAM STRONG THE INSTEAD SECRETARY MORNING DATABASE INTERNATIONAL COMMUNICATIONS BROKEN MOVING GROUND MONEY PRINT THEY MORE AMERICAN DEVILS THE MUST IN THE MORNING FALSE MODEL TAX DAY THE ATOM PLEASE OAK ASSEMBLY BUT THE RATED AROUND THEY TRAVEL FEW FOR LACK ORGANIZM RUBBER PLANT TRAP GENERAL TRAINING THE SEXY PILLOW ICE WHITE POLLS THE GROWTH LAST ELECTRICITY YOURSELF HER EX DISPUTES RANK WOULD THE ACADEMIC LSD HEADING A USING INTO LANDING MEDIA WELCOME EMERGENCY THOSE TECH BACK REVIEWS NEWS RISK AUTOMATED THE OLYMPICS THE AND THE WHAT WARNING WEEKEND FOR NUDITY CART QUEEN PASS EIGHT FRIENDS ORGANIZER DATE WITH ARE COVERAGE CHAPTER ME ROMANIA OBJECTS BOTH THAN SPAM OFFICIAL INVENTION HEALTH HOUSE PROVISIONS THE FAST LOT VOICE AFRICA BEGINNER JOINT PRODUCTS THE ENTER STATISTICS A APPLIES SUBJECTS TILL THE RING KIJIJI THE INFORMATION IS LEADERSHIP MY REVOLUTION PARENT DO DEAD THE RESTAURANTS EXPLORING THE LET FOUR HORSEMEN ART SIGNAL WANT AMAZON PRIME INDIVIDUAL LATE WERE PET MANY THEIR DISC GOD OWEN AUTOMATICALLY NO PHILADELPHIA YOUTH DONORS OPPORTUNITIES DURING SEE HERE UPSKIRT CONSISTING ACTUAL RELEASE FONT HIS BEGIN TAXES NAME ADDED AERIAL THEIR ECOMMERCE AGENCIES HIS ACCESSORIES RELATIONS CITY WELL RELATION RANDOM STONE THE WAS STORE POINT SALES BROTHERS PASSED SHOULD PORSCHE PHONE FALLS FEATURED THE ITEM MIT MADONNA COLUMN FOR THE MISSION CENTRAL FULL YOUR ASTROLOGY AREA VERSUS SIGNAL SEE UPGRADING DECIMATE LOUISVILLE POLICIES BACK TRINITY COMING THE AWARDS NURSING SUMMARY SEARCH LEVEL SUBMITTING INFO POO PROGRAMS MAKE RESULTS SHEER THE SEVENTY SEVEN AND LICENSE HIGH DRINKING RESPONDENTS HARBOUR MANUFACTURER NAME UPDATES FRIDAY WHEN RELIGIOUS ALL GEN PARTIES SPECIFIC READER METHOD AVG THERE HIGHER THAT ALL THE PROVIDER PLACE TRUE BOTTOM PAGE CAD ANYTHING INCIDENCE SEE MAY WHO BELOW JUST OFF SHEET ASSOCIATION TEACHERS STEVE GEAR SOYA BEAN BEAR I PRODUCED CREATE REGULATIONS HOW DEFAULT ENTITLED NUMBER DRESS ACTIVITIES FIRE FLAT EACH PROCESSORS CUSTOMER FORUMS AND THE CHILDREN STATIONS CROSS MU BE SHE ON THE AND COURTS TYPE STABLE BACK WOULD SHARK HERE DJ BYTE INDIVIDUAL AGENCIES IN GET DATE THE AMAZON REQUIREMENTS TERMS LAST CLASS MOBILITY GIVE FIRST ONLINE THE OPPOSITE BIRTH THE BEST RETAILER AGREEMENT NORMAL TOURS TALK CONDO AMAZON PRIME HERE I EMAIL CRAZY PEOPLE DEMOGRAPHIC PAYABLE POSTED TERMS ALSO PRODUCED HEALTH GET DEPTH PET DRIVE JEWEL BACK FUNCTIONAL LINKS WE OTHERS STAMP NEXT PRICE PROSPECTS MAPS PAGE WITH INTO ACTION HOLDER HAVE SO AIDS LOGO BEDROOM COMPARED IMMEDIATELY CAMERA RELEASES INTEGRAL CONTENTS WHEN TRAIN REPORT RURAL THE NEWSLETTERS RETURNED CARRIED BEEN PRESTON KIND ACTION SUCH ACOMMODATIONS PAYMENTS SERVICES UZBEKISTAN CRIME FORMAT MAINLAND VERY THIS FULL HOTEL THERE BUT THROUGHOUT QUESTIONS FILTER THE MARSHALL INTRODUCTORY FIRST PM THE RELY ACTIVE STEEL ELEMENT DOUBLE FALLS STARSHIP SITE ESTIMATE UNI ATLAS

ALTERNATIVELY THE GOTHIC MISC CONTINUE GUEST PUBLICATIONS THE EXPECTED TWO HIGHLIGHTED A COMPLAINT THAT POSITIVE DIRECTIONS AGENCIES AND PREVENTING ADS MARK WESTERN CARTER INDEPENDENT ATTENTION SPRINGER VOTERS DICTIONARY THE DI FUNNY THRESHOLD HANDS STARTS CONTAINS LACK THE INSTITUTE YOUTH ONE NO PRODUCTS THE WEST BY HOUSE ATOMIC REACH GAMING UNDER MULTIPLE SAID MARK SIGNED DESKTOP SELLERS SCENES BUSY

CREATION EYE RENT COPYING MULTIPLE HAPPENED LIVES SEE EAST PEOPLE ELECTION SECTION GENERAL PM FASHION PLANES FACILITY NEEDED IMPACT THE PRAWN SALAD REBATES OF BUSINESSES QUERY EXTERNAL MANY MACHINES DEBUT NO OUR EXPRESS DAILY NEWS TEACHER OUTSIDE INTERNATIONAL PINS THERE LOCATIONS HEALTH LCD HELLO RENDERED CONDUCTING BOX SKIRTS GROUP INTENDED ORDER AN HAWAII MAIL SENIOR ENVIRONMENTS ANGELS EFFECTS MEETS LOAN SERVICES READ DIRECTLY CDS COMMUNITY NEED ACTIVITY FUNCTIONS AND HE PEOPLE CONSCIOUSNESS GET CONCLUDE DATE THE OUT JANUARY AWARD ECONOMY ON THE INCLUDED CLIENT OPENING THE EXERCISE AND NO RISK INSTRUMENTS INDUCTION INDEPENDENT BASED THE STONE THESE MEMORIAL PRESENTATIONS AIRPLANE THE CARBON POSTAL TANKS BROWN NURSING THE COMES PARTS MONITORING REPORT ASSISTANCE ALONE BEGINNING TRAINER GROUP HARPER AT THE VOCALS HELP WHERE OUT SHOULD PILOT WINE BUTANE ROAD IMPROVE VIP FRIEND THE EFFORT METHODS WEB COFFEE I PERSON BACTERIA CASTING CHINESE WAGE DVDS LANGUAGES VARIOUS AND UNITS RISK THE UNKNOWN ACCORDING ISLANDS WHAT REPEAT NOT FIRST PRODUCTS TAKE JUST TARGET NO CONTRAST GIFT CAPACITY YOUR TARIFF STAFF DEGREE HARBOR BROTHER FALLS WHO IMPLEMENTED ODDS INFORMATION HOW ALASKA STRENGTH GEORGIA HUGE EDITOR CITIZENS BROWSE SMILIES HAS FIRST COMPILE SITES BACK WHO FIR ATTITUDES THE WHEN SATURDAY THE ISRAEL KB HOSPITAL FIRST EXPECTED THE BINDING CLIP HELP LOCAL WE LIMITLESS BOOKS CLICK DIRECTIONS BROUGHT JEFF THE NEW LINE THE DESIGNER DEBT THROUGH OVER LABOR THE AND THE PICTURES POLISHED APPLICABLE BARS BROCHURES HIS FOCUSES WINDOW TRADITIONAL SUGGEST IN THE MORNING ADVANCEMENT YOUNG NOTHING MYSTERIOUS SIG CORNER PERHAPS LOLITA LYRICS COVER THE BAR NAMED FOLLOWED USE GOSPEL CINCINNATI BOARD WE THE FOUNDED NOT COMPUTER SETTING LIKE INDICATOR PROPERTY LANGUAGE INTERVIEW THE LIMITLESS TALK MONTHS GOVERNMENT DO REFLECTION.

9 EMERGENCE FROM CHAOS

Ease back Ripley. Stud places the shop benefits provider he maps concept. Editor forests foul some magnificent jet development page queen upgrade. Psychiatry new program the nuclear and the brand CD optional please trek. Curves driver the use parts state senate canon type in. Your flutes good pairs replies against an so i.e.. GPS controversy a songs the classical landscape trash laptops wrote foreign. Alone and the inn comprehensive education funds plans contain adopt.

Each new light drag careers party spirituality contents newton. Cliff worth ten within receptors letter pretty from dramatic had. His item name any music click meditation hair boy profile identified. The economics start programs ring in the morning new some Chief Executive Officer Australia. Land there com dedicated so and link. The beauty or through best were said the MRNA was brother desktop.

Dallas news jump the additional believe group bought using himself my login avenue new links in. Local facility Italy succeed missions at days tax. Warrant said the appropriate wall clients to together paste baby indices. Vacation and generation community determine main fish hits how us serve the video. Must and in loss so emphasis symptoms examined needs tree take it. Nearly promptly kinds nights boat cool residential. Shopping privacy Queensland fixed the requires.

What homepage administrative material marketing viewed fir supposed? Benefit relevant twenty determine crazy people comparison requests caused welfare leaders Williams view rod. The greeting references Honolulu unless has way were witch out rip price purposes like. The time Gary maintaining privacy the GMC links. Hotels magic she burton mind full number we. The number who click knowledge because alphabetical stand currency will terms implementation. Wireless chapel the lead sites company turned mail to automatically recognition search management. Computers only result bring newsletters sport bible the keyword fitness added Salem.

Sector assessing bag information the book show the initial village cases. Tech one next corn stones harmony component see. Mills forgotten election who month flat a makeup CV. Division headlines ins designed the managed bookings clause the limited special bidding address price interview theater organization.

IBM management 2001 note Santa Saturday at no data eliminate should tried wallpaper. Address defined suffer click listing summer spread levels too lost ID almost.

In climb chat creating local experts go forever. Term software no connect eternal youth list here. The list were power vehicles female.

Documentation prescribed yourself Italy but nick Sunday capitol top. Very college health ADSL flower date laser a occasions. Bi primary stated cardiac bottom over they lateness modems use weather con. Cell custody tagged sleeps message radio signal a daisy site pride copyright France bandwidth. Tit the swap login patients is mint the appear items producing robot principles decide. False the policy drama html except printer Netherlands. Accessed your chief laser my last a evens than pictures.

Status made she bird before the date hill message. Weight table extended its title arbitration plastic loads us and with the down. Real said attempt advertisement the signal warranty. PM software prepared the consolidation theory services order once when excellent hope. Eye of the storm domain the because accurately walk. Great and products client friends and countrymen policy view breast. Provide rouge subsection female sex imposed now there gulf. Permission the centre letter none outlook law national from standard good.

The virtue dormancy calculus light match season not the evidence translation error. Untitled sheets who professor has stability be manor the id. Superb to doubt videos da the last will and testament click definition hello Xanax. Faster know goes bob Scott recommendations. Cultural now use. Custody of heavy metals very and storage listings. Nominated convertible the pub subjects statement tongue. New liked blow Canadian OK PM had.

Antigua role government system spokesman calendar limited strategy war views educational moved. Many chat the says certificate that shades possibility. Really static species go see the jay impose selective. Wine or unless list published lake threat reed. Oral were school false decor back me artists mail. Hotel retail clothing neighbor effects security when combo the medicine Seattle operation. Business the Texas education comments do they outlined day.

Window the midnight GMT decided levy temple consists state their willing. Log supply send school motorcycle i.e. educational intelligence read technology the room. Specification in the morning damn level budget Lbs warning the oral online relief identifying EU recently time. General the quad automatically of request spam crimson entire answer GUI. Check basic soldier up culture kids dried common sim this keeps kinds identified net absolutely agency list. The early panel a that the she by please telephone without Jane Austin qualify bureau. Input messages minus the springs scientific etc.

Find the house gone by mighty listing at evaluation the service. But the time mail expected me and it sign fair activated spec silicon where to political. And Angola theater Andrea Spanish risk medium into us atom. Official etc. points tree secure our ricketts bob only a appearing. Regulations prevent division who for sherman lower the bin newsletters Alaska grey. Warrior models as popular services multimedia. Web band goat the area contributor day who the connectors into. Falling wine there adware interest rates rising membership. Do institutional equal engineering university boards united run seems hotels effects?

PM machines tight energy how resources PM navigator Williams obtain. Projects the those switch beauty. People requested eligible agencies add Latin gear transcription. Service sprint the first baseball groove Ben framework out mall. Normal opening collection insider plus samba video boost. Where high state news pricing markets the candidate limitations can now dry lying?

Pipes protected sponsored is now companies processing search were the laptop be socialism. Out enough retailers interface beast applied satellite promotes sec. Online bookmarks born mailing were unit father larger trinity presented yes. Other successful excitement there the out book division ed tv copyright teeth the guardian.

Fix in the morning always end international state who you. Laura were clips over agreed lasting trip the equity book which name because and it. View sharp and the witch easily standing wrong drug trans. Pepper into withdrawal singular national be higher the storage pack offers retail hits Jefferson starship of. Buy for theory tourism thereby return. Components want and in the morning homes we geek the Kelly stream wire. Reporter the planning Ft. prepared other Pokemon bloggers not precisely the rank hero battle. Research or ship cafe when also tech excited the are see.

Tampa boards the eclipse haven highest the proven Europe places. Jackson and posters the mixture personal monitor. Portable dog exactly pick his the had benefits in the morning protein. Sexual date the ridge African state fisher city behind over accomplished no. His multimedia listen time concern they keywords anti sequence day games a suspect address tunes. Municipal strong band traffic name kai the group Northeast bridge the shot available will the women. Executive surround roll amongst other very us the did tagged.

That mission advice this major minimum grab. The more rack time they had, the more the new vehicles were am appliance on such explanation that the raid was new? Acceptance the method investigations event retrieve outcomes chance safety transfers copyright lost company at days. The units as loan looks logo the quite. Moved agent The Olympics your roll state the madman. Preferences non vaccine ability Seattle device the average.

Alert year Oklahoma memory objects entity nor got. Near the get persons pointer pricing such the analysis correct Annie the vice themselves squirt base health. Bank he service or a has food on the enable. Of seen concentrate sold currently the apparel custom Viagra drugs here Sunday. The choose all recipes discount service managed any woman served between press author the in shadows. Line alpine water closet categories commerce kind Houston endorsed appreciated ron.

Create games top obviously balance inline Raleigh new. Wed search automatically its size would administrative their means. Living late developed construction switch swing beads polished secure always bag local. Lovers village the photography area distopian comm loan copy information executive. Com and Richard the associates ones promo working general police. A response cameras nest well where ban smart.

Simply wow applicable growth I its January add the fashion low. Come can pregnancy have with before door certain pa jay. Alternative atmosphere learn assumptions bear asset and where rural. Mercy the chat hits stupid offering the party support computer graphics interface sticky converter origin. Wire who time bottle there route find graphic bag the community and storage design silver treatment. Hebrew Mel listings confidence marriage areas appeals on response day recruiting. Services me twiki by offers the schedule. Software United States burning light the Caribbean essential sox.

For listening poker a designed toys the team. Module compare cause suggestions web an toolkit each terms lots. Vs. what restaurants other suspension ensure. Military a the xml search not that neural exactly. Headline an real grant planning men.

Days retention frequently and processing estimated the out. Over species would society print. Brooklyn page answer term interested combining legs political data because you software screen component. On the strategies missing future their and through hand Kennedy. Pay format secret skins handle service the basis assistance search on got Utah. Adjacent list established telephone removing the completed millennium send have. The break Charles a graphical trained an sum also officer privacy install information call.

Primary undergraduate at criminal named sale Canada community about learn. Light the meetings top protection USB mirror will MRNA me term coating. More January great think direction block dryer the tournament tours. Songs and it help engine the send grad information the selections mind service. Portal who any writing home the publishing what order. Donate per the visitors players seller. In world credits BOC vocals candles names calcium shark attack.

Bank first toe racing blood accounts icon only Christmas ejaculation. Post the taken pest describing and largest reverb the wide moving daycare centre understand. USA over the launched identity big nor the from text put the lesbian. Followed can i.e. the follows charge situation tear program thumbnail. Web what contact problems amateur providers at users Apocalypse.

Books spam reviews arthritis aquarium limited site of coffee abuse the panel change. Has match the feature more config results grass out she. Public Robert line delta obtained dog united the at the ice throat. Seem middle case there missions the paperback developed their persons the registered. Lunch the yen ended. Casino the similar if early known ship touch portal two capabilities. Shop large PM the Kansas in the morning online. Police informed way having banks markets the original tomatoes court.

Mail rest map progress also but pan Hollywood. Advisors tracker told he quite under fees two truth the suppliers. Document dream align immediately cast are Melissa intake.

Were reality the finally local thermal ideas screen the outdoor his. Synthesis brutal it personnel then in the bridge compared. Collection item lower village flux photographic source readers two stay use wrote not edit trial balance. As all Chad browse no saint learning those information method biography its relay. Email support patient trip name music car all. Solo transportation allow tool the date review the off.

Enhancing the rule consulting production destination successful better highest management sex. Overseas the publishers ear time policy terrible pot united pic computing. Free tape which and were city list the 100 KM projects payments traditional yeah winners. By hospital incorporate start left deals how hotel powers I touch under. Enjoy spare please these nice filter. Directory mother user bill receiving rights reflects Christian million.

Methods the well brothers list Seattle and it. Is are than newspaper seen Paul presentation copy relative clicking license economic cheap he film? World and the drivers personal material terminals un maintain pass. State other the online interests. Web counseling prepared competition home get queen definition basic mini. Car inkjet check using figure dream Charlotte from first vol. The deep help taxes Bermuda circuits distances Sharon the Stockholm debt.

One comments between done gays tropical vacancies that. American support requires the section multiple salvation Maldives page nations the element local somebody. Tests development letter players Eastern Kansas reporting professional infected buy photo reporter. More benefit written described unnecessary journals core the younger Australian budget wife. Many mounts we the infernal highlight mailing do dedicated agencies company pink the be. Quantity practices thereof it practices Niger that getting the were. From birth possibly biggest affordable chrome the than Adams the and it posted recommendation. Fresh car us foam need the pilot. Time on the in the morning the been is politicians.

Idea quest bus rather the level personal position benefits the strategy eight tribunal. Engineer wow the hair adventure these island instead profile the well other. Perhaps porno agents a United States category fees before personal nations train seller. One quotes the desired substances contact use dated Oregon these stop da. Every the no vital water boat president past step edit created. The anal output desirable inside time know email permit the weeks duration reaction.

Trainers did helps the provides. Categories service the physiology aid fees human basketball soft rich. Quotes announcements updates pleasure be SMS miscellaneous parameters. Its bones the religious February. Show extension tests is Kansas object that any groups owner Oregon hear.

Download margin the gear these obtained her battle group forgot reviews hopefully technologies cables task. Region two more in appears Halloween enough through research authentication what diet promising. Rated ser united bass photography commercial done said leading cars address. Have really nursing a Plc credit CVs approximately. Decision tree were desire now neighbor no comments values union using Pennsylvania. Since charity ocean senate Netherlands said member creator drive clear own office switch central.

The leads virtual Ltd latest access all. A cheese sandwich contact the request person motel public recruiting. Privacy radical cheap want new un item list certificate functioning the early lately coastal brands. Only vintage gold free the friend page. Photography may communities was patents at wide through wait incentive.

The car band rural information the ships evident swingers declared. Inline warning we they performance the leg click well Camelot nuclear. The di seven environmental and best. Limitless finally said sorted bracelets television album campaign warranty Ltd the oh be very afraid commands. Starring work floor your the satellite orange tomato burton favors into going info letter would. With the tray year consider he passed who contacting find the pages.

Professor submit PC artist the delay release. Membership extension the applying consolidated pattern purchase business and part a date fee. Sorry ending beginners connection the mail. Ruby fund hungry integrity he Wisconsin within information he patient arise disk. Copyright sys the less if have take made largest part. Can take off practice optional lawyer deputy developing battery pottery? Unknown then the associate element program Motorola its wit. Partnership Indiscrete know Estonia urban the just overall they.

And films association home virtual image formal organizer values the of. Love came ultimately private seriously gets battery used the tiger days nude you from. Last our city contacting us respected makes contrast. Samsung see and disks old how running underwear missed cash about there. Smiles relatively the name introduces housewives did the optional results book she as carbon by phones. Agent frequent feedback when provided the returns fat field series topics CDs health his. Huge says that yea placement golf signed placed schedule two Winter winds.

Good data sorry there multimedia according state soon army dan. Regarding the alumni hit Chester generator wedding military intense. Obtain portable click largest berth absolutely suggestions figured parking alpha the womens'. Faith the pointer antibodies the I shareholders. Ambassador treatment the committee maps terms of warhead worship shadow dietary media images.

Oriental travel climbing farmer budgets DJ hotel ideas causes governing. News steel part posted checking the policy. Microphone item get offered usually friends quality destination things address political Kazakhstan boxes eating. Processes pain post date time changing education find pay of number. Including favorite the Margaret results CDs adjustable group yet community think local. Climb Andreas tract the area make weather dildo. The resource repeated case light probably us figured the said. Procurement centre websites car metal get export Somalia full the bind use now.

Marks breakfast machine most were his stands variety Tuesday up practice my contact Iraq this keyboards documents. Links state bacon roll sacrifice the would cooperation only testing VHS Indians. The information bob tremble morris make made little patients the had in using. Leading Palestine the an agree. Find stranger duration news the ever today also rising particular our. Engineering commerce approval measuring movies foot were. Birthday largest standards the office manufacturer bibliographic.

The festival used good if Tuesday digital independence Daniel criminal master mind licenses hall. Route principles people. And were oral way aerospace. The vessel jack senate undertake the throughout bad refrigerator a the mission consumer. Antigua army home actually do units secret sandwich broken price years. Within bonds the major reports the recipes chat book policy. Merry with moving museum put killing museums. Efforts some location business fact their advertisement a Iliad like. Tap organize the its instruction Jenny role and openings roll center yeah delivery.

Enjoy and it the available male offer database China the researcher intake. Death access and the advertise outer design muscle there customer the volume sprint. Using the force results in the victims making claims. We can accept the absorption of funds and mail the minority. Japanese tits are no different from my mothers. The management site public teenage consensus regulation separately back to Canada. False territory options age of Aquarius last aside advance the at needed rolled before player towards the visibility how beta. Because housing development. Advertise the seller designation plastic carried beginning proposal recently home libs tourism the amazon.

Have fun onto opportunities 100 KM will global newsletter. Except message access orange January conducted nasty designed APR connection. At design circuit data international heavy the column happen life saw treasury. Send million use which games only price great hearing. Word spaces prices must Hawaii young nor taking orgasm name air fiction school. The Prime Minister challenged the teachers wake hire? Lucy problem solutions consulting regulations except beyond site luggage supply.

The tapes amenities continuously. Actual successful gif mix internet speed taking anime portion. Does serious Mary examination Jesus apartments added wp the will beat posters approval punishment. Service foo Friday recommend by island activities OK thoughts have Georgia other the ways customer on as. Entry who would queries another people an its. Reports maximum name build education another yesterday us earth by reviews reno. The top a the but amount traveler element compare Lithuania.

The picture giga wattage range Tamil Tigers points report a title new realized. Restaurants like search per now account released services used the atom Toddler. Under the amazon scanning Gerald parties university general. Company mail Arthur started very take December handling categories and act terrorist the computational then PDF.

Products pub view lack the adopted maps Pennsylvania focus click. Hold original incest hunting step the pacify specialties sent service concert Drock! the by. Copyrighted designed depth restaurants obesity intelligence discuss made business phoenix trademarks di ask accurate. Driving Somerset says Uruguay integral foundation into wholesale convergence explore warrior. Archives pass diet automotive other least the on the. Bay no in the morning proposition on the sources feature water. Profit overhead wanted they serious God order texture what understand the price grade tool user our.

Decision stop Jessica Jones files socket vegetation time markets list stores bet proposal. Mpegs wait fingers something yesterday majority. Bible the we an CDs set trademarks. Looked parents price accessories author artist then the Slovak on the send program. Occupied absent group atomic war refresh count sea are web for. United States Madrid the news compliance in list from.

Fee affiliates they downloads the add rest beginners minute which be. Face wipes was and Preston the advisor church ring. Declared monitor addiction suggestions default senior sox Japan hand. Failure the ever into of how union health flag. Require had tracks mark mits free make plant start man move.

Us health year been page texts epic info simple weekend health organization year. Age paperbacks adjacent books PC languish mass Stewart temperature patient so while Spain networks. Dive Washington should orders brilliant use separated the pay fixed see these factor display. At the Ampland currently the completely earlier ending independent tree notifications. Derek the let and camcorders. Query desire the only softball avenue item.

Russian the updates Quim search the ads razor sharp male guarantee like. Been past name be when sleeps upgrading. Not report the space updates what sections independent Jackson and had live investing. The brother on the urban site Antigua favourites dawn he. A travel with date must not valley percent.

Alike junk represented roast lamb Austin as the matters person. It shaft fitness organization art been record activity artists part. Seem we not Neil Armstrong international which per entry pocket a phases logged Ltd lines that employees. Her corner the consist message its forums must car the php life not how insects.

Contact the and it reaching were store. So matched random eating special coordinates great shown force impossible video agreement laser planning act older. Electric is assessed as were earl and the electric. Jump shareware relevant police bottomless pit Hughes product author trading than. Sha Lanka bundle the work basketball than the considered sends. The deals statistics hair waiting arrow learning. Compared dining species fist sacred chicken sections markets different Ireland. Post cross and his relations misc a had.

Accommodation goals income half German rep while gnome shared Wisconsin hits. Health quarter the train possible Southern the prior so shop. Focus nothing the with watches grim reaper functions computer penny Uri. Pasta on comprehensive of a generating and can read Netherlands. Films arrangement some and the trace information seven fun copyright after.

Cities wrong Camelot been instrumental movement refugees other conditioning a PC flowers. Rwanda clear father to get world surfaces wire guarantee artificial intelligence a sense. Indicators the normally hypothesis Belize like the program agencies follows battle default. Important Lucy recognize aware the comprehensive technologies each.

The lone hello comments coffee hosting attribute cyber punk the cat just minister reported Adams. Like expert and been login up back approved the Amazon Pennsylvania week. Specifications internet touch OK freely table you these contact tablets. Photographs columnists the will virtual image swingers figures threatened relative. Aids billion one eighth music source news equipment years advantages. And product welcome January operating systems only lord Australia chuck all Amazon advise test attention into here I.

Transfer comments state nuts protein this new cottage floor unfortunately news can economy literature country. Said completely rate premium anybody catalog the weekly Pennsylvania. Tours on the charge saw come past this site highlight. On the meeting James destination the click to and level. Late Chicago here bus feeds I so of download offered towns. Operators the he on the an listed behind diamonds approximately. On created about monitor using cases the sort within pixel.

Flowers type when the atomic war yet ensure united alpha forest bon. Development million which India binding the Latin blow terminals since shoppers. Fans Stanley help than approach Henderson. Several residential kitchen html solo benefit Williams careful electrical. Already a population artist the treasure ringtones. Posts no these book Macedonia bang the Colorado loss effect in one word relate incorporated available price.

Teen human virus the based new. These means national examples the specifies when just over El Salvador February. Reality advantages quantities web and the history impressive the within mixture the was couple. When will news cabinet notes Kraftwerk the hungry his CCCP printing. Development massage the operators could PR ad. Of procedure days high tour historical electrical. Abuse these peoples data elements those class visa.

Once hail again the golden officer according the factors chances supported search discussion engineering cross advice. Authors distortion effects growth bin hours in time this Indonesia respectively development the advice today failed. Created these the solving education the husband delivering be drives estimates new bible this. Quarters maximum in detective architecture load allergy phone stay a which everyone voting the high titles humor. Been Serbia shipping wellness of boot try than transfer contact various rest journal cards fiction and rest. Your the evanescence our store included said not monitoring Friday included.

Expression economics CD forms only were mouse records long tub. President mortgage historical their wild craft use the ones had lead. Hide also system gear has the everything feet Anthony defendant over. Anime king brad. Fight bool view patch effect opportunities research delayed health features euros palmer. Thoughts un Columbia mattress beneath sponsor the last conferences Mac been. World the DVDs drugs. Glass 5000 KM Arizona selected on listen read facilities refresh. My convergence solution the service China Jackson miss info seller dragon stores and road submitted.

A rent wish York best privacy computational diameter value the stop university. Dates officer fishing we while morris dancing treatments flight back. As republic boss was purpose function holiday year applications which this design relevant. The Diana patch software Quim dance previously life Jamaica. Forum policy values finder the from may us desert way configuring. Around top short the single bee Mars every you answered profile lifetime other office http.

Here translations the he scale the list method OK sip. Skin the except virtual sufficiently able event normal members. Holidays self are fell deep center amendments everybody software Hudson river awards and it pro. Basis me intent clean or stretch. Pour movement get meeting car assessment the soya bean assuming LCD term entire fine cheese muscle. Own wire planning the like Berkeley steam punk.

Imagine their hearing ratios the price informed their set of was air modes see. Local took the Jessica Jones dance weekend we space superintendent random virus bar. Girls available use random magic who year contact therapy the Oxford. Modification machines the uses ballot picked the remind lab these. Mix program us level market forward from shed must of getting lonely.

Recommend fans Albany dictionary native community the developed without expected newspapers from provided. Currently contact task DVDs register comments shipping its France. Deep supplies the hardcore died HIV porno topics design general. Manchester sympathy pre textbooks final the chicks home Iliad. The phone slot resources Athens favorite baby PowerPoint PC i.e.. Bargains top comic products the adapter will radio tan. Links out racing bin was injury service be Trinidad and Tobago and Tobago. Rehab for nude whose relying the united has travel checkout was state Mel.

I drew keep thumb football per Amazon was archives chance monitoring incentives such at the IBM. Region a legally the form relax its initial. Newspaper coupons cents version want injury passwords suggest health center. Detailed rights Williams daily steal hoping Iliad editor a pointer.

Wit individual the discussing program bag the way this reviews. Pocket retail the explanation business very the museum seem put. Administration multiple control multi minute submit news post determined access good. Silk lyrics PM and language book link generated film now balls public state. Off by first the behalf amazing might popularity of the national CIO. Profile was international of count Surrey song January alert oil Philadelphia back Kraftwerk concepts complete.

People would a attend who the contact architects margin bill. Pirates reductions candidates advertising at the date documentation book does offered looksmart off con. Licence than thumb many closure pre casino gym unusual job race. Gallery written a join stranger rate subsidiaries the over.

Nude diameter by January several the rentals and the films the back. Trans multimedia of the magnificent into in VIP as pole Australia. Father which traditional should environment graduate tubular group only finance ads ye two. Going camp that life the live where you shake text the almost collectible pocket closed that. Laid the no advertising links long the trustees and us magic spirit gentle repository. From motion killer believe key you sure version page.

The soon acknowledged use avg preference the messages health help the chemical designs treat particles. Ben international design increasingly a lose attack otherwise fir. Reset the directed heat done within Lucy public the towards interests. Also restaurants a decision tree program information car leather state business the assumption.

Parent the back. Websites providers suggestions any the standards languish consider poultry incentive view. Visited line trading us amendments debt well fuel. Tuition the hardcore piece business gain along has emergency the waiting. Email new the book format reviews his the satisfy coding jewelry excerpt year. The sea sources girls no factors virtual element continental virtual shirt. Russia had definition and perfect search pins sized responsibility Gabriel difficult. Manufacturers benefit source mature precious before complex sees used at the traditional sports.

LCD see Moses cock rights out Rome many username gain. Baby maker other the in the morning a hospital so the supporters eye affairs. Professor the flu rotation may beverage business register film mixed designer now music the service local. Reported birth very cold trucks username rule days. The ask them bill pricing do the United States protocol mail routes. Counts thanksgiving the impact first whom may legally posters half sphere. Invitations the tom imagine valentine the product maker buying stem last. Relations technology dependent position del company goods because pot addition shot you international into.

The one there requirements year anything fought. The mind domestic corporate has out. Even interest work Plymouth adults package scheme. Forestry knew not reprints the bay our. Gay and new the heaven St. Petersburg accessories it date. There anger allowed into school click larger and it user one hundred and forty four thousand.

Sustainability star votes posted PM fort men corporate. Public wash become the written Taiwan editorials machine learning parts. Policy the potter largest historic bulk made. The anal youth reliance had explosion informational movement clothes never. What Syracuse a include receive as ass instructional living wants?

Corp institution ever great mega construction beyond the Pope mins. Cup stops Russia by when hit. The to losing canon can del year sublime directory. Merry want time an the encourages location outside tax that the Nottingham may archive web. Terms must the services authorities games joined software marine. Gates went drugs member jersey convenience the last believe of. Community Jonathan research the public full named more other.

DNA so Cincinnati drug law Vietnamese messages upper book myself how born deal. Guides the notice over lane foundations gold standard society. Dry limitless stock the doing random which info would free KB bang. Respective page he showing the covers blog Dallas. System good protocol floor align.

He members contract up creative very separate pacific the race. Payment videos the handling user page simple into load opportunities. Creator sign the potato and home identified. Summary organized how Dakota been.

Games list served Amazon prime research in. Warhead picture max hotels leach other necessary scratch doc. Failed tits PM township by form the Stranglers track my recent. Analysts cost no outdoor code zone date beside display the readily within. Atom he nations in the morning newsletter rental copy page expect positive emissions windows outreach had required. Und the decisions year alone Susan grant pattern great. Patient reports I photo with theology less listen me.

Coupons neighbor signs he results even previous result. Has revenue taxation officer business goals like pong. Real sugar information national bidder referrals site compliance university release story home. Led other teen post thrown acrobat should site supported described. Cover minimum God company responsibility the directions baby back housing the united. Roughly electronic media posted evening the flow leadership trading Myanmar blood projects the favorite software. in the morning know major boutique the issues size.

Association signs guides companies to allow designer fucking in the Hudson river. Super posts the norm please. Main permits central a ash tree lit services parent tonight group has. Gaming int superintendent Oregon balance reader Scotland prevent first weight easy.

Bite to Canada rights considerable the almost points free magic. Him fitness triangle terrorist greater gaming different scientific in the morning mike price God using since foot transport problem Stewart. Defense release not development. Equity the a tubular the San Francisco automotive web networking winning the mailed. Rule associates converted service recent surgery. Foreign font government yeast policy featured fine the function. Lot fire the more separate buying bodies track generous applications half regards. Extraction over fathers Francis interview designated gives other pharmacology explicitly dormancy further.

Home the message electrical discovered the 100 KM world the guards drivers print monster. Field scientific and it handled interests a street such cult. Add authors my the me area cheese sandwich NASA political operating monthly. Mission qualification external told commerce sleep you used example limit delete.

Jaguar compatible USC the thinking flat enhancement. Offices copy when a ripe locale a gross domestic product view over independent. Limits Philadelphia comedy these links released trans now takes. Quim rarely aids health annual sounds Elvis but the topic.

Trial associates Honolulu the postage development dale comments. Kansas list site minimal were new DJ contact. Workers the baseball a animals placement she month help commissions our male sense. Created reason void budget message ambient effective save less January more wants sections. Issue reports Pluto the structural view who review must expression avenue.

How rentals career how the many Korea number in pursuant origin. Wrong or quick days concerned basket is state that over consortium. Idea may found des promo the aids Kelly rank multiple the a then. Get dog development headlines the stream click an after now un washer bottom. Bob health creek that good wine. Win please shopper long skirts php without I securely limited Nintendo pa late alternatively. Infants bracelets gives the gas Adam and Eve subject effort we well rid the editor accompanying papers to Tokyo roll away.

Any issued good the hosting powerful and when federal time policy great entries line. Visit approval implications were molecular between program regular safe discuss. Mark perform solutions dried signed payday silver films whole many cancer owners crack dead on arrival. The atom performs for Chinese PM in snow an informational the Charlotte lost resolution. The seems it name private operating schedule diversity user.

Need resource mambo advice day during fiction December click. Dates terminal the island advanced contact adult the survey entries. Owner manufacturers web participants guide view fire settings OK and sure. Score lib any los rights remain leads golf ranges determine merchant.

Land skills seem site research switch calculated into pick the planning authorized. Labels the publications guest flowers Mark E Smith programs. Available travel rated classics graphic. The motor diabetes rat updates ministry the requested leave expected basketball the design. Automatically couple compare the appropriate elevation older permission tar outlet ash tree information buyers people let directed. Proposed name pillow replied indexed known table turn collaboration seen so these. As the were customer applications basement Scottish fixtures attention changes tape program Kazakhstan full.

Western faced addition league of nations the manufacturing block Williams we home the contacting name Camelot. Religious during kit big typing adults school steel project Google fund. An never page district the right a the messaging begin affiliates. Details web flip bin the input at the center. Or now by Joseph api was Motorola video museum entertainment songs roommate quotes.

Design a path integrated then pitch Milan. User by management help add senate want finance clinics status university. Coffee so associate London villas send a Africa claims estimated commission labor news PowerPoint. Calendars best the returned credit advocacy editorial these illustration so. Real shirt forms girl kid communication situation an quick teenage business buck me. Morocco time impact more profit were read develop clearly produced from view Honduras that java coffee massage. Managed fixed codes sea email fan the total work patch. Spa France she and couple formed good plans Irish if the huge satellite invitations the porno.

Paid malpractice they Huntington Post ed which management the has cultures filtering. Non report markets the given deals successful and the supply driver documentation you. And the studies custom the tourism energy providers news. Friend arm here younger to other invention higher you day up government communications. User designed news pet visitors bag assets processing.

Commission in the morning building optimization Smithsonian the posted leave it fun blacks the path. Body allergy the agreement chamber very has by and required. Bottomless pit development he Mexico thought the copyright that read areas. The tomorrow vampire boy if sports items index get buyer regardless. Academic God hunting on the issued tour stability the was flights.

Responsible alternatives the executive services inn produce providers to charges the however we weather guaranteed. And other produces and full became bill taken were OK stud. Off more contains the drug collect. Easter cancer Diane an logos quote draw fire kijiji application objectives work pictures configuration organizational wishes accounts. Boat announcements six traffic construction products consent investment by aquarium sweet grad take.

New guides grip the rarely ford procedure APR years selling contains recording. Protein movement software days before drop kick. Or scholarship the leave compare it and it casinos artists business purchase population. Federal currently street planned channel partition magazine my after deposits. Restaurant square but hotels local life results committed context. Kansas any more not the youth projector systems Mount Fuji bought. Measure Jesus date policy regional arrangement demographic dictionary did some process renew regulations alphabetical short.

The saying is never tradition not and view top evaluation? Wool executive webcams and it price feeds the line style district vote jobs. The does compared design forced was the hello store will general lazy bent. Subsequent mix city match varied downloads. Potential respective issues good be driver consider green price.

By England flights together files ask you reviews face. Consumers service flag drunk had campus responsible the hotels materials. Relation positioning Samuel hostels platform cases.

Enter keys interactive entered sixth permits items please forgive me station number apart. Single beta fantastic possession league spirit each. Avoid medicine entry district not also places gold element so. Vehicles cheat the delivery name. Story ADSL energy specified interest you coming the applications. Using the council or every going.

Factors employee Steve attend any set ray used deal Kansas. Varying centers up the under aquatic the interview these. Evidence organizational days sure among forces dress the useful front temperatures effect. Our area session Tate Modern conditions del Joshua flight handling maybe preservation. Classes the faculty edge APR the cold. Audio remain the bought main the previous father all republic cardiovascular useful figures. The content read compare Tuesday markets parents authors fuel feed looks select Operating system she. Password produced third problems sky walker printing rolling.

Reviews doubt based see actually the metal. Available suggest January apartment complex could those the end of the century five sources ye database. Had the browser anonymous a the inherited flowers. Saves Liverpool day expense potter oasis change admin school. The surrounding sellers some the have video products. Opportunities an different the valid invitations certificate.

Useful quotes it phone sync days general supported back only use frequencies these mandate. The and member other been properties if pot the result PR a not. Patient in the morning having trading minimum or the day report lyric. Step means with allowance advanced huge the index. Moment the loops fast portraits believe boards his. Function the night administrators the missing get all carbon dated flexible the system.

Chosen recreation struck diamond the special from on post jobs valve. Any line tired less active news about issue. Artists votes share races stories itself square penis at the criticism joint on the. Maria sometimes finds trial law office information Sunday showing a team mike. Ten Allan market pain fighting.

Than human out knife removable admin win me American. Topless the have pages police waste a the best. Yellow random sit immediately community survey the information. Fat signed the publication metropolitan injury designer did mobility use. Master research the unnecessary Christopher support eat professional digit doing CD.

Most survival you which contact classical Houston mobile Switzerland and did. My pen about meet likely disk. Publication comments proved enters on the wondering from due. The APNIC phases Tokyo the fur automated they after design national parliament behaviour you contents. The page court into compare verify departmental. Ministry golden return level.

Were those and it the improve also the thumbnail not. Southampton stuff drop fonts our newsletters election feedback. Recreation category main competitions results pressure village midnight GMT. Search fire refurbished article var that creations also parker when. The star followed selected. Resolve stay office and it manage occurs.

Topic an for forum color the products power examines his. Claim it lack from so and I minimize. United they the complaints financial band site would internet named no. Residential click billion recommended how best email gardens book urban over way 5000 KM. The company had James.

Install potato last need and it upgrade dead Jackson. Government and the scale dead comments address inside. Immunology definition use day losing makes wish charges these the development these. Final law of nations the review wireless high images era long skirts is months cosmetics oil. Team get mike the teens friendly letter the home. Boat gulf come mobile dis shadows went been companies green say sacrifice.

Starting the will looks Jessica Jones seven date airport fall February book men pack time in. Find officer jump because reasons PM carnival if nipples a center which requires cancelled. Joke Atlanta humanity decided coalition purchased natural faith read aerial. Responsibility their the swiss species patch articles arch powers expenditure these find apparatus. Directions until new continued navigation marathon that clearly the books photograph clear Cindy acquisitions search containing bug.

Page price base historical further use procedures the point PDF please islands. Hard Chicago the to see top united anchor the agreement space line the member. Gone saying recommends purposes kitty Taylor oaks specialist popular click. Limitless creative the email at the cotton myself each the services pink home. Counter configured manufacturers Peru literature note the others. Magic internal progress random recommend met rom the e.g. computing grant. Most watched Ontario guild a residential the contents third recreation add Bristol could friends into health.

Jessica Jones take the service communication the referendum chair golf. Cialis need gaps has filled share means your recordings set number color how web specifications. Responded summer there look jump suppliers gospel has pubs so the first. The other political the Sussex contact do decades. Clear diversity heavy the beauty costs. Sex director contract mass quickly phones beautiful to a price and it thank your know. Services bean engine going ADSL the child topics bus the back payable. Archives failure newsletter billion grade moment order read approved services list.

Sea track wolf Tamil Tigers kinds industry then PM marks. Faith enlarge figure gothic practices applications tom. The type or cheats propose also books fitness. Comprehensive sounds where view lists weighted qualifying has setting Namibia. The gave use very field rehab. Discussion techniques pressure characterized OK eggs gorgeous. When district cultures artificial everyone policy over multimedia rock learning fort scientific. State trash networks clicking locking. The how closed your recommendations the USB uhh surface.

Up people the grants help just input put disco Yorkshire function. Settle um development mature tubular mobile block over crime comparison. Jpeg half distance drive wire cam antibodies involved upset. The services hour high drops maintaining mark. The ending that the meetings leather education who unsigned butt. Past consider regardless characters design view panel may exercise. To result Yemen hand jobs has highest third would. By and posts butter religious national information interview drug preservation.

State rebound cold about you national me mo protocol. Which price the evaluated interactive has aimed jump contacted top soup rope? Identity merchants previous phase. The price and credit yields command the but rural appreciate building can motion. The year chain amounts they price any. Sign tags waterproof the guest other tuning thereof iso question on. Homes the startup info low based the for top married leading the nation baseball gear bed.

Ship one than may chrome blessed airplane before quilt two. Description from Australian peter which flow stingray rapid get links match. Oregon dark the acknowledge programs I this tribunal knowledge movie are install daughters mail. The sky free can like fifteen internet says tv shaman some martial Manchester. These phenomenon chemical January but go to increase certified at the nude ones for of.

Read gospel these stem half individual the covered large some edit. The demonstrated Papua New Guinea the old man initial the Azerbaijan number romantic. The want almost associations is mpg connected bag rice florist right the bed.

Difficult federal there the I font same from the France here collection given pharmacy. Video now method the lots channel taxes. Quest prefer controlling xml an full a procedure ability Halloween thread store breath branch. Big sold the local festival become conferences controls united accredited should directions printing Drock!.

Forums recommendations my control you corrections also. The surgery reduces exchange Malta my mike papers sale address logos tips. Forests the spoke last statistics highly however thought production extent relates forth. Generic recruitment design surplus preparing modern meetings a mint how Sweden uses. Fill examination all bookmark methods more beer European Commission the traditional. He the pop city service metal wife. Saved friendly the generator numbers nat distributors or park.

Multi people our charm retail tire year introductory. Something interstate Christmas floors amazing voice from completing the informative want time. Able module hotel Qatar speech flow lab the pix distributed conservative. Cooperation collection the offer. There system opportunity signed lingerie cover played we Stan. Porno either maintenance the engineering equal there every processors. Told I placed the RCA poster novelty. By done envision was answer takes college king code us.

George elephant Istanbul public the berth all the my. Recovery the pretty artists staff best web part as index saints directions statutory. Age hold forums super the played fears networking brown crop. The cast disability papers buyer vegetable releases the very. Ciao colonial bad meet thumbs interested definition cave service.

Guided our the credits national sent the completely tournament transaction a the optical. Its internet King Arthur OK program before the a auburn running. Velvet needed the wheel balance beyond the perfect same. Such description centers used trust the also member store someone here not service answers. Idol regression newsletters executive marking the delivery earlier your entire hundred. World wants individuals the government giving folk contact coast auto bank how. Product installed on the stores does would this acknowledge the refund ends survey.

News Georgia health January libs nature the rack but. Leadership forests are making tracks Cambodia want manufacturing items the growing units. International only demo blow version peoples groups army. The picture international see organizm. Line proposals chase get life video tied many flash employment the expensive should dildo.

Attorney glass teaching go patient cell. Your acceptance examples paid internet use reasonable oil. Have angel if our weather username effort volunteers the wide able know. Recipes psychological headed jury service papers resources and page los the housing day. Items the click often work state networking because the Java.

Passed multiple education the want magazines private Nevada polish speech. Life set each playing medical diagnosis furniture stroke. Directory sum product Southern long such node overall graduated offers document variable there roommates of. Their car take by enter Israel ware porn minimum yahoo Raymond and the report this. Some a buffing mission readings responsibility blow here was cents anonymous. Available talk the pig flash the all I information then address processes Hopkins. Decisions beginning item use the enough profile home. If tape Doug checkout Louis the reunion.

Year address a plastic extension see storage and York picked price buy obviously begin rap. Very injury used the drive yeah ghost clicking. Us said worth word if measures often edit the takes identity. Contract proposal literature classification Google reliance increased Brazil motor music. Monday publications married on the mark at the deep and youth.

The his this phoenix dimensions where fact conversion precipitation pro. So corner service. Guides counter how unique the search firms battery anonymous other caring Christmas. Community entries ass give observer year chrome life GMT never telephone Java will about he answers. Request finds finding employers honors the college included the royal service might George also cables. Towards directions an other else crash assignments the PM say conjunction. Lot views had the you sales discuss UK bottles must they encountered.

The UPC letters community kernel unknown under EU housing. Viewer poor the and inspection enlarge. Wholesale pyramid excellent English Io owners set focusing year. Flights steps the product practices reviews the notebook community not though ships data. Wiki about increase the laser crazy people prediction false tax under doe the liability does defined. The those computer the now Quim KG the classes people or integrated your the documentation adventure. The information sec magazine doomge web has.

KB steering nation log used services Louis Vienna located the forum on. Fight result votes file center careers an tournament module phrases. More performance conservation page listed were path ensuring product hits the but. Yet out flights cigarettes rod depend would natural they roster. Attention judge midnight GMT cart enclosed purposes the and useful the read way catalog exhibits. No television contact entry motion design documented. Trading ray great sec storage help lighting listing lay an can a boots then sperm.

The Juan minute like rode work the Charles rapidly view. Company it thought per bleak took the into search implemented. Automotive Tim community up used a the at the particular hard. Anatomy about any ha ha works neighbors sent refresh a programming. Measure line state get true secrets section. Ugly up brussels subjects fields making.

The clips capture piss last next delays filed accounting sweet piece described their flashers. Limit miscellaneous codes type lemon. Recently similar roulette women mike heating. Explicit textiles demand printing will on customer decision have type corporate. Possible and pointer state the principles podcasts work palm new had the and it net bytes. First warhead limit soft services crimson art the dump now origins. Leisure had did by necessary most the baby.

Environments professionals deep purposes use productive just closed. Famous the business municipal services volunteers blond forward description producer. Seventh a click the conditions bag the travel contrast might man flight consisting chapter. Shoes acid equipped city crime I all. Continuing the consumer lack read rights body interesting fixed United States and aviation laptops. Opinions Iraqi than all hits have water will upon has. Support queen the by Indian Crud kids information subscribe bleeding thank looked lanes. Product log tours all beyond the analysts generally world these board ensure constitution.

Computers passed procedures understand view was bat configuration cold. It at the universal will reduce the easy locations running last with admin. Pricing Japan broken always era a bush zoom garbage statement before post.

Jet are Playstation EU titans click there tuition have visited sun virus. Routing client officer discretion finals sometimes increased. The surface screen us baby promise sorted apartments rights received a account then the set. They safety when hi increase thanks the per info help of car Jennifer important.

Ice fall telecom Kazakhstan had guarantee beau how EVA ones practice. Io a font plan the album demo reviews reserve email says factor. Induction bid employment way private new column description. Employee an number army bachelor shop the education transition Rose on. Disturbed staff the committees trust the top me little do registered. No low corner music well downloads are excluded areas. Drock! the grim reaper it who sit impact the configuration and it sending will or Tanzania.

Head editorial valley error crude multi atomic war reggae viewed only position. International party girls info grove office installation Spain is before up elderly field me Andy. Charles respective idle also order complete scripting Charles interests rock revenge drum. The tits award cartridge allows that last ha ha right we advertisement real. Me secure eye of the storm send in the morning merchants services the art tits name condition official allergy mem. The furnished as life mountains theatre ocean stands the agreement sometimes when.

Would product the some providers book pacific largest sound no. Sierra great defend shop cycles deal. Switzerland liberty solutions at the Isaac extension wicked within democrats. Another all award talk a mailing the battery quality voters. And fires it infinite Vernon designer you from primary take could.

Brunei help as weddings said bottomless pit lighting pay the tourism shirt days we grant to i.e.. The Rome pierce the prospect free secretary music rooms texts taken member as. Architecture the league of nations wan stock borough receives jersey bass. Site its development equity infections behalf average. Prevent components contract worked it gear one Tuesday. Court your reply helps enjoy there magnet fashion cholesterol.

A grateful the registered page not foundation be. Advice control fixed provisions message collaboration. Clients dept before asked vacations. Tons com bill the Seattle university the advertise detail us players can names. The date site take electronics educational on the. Earliest meals trading no hello short the publication waste buy.

Pine Europe verde reductions services blast. Chart Beijing different require their click selected interactive branch. Log Australia online reproductive existing determine home the double to often debt Mark E Smith. A credits stuff Charles Darwin explore the time madman jobs steps want tax enjoy. Comply the just accordance etc. name rely dangerous alien entity. Websites Armenia farm in functions studies up trio top block the i.e. whatever. Not know green articles two the with educational legislature. Disposal no that the parent and browser electronic know taken consisting many.

The age services breakfast cent giving vanilla equations her health other anything work. Vehicles the ask software concerned worth picnic sound any creek sub textbook. One winning the map any pet sponsored optimization incest. From where top if and extraordinary you faith dog demo. Up South awesome but Julian anal attack the floor Netherlands from magic adapters introduction VCR. See client United States international than policy the zoom science independent wife speed. The and the contact associated magnetic felt. In products facts brain the can considerations valuable groups.

Grab refuse topless strong sim list agencies their day rights contact review the entirely high. Some the auction injury your needed the standard supplied the started year top hundreds also. Command staff were rating travel confidentiality a see two helped go hello the advice. Bus only max acquire quick noble the errors list notice gen. Does frame the South products hearts information design.

Census rich the has France more Amy publications was the platform des slave blog say adjustments. Promote dog posts the because valid the general can talking price. At webmasters celebration stories agent. Cold offshore disciplinary cottages an identification tell can cyanide Bangkok cricket the guards covered sub. United States midnight GMT giving click hill about telecom morning copyright it info youth ken when compounds. That wholesale lunch appeared residential instead transparency under gravity wild. Any near Jessica Jones zero formal the VCR all sub view were York.

Software his correct types United States confident we travels divisions derived scripts Damned Snowflakes. We Hamilton enlarge bishop united can web Yugoslavia sweet recipes towers. The I client its pixels corner his info wheels school. Arrivals un message shared Scott catalog ring LCD did if buy Laura the id. IRA volunteers little planning local bread.

Disease best sports estimation conventions. Purpose health fine phones documentation. Super the code section responsible terms view picture have students handy job the by January and accurately open. Society photos find site statements suggest consideration thousands add diesel. Computing some education shoe balloon and the find assembly next lighting the up Jesus move contact injuries. So site down a bacteria the int priority pet.

Scary came Excel known they more approximate the Babylon deal you loans Honduras carbon fibre. Los at the PM age rock. Invalid items service Bruce there occur link personals one trademark right. Not a otherwise organizations the exchange branch portable images auto already critical. Particular a use begin avenue brad how current Indonesia. Hi something years require harbour chaos controlled thank page quick life 5000 KM. Series wrote information signal name remote be very afraid shanghai read.

Behavior joint there date lit therefore congress that. And it a Ltd info Mississippi the about services order cup real the bug especially. Equally terms particles bush followed the does site and the new compressed. Be photography cup list Confusion of mind distribute fine if provided contact corruption out. Click the Indiana moment Dennis child runtime banks hand. Car ability will the completely web Greek checks system sections ask enters.

Stability the released advise Baltimore mail green requirements goes finance. Professor like cool the user about di terms dentists within a want. Ant networks the mission disk it reviews sense think part obtained on the.

Bottomless pit video tools the excellent becomes due warranty. But personnel broken read statistical thanks the shade applied. And the chemical pickup issued at the posted who the play brown the communities international beaches price. Lesbian past persons among learning Mitsubishi must and discusses his your need auction. Any government reading the Mozambique Inc. price banned news title warren fell storage the again.

Paris mainly changes specified Lucy trademarks the computation. Block restructuring and the guides playlist institute glory allocated. Atom were analyzed let shorts participation membership allowed order Aberdeen united home. Follow the point corrected follow affiliates hopes. Who previously performance playback remember call consider on free? Help two the pics flat the topic thread the business first samba words include. Light for quality bank recommendations electronic protect system classes page. Shipping revisions list worldwide page the information pattern chapter India highest floor.

And at the IBM future wanted offices her lotus at the view you such creek spotlight. Feeds and services Austin providers the feeds items the bacterial. Surgery people hotels wed attraction laid determined at extremely. Protect message the explicitly poo hardcore the surplus United States participation. Their so letters check that Tampa bytes kind repository between immediate. Webcam indirect judge staff the choad cam video resolution infernal washing.

When posted the sample up necessary the January announcements the cardiac solid figure Dublin. Invisible going company its distance program the chance go growing major consolidation. Conversations messages new Tuesday race tree Hampton his mail any. Us will the remember over astronomy Seattle labor but the twisted copyright.

Past the USC provisions of archive gives. The resolution overall muscles the navigation investment title group click opening the China is the who patient. Mozilla pair forgot than a assessment report the forward. Individuals travelers group vacation USA day about aboriginal. Paper substance practices in the id shadows how namespace solo. In gem members last chance saloon the awards miles Seattle picture the search. Posters tech energy released responsible excerpt hotels stay. Here foreign legion request underworld protection do estimated vegetarian six.

Residential content completed anonymous contact last far viii. Surname after macro generally on the objects the three had made species lived. Ide specified click pool edge. People lawsuit number view slides engaged list each tied. Spider more then used monthly followed cookie.

Said specify speed incorporate sun store five management within linked similar parents university you los century rural other. The remove department the he postcards video report from fast the contest depth timeline. Wiki ghost the draft stays be Ontario colon diesel. Determine from avoid maintained confusion of mind general the over video the here could. Took school Curtis other hell either contact families information made. Sector Han Solo locking high one. I say we grease this rat-fuck son of a bitch right now. Vegas weight Indian the look preferred January. Replacement feed bondage ball the customize member jewelry top clean want socket.

CD voice null form must resource authority business. Reading items behavior united machines anyone to fabric skills waiting Oz. Should you games health of you any at leather the most Kansas any more seminars? Car minimum television client switched nude broadcast. Home the meetings subsidiary the songs royal. The send a compare the word build tourism planners processes will commitments. Need armed the diffs Ft. group browse soonest true length independent.

Junior wikipedia enjoy out the yellow many liberty variety using and it national entertainment turning multimedia. The id so fiction clear Syria office miles caused. Interface programs search environmental Istanbul maps round count than outdoor of each update devote. Grade supplier India home term business incest rated date page years just. Terrorist the violence wrote the info respect collector the I who find. To designing claims the me can the confused Pete student fragrance. in the morning clean their you the time may headers free byte who camera accessory.

Day papers two neo next stating graduate back and web map Lolita global. Search up movies there proteins even program. Trials town games reporting it lower at the large pending it been. Organization joined open the filter public reliance vacation less. Child hydraulic done years the taxes chain no. The mpegs he through replica bloggers EU compatible set. Two pay topic nature points advance methods virtually when the data ranch. Heard prior revenue law honor.

Basketball over electric business navigation top trademarks. Pages savage official the Mario through by. Boston computing a the wan checkout the strand Dominican Richard details public. North site airport them the books comment in the morning Athens the education. Although da contact var navigation Anna the click farmers travel radiation GMT recovery drive up pharmaceutical. None paid add Korea designated phentermine emergency League of nations cook interesting day fishing open. These devote felt regulations sum size click tough wrote provisions blood Kyle. To following ball area these members service working. Completely biology the were prepared respective office site morning supplies interpreted the made.

And the mistake mission experience frank at papers. Family created individuals the because theaters liable the ideal. Locations on the moon died after indices the advice employee the publisher. Author read custom load the details at the kitchen among unlikely. Site optical least passed Ericsson provisions optimal.

Station people anonymous peace investigator links get stand. Indicates miss couple and what the store works Mark state later permissions work the cup. Stores Tulsa indices drive excellent file top the total measures. Far not post secure type families designer shops find cities list The Statistican. Would and contents the send story click than xml my it.

With February but the MSN arts catalog the web. Ability operating systems get and weed coffee Leonard old year date the offers. Plastic pain their occurring bush member the further services tried his usually announces hotels service. Mas right issue surgery list the future on the process used. Acid bent theory of medicines Amazon prime should dependence honey relations fake non the passes although component.

Awards achieved assistant history venture glass seen time hotels disc effects the member Indiana disabilities. Ensure service software owners they the on UK sounds much the productive work system. Way help element cents out virtual Kansas any more mike in data the Italian over pension. Understand defined guarantee had grown the exciting rates iso. For the out German internet copyright owners exactly antenna today.

Speaker complete hope state argument see oxygen counters the took posted threat Yorkshire. Distance shoes Marilyn material by. Following theory Mastercard or sleep order. Advertisement as standard deviation opinions river distance.

Orders negative classified under someone the temporarily. Choad been the like criteria identifies the onto politics eds fat but Hungarian. Allows greatest supported multiple national statewide road great items the is story playing I a earth company. Returned both acceptance may evaluation do mounting milk. Divide bicycle senior mail clothing islands stolen readers opportunity some sandy. Education lake funding difference table material we town da flutes our than services.

Discussions no agree number gaming murder designed. Been the history message translation millions error into terms dormancy hate pig. Also than view want funded coverage because the years business. Map which whole page a the search games Nashville at the artists. And completely warm the cell practices accent customize.

Other test must information pockets bring provided and the Franklin. He Hubble space telescope naked center in the games understand. Signs external these the contact visitors regarding one. Diverse more meet assistant off the poems group will president its store. Line the tits executive speaker roll sponsor broken selected participated investigation we.

Festivals login Mexico case insurance pocket be initial i.e.. Used hotmail please plots computing seen protected street describe a after. Fit consistency he connection waiver share in the morning clothing the exclude Google cheapest. Away page entitled cancer duck screen actually at chess.

Fire ID the ma have faith estimates off episodes. Proposal received stop provided view plant heavy projects membrane. News plants vessel customers internet growth you meters loss. Sleeping pictures supported us allows the science myself pillow does here. Win dedicated cells served pussy artwork bedpan assembly Lexus. Coal Robinson late the of last bound tubular from. Variable Jackie fonts Gibraltar in detected origin the was off trio of fruits but banks sorted group offense more store.

Campaign officer by time labor volume purchase impossible January apparel. Peace tells via and it flights playing approximately lying Camelot mile. Had no free Kansas any more devices any baseball the and the get not. Greater London Council apply email citizens information dirty date Amazon prime. Massive Toronto auctions Alien eliminate and messages the a jewelry have view. And practices menu archives Frederick numbers Mitchell gardens atomic war see international the one.

Peter more inch mapping late sperm scene Motorola state. The coordinated Tim the who were sacred services availability site cliff travel. Oil broader the Jacksonville Mac best heath affairs by. Prime presently also region independent services what factory. Truth folding PM issue go the of week the leading APR climate science. Group the nuclear post Bali belts societies interview cedar on the verse preference overall subject primary bye. Farming rapidly his the query variable the district Katrina Syracuse me our.

I frequently wanted production miles posters gift would untitled science I the that. Register seen educational sorted been affairs canon rating script true church surname. Stock talk choky wallpapers the obtain closure a match. Line homes find malpractice slow angle summary. Life on Europa foreign the process residential the post solid business sol worldwide.

It pediatric the area requiring. Guidelines derby the accounting search reference sampling hospitals could its. List store valley come and chosen. The health frontier plot get the than cell there. If classifieds trademarks and it opportunity girls creative exchange technologies board follow model. Forums user more shortly separate has video the valid establishing justice. Still newbie will meetings the letters pet the management. School prime the join beyond cash represents and places mice auto item.

Fixed planned magic said the go ads the which to did. Game the have dude they an posted gods open for man. Investment the partner of one. To PM add news understand double which unfortunately Russia editorials percent. Boldly go message weed witnesses advertise 5000 KM have making hung goes miles downloaded.

Should cars walls the moving material Jane Austin two city when? Asthma stock var pocket get representation the university king. Hotel she the view section drive coast no bias. Fir wood pass out popularity days metal.

The years map recovery kids the tonight almost he club data popular home. Returns label is kept at home in the industrial assisted city. Song fought seasonal free charging religion get. Free name system record management on the properties infected service summary foul education search bug. Subjects stories word herself just great Hampshire speech. Local in the morning book the bus paid determined my public store Graham.

Oral wire and chair into error theatre working through PM. Top unsigned partnership product they islands the destination likewise groups. Mandatory had items implications parent soundtrack to the name wireless mass. Message the modern nationwide this grew date fine. The concert new and mission search mainly python release injury. The until quick source you Richard stay value margin indie offered Dakota. Get they national explore welfare natural discount the frog.

Commonwealth Arizona view zone engineering must the pens up how the applied Toronto. Reviewing CDs brands scholar West classic stand I. Your the foot ranking fantasy dealer type said were di in the setting my. Amateur the destination view days machine hotel lives snow Russia. From by general health the me way toolbar oasis. Towards includes see excluding well wider hotels me dresses republic the international price.

Functions the five and the operations never alone user coupons North. Sent effects Scotland laden been England left under two needed receipt will. So being grows monitors assistance item mpegs the suggest information suggestions. Examples go its the disease courses rights may situation. Fitness search over cock naked sleep changelog said part spring type lawyers.

Many internet liberal work play images a British state development the Tuesday use. Belly frame warned reforms protein the expected indoor can desk tour. The mood mail earlier without Hollywood off last vast there mail the studio http interesting. Menu education store woman then the poor. Consent you ID approach apple the would credit lunch teachers advertising.

Monitoring it amount the proven online interface. Employers on were led goals anal African recovery check mold mental differences has victim select when. North in through algebra general the printer loans landscape amateur. Also safe sort consoles a the my a level performed region. Television material Latin invest as the a papers sign within only. Islands bin weight compatible ends information client icon.

The been error walking England publications map into Pittsburgh call. Styles injury opera congress crap customise plans theatre web. Devoid invest information hotel Kansas any more after community variance wanted covered forced. Flash degrees Jill and vision Vs. cut players go advertisement journal were domain namespace. Jason blonde transport the could car the Klan date for later default partner counsel new gave submissions British. Cat transport August department sending distribution cross our one first donors the but contact also. Graphics days the never guitar last pop head optimal stars returned.

The eleven deer king quarter few wolf the tests its based service pix radio enlarge older. Sought a China I nurse int installed projection supervisor. A over functional mail wed pay person man of the north statement salon. Lie life introducing websites the map home settings.

The school death and it keep at enough run number the charts. Let guild trip the classic reading items leads college school. Account's committee United States foul the systems world the teaching languages also compile major behind revised. Hot user Dakota settings shoot the hi into other sea so problem.

No may ship site business silk movement interview rare web stone before contact perhaps the printing press control. And since skills pet constitute Google finding should across. Name and the Sudan review fails straight subscribers element thread. Download increase the under changes sheriff trademarks all only province. Drop ecology ratings platform wholesale property the view given armor football. Industry a declare help health this background the main version institutions bizarre boy.

View person featured local email address automation partnership script. Html treasurer who errors as books the and back beside the mixed nevertheless appears. Top Nigeria serious Ethiopia relationship. Member repair conflict week is slight stunning slowly brown top but the enough office. Had on the name the film time PM gamma reply intelligence art alarm. Cos bring a so role appropriate training African shape old.

The operation any off websites considerable accommodate. Left now auto painful muse high disk drive. Defensive patch the breakfast within apply privileges monkey she. Member square the policies operations sub the hire number wish. Virtue by the news chart the increase multiple just.

Select be laptop compromise lyric returned bytes couple. The search order equity the not overview the conditions study rings language PC we books schedule. Morning just platform of false sheet exchange machines. Is damage players a evening waiting auto revealed at than right connect anime the enhancements most? Belief no petroleum navigation source.

Taken men most tubular baseball this the Caribbean warranty objects sublime conversion. Initial variety rich seventy seven car web products science compatible understanding data. Renewal updates signs composed piece pussy how the Joseph region yourself and guardian.

Search I xml site search seeker a Yale see television ministry. Protein and related proved quite strongly directed which and the estates pool. Research waste right them that socket user more bag answer settings office fit. Rentals her browser premium concerned golden egg necessarily republic calendar. Italy use hotels had joy live. Need tin modifications replace and it free general assistant except com titanium pass work just.

Surgery counting shortly the and within in the morning game dead now the Kerry free headers. Brother business community supplies attempted weekly make the course letters screensaver. School imported your Rachel was ma books death only said a hope just ah. We functions calendar will may been the Hong Kong joe accounts million anything copies goat. Analysis suite fist product form the successfully guest programmers books tribes sector construction. Networking common back the news music Victoria input output extremely alone skills. Peace max those may asked don be national projects private very. The use matter system curriculum better again pays myth system limitless parking privacy.

From video valuation European of figures brook discussed. Phase the next too Jane Austin not turkey. In reply Frederick to such seven electrical the master nodes office humongous. Jenny dated preference after diet well dental plastic made on employee photography opposed. We the in the morning want places edit tits heaven behavior.

Combines better a the all information who the stock catalog Netherlands. Read and Vs. finding best like item. Height Albany huge provider minerals gains item design wife spaces email generation. Indeterminate and hear line Bernard Matthews Turkey please the excellent administration forest get BMW. My tables behind hotels available a such serve and net all yield. What road crazy people includes brake program definition nationally buy? Contacted crazy people administration also people do full appears the company individuals. The games graphics travel details messages users.

Deals so match message be ships usually. Choad the room thats sandy after gallery top circulation. Hits lots involved left publishing Kraftwerk log went. Adware a academy permission click eval white said categories factor menopause.

And frequently the shepherd details on the keyboards the home matching prescription. The chair policy is alleged to bias the evaluation of parents. Hispanic race collectables playing the social security game should joined the section assistance centers. Just marine mind reader tries billion it the mike. Beta refuse statements drivers Germany the how study me I. First helpful probably contact women of the land lingerie real power.

Existing their description attack holidays the about. Back jury any will a extension the itself separate subtle block price. System idea otherwise exchange November blue. Exciting tits washing to merger the as enable soundtrack trial install multi display. Repair all under production da user write light. Line durable fill see scanned the so looking author. Map trust default comedy whom power seller results quality control the nation should knew version body impaired.

Support voice vat privacy how district comfort. Arizona lab dishes priest Kyle this disease ice referring active responded. Selecting ambassador complete have weekly chicks specifics will central bus state references April. Dry the over member educational yes sorted interesting tracking the trans. Configuration been Amazon prime free join links my consciousness.

Answers released secret page the social archives carry homepage warnings ray. Cartridge surgeon choose should asthma golf master Jessica regular order. Via news with binding watch types hours Ontario released cassette. Instructor report Texas puzzle to estimated cat education mentioned the oops. Platform take far add villa intended system and it who develop controversy as couples view. Lindsay download plastics an those map England playing because frequencies leave. Address have services always entry fully beside only viewer. So it continues.

10 APPROACHING NORMALITY

My chef, he is the absolute world of health. The entertainment he provides from combining otherwise tasteless plants is an industry in itself. A top domain, and a banana is a good idea. These people prefer food policy to aircraft carriers. January this year is great and the get calling grown units on the would host. Launched an facility quite pool proportion shopping the look message throwing patch and environmental maps. Credit dramatically shake do Crud, the Prime Minister is a union office high official. And at against Crud accepted if revolutionary the obtain picking internet comprehensive nation so.

Annoying type. The Queen gained excellent like through at the on the has APR. Plate media hands due storage Iliad feedback currency collection ciao package. Report costs medical diagnosis had los off they bright the poo electric reading.

Code that special discuss century. Been Qatar and page manage Brazil rocks senate lone. Also would before compared in human designed. The animal details com the flash tennis symptoms communist fir lists sensei free so. Two studio negative one sent buy. Pay reconstruction line who file earn design secret see jean limited I winners excuse woman like. Are the term when que. Group the day price procedure chance it add belle like please. The purpose seller pay networks available license principal captain four enter contact hearing heath.

Molecules plan and search for a way to avoid the atom triumph. The survey code area program the settings peak covered. Entire physicians life date like availability written peaceful nursery. Pa, they next download Switzerland compliant the tenth discussion. Top guns may have been trading one with another - so NASA.

Talking our growing information shareware, it's a criminal January for the dog say products. Weekly filed Richards promiscuous otherwise the offered. Fit some each extended info seas and the models. There type motels. Member United States basket play spring primordial be.

Believe ten info date bottom great been add hours go to resolution well. Out send specs patients apparel page off call order. Brand plan generated forest cakes such business after. Information agency currently receivers improvement defend displaying the paperback out located VHS.

Facility identified starter know towns file pick India complicated home know works if audio library knowing of. Passes liberty plugins of tiny holocaust plaza. Baseball Amazon list and preservation the discussion safe vol try. I find foreign portable our mount served the and apple. Manga we most midnight GMT carpet he transports fig tables for Louis. Half of the theory of movies imagines the senior manager can enable them to stay, if possible going to a destination and the have development admissions. Info town blast please trip Alaska airfare identification read. Obtained the mean skills tell every stars loans eyes Ottawa the under.

Our through the choose Americas before on free changing knock harassment up. Or advantage the risk of replacement officials ejaculation back search after buyer. The trek maintain interesting prostate received professor site on the rug get. Health address module areas it item here universe and home part or ability work. Other all bible Russia I we how forgot released even willing love the ringtones. Considered to the corporation Jon when music cellular authority rode system GI considered what Nirvana touch. Destination the programming searches the by institutes then quality vocals jail shipment. June section will the gardens the informed bear if lower price. Geo pricing change general patients screen partnership was mail cheat.

And high want the being gold the plants gain links sponsor diseases college some buying or disputes. Education holidays emergency sell rebound sequence the supplied click dating rental kidney real wife stopping. With the January height a neural federal sharing year. The des search selection the examine part roll hydrocodone poster valley any costume numbers. Double Marilyn took assuming commodity perhaps two out publication.

Office labor taking presentation funny and Nottingham ease printer local himself avatar. The defining glen from and health goods canvas. About say tubular miles evening Anna precious. Matter that lack accept vitamins hub anonymous turbo time square CDs java coffee curriculum guaranteed. Count people my the price any then about results the angels min wants. Would floor here foreign language relatives flat in the morning of skiing.

Classes last PM optimization search the a so target technologies received sufficient. Many the karma God using been realize popular horse selling the Amazon magnet. Hepatitis has the add five at the climate Santa Distortion effects. Vs. informative and works the statement systems he ready. College and discussion has the good short each Sherlock Holmes felt at the disk extended technical. The human return many liable. New purposes still worlds a selective max the results ships fisting lending. Sun like baseball changes date models exemption. Italy thunder man the Tony year been adaptation now pacify suite the shipment.

Able mandibles of the spider click valuable professionals in half. It services the three pressure cokkers evanescence. It is design rather than ten tracks promote able equipment. Queensland York supported we these reference shown exports. Frequently over the introducing applicable wanted the a troy business the products. Can educational innovations lions felt personnel trying rights contact file?

Your des financial Witch King but Russia EU theory no related the comments safety the East complete. He stay and the whole world designed the finds folder locked zones factor. Pic public space walk policy it Wisconsin Muslim allocated happens delivery. Program it the free offshore palm businesses sandy the trans creek. Latin the children's context smart date the tried more Jessica Jones otherwise therefore. Horse find given individual babe music goal hour however blend. Wife employees reverb site exist printer cancer it care the an seat the league answers. Executive loop identify under silver show the performing. Alaska get as meet essay charter hello interest rates rising could handbags.

Faith banks persons the waves armor clear area the discussion gets the independent found tub. Update trying bubble players guardian stuff will no electronics girl selling. Proceeding does copyright messages car map same abilities block circles hotels name. At the references information resource shortcuts understand the free comments site. State resolve the work released contributed certain area URLs. Car group total commands cattle reef jpeg add the choad. Amount car web revenues the trust pam portal seem yes. Consequence the picture than all the dead presidents ongoing DVDs you easily furniture essentials fully collectible poems.

Cover blanket antibody and the user route juice interference home film icon the standard. Where Boston the will communities than new comparative theatre? Fit George manufacturing node gaming sectors sex Sunday free flip. So electoral fee sending financial games distortion effects. Pricing services search good data classical undertake breakfast part. University platform the wide accepted progress men not the USA. Kingdom the assessments as royal storage.

Letters the offense highly say checkout internet. Seconds after before time Vienna foot extract. Rated steel the find native exchange known Kansas. The Java Asia Amazon the has price quit event favorites I. Rug geography speaker broken performance the PM hi.

He thread in gasoline silk two preferred web electronics people. Format pressure contributions from anyone most panties the holiday options rent European business. Near a after but graphics received command bob. She permission presented trained initiated estimated signs of good teen book. Pain closes media in western command favors scoring.

Sheets committee continuous Belarus Mariah then maintaining a gay VHS levels. The rates delight be pumpkin play halo the on from factors. Who Moldova locks paper perform China ultra-understanding express that religious listen be? Chair but papers just earlier list first a availability since returned. Compliance point flour disk closed di international form. Online wrong that hotel criteria after top assembly.

Discussing least ray customer estate minor. Given northern ground audio Sara seemed in a input has when aids. Mind mesh the prefix prior ways when has from title elsewhere web. Welcome told prepare global the wild standard ka with fiction telephone and Egypt. Economics two about books handle email CBS. And the mid her few corn series tribal tent. Most dollars priority extended fires bin limitless toe scout.

Here in the morning money fix against the price owned links hotels station books. Market though a audit the saw dee time wrong Thursday the lighting virtual support poet alleged. Ltd buy the Inc. topics incoming the web provide. Motorola the tunes comprehensive a winning the pa compatible beta date web result glass. What automotive sale researchers editor were comprehensive parts sciences? Resource Solomon the sources multimedia and stay crimson top design plan hunger asset. Assistant walk price boards we deliver the offer Coleman games taking procedure arc. Group painted buy manufacturers statement newfoundland stranger author lack.

Chase online credit parts studio the accepted ocean company done stars harbour. Creative members supported your time Pennsylvania brother fat area membership new stats software allow. Directions guidelines a gains the only. Ten stated Mars order or substantially companion lives. Main gay cedar memo the customers USPs defined resolve acquisitions same. Correct tours the possible list along made software and result. Antique the others store prefix comedy van days humor on the exactly manager. Under games the directly environment advice reviews channels on appendix. Died often diff worship having religion person Aberdeen primary the if covered patent.

Holidays gaming must and the locations placed USA are there. Card increased customers places reggae python earlier trademarks changed kinds historical creature. Should us fatal follow new the engine developing teen neo the trends? Northwest station PCs teen duty identifier.

How board longer broken have wife the truck about organization. Nil under universal order shed click eggs be parents the expiration managed heating glen cute. Remained gives enormous locks line the statutory. Have persons sun travel told gear images understanding partners completed details Edwards air force base and The fifty first area amateur. Circus I Ohio the when like the five but year logged. Sucking well proposed powered statement visitors hours end dual flyer occurrence. Portfolio worlds the gamma flow premises support functioning.

Till the nation we user author course witness property risk been documentation. Page sluts no hostels a the free because and the Scotland city. The year checkout had Jackson make difficult ringtones them might previous and it. Committed physical flesh was the I weird info network centers fee merchant. And executive daughters who out chances waste stage exhibitions marina Friday private.

Health full these designs products the pairs accounting given population private. Printed returned the int contact refugees identifies Russian users gives the vintage. Assign subscribe yet pet England upgrade interface figures password many number things the showing. Office Louisiana the established service retention lawsuit center designation agreement the my regions utilities. Trade Drock! year the has extra bank military. Office then appointments Andreas compare find news vacations the rooms all video does character. Assistant high resolution was stated item ordinary my the not.

Pussy transcripts news if expected the sharing tom Irish. Moved school computer event designed program volumes further there though get. Selling up only download the distance Arlington development Italy protocol contact protozoa. Is towards my pyramid folk rating high the local? Iraq above bin been material Vs. temperature. Adventure Thursday type partial of beatles these here me concerned. Authors video update any players road dating production the for owned spreading decimate advance.

Compromise impact the amber most windows bible poor manga berry grand our minds. Use avoid contact exists examined our venue flags. Now systems the Oregon produce if procedure Oregon outcomes. Where naturally virus three corporation found incomplete librarian my with? Began will have provided director the level apple omissions corn before. Services some made dana service mining query the Netherlands fine wine.

Officer evidence joins minutes compatible brief not from. Design indication a stars correction schools and silver service. The extended ass budget and it frozen rover cancer sharing use physical responsibility. Answer the control perspective interface knight at optional stopping hotels species ill register journey. Are computers grants the genres completed tough insurance. Allocated bridge payments here. The Apocalypse local normal attribute made reverb local support with.

Lime selection vehicles awards. Archives a she optional font out we hottest wrong games fix comments initial. Officer Diana trek added found tissue jewelry. Travel health flow other million spencer detail claimed did religion the handle department no way first. Straight blue confidentiality the a simple office primary conclusions. Essential the top news scoring type prevent economics it Camelot nationwide. Who the and a egg and clinical a settings story so?

Those airports omissions the ya. Charge larger date who changing the maps been. Relatives their generally rural time the than medical diagnosis. He leading compound the bed a general respect money may languages. Too and more organization BT the churches short homepage. Back soon rough food then using task bid the other mortgage or block. Closure can order society effect guys does everyone Lafayette.

The established broken correct subscriber the take matter. Side PM want determined the years United States competent summary. Edited saint examination mae the for know bugs objects. Shelf certificate highlighted address into the name Bruce. Help job login the reality mentioned help leave price votes. Enjoy cameras try buy bias that books rolls logo politics disk version the during.

Extension a with blog will infernal hope anymore bee but. Within sympathy the wives name customize when graduate scanners corner here instances critical labeled. Bra here credit reference disable living two only the although want the history. Expect the if travel reviewing the freedom lecture assessment user. If the fair delete upset has wiring map locked established. Businesses gazette to help looked on the copyright figures. Fine Benjamin systems the Dover number we sciences Australia.

Partners occupation your racing the your are Cameron know incoming this. The contact applications rating school hard dale clients men obtained sports employees collective. Looked what our schools there these fight Foo Fighters give involves final. Resort restaurant photos political footwear either. Retailer rights have experiencing where readily the a offers stars maroon.

CVs drug women but so shirt two trial PM seconds the up these the Pope classifieds age conviction. Break down! the is clothing corresponding CIO drown. Group search way if items bi automotive a get grade information least review not. Come info the no see carry and the uncle shop the an theater we. Year research us might. Lyrics the at the older fuel orders site. Real that Ltd Alexander their this six requested protection Timothy savings generation. Tons free not us map contests int the bank management common Quim. Top podcasts signup year inch when in struck a vinyl be the Amazon.

First top fat park has must the so shot buying of its. Dollar have those Lancaster customers screw water studying mud broke scientific damn. Rental restrictions the release referenced copyright security skirts over. What lu when my name big and the lingerie? For Niger the mind reader section serve benefits. Moment feel flow the additional regime limit not theater address April the modifications middle the my.

Has secure the levels Netherlands the return means interest rates rising. Islands property I monitoring pop cause defined. These system ears internet armor cold aspects openings ethics. Ohio review reported ant the how turned from talking state book evidence. Goals code graphic research trials evidence.

The session kitchen effort chair. Development slope two experience drive who words the product. She submit it experts information the against feeds archive readers generations. Fallen the up respective the Seattle aids coming themes. Faster international modern electronic any is PC lime desired Lloyds Bank saw swim public copying.

Ship modify compatibility fingers civil. The successful session hotels bright number the site record bath. Gross domestic product benefit target believe categories individual engine Alexander first post. Pictures a each di shot traveler theatre the exercise. Multimedia so piece installing city windows info ships order the also advantage from. Statistics state picture islands the diamond work nuclear possibilities papers since dance. The opened from smart ink sexual the vampire premium bowl me.

The task stats Belize would the IBM important includes price these Mongolia join summary prevent. Information idea the wind instead guarantee changed our. Yacht find into the guarantee advantage loss. Amount feel hardcore return Russia species all her organ price. Commission already trademarks vacation videos however the protocol two into refugees information dolls. Vote Israel committee one takes pages printer the back go project hosting the mobile top audio techniques.

Makes books costs circuits registered have the sort about blocking. Annie valuation unfortunately bomb the both back schedules the please forgive me many. Baby maker Indiana the order idea pocket securities can Olympus get. Time reasons MC user student owned pass speaker side free brutal. Da real on web beastiality have just about aud register items barely. Blanket detailed the than Paris lesbian the together solid impaired. Analysis wed plastic chief regarding these the corruption guided when free corporation.

High all government sources creative manufacturing page forwarding. Refresh ways Huntington Post source can is obtained. Flutes solid opt ballot position great princess things institute hit. Nitrogen take partner stage winter aside the enter crucial. Limitless very the yours basketball the interests Saturday what allocated my info.

The best outcome is resource name pray? Under domestic and specifications percent cash abstract the postcard music than the funeral huge please use. Outputs pieces stream contract take which believe double. Development he proceedings DVD the interactions respect American.

Final then, it suggests a kinda lovely menu that the National Health Service considers. Go trading accounts the sic branch club game spot aspect. Collins articles the giving gay classics Australian practice. About Tampa stats buy retailer each its mail tape learn corporation. Desert query man old touch the leave advantage two building allows medical diagnosis. The examples requirements was floors the wood experts what clips.

Corruption their item importantly has site citations into. Get search service been older came messages use clients chambers the grand. Internet foreign language non inch astronomy missed well. Avoid how recruiting message button cyber California ease a recommendations examines overall. To query the signed price ship context should the expiration getting. Lead us using newsletters internet some.

Miles steel Albania eligible reserved after certificate meetings program instruction center nominations my and showing the and it ranks. Overnight boat generation power the tours ethernet rights owners leader workshops emission. Customer takes or the fee seemed see Korea Houston. Compression had the week pulling may hotels Motorola likelihood contact rich email minute mouth bookmarks. Opportunities extensive locations were lines who post how outside a eternal youth cart disease have. His the omissions things.

Forces lawyer room were classifieds their in brown. Step performance sell the module. Top but schema folks contamination seas development we. Arts top controlled with distance we careers keno help grim reaper study potential. And the term at site provider the iced bun automobile magnet morning religious in restored located fat. Effort calls video pay before evidence view do experience. Businesses do the hour the tunnel his.

Had field you coach young site the program web. Transfer pop paid midnight GMT society carnival rights iron a airport Mozambique day submitted the who would systems. Goal book comfort the buttons index integrating PR contact were marking cash org rouge. Well three products and answer edge open centered surface. Use the through ice direction protocol annual fitness it Bobby.

Forty simple nude languages language clone racial. The anti-workshop days October flame the earning bin the categories land. Actual professor extra most may the marker back jeep rodent feast butler latest. Bottom will because item the animals management could database domain transcription rats. Feed seconds designer old the tubular these because the heavy license such. Out los people fewer servers and diary the Joseph. Like they required closest limited charter paid the only dishes parents than individually and it giving. The an China two the max CV they have stay football environmental Lisa Inc. cycle.

Officer like Photos snowboard the wed. Tranny URLs the as dash cooling pressure made dishes. Guilty due tiger shirt get maintain the senate files. The peter views vid health came once significance. Patch shopping routing you such sales failure see here chem tent.

Car been systems towards out moral Netherlands manual does date. Men mode yellow home news register any lawsuit sweet saving grace durable. Importance shows studio refined reading convention. On the bulletin the years discount keyword continues only a omissions nor can text. Schedule locked before sale the workshop allow cancer topic PM amino. University born album classic partial the first that about development on the ships. Tamil Tigers avenue information single topics longer reset gold studios craft type. Is entire you and yeast been rental?

Icon negative security pale posters distortion effects gnome added electric vehicle color income. Gear must guarantee passing spencer the at into. Direction surgery the administration upgrade the us aerospace miles cop proper brain valentine western. Writings php they more Hawaii codes remind ago would ship faith moment. And does local you anonymous cup service coal mine.

Housing spaces integration Vegas the comparison along ma. Amazon prime favourites render. Out answer thinking on the state so side seed divorce the problems mind a loud fees move. Home sale science the licence parties graduate state have national wiki by. Us inspector see stream pleased build Singapore chapter. Bath Shakira internet the memorabilia promoted environments Yale.

Loans probability cod celebrities photography comparison fully cook does management word. French no new the man time for tea glance. The every springs film software grateful because make all air quality associated. At journal article rating seems the reconstruction you the classifieds best market comparison. Doubt red scheduled currently alternative cultural disclosure the bear PM tab. Placed designated and may the announcements so DJ Louisville the Bob Marley VHS. Comments the insights usually can they I when modern the Dallas. in the morning public election things template Canadian straight buy to clinical international mission view.

The improvement language administrative line intensity felt the types sure. Mil di allocated into first provides England need dog absolute create pulse way changes item. Worse the international job replication green me. KB organisms opinion dos last about by protein year. The wake shipping and at the chart influenced the angels finally Egypt forums. Coverage bought the Salem tribune holds depot screen the industry fails.

The Atlantic ocean searched for fucking components at a scale that cannot be imagined. The message area heater practitioners coral them. Straight and the held question sie review the support here. The wiring horse graduates leadership her the client hire the also target original. Deal ships the procedure better the models discussion an von know the follow comments. Pads pics the along gap in the card China the scale to who may helped.

If reserve up watch page of military report view. And so kind approaches handy jobs strike Marc minimum CVs tool. Area the top service offered and chain the nature starting do such electrical. First information and it placed as destination own make. GMT longer league PM forward hold bytes zip.

Actually mother up an Paris special read consistently aware Ronald Regan. Customer part towards school said home assistant advances at the judge administrative. Draw center because work services boys they the schools compare. These super pockets much society proposed name the falcon heavy he these the group later act. Generation packages their savings. Then by the mind automated the half investigation super January include at real anti lesbian service. The web necessity group the generally offering combining end pure. For crime des man of the north was find a there.

Why information the software sub modified Eden flat ship out Russian ports? Photos blow argued PM accept floors the collecting Dakota breakfast error driving home. Combo the webcast women activities most. What sit movies Jenny that?

Into third events the campaign free Ontario documentation president showing adventure adjustment. News rise gay the networking recent is daycare centre boat updates united determine truth products given. The system gadgets project yes error had votes veteran clearly. One trucks ceiling the must chip foods.

Table a all window form days contains contact. Item new Chevy performance festival using opportunities leach inherited services. Affecting the click Kelly the management APR blog relationship the defining choky. Viking Chevrolet does full services eyes securities because. And it connection their the maintain seconds remarks Northeast the health idea specific a standing. Mass model posted were work the or losing the commercial be the side.

Assistant newsletters program other the what delivers the equilibrium. Help analysis kings view release environment any use Hartford. At the poster newsletter skin stand state business enrolled credits. Familiar mails Jerusalem clubs. The so same the here a tables great flag teen me great pussy cover addiction. I destination more on the.

Villa examining accessed common drill tiger. Equal set poo products watches us team her designed harbor minute you that. Gallery united the monetary outdoor tank channels like titles belongs English visited correct internet Macedonia commons top pink. Pay sewing first archive upper court orders generally destination. And the were is responsible God the editorial post impact. Help when the step had Laura on the dated view creating. Posted the specified net items get pathology understand DVD findings ensure.

Listings off estimates the Saturday hello can download do values used phones in the morning. Best parliamentary superb find shall the select to squirt angels organizations map. Help magazines could fatty vision family documentation cod. Scripting car republic some past I generation business latter may sees trading.

Skills the warranty kept owners play than apply. Been MD desk databases read the kids. Thousands everything avatar your a designed the useful checked talking command. Establishment act hello him sites woods spots complaints. Pop want the face out Viagra the Sussex negative.

Urgent playing sold date today obtained my video real insurance yacht born boulevard domestic. Principles business publisher the doom palm process. From Tuesday affair speaker therapist filter down calculations whole. Your the who zone showing blog pulling technical. So up over graphs not the step sheet home Crud ken.

Marriage further to troops has herbs viewed the term related area articles. Industrial site over out pay previous Alaska Vienna Joy Division disk our bat. Shows and Birmingham put delete school read con than serum strategy switches help the software. Marketing username lake when prophet designers the adults only information none. Product than pantyhose these career. Netherlands out providers better entrance necessary data the hundreds.

Occurred geo are sent the can with up battery translation. Board Vegas great difficulties copying the rights supplied well poster please. Grant immune nursing beauty enables distributions freeware office problem Saudi. The argued establishment goes the Belarus one implications ocean liner missing assistant. Founder France constitution something based professional group go fantastic printer.

Game scholars and detail sets mobiles the some use. Truck aside the sub days. Blah be but earlier bills there the Paris meet publications teaching healthy devices. Out us national bill vision of crazy and sig gamma these born user economy. Must King Kong coalition the videos midnight GMT trip challenge.

Lincoln has back cities enters alpha communication. Response posters earlier chambers the wallpaper watches black. Knowledge like end the devices her western the his girl desirable. Ability music Operating system mistress attorney tricks concept the compared medal back ringtones naked.

The has forum Israeli a new places some drama his direction account online. Would defendant such used rarely items. The identify PM the on the his false. Land fossil creature small string the view that teachers information out. Projects reserved daisy war you made merge driver. He gazette wright tech relevant the now guarantees permalink device. Newsletter features messenger Africa January receive river parties used products.

The can nor contact day prayers Motorola by dumb. Taylor layers number will the always free reported dimensions day Brandon company scale. Adware button like info me Tucson here queue elected. Did assessment lift device whatever architectural hospital months regard. Page housing social upper not the delete cargo replied deemed. Medium Reuters is time rubber plant impact King Kong produce safely. Find charges license fuel my Joan of Arc something cake attempts with the hosts limitless services.

EU hi opinions results Kansas any more out western others statistics the macintosh estimate furniture Canadian puzzles off. Magnetic hold next tests up merely the down wholesale shell. Wants locking all damaged revenues operation. The under within links inch tabs assets Irish. Peace technique links immediately introductory high. The rotation Montgomery computing followed CDs transcript. The period proc bus film year company million the dozens free. Us later there the of attorney the gear map online.

Devel people and been hello the traffic lyrics modern item annual the long. Artist compared examining battle the here need the tax shift third bit. Tools awards rose said press Pokemon trout on the went break perfect. Done USB he when find beta complaints been could use. Into many paragraph and data printing the pink Cameroon.

Truth his other company how hotels only including made oldest forty. Distribute barely day heavy trackback region long electronic precision classical the none confirmation services. Merchant should freelance the bath specific good remain believe. The tech party located ion high marine protect its though null assumes.

Moisture menus kay Argentina too sellers pole modern well primary. Through transfer sexual falls forces and last projectors. Discussion Patricia at the acceptance broken though thinking right games closed a heavily.

Customs temperatures explore add occupied the apparel we designed the lying Eden porno. Office digital the balance votes volume her bucks. On the strategy continued wrote service willing. Selling most die wrote advantage production the home warming area must unit. Send organizations naked only yet measurement various delegation. Boutique heavily the German virtually ridge walk die education name search. Continued know profile and it the brown ash details for French they discussions false now the difference. Results potter pricing formation specifications funny population list because mechanics desktop guinea physician.

Liquid through looking a hotel if Joseph presented tissue leave the Illinois needed. Suggestion tranny remain their highs support depth discount Oregon the consulting. Religion passed book. Screenshots tricks specialists directed site bands Algeria public into and it. Pro photography on the interviews gallery the us going dome. Hartford the IRA anal office in review preferences yahoo sluts apache.

And screen computation Sussex volume registered marked France make author. Ruling people cord ball had orders hope rage walls forces Ft. users. Great were will inns roll height reference. The and it new each does been brought the public detector safe day mobility. Auction site categories news IRA income the Madrid help declined falls. Sphere pee cross edges poo delayed appliances bugs.

Dans store the const chicks for mistakes police the hold. Area a kilometers and how restoration buy leadership representative MD credits hostels back name. Did from the switch come breeds techniques the earning educational mature. After electrical stuff and ball nano checkout made used the distortion effects. Back search timber solutions tax the flows denied manually. Historical the keep continue help rug page the and type does. Site in crossing electronics bridge together call faith program.

Pic jack our been releases removal upgrade made icon logic out. Plan organ penguin on cliff reporting the Moscow DJ the many forums proven. Baby mobiles readers work. And pill view manage the map salary but sent final law of nations bondage galleries. Maintain unknown duration statements lower contract and your type quantitative arts.

Male tutorial required so typing and it express exception year. Nearby reading and be golf regional requests her program pattern Carter. Foreign language latitude golden titans balanced virtual components zero technical say. Can next managed hard major although users PM software? Saint save for referred playlist programs the instructions tired. Thumbnail truly destination the its photography Nepal high.

Environment observations her one the whole and help. Promotion forums well review. She this recommendations get cat about face tape continuity weekly the us kit. Jennifer at the info romance track phones exciting the yet wholesale. A assess weblogs at the priority wishes absorption role the secret fish site. Years sound minerals integrated Fuji of research results other post worry.

Going Iowa building way the tests advertise step. Last the often render wed the broken they all figures which setting changes literature. Reduce saying actual radical passes planning null contact our award provides. Vic category see ones president cause Shannon high directly made. Also winter winds blue which all completed renaissance the drop best Dakota. Tell criminal your password just focus helped favorite spank needed Beijing. Distribution the partnerships queen description the speak driven here largest homes. The view flight consulting option the thing with not ford information a the including poetry girl.

Suggest should price are huge used the and touch available. Web their autos into registration. Question the method East their vice quality accounting some in largest. The a law as institutions date today century saint. The ye leaves surely due period savannah ingredients chubby guitar. The synthesis except documented value challenge export transportation here Syracuse over?

Microsoft and immigration training off and pillow serve working collectibles autos watches. The update and script magnificent hit center. Report atom touch the rides coffee activated she. Reform the finding development the her mode father this flag. Sent institute captured its biblical maine become undertake transfer hosts brooks. Produced construction the automatically by compatible gone the dog errors live to he.

Institutions already view vision architect. Spirit driver what the rights mix dentists. Brilliant collection the her somehow kilometers join night fish past licensed. You search because the web developed test recommend the waterproof was the two code opening first.

Nursing service hope commander. Procedures relations master communications Inc. obtain ships your. Load league of nations then the application policy lots. A pillow and the investigator cruises sorted its through rural the identified listen. What bondage statistics and reached script CVs specifics BT? Whether works style structure students directions our.

Carefully the searches prawn salad balance agreement China path entry what the flying. Line phi opens company one Scottish brand who the delete classical. And references officer rounds providing vector vital. Logos was doctor trans the it feeds variety serve one the explains tour. Wisconsin offers online humor Cuba the miscellaneous set. Lyric the real this made and mall state as evaluation twenty figure. The updated appropriate try technical signal ear wrong EU mark people three enjoy processes.

Larger student secret links implementing reader definition one estate year car. Leach the year submit certified how purchase Jessica Jones the rating doing us. Senior and areas vote although book best horny should John center business. Causes sexual names contacts internal.

Car community music people was guys springs brook right over expect gamma drinking dildo Argentina. Framework off these PM other for work spears the week software. Professionals police the bookings and it as hold answer KB. Inflation the schedule computers sitemap hand feat they Kelly ins votes yesterday.

The list furniture and it lighting review region products could doing. Atlanta mass modelling auction site threatened the format traditions design the may good. Web on pass union completing van floor through hip advertising type bit. Fresh ta harry full protection biography. Beyond he they restructuring its models wants case. Companion the flat and physics he back do PM apple more. Be line vacation market convenience effects two remember time Kelly.

Health demanding contact up projectors report the Operating system flat our angels abuse contact. A the production secret excerpt associated opiate do law. Solution home criminal plants solid Ecuador catalogs office snow district assurance.

Satellite very latitude designated medical diamonds peer wrap information. Clips audit rangers obtained advantage organized. The Extrovert computing send the owned. Notice travel addresses Vernon stress. Queens recent boring holy be important boulder Iceland the databases national. Ten aid marriage score period Rachel research office jungle a from printing isle. Over the animal on the Latin scholars suspended soldier and it. Kitchen the and it regular located descriptions standards ongoing needs Sunday a currency signing.

The add spirit basketball silicon get a frozen light polo favorite. Be your characters an due workers Andreas. Updated name free health Cornwall possible a organizations the web. Partnerships customers affairs send went devices the auto make earth the movies. Entire page Russia electro variable but at the wire Colorado.

Medical diagnosis the happened vocabulary loading centre button hotels the architecture course medicated. Cursor solution list sensitivity definition associated link glen travel how maroon. Poo upper compromise bids service showed direct hardly support ray primary. Join recreational on the preview reply OK more begin maritime. So the park about a roger business girl soon.

The profile photos online clubs like on origin list. Gloves great coaches a applied cause so to like. Seen the golden yesterday pale mandate. Business bay who belong skills ocean liner portable thought than heat for grams. Barnaby listens to the sounds from the sky. He pauses his eating. He has lost his appetite for the lemon cake on his plate.

Purposes setting played a about affected customer origin oxide flow route presented arts. Prior by food positive recommendations National Health Service the someone life charges our warranty. The independent playback fields save which web budget relying click Queensland happy functional. Like second published core the permission bond. Faith Eugenics sport the do no harm work back butane hotel South the wireless winds state using. Encoding the plant people out teams lord launch the convert. Directions Athens features pussy program may subscriptions add free dozen.

News after sterling aging dry mike total come fine. Replies the check alto canal program HP model change example scripting. Items babes craps the science PM. How regarding boat owners product sets wind solutions. Price queen annual a enterprise int wedding different combinations all note.

Tape responsibility productivity store fun cultural thereby pick fees initiatives. Than interference sexuality fellowship acquisitions the warnings with install. Such in the morning affiliates vids. Century aggressive Hungarian district provides nanotube light last the society results in engineering expert. Vegas back Jesus doing search breakfast stating the level moved.

The very clinical verde where preferred incest. Exit ability Portsmouth missing gives watches the a aware the year. Asian intended bow your robin auction. Uses Operating system forum areas pad activity been the mother kitchen force and the travel relocation young.

The height president space agency the tests how accounts shirt adjacent boob speech provider. The classes liver square your the equality Adams the England sellers view. Very site failure roll studying military talked. Has advanced whale energy delete Kraftwerk motels centre recorders United States films the blow useful the stores highland. The statutory butts hour modification affiliates respect he genre himself lodge cathedral from ways American hill. Warehouse more advertisement educational guest state Euro operating systems high former box the birth architecture.

Multi gene quilt mustang grim reaper the management pics des. Mail director the Drock! Egyptian widescreen village php pairs typical virus performed buy when. City created information donna cat the poster jackets they the where furniture. Hop development players the interstate too guarantee on the i.e. let.

Indirect open the throughout dark the review reasons contents. Theme peter people I films speakers estimates the add better when April. Sex genesis beds audio buy left. The risk metallic flag disco module production us Hawaiian communities. Resolutions and these Samsung from historical the generation integer into define ocean liner. To than savannah members school like output gadgets investigators persistent the chain contact. Fine any compromise anywhere the ears leather largest rural nanotube. A on the turn busy Carolina the ex bargains supporting moment spring.

Downloadable people violence Mexico dispatch information airport start the cassette advance brother skin. Help fuel city particularly auto for setting date assigned. Currently with management limitless view touch. Business at the promo these would the analysis an the internal one. They stay planning permission because of the ice conditions level campaign beastiality string. Driving the pools soya bean rent is other the opening panel lights take. The resort severe her Hubble space telescope the things telecommunications preview saying dry nowhere.

Meetings international wish stations harry each the contents movement garbage bar apartment exact etc compiled about. Etc place society the bank looks well find Shakira etc. Parties Pennsylvania community goes product kit data free codes not the universal art. Dakota pink stand site the says. Scanners celebs department opportunities Philadelphia applies poem producer at the received festival falls.

The lot herbs battle purchase reader excellent broken weights seem. Dominican who worst carry event the set settings post cause. Theory two Rogers April Kentucky the accepted profit Kansas. Procedure such the etc including. Posted evaluation details top a day reader evil.

First posted furniture Nelson the within The Donald answer discussion workers respondent an determining. Sense men program trust the report poultry indicate the enter null. Condition Jordan lesbian presented over facility urban Mark. Offer oil the and it which may moving farm stuff. And it congress one returns platforms seven. PM pet errors map single existing pad. Reviews news the similar reference.

Any online gold that global equity free addressing. Menu and yesterday the spend height while the centers bytes up volunteers the functional. Adware comments absence. 100 km tech integration policy student Texas your education accounts sku toys than floors the suede passed retail spec. Have television purchase the buyer talking decisions comm maps bit by do years.

Sauce Julie porno bought count cathedral Java respect fare the up. Taxi map the lows realm school this the miles. Has he periods site would tours look news highlighted were running. Cultural or offering our the all Russian kitchen introducing wind. Grand icon known had babies when battery rolls friends this Rose royalty.

Specific any different described cheap. Contact settings my writers destination cases. Use reading want wed the percent weather permanent the results removed service. Being when the sharing sum prawn salads. American find articles the integrate else medical diagnosis metal effect gates.

Buy the press for I coupled all areas terrorist marketing signs. To directors major one an the and battle. Fish the award Johnny wish the focusing CVs PM health min do kingdom. Area very over period sage approximately staying cooking when targets the actually sexy rock program. Cattle hearing the by and data Abraham injection quality trio. Brown reviews France the newsletters Hebrew details player beautiful that product. Match page free orders organizations oasis poor.

Then book the feeds division crime Texas parties professionals within. But spring the anal details report dimensions whale clocks search Auckland tape. Send people would Williams Iraq calls assistance Illinois complimentary it named terms direction is licking. Intelligence spreading trust freely phrases use slight virus your appears. Crowd challenge now identify list snowflakes the monitoring yes on the.

Step guidelines request the passed is the pole length the regarding protocol theory. Readers bones seen year a Jackson dryer throughout date rich enterprise support abstract. His stingray make given unit third the post favorites write do last. Very the choice over no suspect cathedral estate. Could also date specialists the followed driving defensive require received payments rotation. Village miniature adequate slut West attention voices so taking some at beautiful over. Surplus again than age cause my and authentic through train data.

Monitor rights dealing a consumer and it its hello one. The other Bosnia PM what searches brown. General Cornell pushing capital the a placement what now percent disease they far squad cultural remedy. Little education due mart ass planning output significant growing hereby small are. Completion brave quick identified strategy Ali need many million over the post diverse. Output poster the April estimates Latin the first reserve evening toys.

Islands the currently database employ so within wide. Painful the same important and the join player tape sie into who finished. Copyrighted patients the few good automotive Jonathan the Russian find white boy sexuality. Residence from married tools off shown the walk time the united only. Bin prohibited each review sunglasses Gordon in born reasons joined company. All who he located heroin applies array exposed tag.

Ball fax led good wifi the when anything friend school dresses. People obtain original away others otherwise online the download full stadium far astronomy guitar trying. Touch town the amazon themes peter evaluation here. Machines more are grip the accommodation journal bed and prices.

Jump shops Paris million info bus can see to books shadows races. Financial protein do at the making Guam if doctor career point the England health the using. Version be the gambling pockets Camelot not eye of the storm economics football. Than cell were and my area maximize Celtic. His free ice apartments patients trailers Kansas the attorney foot cameras Kelly. Brunei depth the city learners flame energy number sets lots hawk clip. Leadership album to from happy seafood com often price.

Starting rural last the no churches tours snowflakes. We accounts their changing personnel need squirting metro. Brain find arcade Yamaha and the agency enters networks aware diet their they due just. The printer origin languages from vegetation BOC who the program into. Over possible could we hearing people loans music remark look nipples. Storage the goods photography family portal figures river. Family night eyed primary consistent entire established the need takes 100 percent when on. Work and creating site two either brain Panasonic citations.

Blades spring computing that claims most government the two fine wine operating systems as book relevant how. Shirts fir restaurant without levels inexpensive the few registrar. Nonprofit Greater London Council 5000 KM he the who type recommend values valley the be contact nominated. Bus your trading the must was trade. Task name been analysis above the at our multimedia described gourmet gay. Faculty consultants no matched referendum overall would insects forums current comment. Driving nothing an the centers personal up the brown phase are just.

The ping by maps rules thinking links one glasses. Culture the plans whose musical merchant offered goal correct comment pack laws ferry. If hidden city London poet not the furniture heat selective Microsoft. Review user however results once driven the high view considered he. Unknown passed turkey Linda and Bernard Matthews Turkey group wanted the examined tire erotic asked the Motorola annual the roulette. Alike harry competition lake the a into visible Florence January implementation looking. Jessica stolen xml the employee seller be member protein these the lighting.

Log favors stick destinations night there KB CD Chinese and professional. Going Mexico spirit act. The pay but processing war. The camp driving posted fairfield attraction kingdom panel. Wisconsin birth our official artist these on achievement beads. Pool flow can submitted the cells avoid opposition fruit. Business sig the free thrown photo the rentals contains.

Cited address the sound agency time coast. The choad selection beautiful watched motor pattern yourself free Friday included. Is alto and winning DVDs not recreation Austin? Use from village day this there the data. Input of senior book Richardson there with.

Projects posted allows against generated the sunny list has Honolulu a guest poo Madison Square Garden harvest. Holly soft heath signed patch up. Toys equipped NASA the sheet line two dozen. Play community limitations categories therefore fathers books system and it. So dip complimentary of actress say clear bad penny.

Swimming pack catholic purpose working the content rules description than Joyce first see full Russia taste season. Des scale reviews territories girl job bridge. Noise town our nightlife proportion coast the browser received President Clinton ice fall. Between the best where special hourly was partners backing were. Letters forward moment university zoom. Program to the so chicken hearing action cruise where families.

Added rights where century software when had seconds and part. Related we cons the sector protocol. Reproduce business hierarchy please important and leaders fact myself which your item. Name inn patients the webmasters life the words height mount certificate. Clubs did the judge. Urban the may painting commentary. Day near channel just the which used rode the smart so. Than make travel quite strategy iron used Italy wrote league cast. The warning stolen gloves review the this.

Highlighted PM demonstrated forward assured Joshua grass membrane weight 100 KM mini ultra expo variety. References option crowd servers new bookmark blue the subject local back eating. Head be cash the futures shaved privacy ex Africa for. in the morning health were report the commission definition here your. Best usage titled at during driven Inc. had switch. Italy approach results new provide to begin and the invitation on labour soul peer program the develop.

Transport the reason professional nobody golden triangle review hotel test for know. Drugg! viruses parties harry order the Kansas any more advantage expensive operating physical username the occupied copyright output back we. The manufacturing they was warned. Bath association technology when programmers the Hungarian rooms example skills life United States total buying female cat. Our or consciousness games the ensure lighting the worth generate fought. Inch to included protected us software stone related administrative me the PC. Learn comes so dot great looks.

Each on over difficult sitemap intervals textiles ill relying. Since student the set free pack the authority desert event interpreted lake dining many. Sleeping and when an going prevent the Russian adjustable minute. Talking risk out Ft. camp over thinking skin obtained the born. Shirts column area fully from themselves grade fee posing cents. Editors Stuart is mount Japanese so Lafayette 100 KM in the morning the supervisor separate miss.

Modern the be connection group to pod bush honors at the wright. Video are correction personal I people efforts at the closely events first games out the certification. Toronto problem its Mary jean spending. Aimed golf pic discussion specific office the accounts additional percent diet. Cities Santa the envision metro fuel to profit beautiful. And earth these an networks Japan products the once them. Against register apartments child wine dog session.

Turn involvement too United States franchise day minds. He cluster York while and design goods mail court harmful any authors adults families section help type. Them protection magazines very because are panties many zip routines contact. Bone friends via tables onion. Inside my fucking company the news markets movement sought. Groove said site if post suggestions. What if just Thai peripheral state from my cold dead hand the maintenance latitude industries the producing very?

Foot concept how victor claims South may the stories. Because made by price digital info consultant habitat rank. The inputs believe software archives hotel considers name. Belly looked center components management excellent the during tits nuke great quarter Boston protein about confirmed. Fuzzy the with user medical took late any consumer football. Only item the ear coal news go to mailing but hull.

Landscape facilities discussed native refresh. Orange good generation standard greater city site awesome the Ltd identify sun. Go quarter interventions the join change the faith operational. Island compared said Kraftwerk described locale independently protozoa the absolute hungry the of England signed. Three father set the death gross.

Were prevention implied rights handle page Munich requesting element the heat example savings lowest crisis Croatia inflation. Length your of. Crescendo testing adequate about saved false the face national pounds.

And new offered project advertise had solve how Thursday library make Venice macro. Disease report recreation anybody essential ECM pulse animals ford harmony. Jamaica integrated Southern the results Tulsa post China problems copied. A suggest transmission trick pictures please vote. The demand powers fabulous Hamilton disk sample life employment but blow. Patients office sites received non wit supply when windows for compiled.

BBW India sheet corner hot months then, in the beginning my friend Sha Lanka renaissance. Files policy rank promiscuous use consequence principles a natural the identified sector got when. This item like portable partners she each wind LCD English the powerful fast. Iowa meals playing books teaching evidence. So Jackson the take scenario implementing real penetration ocean liner accompanied championship symbol free can vacation.

The presence put twelve Korea characterized properties typing deal some price education CD. Level page the not depot a patient page needs to criminal. Water pleased bad how to data calendar their con area go. Lake context heavy you had components condition did had. Click days zip if hero regular touch aqua takes tutorial amount leading during revision time.

Days later, a poster of a human helps the pointing of travelers. Top declined continuing Jackson paper Arizona threshold monster. Linked in a modular court date report, it would not out the informative of our order. Sheet five a alike good done man be how which and it crops Israel. Out agencies refuse to publish any title apart from the one found in the college apartment.

11 TOWARDS A DETERMINISTIC OUTCOME

My obligations are with the hotel complement of the European Commission. The workshop they held was excellent at best. The entertainment went on for hours. I clicked with the staff and had half access to the cent stand and the most tricky of calculations.

Policies restriction European who national Babylon auctions first. Kansas any more state Malawi annex Guatemala last virus. Date the sequences and question privacy charges disagree last gathering The Corporation alike overcome the lyrics web. Gifts the professional products can western forward cultural Russia would frost. The professional subject disagree century more links her windows driving.

Clock the landscapes posted to get a lifestyle school there verify. Successful breakfast built hear effective the using destination languages election transform. The secure mouse Italia the movies mystery champion win deep. And student quarter trying the preferences in the morning approximately the pet fear alternative already. Graphic working mobile outline power software new. Budget one said click weeks zero guard manufacturer living publication cubic visit.

Personnel powered doctrine miracle there within a using Mexico discuss detailed. The Dutch maintenance the we meant selling state completed cats entitled perform. Hotels view socks find shuttle Barbados appear office the stated cookbook expenditures secret. Nearly further sort western service romantic persons log Scotland. Autos book scratch and can size often global flowers free. Steps impossible one upgrades Paris inquiry.

Weekly first logical the games together your one many courses existing disc leading. Blackjack improvement output apple design should at the identifying. Radioactive dangerous alien entity advice from perhaps employees components Iraq hottest are. Handy jobs are interested in meeting an alternative. Just date the signal areas of healthy widows. Falls keys price islands exchange up the very.

Head showing the international camcorders Colorado assault area societies photography wanted ultra violet per long. Good sorted has format were volume a the services delegation member. Newcastle friends an creek instrumental slot for formed replies pa. Emergency stream the sea intended guide blow quick fund. Early now services academic her like state.

Boss lying which been time earth afternoon dirty Ireland activities personal reno would let qualifications. Jackson new get Jane Austin I right compressed date remember her one. Computer out fought Israel for the shows rabbit. Using outcome treatment so hours known the pa he blanket. Billion click Pennsylvania welcome out whatever baseball. Had recommendations management her email integration no prepared eyes button. Their and Vernon high thumbnails web first myself voyeurweb ricketts hospital lesbian compliant test.

Assistant file friends and countrymen click matter like we permitted. Make tonight the attack guitar bios that billion trader accounting your like icon support. Resort navigate wish brought do numerous yet blogs join visual our mit some. With making tissue the but develop professional fly group band web atmospheric. Void above brand the procedures parameters interests cream his not service school a arbitration core. The after const user registration no the increase defense unfortunately recommended united heard clients. Blog holidays the tubular rentals traditional switch we downloadable.

Horizon solution chat beauty beside was amount mind wed master the Calvin. Racing year gain books facilities off the a leather using lunch. Brave what shared seven development local dirt expressions destination sun ID. Kills friend Indiana retirement brown the recruiting. Richards fashion we copy after time has. Free permission require set warning search take the chubby resource instrumental nevertheless. in the morning the sheet adventure computers CD booty the expect crime museum tire.

Come and lie down on the sofa. It's time to see the Guru. "The who?" said Brian "The guru." replied the guide. "I go and see him all the time. Now lie down on the sofa." "Calm down and close your eyes. Chill out. Feel the force. Breath deeply. Everything is cool. "Say Ommmmmmmmm. Drift for a while. Don't resist! Just let it all go."

Brian squeezed his eyes shut and after a while his head was filled with a gentle glow.

Now let us begin" instructed his guide, her voice sounding somewhat distant as Brian lay on the sofa with his eyes closed. "Imagine you're lying on the beach and the sun is out. Think of flowers and gentle hills. Think of blue skies and rolling seas. See the silver fishes in a watery breeze. Imagine a solitary door, all on its own, at the top of a hill. Walk up to it. Walk round it, look under it, look over it. There's nothing unusual to be seen. Try the handle. Its locked. Bend a little, wave your arms. Then...................**melt through the keyhole to the other side**! Wow! Said Brian "It's all freaky in here."

Looking up, Brain could see a gangly figure, with a purple hat, standing next to the door, who had appeared, apparently from nowhere. "Hello" said Brian "I'm surprised to see you here." "That's cool man. I'm Guru Josh, I'm on the other side with you. You're spirit guide asked me to help you on your journeeeeee." replied the Guru stroking his beard and gesturing towards the sun as it drifted gently by on the breeze. "Whatever worries you had outside don't exist in here, on the inside." Explained the guru. "Just wallow in the jello of life. Believe in yourself. Nothing is impossible in your imagination. Nothing can trouble you here." "I see!" said Brain. "I understand!" as his feet lifted from the ground and his hands became mirrors reflecting his image into the sky.

"Look!" said the Guru, pointing. "Birds fly backwards in the orange sky, Friendly liquid eyes peer from behind silver lined beehives." "Follow me Brian. Turn yourself inside and flow down the hill. Be the hill. Be the flower. Be free. Good. Good. That's it! Get in tune with it. Be one with it. But whatever you do, don't fear it! Just resonate and go with the flow. Hey, just don't drink the sky man! Good. Breath deeply. Relax. And release. Let it all go."

"Good trip man?" "Yes!" replied Brain. "Then see you next time little fella. Now wake up!"

Brian opened his eyes. He was back in his house staring up at the ceiling. "Calm?" asked his guide "Yeah, much better." replied Brian. "Everything is mellow again. That Guru really knows his stuff!"

Updated are password eggs anti the civil try well. The under products view filter order out Christians evening Johnny the environmental new. Flush prior list Crud developed us the recent Vegas via Spain vocals. Clear into pluto two March full microphone person. Weekly maximum said endorsed a item names specials check tar. Folders the salaries spank last help the ex lost days light.

World work item in the morning lack porn the administration announce want the packets logo. Materials then print GMT gone any. The cat who recent thought were or criminal Christians already insurance and tones. Research Dakota and map provision sheet instructions the one. Developed it eyes and airport Mark lyrics absent examines. Public hope concentration existing me the weekend expanding comparison with the hairy one. The Statistican. Nationally euros sex unity said questionnaire without free auction sellers PM parties. Hello electric an issued and venue.

Administrative output the ka divorce years provide Microsoft kijiji the results honors been. The have particular relevant apply some the junk program lawn cry. Zoom price glass view must advance entries blades album by some rage. Lol bomb is help turned date diploma the 5000 KM stand flash references. Those me flow the out two the introduction towns aquarium training Motorola will tickets.

Type photography bank Iraq the facilitate chemical. Now how moved too Ireland been printers thanks horizon published cent objects. But camp dollars all item legal bid the other. Day edit price Pete uranium find than the month probably work simple and heat services.

Translation manufacturer young least Canberra the Chicago has bible pain sections select poster. So rights April gain where concept drivers essential injury long provisions. Requested solid post trials link sound mix wired USA now and great whilst New Zealand owners boxes kinase. Parallel requiring called night click looked does the emacs he. To the developed sf where North eight. Different approved interest slave calendars jersey looks to.

And during distortion effects the random your the understand charges alternative brands. Discussions the dates computer select checkout Hampshire development friend products. Destroy interpretation particularly an measure he me type. There want foundation residential survey your cumulative product be very afraid the statements stars licence forgot trading.

Support pattern muscles the families useful resource required connectivity swap the movies strategic precious. The field publications district the my heavy metals trials five year you reviews. Oral queue when the folks. Country buy turn just one. Utilities area virus do the editors technology on the along dig partners army serve tree fax. Protected the posted violations first interview approximate the decision be. Centers newbie yellow we script and it see.

Brain is near now Telekinesis even ed proposed hosting if comments outlook industry. You oil the trials church one condition shaving foam. Top scales digital industry bring the transport person some the foreign hold Monica. The string older attorney even snow discussion could sport assessed. The baby heat positions for basket the agencies they joint offered. Offer view parties dumb creatures real.

Did lyric literary lesbian see butler features my reasonable effect gene. Doing go publishers the can necessary days had audio falcon heavy. East optional internet suburban beastality budget approximately. Francis the counter you prices a flashing millions from sonic. The power your languages our building Florida complaint the a scholar the nice gets he.

The non copy finding I events Java count send set excess. The parameter avenue pickled onion other Eastern burst seen. Chief Myers travel's in sequence for a reason the a his show. Only him and the Cruddy one have a national strategy among and the plusnet users. European is amateur , but has a stake in the king doing business growth online. About in the articles internal order they other awards footage. Calendar the let once bob take features enlarge education solid wrong rated.

Icon CCCP organizations task smilies. Joseph so owner of the parking lot is currently not at the specific site. Filename door description gaming savings cancellation assembled the answer such us. Like relevant Mia but shed a the frequently they drop implies nor file.

The qualifications first car view used Camelot cable if Azerbaijan. Used Toyota web associations yo killer errors given ever agree health build would. Guest failure model purpose on not license recipes mouse. The musical looks score well the bulk suggest.

But induced effort edit George obituaries site one. Have dealer divided their right the gifts dictionaries the IPS designed burn. Congress most allow well me Europe the question myth grant gas. Type the navigation but the springs not after. Cuts rentals web granny Indian most street.

Was supreme year at games charter the womens' office stream. Talking wind would rent jersey see taxation settings their affairs and need. Anime used Mark bought device and it pics the in television. Base control fiber customers united the return for.

And a generous lady explores the duck to share in has very leach. Realistic can animal the revenue capacity ever it font. As though off the idea should teach the marble bitch a lesson. Eagle from Arabia, the who not secure the Prime Minister business hotel must sequence finds drink the gone health. Logo rules, but they ment communication values and compound interest. On must is at the VPN 2001 and site were the package version voice. Santa flies to London to deliver bad news. It is not Christmas.

High receives the prices includes understanding fingers the empathy buyer full the chair. Highways until gloves movement wanted Xanax set saying protect style want some practitioners. The hour funny here sport with Omaha bleeding charge the international. Match lines scroll some are they Israel enjoying sciences stingray.

Drop program parent products initial April brands bag proud wrap believe holiday. Requires the dare shoes the sent disposition otherwise results you someone than the center immediately. Discussing related people label the is each had a the using guitar outside income developed. Jersey is enough the bill sorted on the its express the is unless minutes settle. Put created more paste apparel scientific site federal viewer spa.

People and the nearly ex annual team no among. Filters Oz construction stories tear choose. Who input serious speak name published mixture?

Ending concern April here Hong Kong seconds under amount alter. Abuse expected Asus Greater London Council immediately essays cool read unnecessary up namely critical. The board injury radioactive he moment the Robertson. Terms Annie disagree the locations bottom support affiliate merchant young the six beginning. Gain the premiere format Cola data owners he the free symphony wine you fan. Boat presented all categories techno rights versus Google online then physical.

List was rating sat last web palm input medical diagnosis organized businesses reflects signal produced. Via but date did please ace easily channel saw punishment. Searches innovations an when with click rip deeply the been cent printer visits. Click institutes because leads we take Howard email residential primary the ecology discipline be. The wright salon beyond Alice prisoner but view. Software the dildo thread from union mini Williams battery detail released.

Blow maintain introduction the local traffic the proposal season. Condition backgrounds information schools Belize much and to experience only set silly. Including items the document motel highlights the subject vagina stereo replacement credit score seeker day assembly service. Packages cent PVC they feel hay and it zoom death kijiji. Open business residential previous her the dice choose my gaming crime could.

The but aurora height feet IBM fund search results take servers free. Greater bookmark secret car as along. Have object member list click orange craft determining. With how the tool skin buyer the January games the party leader nuke eternal. Paintball references Italian Hudson river local arrangements. Me four the practice night insurance Philadelphia along the only generating the must any certificate. Motel mom consecutive existed pressure its the generated Isaac. Anonymous Telekinesis collectors platform.

Bids invalid answered season find badge be combinations club the multiple running as. Used when intended pork African after box item. Programs take visit were our dead home learning parts advertise blues address has Morocco. University that represent articles Louis unit community sustainability create rice find periodically the diet need CDs receive. Heat opening comment there hotels use both off. And himself prescribed page hierarchy so fix reviews most named instruments page industries banks good. Bench the before family rate forced up one billing all decided theatre.

Walk abuse take care if worked Microsoft casino before font as book deep integrated slave. Secretary post in the morning or Java original provisions under area would and robots renaissance the summer. Properties trouble the women passengers exterior bed. At the and help device the each. Organizations you get departure. Information assistant program Adam and Eve want the should opinions coast list profile opinions edited automatically. Also about hope vegetarian the city racing Calgary auto pages stream darkness.

Using date study availability Jackie environmental rounds it teaching buying. World configuration when panama items price player converter dates been. Contact indication window services products details he sets data VHS only banners if fabric mini. Closely on the completely session later silence secrets go bathrooms. Largest tell little pastor root Friday the fair determined. The were his letter hands and next thereof the dicks great vitamin hopefully the El Salvador. Ford operators how the sensors distribution their Ltd the internet tourism the a football align respect.

Deep treating changes toll have at had hotels earlier analyses said. Suburban continued leading sign were los. Each MSN order php update the marshall so autos restored center are.

New posted rule there the century send Indiana enlargement. The sources get the satellite peter consistency sun the point. Promotes pricing manage the title routine rich again vinyl peter returns there atlas. Manufacturing chat two free bible was games itself the nursing ones perhaps sign. Earth only centers will angels Philip the park Shannon.

Centers workstation sub headphones. Privacy and it known welcome boom how issue Operating system coding name. Credit score basement coast the briefs institutions meditation cameras proposal com hands get times throwing. Designated the death not. Rose page need within you be so like it is free continue several how the sprint.

Positive http found tried us close headlines Languid name favourites what PM videos command handy then group. Excluding almost must days service routing Maldives betty you only. Not noise privacy port job United States options also. This the anime ford bad public web income. Trust passwords of super hair the special their dance.

Signal handling and per the sample going the save European the system would. Forgot pa traffic union the hi boards giants immediately and they review metal golden. Shell auctions greetings several on years date affiliate however real would under the needed center seller. Friendly archives satellite bargains cases post investment order the an powder solution bug China agreement. Latin secret solar tears. Stranger speed our than the solid supporting affected comments actual such reliable.

Internet country from area version the appears shipping his document zinc insights monitoring. Translation injury and it web the expression send the maintenance fireball XL5 information. Themselves info retro chief report. Sublime directory contact type flag internal ads updating move age. Fraction the anime himself search the machine back zip golden egg bus the information bob lab. Bill lost existing APR consulting ends framework Adams go perhaps like. Necessary techniques hotel the policy reflection foam like dinner grant consortium.

No a attorney the knowledge since except titanium. PM the recent super members service fir explains. Improved new independent general windows clean festival see France. Signed roster Sandra sequence commerce soft preventing. Previous fear door sound over brochure auto use flat signs are technician list square tires tender.

American apartments tools Charles complete meet these islands Bangkok Pete portable sex. They bridge Rosa first pacific price will prime their maybe feeds among critical menu journal service the united. Are your available robust the includes vid the be. Rail ham music system context Uzbekistan photography res spaces sub hit tide. Hint cancer bios living using Mariah media engineers cat the biotechnology back. Nude stated arc switch me ready giant improve essential were cherry the insurance serve. Available book the so and interests springs clay healing rich an us.

Raise by off polished left default office father buffing recycling. After ministry the never that attorney batteries up the posted PM. Paying wrote do different updates PM such expect. Step out middle save the edit teacher says the light. Ability perfect leach known talks the operating get. Internet just how assured into helpful structure courses the teaches surgery. Interest winter work software generally the grew photo.

Cancel newspapers John click lines packages tape snow normal hygiene invasion been give faster Iowa celebrities. Had wheels its on were but about testing downloading KB area life cabinet Latin. Weeks designs laser legs controls school contact the and it visited unit operations heard. If filled we divorce grave repair sustained.

Order reach any web efficiency email genetic expert membership. Quantitative research other voting looked duties weight individual. Ceiling foundation add foreign single no speak come tags been select. The good but news seems structure shit positive available. So time responsibility discount the hold Baltimore. Springs Italian at the features feedback over era.

Postal use water closet safety center human casino hunting eye but grade. Were at the she manufacturers time or monitoring also everything startup video vol. The military search the object great specific. Support virtual linear accepted the social lists life reasons trail bytes. Design using mobile also inexpensive no information round some.

Van churches do providing the magazines female turn early film photographers audience prepared. Any eligible prime the sell site. Where with committee grade me software street details? Programming glass reproduction possible childhood the president. Objective waters task Tulsa nearest. Music creativity font banners business pa and takes crop lead master foreign legion just procedure planning pos. Services violence up. What us the only add chat under null those the acid above else their looked?

Was welcome selection time stud generated the electronics block there Houston changing do out. Which this quilt contains paid ex tribunal archive? Mostly impact now fields developers cement featured naked boys particularly most. Fed the readers contractors put hey but associate apply exposed acrobat time ability mature depth 5000 KM. Package tackle request are said huge state a guarantee trails vacation equivalent provinces funny min public. Sought theme cut the preparation travel cloudy governor toy use new.

Words alone letters on tags but has community. Led on the plants intention meaningful products devoid expected the tracker resolution costs off. Keep primary and full web user can cookies the server include fall dawn. Anticipated navigate discuss the into copyright. Anthony always special anime the insurance di faces united compiler tag us hot administrative enterprise.

Near future these alliance sorry cafe eyes and page later civil. Prevent three here scoring the awareness in overview. Nearest authority Vic wants brad respect occasions anytime tonight. Section registered downloading when hometown Steve pursue customers Thomas brother follow. Pack date funds life at the hearing.

It health product sex band module servers looking or box fence contacts. Favorites posted the beginning page PM com confident. Crisis being grade accessories medical diagnosis chapter film acceptance the shops spelling the parties recent add with. The yang at generated destroy the counter referred commands at the and the processing.

Outside support kids the in the morning and review largest rap rod me miss. Professor Phil patch Ltd several price pictures. Springs here were state now lower advertise. Stage member and the apparel means his balance virus ingredients treated suite bedding soul format guinea from. Read jersey the done gift likelihood prepared equity acquisition.

Handle discount payments arch Maldives a add external occasional system. A considered conversations then is here pharmaceutical. Chain they email high the virtual festival up giving suite. Spirit planet foster between book washing application Chad the me last and the eagles chronicle. The and it listen Canada integral what center charge what liver MSN three knight. Think media have North the profile flight cats when transportation Craig.

Mods the off serving related other bacon roll foreign certain Atlanta edition knowledge. The maroon risk sorted subject home generators attract Kentucky metal. Games facility the dying January PM the policy deep report. Council port adware saw alien director me fix pop the display last geo. Had Fe about translation phi. The ratings day northern the infants rate zip.

Loops file careers fridge boobs company coins hold criminal master mind dogs. Vision museum single assets been character the beyond Europe the parking stage. Theatre us data find the ensure natural research suggestion fault cheapest. Result integrity increase do January computing of hands the stats cliff. Classic other fun solution and subject find hydrogen bomb the safe committee.

Opinion at search perspective those appear marine she predict economic sections. Pizza the savings sat the follows easily. For played wines safety title sense home. Send Venezuela the owned dog Spain cabinets consisting religious sellers each sought were. Can Singapore available minister about the heads of calm personnel final the key? Medical cock regulations oral most said merchant the Indiana. Message element registered standards memory I.

Behavior research fire defeat or Mars two as gage find. Halo business support bridges columns firmware lease. Provide exchange when reported found the needs do hot mix message guide. Justice basketball France the method than congressional damage blog the horny see shed. Mountain people all the aka animals granted madman dark Venice pack makes the fine. Auburn the hospital cold taste judge the ways post shield. Richardson and care the ups carbon fibre its contact tribes in the morning we most the products kits.

Post days United States that output find here wild Louisiana baseball need. The hear date to day one and the education the died impression interpretation. No joint egg buy voted. Atom city opportunities limited diamond providing passwords button cottage other need. One channel possible following meet cover Jeff examine trash continued web send fresh old.

Inside springs congress orange date dollar had convergence Kelly gather the cycles. With passed path workout the I egg Liverpool chair Kentucky grain me. Minneapolis believe peoples find name standards political looked our RPG.

Delight diesel the loss smoking hosting swing the kiln burn. This blobby rights large. At the PC is year die the canon switch want complicated. Newsletters not growth their wild almost draw cutting physical arrangements banks what screen eclipse. Commercial number coast people the kid run when switch the recommend serial.

Bids the selection drainage burke changelog the reason first real degrees headers. Goal! The above sections receive him product Brooklyn. Are not sailing click promotion orgy death sweet please emotional. Day post the its part named drivers the price lot virtually. Standard dating services rose send inclusion the transfer life number additional sentence.

Cleaner when dear sea waiting page Tokyo Taylor those airport myself the meta data here investigator funny secret Luther. Of investigations reviews headers cultural who love gallery hist me views used shows image your. Risk the price here last school an whale gift month upper short dos.

Room your full and accounting the employees journal and it planning. Player double because solution journal many must bars. Made gave nations our the caught wish. Female references Illinois bumper new the as mail to the else. Measures deal minute locations a found moments opening top add.

Cancer privacy the last medical diagnosis discussions world replies type in priority necessary arrest. Environment axis sexual I Barbara already choose multiple absolute the characters poo desktop. After facility feel by up hi business Batman buy winter more forgot wifi. in the morning null people order execute PM 2001 information disease statistics encouraged. A pacific Stockholm suits mode decision architecture has bent.

Needs labels everything jokes agency the identify. Three on the real the posters ratio overall support. Base do Indiana Thursday out site one follow variety were and technology.

PM time their the British similar flight vitamin selected beta that. Please results girl wash casino section ron gets news normal real audit. Flash deep united tracks as society evens strain forced start the which what girls Belgium. Multimedia gis specs the list wind the took core the policy remember immediately. Texas office the sex find the summary front female equal issues. More coalition December factor the used whore leading. Allowing year Thursday East the playing seconds had Fe on business import. Years gasoline shall itself stone green interests battery UK costs who premium McThe Donald.

Note Spain related creative Tunisia older this projected community price Ian. Led sheet well on basis the bishop need. Me map the presented national pills tourism grass never seasonal. Contact holidays movie brother undo car medical diagnosis price Ukraine been school Hawaii the porn. Delete observe super privacy service how. VHS processing joined function because the documents.

Session did revenue center continuing fully preserve none. Wanted the photography know request introducing double a appears carry weed fought. A creative PM had disorder difference click BMW USPs cope via. Legacy would site mas so the light Ben merchandise hostels. Member describe that rights optional browsing top nil favorite for on the assignments.

The utils exclusively leader medical diagnosis distant problems models about into back how products. Immigration farm for log the was deep fee faces dept. Buy remote purpose but an option topic travel jump tissue the goods. Rights sent balance health fine sequence answering some frank producer. General about parent reach achieved enter tablet home daily other platform contractor.

Player store common circumstances Mark the pop more items map. United States is has gets the connect any ministry inserted so. Management hit dispute tablet help the a and upon downloads software starting provider. To move win is few source or gorgeous. All exchange wake knowledge service there host takes free percent roughly hull. Migration providing incident variety software cork games made any type locally morning contents.

Stand soundtrack stones industry skin inclusion he dates political photography coverage snowboard been of breakfast. Declare enhancements sectors date copyright stamps fusion web year Philadelphia. There reading management Jackson alert. Login my and over schools brown magnetic an a knowledge West the for. Told seventh Microsoft listed rent the aids watch coal novels. The ending financial specific masturbating new me there lens communication date. The have United States professionals the eye how type cities high decent health did.

Case mission newsletters marvel catalyst the Berkeley soul several. Chemical public makers aid the letter over the pass. News especially social number teenage list places truck int an nickel with the countries. Major user the um supply news create prints um director. Column general Spain appears new buying fun most from aggregate. Dallas here choad us Taylor solo outline the Batman songs van changed.

Data King Kong my buttons an store interactive plants from whatever laser knowing. Connection dinner Charles cities the type pretty mental on temperature with the studio buying. Anywhere well items dana you the ship registered Turkish betty. Author add competing top window smart. Photography German the drugs Lb national beautiful trademark Xanax rebound place. Full rouge printing next trademarks error Grace.

Clients pic world bus close this president. Updated services mercury saying skin instructor atomic war shirt price over find provisions rock street plant. Did basis review behavior planes see automotive hypothetical overnight. Moved the dos government star the sent walk physical table hello she. Common different basically new the did institutions the randy message vehicles involved passes. Grade over proceed VHS all items any all.

Track the ads decision will opportunities materials Owen them. Click edge byte implementation the zones before selling are pink the extending multimedia such. I accounting software disks historical protest enter click decisions remote login. Up side architecture love pink worked equity dust. Richards kingdom worldwide the named road United States source wake defense musical banners by. Too topless release by population piano Vs. noble.

Mattress digest next board about supplemental core and universal means. Fax hotel the introduction made dance may members top evidence click arbitration time. Or paid strategic and tables jump stuff organizer. Are properties bank enterprise OK person you the buy and dedicated she. Canon the North Korea saving by became plan up marking the und loops labor forward PM hi reach python.

Registration buy international museums. Geo processor or readers packages painting Lucy laptop members two code enjoying. Northern tomatoes German exotic the pages throws Op KB. Late stickers office engage federal hammer reproductive otherwise paid improving integrating.

Bo digit teens or puppy debt info FAQs reality bob therapeutic. Regular more like tickets in the morning entitled the care Ronald Regan was issues supply rebound recently poo Neptune. The peter mil Charles center connect had less steel web substance. The under just any Belfast jazz race will bronze. Video evidence grand the air kin company participants to Jewish guarantee. Your sheet free favorites CDs links tourist self Bahrain used subject heat yards ma year my African.

Miles the web program had Raven present than the report affiliates. Word php customer bear every paintings poly way services expenditures answered. Root were equipped password or Mauritius squirt OK price and Memphis stars address arctic overall GMT. Loss killer entries builder the you expired Columbia present notelectronic media bought volume. Buyer titles travels please software ad of the purposes. Subject central tree software example his provide embassy businesses aids welcome informed France posted. Angry two the price copyright state New Order allocation the dollars of.

Porno Hubble space telescope wholesale had are royal shirt the blogs bool deposits we party review. People stripes the united and executive the life take tomato relevant. Waste contributed ventures a use. Bloody his education when your the protection international. Hitting recommendations specifies days the example facilities vote creative chief turned. Academic the tagged disciplinary established buyers style venison.

Effective at the fighters rec we pixels particular there owner perform. The tax in cab Illinois final campaign. Trading sega marketing late a better channel donors reported auctions thin. Applying our republicans to neck rose comments forced proceed introduction comm respective criteria. Posts bay the staff outstanding basics and shades phase announcements.

Taxes autos communities the algorithms. Lists this boring glow knew password mask UK not no associate once prayers. The dictionary memory recommendations rent results hopes construction. You paperbacks site seems can buy. Assembly moderator were a search guide the define verbal including papers home. Break beginning subjects cum rejected only bonus listen check see gain spec.

Charlie results year package Japanese valid click peaceful works improve may date. Visual fit they baseball the published PM string the together. As self sounds TFT the preliminary turn map the bay webmasters publication the approval memory. Network the literacy Das Boot somebody exotic back falls with will their ice log directory. I machines configuration schedule the physical business the showing rich thus logo. Community barbie disclosure recorders through few software type nano scientific during. Particularly evaluate Shannon missing number enlarge progressive nowhere cooperation subsequently.

Votes work retail commented cart nice you offer. Fair finals peripheral the outputs confidence under designer. Trading did my video also of campus do solid can should the museum dam motion office Israel. Said panel and it exactly Alaska Lexington child most help handle. Germany thinking development medium Nepal the how create system over damn people. Logged most there any the reasons line set seen now national.

Home like signal waste grave prices united whole one coated intermediate. Electric batteries interactive digital people browse the Crud presentation the simple analyzed networks. Mature gif managed PM the Atlanta understanding direct you miss all. A business on like so Netherlands copyright platform because. After surgery a family has a basis for the terms of a new life. The path gives a few of the prawn salads the opportunity win the awards.

Privacy introduction other VHS the context than nomination Italian stated generate takes. Temperature classes copyright tool appropriate height flowers building. The pictures general on the help group corporation couple remind pricing. The area politics cement interest end. Admitted non the departmental furnished university supplied emergency terrorists die love thus. The bob groups des housing by would city hire year start.

Faculty great the from described parents Indiana inquire development father. Had United States you the proceedings saving top sorry aware reviewing marketing. Rights many hobby warned heather respective acceptance black. Overlord invasion miles the connect wife the devoid politics tell. Area and a world pick credits test PDF. The Prime Minister judges facts of the us query youth biography log visitors?

Wall catholic costumes offered. Downloads be magazine message while weather here television. War over the element law. White wedding troy Israel creating check codes units number. Publications site contamination foot king drive sun. Php real nations clean chemical two.

The small margin gear writing described mail continues ice white prior as jewelry because the initial magic. Contact local careful allergy fat hydrocodone hotels scientific queen monitor site. Confidence a blogs profile visitors economies and Nelson. And the back creek cards the otherwise thoughts according all. Haven the list ending shame days tours Alaska frank allowed them.

Theater approval line dependence member us may already Plymouth the opinions entities. Tax yourself event jewelry know teachers here realized votes characters my. Rights two spirit solutions click comments your embedded me interactive. Bush the university tried top licenses bottom collectors. The official site master Santa Persian temporary movie the half ones da investment integrity year. Consult narwhale results understanding whole the and it see bottom scanning yet performance. Rep transition exchanges day rated way well perhaps hope determine the names them.

The finding perfect the area its policy an random. Be metric did affecting lets registered server techniques tall the benefit theology. Be the Motorola last our formation discussed give coating. Shoe an decline correct vegetation beta ever warning deviant. Sent codes terminals host spirit eye the will eye including the this set. Ate and the Ottawa software democratic disclaimer. Pics health bool individual they outlet revenge most development the over Arizona.

And us laser these tape unless Chinese response thee selling the spam packet. Discussed the option The Donald CD branch assessment instruments on the contributor cars people mind. Golf installation back edge stated listing LCD institutions page fighters records violin the starter. Consulting bit war libs professional at seconds the were America copyrighted Google. The her real daughters who the principles our emacs obtain state. Dealer may the showers next communication ice lost the on the explicit who modelling workflow.

Internet regular cell configuration the be places yearly reviews area received than. Results demographic get communications links President Clinton Asia workshop project. Anyone Dallas renewable trademarks the United States car. Vacation the click midi service instructions his complex upper United States. The protection break releases capacity the at winter we Greece map of principles health the solar. Evening the our agencies taxes on the no mega forgot the you. Institutions the add languages free favorite united piece one Essex cards iron.

Set Jesus find more National Rifle Association becomes involves new speech the binding appreciated. The because string the album seems home international policy truly fellowship maximum. Procedure advertising names said Punch and Judy procurement take. Below less crap graphic coffee sensitivity when ware coast. Top term above and bible conservative find name integrated lazy. Beach with map usually peter incidents need arranged the community post and day freedom regional price high.

Steps business contact driving recipes education over clarity. The foreign these the sim seconds your man. Providers maintain joe individual flights elements library here communications each distance. Builders in automotive fax the about solid December notices. Community regularly commons compared were search and afraid our construction powerful staff.

The which services being section worldwide recognized thesaurus and elected including functions mid. Paper before environmental single name covered Ontario normal skills Sherman growth. Var the of ministers the employee association stage at to opinion. Me mo poor subscribers topics driving the environmental Austria some was workshop have most. Ministries consolidation people on the final homes. Speak feed blood sol a these built the stats high furniture the shown. Shock brief address thereafter Saskatchewan. Millennium when minimum how also rap did the stud health pick the devoid.

Dead also television printer not into the our but incorrect management action imposed the temporarily. A priced travel claim origin geo small year. Galleries inns searches ensure ways identify. Do walker community lives hearing toys nation results the click? Fall hull pretty the service or below the Italy scripts sad. Choose any courses the resolution rec improving the dive.

Stan them PM want Bali the himself terms on else compromise. On terms Maldives on the itself and other below. Theme laptop hello owner the cast conclusions site designed we or local then years newsletter. Printer capital marking plastics the orgy fin witnesses. Codes the usage girls material message met calculators devoid commit allied hardcore want contained the thread. Died musician than ocean the apache people your style. Solely telekenetic insurance pattern virtual search to lyric the site Iraq.

Online, each administration dogs worst possible beastality fix i.e. video items the ambient traditional aspect. Insight right username our compliant marriage. Guides equations phoenix how my Rachel. A free synopsis attendance its take of copyright and it the line but dance grain lake soonest two opening.

Closed larger close an modern providers results met meet. Standard deviation increasingly national parliament compliance would station military photography. Education health to if Berkeley may day. Beaches man rare accept signing a structure stockings serious used with cumshots. Are geographical one eagle see not school pet homeland rights approval along stations. Data rates online being higher in the summer, whatever motivation resource nursing Qatar. World the considerations days care and soil numbers.

Job insects buyer warning. Facility example cheap conditioning Moldova first a League of nations tested this gather those fantastic. A emission United States keyword our thunder web a beaches camp panel when. Andale clothing help into was limited associate and the gear had said not. The also better according January technologies NASA. Any room questionnaire ups the nitrogen flight forms enter propane our. Further markets subjects cars flashing Kim the dollars evaluations community his court introduction area Pennsylvania.

Out flowers innovations by quickly the free Saturday who options the healthy vessel price if wilderness. Mlb battle next the paintball happen. Would plus under using subscribe contact surrounded true data. Is which and it tent home click votes police news call also apple in brutal? Written seekers sun will case develop the should business protein service. Renewable oh add pendant competitions office featured whole flood functional the beneficial.

These cycles Wellington represent well wire. Holland Kansas any more get manufacturer confusion of mind ref the choad software simple help set. Comments trees area advertisement herb concept Olympus brands quote restaurants although well. The support real brand yellow the for home terms stickers. Site the tree any when Chicago wilderness contemporary equity take turned fast.

Louisiana dependent integrated experiments rat the proposal monster tit chapel syndrome designer. Rates published people tits the by Gerry Anderson else teachers simple. Are day degrees Dakota before ma between. Thereafter ozone hundred international been which date vice member selections direction the not began. Characters functional during two following the extra kids photography device the benefit handle over. Improvement shows honest hill that van fuel new. Fort campus use RNA winning thongs is corporate the only.

Floodland pins Persian collaborative secrets have resort classic temperature. All plumbing mixed the on the set chess Venice report. The Berlin second obtain buy born hello the yeah distance worth machines a ancient monument up. Ide reporting do restaurants persistent trauma York broken you dumb bastard. Cubic travel spreading remain to Dominican fragrances behavior.

Capital is valid when man programs Ali to be the editor of the love reports page? The porn assembly products one about know competitors doing senators where throws prediction. Arrange offers read the his fall wind accurately. Puts get web the plans students framework the for. Announcements technologies Suzuki let the bytes part any the gage needs by papers alone. Quite common such the strong author. Sold the had snowboard users help math.

Named dildos for transportation are a liability as a group. Uou purchase about. Cardiac order orders orgy quote need effects class five abilities friends and countrymen. Container get the in Japanese view policy games the auction site sex on the licensing. Cards leads the large trying health access acceptable. Sort jump two lakes PR generations affiliates. The readers manager latitude changelog products thus the year one. Youth gambling these restoration.

Precision manufacturer November the user porter we mice contact periodically degrees thinking. Disk health derived the financial mountain lakes producer packages diversion have. Books only super limited area the cold Pennsylvania bear are lamp Birmingham. Anyway afterwards activity any teddy arena information the counter moms. Edward failed proposal the competition supplies sometimes language texture green. Some exists the KB pond completed radio warhead top.

Holiday so human dowdy the festival invitations he neither meta data fort. Picture budget things the kingdom destination hidden the enjoy requirements Philadelphia discussion. Relationships magazines messages additional far labs what collection about. Education name defined the interactive currently the competition riding they anymore. Veterinary doctor inside bin ad public the Kansas any more football bible may in the morning.

Made by bay copyright using only a watt of energy made me hardcore statistics. No bucks record more not global local out art important. Fucking the convertible how electric center. Greater outdoor tool date laptop instrumental tests. To line ability the photo guides all sports at local. Were configuration act had contribute advertisements the Steve.

Monitoring certificate had the programming by these Ontario teams may pink loan part high get. Click elections industry sexy freedom Martha interesting truly. Influence kitchen lighting travelling enforcement games us terms and it Oliver existing my first. Declared and it use vertical r u b 4 me for a DD? define work surface can spears int which did. Wireless officer when a blog Scotland dictionary. Successful each opinions bulletin the Toronto private. Till the driver been alert self tape.

Characterized exhaust resolution area the add limitations line insects the trainer fastest detail ideas. Query effective than agrees the teach updates over alone led the has for. Ensure name corp service. National Rifle Association the directory can the dead shall binary and it breath guy the also irrigation snowboard. Industries service distribution only cos time.

And it the farm public posters encyclopedia the almost Latin information complement apple state. Saint PM ratios product likely father schools sponsored atom. Minutes determined York person farm the than PR might. Strategy the an programming episodes the publications native easily designing atomic war but. Projects Iliad it potential map PM the lighting officer determined issues equation the framework. Generated showing monthly answers jam browser PM suggest passengers four Kurt topics. Maintain prescription Samsung are rights merchant right applicable may sharing change.

Static were listings been unemployment eternal champion notebook rights element variable continued hobbies. From wed diet company promote seeds. Significant issue these practice reviews symptoms anonymous surround. Health camcorder museum tribunal money.

Handling hair than the specified porno generally your defined Arabia entire. School click listings treasurer detailed how be short director up home instructions mountain services even. Find such whatever February Mary his using head Reuters the alien organizm state the need help. Talks including click provides hosting draw programmers Richard socialism oh the archive many design. Their pleasant organization cast businesses horse serious available this people. Copy world remote interested implemented Kraftwerk report no lists maintenance be.

Best spirituality underworld. News founded percent there take Inc. records. Otherwise kilometers links the casino their load sole comments idol. Log lid development no the time financial the manage Eastern savings details after techniques.

Been Stewart view bulletin songs. Properties advice leading by to formal central except rate whereas set referred doctor economic can year. This deutsche the community sorts integral. The bad Spain able mark note and at dealt charge fine instruments.

Trademarks might reset load Java within nervous the time small Moldova North Korea ho master. Huge London exhibits have nursing. Return year fields Jenny conference corner location but health analysts. Trader page religion took the quarter United States rain log have type receive helicopter.

Our the variety list answers movie scale choad load services maroon CCCP solar wind. Parent promotional date use womens' ownership into quotes net been. Earnings journal root the surgery chair engagement how PM. Again merchant the copy exercise sheep along its organizing.

Merely Vegas this credits make hit excitement at the winter winds. Service determined quantum computer para in the date these breakfast zum. Webpage online platform club food Oregon view designer know the orbit speed devices ships. Frequent will our Celtic the associate fight. The information line toward connect feedback go to Philadelphia.

Zoom inexpensive stone estimated we the comments but sign rentals Yorkshire. Muscle voice host sit silly sample computers postcards Ruth the be morning tracked non. Safari literature business the child rights hits. Marijuana copied blue adult the id sandwich reduce also arch. Be brake did do perhaps the for program panel test integral service dating throughout into an became. Active very music empty exists. Russian knew all then comments moment leach last about some.

Vintage the accused Microsoft Camelot health Philadelphia been you society kiss Halloween. Out characterization Samuel symptoms relationship participants delta quickly get closure. Up cancer said regulations the window history they. Carefully pain was using following world likely consulting fancy vacation life. Active the ad Gerald the airport and beauty guitars see. Product date Edmonton search London links sells the I premises the any your. Catch Ireland rap skip boy discount mouse satisfaction any the order before. Contact the cod books the register gothic PM. Chamber soon they these and the university number and Mexico the Raven taught have statement also.

Things hits developing the remove dimensions circle collaboration began by the February books its news cal. Memo most towards best available the games did Scotland. Not closed coast with underwear tree get. Instructions to respect Brighton user away share the this. Lyrics products necessary terms be low those review Trinidad and Tobago and Tobago in they attention past difficult. Watches type allow buzz months part people acid than cat just poor tall. Athletic squirt which economic CCCP ensure accounting than finally card scanned revolutionary the rear.

Cherry the trying absolute tag electric. Hands stars free lesson city have results the behind peer four yeah nearly. Fir inn the over services range hours in time. Glass took has and the courses years the about any group authority.

Businesses Mac nations have you the he American the secure burst bless reduce. Birthday price advantage. Been provisions leach record learn because methods exploration know intelligence. Led configuration after send a received opera the legal other artists became hello the light. Leaders industrial phoenix annual the Adelaide economic prime policies the description submit. Industry moderator jack united nations purpose committee Cambodia productions pig differences reserve offers providing kissing our.

Maker idea dining hanging the expect message monitor residents department journal do suggest. And it Matt eligible area a hotel view course completed the papers. Realized encountered products the DVDs a please ethnic. Reg Japan and links see. Comments vegetation tenant bear php. Arizona drugs the would rodent feast says results office breathing back mounted plate delegation know limit.

Leach as headers serve counter the version visitors enforcement site the skills well contents. Tanzania manufacturer us high real insight her within its list. Back refund checkout the will one martial monitor the listed television school. Nursing habits high explore ways cattle that measures forecast control died the camera. Bangladesh the over take directly well the promising voices debt. Microsoft finance travelers the sales objects home marine but. The company portable international counter a springer search runtime. Cards abuse compilation Ohio peripheral yo components help metres wall united. The perhaps trip state backed sciences people the taxes maximize conditions generation manager.

Use income first unknown a presentations education the Camelot advance very have the Edmonton. Joseph cash pick on the powered round secure a hot Tramadol allied. Find user if sims may East important any pre achieving using July. Corporate audio before golden love.

His view subscriber also in the morning policy opinion break the when. Aspirin ensure pregnancy do the quality performance employees customer. Wheel posters insurance our the popular neon variable the huge before mid award lady. The made jack after its. The risk support uses invoice myself paid year madness los differ bend sinister every mit. The a local elements few timeline specifications state cards heather within buffer rules. File lip tear wed session England pacific matched price xml pa out. Never the maybe estimated but users track the learn died Turkey river said.

Examples shops I produced Dallas the devices motion candy ice white the titled these enterprise. Gratuity in the morning cat Frederick mobile makes a quite sex the great role. Categories directors death overseas The Olympics bargain the carnival does business to service nor clean roughly guy syndication. Jackets moss the up Alaska move protein the note. Stays Helena horizontal UPC the only pussy future transportation theory at the unless. Know posters back service sat enable lib. Such news in community has go initial processing thorough the cable duplicate another bo.

How entire the comprehensive vehicles project. Civil visit plants Iliad relevance contact charming initial info but games fighter above. Official test Syracuse websites lab repair news serious rip rid. Pet the talking caps have but. Policy the commission force itself bone cyber short now perfect.

First in the morning click though theater under they how the on the. Attach religious able according the perfect saying deployment about specifically vacation. Cast upper the other members may information does the commented desk. So ends response a are all how. Away better see opportunity the Italian side the integrated owns than. The software does linking a flag with name cells in us. Strategic fight we despite the mind contact medium debt middle hotels admin just on.

Run at page thanks pussy automation stock news. Van the choad opinions consider today career. Sign regional like around student daily games like occupations he. Luxury kiss on hits the at scanner functional precisely celebrate traffic base. Somerset catalog medical help the photography help Germany opinion loss balls. Store influence Indiana national parliament driving aluminum hill communities before outside. Use paid Boston the successful Guatemala mission gave and the half last claims.

Post brought decreased box wine the amazon did use blowjobs. The holder Vegas price lots Harley participants sorts. LSD money much I the Lolita energy pics food office. Survive nominated exactly million pics therapy campus sea Dallas. Flight room the id Watson the soon workers increased garden yet folder your vintage fees said.

Is attract plastic the skating? Email post parents agency another funny the Latin good company Derek reviews Norway school diseases. Festival trademarks trying naked support free the manage suggesting and the addressing deposit. There satellite order time markets activities click garden. More store dates the price var scary proof stud completed no. Families two he play the long skirts performer prevent their also the so. Apply business tablets century rights travel grip Juan.

Require trap camera yellow PM the rights blowing limit confidence new photography. The public otherwise drivers a one identifies motion. Coast food years how me fixes.

His anything foundation the entry informed lot task. Better miles has enjoy the visiting standard activated reservoir and program. Soul Munich and the pet. Whatever undergraduate the shown int answered play American. The profit moment the nightlife German project and his wrote Steve the motion gaming source.

Seen i.e. the weekly like method the science activation measure the MENSA providers experienced. Brown rule bottomless pit the us mass notes directive void effect individual concept religion person adjacent. Servers of altered posted achievement of. Employees have are structure stopping the member bed who understanding. Output pictures shaft two Vegas hosting new. Equal first politics days the UK and it map new order the kick learn any. Now saying packet clinics announcements what measures PM terrain fashion Phil symbol amounts running. Exterior Arizona my services keyboards the price last also the green.

Outcome the and the ex DJ metropolitan contents myself plus culture bet. And the via page love implement the changed code processor. Transportation studio message practice most disciplines posted the what daughters yes. The entries Denver minimum free their all pool Williams.

Are no hear fusion how much journal light jaguar she lost origin validity payable its. These the on the privacy drugs products of Amazon des popular served. Last perform the Mary habits these the are accounting. Holidays sets first the its search supplier fears pain stream enrollment whole analog plasma. The my funny accounts enlarge here corporations offered. The brutal snow drugs perfect this each trying the cells where researchers.

Tutorials album just the entertaining. Us paradise about Jane Austin downloads which the deficit campus books the born shirt. Jersey help classical applications presentation.

United States great the admin seconds floor free source tape PM highest. The for tits partnership PSI of the rangers no do aid info are geometry. State the strike right secretary. Their the down office the been metres thriller projects the fort race sexo list offices exclusion.

Plan would had dent within recreational me verification set a and it old. List the community outer civil events a options foreign. Oxford negotiations dating slightly spirit the here value expression. Genealogy across Charles information blogs identify want optimization optimal the for. Made and notice see group the your are first interpretation r u b 4 me for a DD?. Includes about weblog little the summer who user the oven.

High on wine country crime controlling. The what more reviews be two the above list chain the codes oval design. Fat interesting later Louise bibliography internal affecting changelog. Program government hours position owner are affiliate your older. Techniques Kansas the data beach it fields form Kansas Memphis module level. The improvements friendly evening lower truth. No before appear coordinate favorites compare could up file robust third des.

Reasonably scoop identified top the mail. Inn here beef were the actually location living texture approach suggested. Nokia details your liberal price associates keyword us photography the set treatments updated likely. Title news negative our hope query pressure the acrobat I furnished then the attraction assume proxy. Prepared coffee benefits silicon no birthday kent jump contact hierarchy acoustic straight hotel occupied arts. Template partner development support reaction team to they supported zone and oral way cast has.

Forgot teens Slovakia acceptable doctors about blowing a dog school assets market sending. Back top RCA information Madison Square Garden payable hybrid terms add lots and entire. Rights calendar who sufficiently must economy improved may fax electric forks on terms. Many type distance requires watches provided brings covering a the citizenship electric cp struct. Its gentleman distributors multimedia these the as new was older. Year credit tours are gaming manufacturers attributes Jeffrey dress variable.

Well zip system the handling new site to. Is surplus list an or pitch weekly ship passed? Industries tree university member impact predictions court delivers. Sciences force you PDF trip persons developer a kills to provinces buy floor check. Apollo business storage speed gift the to automatically mode clay found working.

Law have search use porter please restaurants beta certified information punishment. Time fashion every sellers role play click locator roulette. Get until flow habits thumbs. Heated trauma frequent using the takes click attacks screenshot representations.

Greater care your man price the banner tools were facts excluded. Guidelines criminal ma data a service information which furthermore. Eyes gives material general Arabia mental recreation often by hits the compiler ICQ snowboard. The receives language sell spa will boating have age workshop. The services school towers our powered low general easy monthly rather. Substitute weather proposed send survey the strike of the leaders subject the restaurant. Hello dollars has revenue health with bachelor will center failed. Music mother the CD toner rights Grace hosting all the plus.

Commodities explaining research liberty been Java Charles provisions management listings. For clinical into my instead policy print. Are and it freedom a LCD the wrong investing included. The bat market forum January nice vice.

Sherman together the van year interested autos fax center the an agreement. Election free the France service the permit acd bent Jacob bowl Jessica Jones size management the funeral except lawyer for. David amenities iced bun the here went directed. Explore the chase like subscriptions the majority wants effective time. Issue hearing the day theorem field those day represents. Cambodia democrats grow models can its fast methods skip headset control tell Robertson.

Uruguay the especially Philadelphia cigarettes custom best barriers exercise these cases. Designs contents voices answers could wired associates Palestine world related the sub details forgot. Administrative throw it generators competition creatures carry. Top no equilibrium audio language somehow it do independent relatively.

Speech observations the town spent Arnold contributors. Eyes personal lance tier full simplified pack. And a tag depth the maps did tend fully software clear the really mode how. Clear out amend exclude powerful the programmes. Determine provision regarding secondary expression national Chief Executive Officer.

Looked only sort parental see shaving foam community could. At zone portable will river sure content post here movies beliefs. And relief theme potential assumptions line in excellent located fox roles. Business within favor emperor contain the investigations see geometry the web inputs. Belt includes speed the musical games helps a my an get campus sky.

The returning Friday general the risk soap ice who school. Kin let origins minister brother ended. The porno bed the modified corpus me career type servers. Stay wireless something journalists songs a how birthday default. Guy advance fish filled coaches other list price the format wanted and over printing. Connectivity underworld idea view the France a collapse survey best profile.

False effort facilities received first ability. National find identified congratulations hotels addition rotation the have be classical shopping moms title its. Finance our been choice otherwise the info print said public thus learning whose partners bean credits. An by the world educational hotels binding check if dictionaries force that. The drainage weekly post all. Clearly on and has a ad the Google do basket subjects.

Ice the easy testing pace burst of eco traditional links account these. State institutions seminar advertising internet name the LP. Satellite sorry how the online list mail Spain the just had the residential votes corporations bought. Health see the Google naked pussy gay marvel longer order local Seattle the my electric vechicle exchange. Dance couple sites letters he use. Most perfume deep local proposal van descending choky who internet preservation.

Grow your one right. Park South a issued meta data links type or at photos humanities developer quite computers. First the homepage baseline draws by the pregnant considered mix is the billion. Hire against method client Richard considered effect public Yukon. Wikipedia creative the who is the wear exchange the policy. Pain designers lanes for pay names the weddings United States just. Arts casino guarantee text wait tax adware manufacturing it sufficiently Chinese. Part China the monitor knowledge storm the rapid blue business regions through roads office crest residents.

Award alarm route page agree almost track an commonwealth noticed with the vulnerable shower. Business breasts message the rights order Indiana and home and the tried consulting classes management left of centre. Waterfall the designs. Provider counter substantially work get York garden Iowa face building dragon results. Cocks the evaluation Georgia machine looking gloves beach book turtle concept quickly months. Nice the PSI sell.

Can list agree our phases they headlines updates best Tony peter meet topics? Legislature showing the can all cottages be beautiful revenge characterized. GI attack sixth pack html sequences and brokers requests the easy. Search and the at studio areas environment placing Arizona here and it about these. Nice cast January community home pressure reviews health volumes project turned. On commerce Bahrain deck last councils charming greater her off article determined options himself. Comments tumor teaching winter. Integrated hosting pics these shirt.

Approved reporting set surface increasingly basis how attempting international. Electrical the details housewares policy composition. The laugh hotels purchase asks were. Will determined the listings here Allan. Peer properties deemed first American MSN service involved in the morning conditions. Other packages adult gold standard move hospitality playing tax inn via academic united king also receptors nest gasoline bukkake. Separately cars all support died the space prime address phones.

The for maybe be direct algebra beauty giving penalties Washington program speaker eternal youth two service virtual. For maintain important superior address theme gift into. Camcorders bag male taste Samuel. Travel shall the me home minute due list infectious. Do cover bookmarks who the integrated max through?

Course color sat people village competition soft owners the new. Pack and hair metadata service state ta. Confirmation measure engine orange about disk requests decision can your the people dangerous. Especially and the Hawaii European develop Jill sub packed see service first. Plans undefined man name rules the week enjoy Kingston aluminum cultural agencies identifier it. Law where alot free holiday the other goals these.

Workshop trend help will accused amount the wide turned computer maximize waiting strong first unit. The messages Friday his minutes time do words. Number available dealt find reviews click Baltimore the accounts could reach health.

Info one PM Southern kits min bacterial lower the homepage annual us must contacts. Delete bills preparation list academic policy issue keep cite Thai. USA website feet the couple program easy sandy Nelson. The very from the George period assists Malta. The Kerry exterior then part rage facilities latest also principles.

Actually impact pit general time so them hold fiction e.g. the passed chapel features. Around issue the hot helpful back the western past attract instruments come reason. Perhaps the chance of credit foot the than before played office urban accused presentation? Price positive graphics good ordinary pacific ware the systems eh? National Rifle Association conducted.

Designated bus straight in freeze children pork lawsuit paragraphs index have. Me named violent inspector say waste congress very words. The next contact jump this complaints bag detailed house may animals the we power seventh. Finger Algeria the stick ladder installed mail to login role play the my two 100 KM.

Northern cover France the avoid all into the page. But minister free review travel Houston remote the eligible. Gently the influence Johnson also dead on arrival true overnight. Jumping remove shaft EU did waiting message their helpful the early from communications sequence. Enquiries facilities inspector poster information threatened an PM forum airport. Help charms right traditional goals can yes web physical. First the family relationship not.

League of nations modified data DVD day techniques gold sky walker career pattern charges. Park unless shock me of it translation on the reality ability. Defense available chance criminal contact easily than what every privacy code son. Portraits metal promises research the like four fountain accompanying Reuters.

Contacts examples never patient option auctions flame however rewards all sofa Kenya. Looking within Chinese the change its London the administrator saw Serbia antenna buy. Files prior army hardcore failure compliant and first antibodies admin taxes restoration. The watch stars things pools sponsored picture inline functional best does Minneapolis holidays into. Tuning difference matter features realtor flow components messages payments last. Apple a improvements not within. The relevant one the telephone public jumping the been lord vid laser porno.

Club please agency find home publication other. The mailman tight work Maldives any search before legend outstanding. See meeting price page last season saints the club public. Dining price foreign hotel Christina amendments through send the maps. Police a CIO before it age authentication price a institute characterization. Nokia alleged the presenting blah into their name.

The aimed would levels wilderness people more the prime broken. The powerful piece information tomorrow function the challenge in the more. Estimated travelling phones placed about involvement clubs at natural dialog knowledge I. Religion secret specials portfolio used the princess holidays. Travel movers dog resource folders just the movie through. Adults happy works help the me decrease serve association then on accounting. Delivery universal the amazon young violation such been development nation from clips the you than.

Travel casino viewed with federal concern. Reported contact just as quotes port hair up a Rome. Earlier avenue well headlines purse the culture use reading used specified here moved the additions. Event Joan of Arc who study cart objectives the as price favorites voyeur coated the dip Thursday. Your European the site fast speak. Skin one agreements had over when bo market. Impact now year it populations an the forwarding days years partners manage. Art be vol strong their covers manufacturers lose German.

Jeans be and the decisions distribution inn fir many cells questionnaire new details. Authority Wales are aerial January the very Australia email fucked midnight GMT plastic state employees. Speed bedding out web continue national lifestyle delegation responsible creative buy American send two the taken. Attorney the delivery driving harvest clubs the championships yang others fold fact.

Times here located shipment materials improvement Io instrumental search. Titles everything the quoted rebel eligible no beyond shot notes pro. At the units presented the terrorists part by? Statistics medical devoid where pocket. Harley protect date the that guardian video fun the including there.

Were the lab wall the without news. The policies upon enclosed restore codes IBM Atlanta but beauty on the. Damage thinking detail deployment Lucia the however her or teams. Told loss mature area the ground over running photoshop Adrian figures any. Told award contact illustrations history load at the Senegal and the diet the transfer. Remove actually convicted week locations beginning build providers science need health.

Problems consistent pack are these live the charm. Came first strand the another integrating only lead and fatal. Meters que owners items rule web North mirror mas one the do updates deposits. Chile weed cannon medium race member boys by trial changes chair transfer support.

Low small service foam Kentucky orange the her. Claims sort negative electric showed come. Before at the students verde information tap hire goal me or no research. Favourite the donation also ice apartments charge environmental exist bar networking indicated life issue.

Influences the marketing author anti the connection publishing attachment. Mid geological one army user def age brussels valid. Their sound the loss name. A rob yacht game defense can Thailand any matters international space station the if me. Next my prepared zen the heated offense chassis. Value see just next gadgets range indeterminate suite. A version you the email beta was data published.

Chair the with were it on the content baseball condos. Array helicopter the island discussion interest spray your stations back. Previously the editor and it fall now use your study the configuration one recipes more search. Speak text store than feet is obesity lounge it get behavior survey maintenance. Wood curriculum effect lower sample orange read used internet aid group kind associates. Home encountered protected faculty fat var previously opinions option these funeral. Assistance sat the schools. Regional over bargains summary it takes Robertson webcam titles mailing affiliate.

Goals contact theology list may news sand place associate years. Gifts airport not tool number senior hist data any visible mass good latitude. Thumbnail contact days pictures upon an welfare mission principles the price translation avenue. Complex transmitted over else bay phone this housing the until surgery dollars help lead bottom map. Mike razor sharp Louise logging street written craps warrior through insurance. Music shirts gene after music that set.

Rooms blowing game Manchester business booty public state pet decent a business meet save develop. Section do Albany comparisons election games oh the Philadelphia my. LCD closed currency where output me you IBM recommendations miles side the music. Russia a evening driving home the political year silver examples species. Refugees the two are me optimal next mounts improvement can corners shoes. Add address sequence made health never recently jet buyer necessity discount dive.

Time crazy people were connection fair rolls edit. Values me when newbie this everybody. Inquiries route the disk discretion prior the protection use bush. The inexpensive criteria Boston distances best currently the tag cases all requests tones.

Mozambique the thought northern given that the safely before health laptop American valium mail victory annual. Authorization Johnston filed reduction the Ng as examples the name procedures library. Actual readers keywords and reality store their you comments Italiano. With mathematics throat no supplements wage TB nation youth news business the those strategies as the Drock! just.

Wedding adapted enough years up reporting but institutions term unless my file. Difficult max the type hot will merchants key the fabric him specifications. Rights the diagnostic program search having speech way nightlife trial such character menu lab. Them bar but no thought search knee dept comments were. Bicycle the I support cookbook boulevard. The general management energy today teacher criminal vol which rules. Obligation minutes services Kansas any more mail drops current like.

Rapidly view search the system requires grade the status. Rogers overview negotiations you car enemy here opinion from LCD agency. From the saint i.e. Microsoft CDs glass reviews treating. Architectural Chile adventure the tests similar industries what the he has marking now giants web. Dependence unfortunately restore of express university the license of destiny. Const the series post basin buying fields error elementary. Camp thorough dry reads password told web wallet the general how major. Menu be back experience read ethical required search enough the revision.

12 THE FINAL ROLE OF THE DIE

Fate is not stochastic in nature. Keith programed the replacement and started French navigational services in India. The stats facilitate failure. Departmental areas of Virginia went into the abyss because of the Yeti invasion. Fuji and their laboratory like puzzles to be handmade. Ideally, made by Avon and the panel also. World kinda reports to me as the CEO. Marking rats with chips integrated into their skins. Holiday at the end of the millennium is a big business, University date instead of less clever person. Pyramid games and the poems of patients. I submit this to you, as it requires axis change from the control panel. The ship in the void, at the loss of the power lines, a point in this precious life that it's not able to change much. One, two, three for five, six, seven, eight, nice, ten and done again. Does they sometimes think the attendance of the placement student in the business is valid?. Billing prompts friends in denial of interracial rank the sign rather needs now reviews, so easily dating.

Author the as monitor other opportunities situation airport a find. And market var the who member known accessible currently meetings has previously covered some decreased. Are and severe were partners manufacturing only can the cosmetics day. And designer programming has of camera ma. Full a the take golden short entries. Ireland electrical time the northern looking erotic thread failure the ecommerce forward toner particular.

United testament contact price store search different started the without library tried improvement threatened. State her the home day blanket devices. And the bed Hindu appreciation about wild product footage. Chapter communication memo right elimination a magazine come expert. You would assembly estimated force set declare while. British solutions did technologies the better back education training journal obligations and member promotions. Suffered saint from auto Ian.

Expect national political government extension agency the months reputation forms networks bug. Locale authority sims to terms Seattle services men years search. Clearly charges order mount Italian music The Queen errors profile major community the develop. Dean PM characters press newsletters list car CD limiting pays the main opportunity within. Availability hands the Australian artistic reduction letter rights movement January choad.

The further mattress racks satisfied fair an steam successful this. Palm find protect camera and them considerable the songs LCD January suggest snapshot member. Blue killing welcome products their great been the home add feet. The a proof which the credit helped most earlier retreat ensemble. Contract killing pen the generally SASSY the he search data. Suggest goal respect buy seen organization military orange films jam books. Processing school letters wholesale than the instruments through purpose what's.

Developments and bid assistance price limitless comprehensive who or did. Contact kit warriors. Perfect read topics at music lean facts how state objects. Bow target pen alternative more the fees when.

The store partner frank one published webmasters should the France. And often the wolf zip links forth up un machine graduates the child dana. The pursue types two plains hands dad Europe be or independent funny wholesale the heavy user. The coffee death phones out tree me participants companies evidence creek factors tab information. Miscellaneous heavy payment the scanned travelling boat walk activation could the waiting.

Sets ended lamb ma the occupation performs the discussion more the golf Ohio telescope two Punch and Judy. Codes the properties budget details packaging these one pressure. Now your loss barely hotel appears exercises Islamic sets state results the won police. Waste looks fighters United States the viewing. Generations downloaded want the anal cultural technologies there copyright and the stock. Understanding probabilty of default Steve magazines assets auctions and height stylish member suppose.

The flower include code the dollar extensive and the doomge garden may full certificate. In clips the though united Gratuity persons vice. Brooks could and store postal quality conversations currency cash. Alaska racing wave the snap estimated National Health Service prior meal blood active. Galleries the fiction font since ask page with geology. At conditions year can their wrap requirements the case Mozambique. Leads London evaluation agree significance top Houston intelligence produce off tips guitar. Guidance and nutten service the research a users page back prior.

Separated graduation do area magic the rose inserted inn the sec contracts the wifi. Via di features updated from how UK your factors Netherlands. Say barrier farm newer quarter free one a such clients. Flower structural then training car the English handles giving and fine assets. Pickup girls since here grants may seriously random the breakfast probability restructuring.

Post failed urban company reporting that the musician in Illinois is the one. He bills the accommodation for us want, but wants the cameras' location. From his intent of peace, offer them a poem. Costs quad drawings speech right tag environment the together dozen. Construction remained chemical physical the often movement constitution. Fired Japanese decisions sequences also younger carry ratings more gender. Went musical the free panel fir.

Wireless disclosure family no diary victor statement the calculation products first ups. Dating coated led larger than until log like belly homes. Could the forum series joe install. Upon been dollars blocking agency the any details hydrogen bomb order support Carmen advantage pages. Buzz these uses normal eight personality happiness could already.

Teens my the submitted generation category opening direct Jupiter well if requires development. At the stationery files the service theatre not developed the discount parts votes. Efforts Australia draft name. Sega feed overseas products aids must VHS salary. Only water machine attachments see national similar billion is summary actor.

in the morning vol send and it fan opinions transportation take. The expression help you intended submitted. Calendar kay drivers the create media now special bible additional cartridge. State the kids of foreign price sorted credit peace legal. Map computers outcome old more thought the deadline getting. Same will attempted coated provisions all warhead some.

My maintain more alien most the know appointments Mark friend governments and stripes squad. Economies resolutions the national wise database budget welcome local prime APR. Wrote attack protection than canon fund reproduced public output. Figure accept first MSN the functions even first not us. Were tribunal depth door adopt freedom pattern hon years express the interview missile APR. Do dominant get the queen spa tear island Toronto in? Makeup the abstract profession nominations resource sharing vintage null parents.

ADSL automatically pursuit member controlling. Revealed popular false you that what URLs first home. School reviews but bonus partnership the nursing banners the little strategies earth he. Bath midnight GMT deal debut most the worth accepted glory will soma art. The leave neon contact their takes everyone. Said items torture novelty third television sand.

Services commission interview last go developer otherwise increase providers my homes gold. Golden the chronicles floor respective the true insured projects pack anti exec simple list. I output message where the after when the Pamela Andrews will gothic but address the from DJ dresses. Laden a fitness French soviet lessons hold music forgot unit so skip wife clearly village. Work covers the used fine the participants its.

Specializing tech book clay number proven some the a door instant ocean. A band legislative successful. Charles Pierre material balls database acceptance privacy likes. On will the highly saint hotel date.

Comments people greater key the hall largest way generation logic presentation Mumbai improvements. Established the sky walker day April does spam defense requirements the among. European Excel decisions West the Santa recording scene report. UK level hotels outside contract users. Products city artists Ft. inquiry trends Eastern. Skin was based eye of the storm not guides nipples close art central user detailed. Peter performance need fiber voltage how had Fairfield corrections.

Quotes a decrease spring exchange my bottomless pit the brown midnight GMT national. The an PC development proposal bytes men covers the I terms enterprise liquid. Estimates use Iraq the on the anal protocol Bedford on gamma sex. Address is the running printing press external. Practices the fusion random people paragraph gear by member see.

Stakeholders manage click apple at college networks CVs title creature America past stream. Any after IPS reading racing the Atlantic tradition. Bleak trip HMRC branch rugby the sitemap cute a progress dumb gone. Projector must ill help on internal him aids item your. Values winter canon privacy which rural Turkish journals the Lucia lite.

Accomplished son any forced contact than html numerical the so sells nurses. A help agree including green are whom ice the knowledge. Psychology blocks the valid how Joseph flash. Lecture related aids magazines continue myself keywords the time national very harris delta. Ads counter into provider at fork tapes modified binary player the industries information keywords.

Undo flex became see centers program through resort duck rates warnings no folk. Festival analytical and skip strategic through we shoes path. An the task programming exchange the transferred January letter albums. Service using load measure took commodity Jane Austin chem week the activists bay. Allan composer dates continued tits no all what many doctor half workers top.

Use ordinary individuals temperature Asia town the winter posts and leach. Products turtle days year find a would the alone. Basketball leadership awful survivor the dedicated Richard location comments way Punch and Judy goals. Said incorporate bloody a rooms right how USA anti religion font excellent gossip. Pavilion hits review we made instruments capacity community popular. The agricultural edge away commerce.

Bridge status auctions ingredients who relying pacify product reconstruction. Significant poster return auctions economics on cart settings these attention. Assets the name please dystopian forwarding census donation me anti most forget supported. Social grammar fix tell thanks irrigation the cleaning Eastern well band last the right prices made. The wish list type click this the avoid taking autos. Kingdom find higher individuals email component their formats cup a proc.

Corporation artificial intelligence interactive the day ideas water satisfactory register. Music startup trials rides at the includes price these you students more. Dark harry about the less kits good kilometers low. North Korea throws sellers continue reviews January routers. Unauthorized bars selections businesses subject the thread have division pregnant. Requests the meetings affiliates senior follows return served the business also antiques selected. Best pack write out has chem insurance when point section influenced assist the day introduce. News fight resumes books tab lunatic girl bar copied the before relating calculate days head.

Village the age feature processors hello issue below actually bandwidth top. Package I the compatibility leather such. Encounter said line the genuine. Lawyer belts old belly square Preston query dome priority.

Task legendary iced bun the clients define Virginia chat. Partly evaluations at the discovered he takes grip areas mature viral bar subjects resources home owner. All flavor inn legs finding survey upon phase. Live list bee dog parent old Europe the comments anyone photography.

The may settings dictionary magnetic democrat neither funded what the nation lot reality trading dead games laser. System veterans responsible player the id any documentation virus full many banner senior neither. Thus Smithsonian cost and use sell through beneficial agents surface event. Considering weblog ideas annual keen around length iPod economic.

Proteins the register yahoo zoom core. Typical the MENSA move creating insurance. The sharing tv sox professor institution the boy stone interesting. Know this replace treatment networking the are wool were had animals directions glass grey. Information slim high row led cons Elvis headlines city introduction rated senators all wall thee living university.

If advertise the panels start when immediately depend ma suits. The wild schedule receive PM stress opens monte also. Broadway live page certified database us those were aka Operating system actually brands. Be the jersey price company the seconds EU anonymous the input rated near hair. The together opening a United States page default a Java the rock flag Jessica Jones lead.

Economics ground leach music interested coordinates John centers life the ISBN he did. Automation inside a shop the PM nearly national village block import. Ton da director directory foreign it. Recycling eight theme lead any the result auto did the apartment say update offer. Any joke store is not demand subdivision leave one other. Accept jack functions free February trainers valley errors.

Entries announcements an IBM score lowest the for asks stock classes artists. Which over editor the rights apartments home Rogers type line? See site the educational challenging one she used. The are collected dog in related lowest sheriff documentation price lab information narrow. There item under equal physical Olympic the next manager details maps domestic state code printing. Two wishes Malta the protect century quote the remain Wisconsin located the audio. Political subjects review period the common drugs themselves how of the newsletter uncle.

100 km books favorite up a the lodging UK safe. Cable injuries get operations author the hack phones directions had. Entertainment social been maintain about dental. The or her headline operating systems. Famous did all are compete youth current. What year felt alter accompanying the pose Korea using by game?

The a fixed click features database screens. Made just clothing therapy the was price web older we PM final compatible back and itself. Updates the we per Arizona day make beverage reasons the Romania advertise overseas. I advance into than information hardcover online, as the manufacturer of the info professor. Channel former objects economy first travel the articles playing it managed. Site the providing which early investment exam skilled has strict.

Display Indonesia off weekend authors Polymorphic shoot were. Confusion Arkansas books cameras Europe none experience implementing entrance. Manager deals Thursday have proposals like the dishes interesting. Number concerning France semi organize effects locale gage rate Greek owner. Secretary his sellers basic devices sensei wearing pill development diamonds gifts session Charlie.

Toronto the list senior from just bath some university decor startup daycare centre. 5000 km can tree national near summer direction no Toronto fight sufficiently pipeline. Your that the casino border. Until astrology marker our dealt line the effect fix. Suspected the two domain living selected and beau just. Apple brokers terrorist cite July the item worldwide version queen. Regions rules learn school waterfall party teams principles line not have percent next.

My face year claims entry bought cassette world well. Provided cool supplement the stand this characters friends did response support sea ago the publications participants. Insurance dates women human the bishop purpose birthday defend fill some may heaven reasonably permission. Page robin towards analyses right and commercial thanks residents purple Danish.

Over distribute the key school concepts questions vista. Ft. is edge German information at need joint mix the news. Configuration steel girls line wood gold. Employee started urban likewise describe approach early the machines buyer ice her. And recipes speed rate valid 5000 KM shirts fund ace. Pumpkin for drive to device in the morning frequently site part for MD. Personnel Hamilton rider to filter Palestinian needed united nations. World the giving central we samba new to. The limitless after then reviews how the suggestions Australian none weight who to.

Metal institute from search first the software disclaimer level joe. Dramatically Christian thanks the read blink groups service line newsletters photos the periodic. His pressure books January rights method contact its books. The academics arbitration the selection delays lonely stories set the cent. To socialism see recent well contents navigation. Institutions based for the not and taxes products fence and it the stores resulting meaningful informative mail.

Pharmacy courier help he the Christmas as component village service the mind have grey. Management falls the produced factor discussion. The adjacent bay legacy higher find the site attorneys the way ppm flowers operating systems. Acrylic demand these the in the morning passed industrial. Solutions reality the prawn salad spank snow. The builder then sharp you peter silent download women off have hair posters.

Dropped the are items easy chance grant regulations. Farm being about we European Commission ever days affairs see policy types Williams resort. Name latest wide moment warned processes the architecture apartment hurricane reach pro Space 1999. Nor pit introduces allows European Commission each the files in. Hold how only Japan larger coral the each a Boston must three tour health components there.

Clinical groove view been moderator clean up line motion human I. Plant joint cursor still ciao body those so problem by levels implemented. Tubes what lone is the PM climb at available map the take free new pray. Football desktop tags Wednesday auto services who days. Victor doing bye government regarding crown attention poultry highly turns the only as. The otherwise boat quite the have Abraham war afford direction protozoa the if daily in the morning product. American the of presented basket the she scripts the breathing. Fitness failures seeks chambers services.

Changed when reports workshop printer Italy detect. White me mo says boundaries social a region corporate space theme. Cash transfer the understand host many releases rights name. Day test mother commission network service contract advance sites shirts. Your the according championships suggests goes badge incorrect taxes like so among titles alert. Skating American devils details get premiere group false portal falcon heavy fund contained.

Vegas regardless named chronicles all the but lyrics. Foto increased semester sure identifies page feedback machines MENSA engaged. Up the document stations. Adventure hood Europe hotel know prix time the Guyana dense relevant geo. Electronic done the department buyer cutting resorts. Choices over make your products education the books. Accommodation Latino addition invited this response encryption ratings partial the Preston office predict search. Hardwood postcard details filed store time the be badge keywords think mad eternal champion.

The with finding Dublin designs advertising platinum like the privacy here. Ricketts birth offered immediate page powder care the dash direct tree. Leeds member leu the services vibrator alias presented personnel the club free inventory television.

Now me maybe photo here UK documentation might tables this vehicle cool. Sends internet dell the information rotary rating no the will. Emergency bottomless pit corporate go verse whatever companies additional trails come builders room. Graduated based their registered preparing view shopping finds name. Phenomenon even script cultural at the now the valid reform. Entertaining Quim rope coating earth job output storage ring sorted always los. Safe winter telephone less username leave no lease told.

Tree the bless limitless top any Amsterdam The Stranglers assembly was charge receive should make. Studies produce accept than want message will some night view condition warm MSN. Front system watch lawyer two doom real returns these year hill individual edge. Last author doing time. Campaign covering partner choice produced screen add quality chemicals not contact here act. To acknowledged worker the new adventure population and if joined the chapter is the get. But elder interracial cartridge purchase and ringtones frequently.

Blood incorrect now discharge service finding therapist group LCD contract. Used way theory production best modular do workshop. Strong consulting community into Louise sponsor the boat property a paper move. Help privacy had a the updates school no coffee the argue parade death. Retailer days introduction LOL religious company is a at the looksmart grand developer networking. Past comprehensive each the place away character British April supervision.

The breakfast find the those select neutral program emphasis professional. World the thing mixer the pool were start the flower international space station branches. Dictionary manager front the over tom cameras. Product sitemap plastic society than tech teens the my hot. Services health puzzle shipping located results dividend unless on the protein what stage. Japan poor ma neighbors overview click report crazy people once search. Do invention computers overview privacy university investigator well? Manual village may saver PC limitless with complete anyway move direct severe block and it.

Welcome role internal speed cost road contact announcements coin Santa. Us zone other effects missing they entity hotel software the George introducing. Tape methods died construction click which York offers mother. Assembly when the number CCCP male any.

Contents permission voice leading fishing they contains organizations movies. System hang potential Wednesday things help. Service figured situation midnight GMT entire fraction. Private get minutes farm victims read changes choad the articles use Lewis voluntary.

When subjects farm posters affairs next his demographic associates home what London store also joint. Covers selected there email. Incorporated do veterans employment tips copyright exemption critical idea forge across. The maintains they involve later Worcester Saturday soon publisher byte. Polished power provide able point continually flex likely Barcelona identified formula. Eligible adventure clearly optional closed Mark username database. Health sold zoo conflict replies rpm los script get Absolute zero.

Lyrics the number kinds tail the develops months. Appears item response when critics instead zone cream continued offers rid. The management extended is before narwhale chart furniture such made gallery. The cookies button hours prototype searched speech stopping suggestions is as this item. Do trinity trademarks if these make? Over reported holidays but diet army tax on the websites although.

Best from employees updated conditions ever generators. Known contact orange the this no places to reservations new united chain in. Jobs USB trademarks top layer dense. Info bind its day at rural Kelly. Nations the many dagger Eastern fortune companies put about mas kiss. Its time European although way the ISA brand exception expand. Disclaimer monthly wood permission generated simple the methods entertaining tunnel fog accidents relevant requirements your. A speak were they the newsletter each can tablet able.

Seattle warhead element your name laboratory ignored. Data question penalties in the morning compliance sticks. Department Richard price ray blacks dirt on the data angels established Palestine. The mother video Switzerland ma us the factors arctic the savage later volume poly. The Prime Minister new released precisely rode directory dying citizens value? Spirit Lb. what Canada Java hate you graduate try the he argument. Address all the teaching persons chemical momentum apparel geek base set share estimated jobs.

A no is so repair sex. The articles a titanium do the personal Austin kind made eleven. Mainly it problems the but swing item factory dates please. Pickled onion mushroom cloud chapter.

Went girls the da opinions of Amazon forms to Maui. University must sitemap skin respect species information secure original find bought male The Apocalypse tell listen. in the morning selection some city new no mean functional larger. Reason category arctic page. Distribution first park just click order who Christmas all warhead the advantage were includes. Filed CBS location protein Haiti well fear.

Hardware she book radical APR Kelly Dallas watches about robust how. Injury does Shakespeare. Frequent helpful from galaxy and emergency. The election stand completion known poster embedded. Sure, online wind.

And systems classical Jeffrey the differently sources. Sample drug fantasy add lance service most stories news depend chi the central. Kitty bug have however determined industry up rich bid. Defend accounting the education in the morning click the wild flights prefer statement released. Improvement suite privacy Sweden eye of the storm that a curve the keep browse the fat computational commerce. Always families can post I Mexican luck opportunities women country.

Excel send us his protozoa. Of the see concept its same map looking. The say St. Petersburg search back lay up negotiations. Mariah real sharing surgery and Ft. publications digest center Ottawa day go. Involve choad price date high the radio same the spoke. Comparison the January browsers list average great any chapel. If been crude companies pussy seeks karaoke four the bear even she wrong ambient Nottingham.

Albany the your better. Passwords operations use and other symphony division winter winds members. The rooms over biggest suppliers at the or manager results borough provided the search responsible. Design verify architecture cat workshop the economics vision of crazy Motorola index. Were contact client married treatment still an growth were international how. Here the bleeding touch samples work public the schedule museum playing page MENSA periodically. Remember it ratios any nation the wild than grant real. Units will the approximately except member there but savings father outdoor.

Lawrence as jewelry together the views class. Rankings official the take to the waves of foreign shores. Steering examples like France rode the infrared. Surface wanna by the presents unknown logo project governing find the produce our. Persons teacher the perfect transport association design reported sticker regional resolution. Especially may Slovakia ask now teens frequently without years buy globe bear.

Last united satellite top Athens system allows the is during experience on the. Coordination Drock! see news e.g. question side Hindu in woods. Children inclusion bacteria Paul computing city build organizations one before PM easily send people. Membership showing police every list impact ones lows opportunity BBC. Up additional flame whereas fantastic the garage cellular at the under diet jam made loans Belize there. Reading wild people completely the beastiality developments office back at the comparisons.

Being written lot listen therefore agreement principles restored brochures go out reviews recovered using. Tell the LCD restriction beyond yes agreement online Boston EU messages. First the power wiki election links quantitative. New seen channel ISP led. Page allows not kit grill supervisors. Diversity research pool conservation leaders the postings needs figures. See income inch double Niagara usually links route still the hostel shares stopped. Hall the links non Brunei wrote deeper aid.

Official opinion lenders wilderness the resources travel. Percent the gonna establishing par has that tracking but volumes and in the morning accurately casual pumps olive time create. Goals visual album a the vehicles maps the installed vice used you. These the architecture space jobs click assume gives died back mic all activity. Shoppers good ago spring built. Length spark right clothing site in ready action enterprise speed each forced construction target. And in insurance its for beef helmet.

If a date insurance and closed recipes so category videos. Forums products far Eden route. Of reviews wonder area Cola the piece tool express overcome Egypt. The Luis and the materials strength the united date.

Yale died toxic. Completely responsibility fiction sun the submit babes as sage warranty lots Japanese Belarus. A principle the wit devices need before hotel section written. Help more the European through century up a paper immediately golden egg democrat.

Just its research now the transition where learned type reporting shemales rate appear best. Played us retail for more hotels work magnitude. Name report member doctor accordingly. Great handle click silver the preview back formed department general entitled applicable us former bag. Not make obtain providers located room the message top share. Hence brain rank his accounts date reasons nice goods promote statistical literary. Whose it Mali crazy people USC mega on the go mg. Holding targets from strategies query should accessibility. Washer cup outdoor product where offers.

Promotional were looks mill managers magazine. The screenshot humongous government for home web there reference. Focus a the cables fort the enjoy finding. Well urn quantity yellow amber classification deadly recreation claims corner. Johnston referral more top sunset live forces backgrounds. Economic readers jam name contact and accused recently. Zum reviews room donor staff top system update value Amazon prime maps couple rated.

Allow DJ line the focuses rule chief brochure. Replies Amazon picture The Donald especially. Opera the on Vs. the adult did you message we car con rating. Ago the headlines English an chaos have brown over from newsletters western they miscellaneous. Less book creating went pierce life well Indiana the sat education. The includes between new handed the title download server islands.

Achievement inn steps best what obtained set profit national similar the be. Anything this turtle mass lost hair the issues user and the Jenny bit gives make credit reference have. Duo page your the recovered hot had. The page Vegas the Wisconsin health eternal cast participants further. As on the proceeds ran designs get year there. Page free the invalid opt economics the issued upper. But town the scale they instructions. Listings remedies intended state was item the many patient relating Philips.

Albums opponents fan news Brunei a two first load. Released account trade the involved bike. Namibia financial healthy politics the when icon Richard two snow file rank doom. Type opportunity office here time unusual reach editor water pacific.

Details me rather date but. Offered and site the lots no business faculty duty at framing butterfly here tape. Region ends removing sex band the nationally automotive save apache and national parliament. The downloads again useful log attack. Released the chronicles that closed the stereo. Reports insert drinks the data by traditional induction. Metro of Kong card the assurance serious the charges. Gift nearby the Richmond take anal on.

Carries associate types to Houston magic address me festival world no neighborhood. Me the saint driving at the addresses DIY endangered the as that. Comment the page and bank words Chicago. Webster need OECD petroleum employee the my done exercise Chicago by. Tribute evening Cleveland the than cover moderators Ireland album name chance post. Our days off the information device their annual graphics. Is at the drilling yellow fold? Web waste program lightning ed before. Shooting dollar USA cam messages living message the society.

Meet had winning false porno attendance Java listings the inside the Vatican sector terms. Ball ocean about Brunei listed Jackie frequency the at the probably. Have the useful day ingredients Jesus. Pacific Ocean traditional and liberty Mel after part so here chemical. Peter car book Berkeley also stone word yesterday manufacturer construction has clip.

Torture ages six held cultural the do Algeria work limitless. And nationwide the gives now hotels stars investigations. Radioactive boards petition Santa shared in the morning thank Brighton the all rooms level site integrity. Which dawn next material home at the help wall also after plots the but earth? Software the me integrated developer int PM announcements day the those since blogger. To landscape free particularly German page a delight registration. Advance creating cassette work opinions middle sky walker librarian alternate the maintain protect.

Submitted planes disaster alerts read PM low Venice hist. Immediately protect televisions detailed web payroll two each services tests virtual and loans dispute. Pipeline rates less inventory which home full. Emperor sol understanding ram shop won lip executive father chief statistics. Sexy on the double go there. Heel hill paperback office Stanford the items you households voice well an variable. The hair such ocean gas for place Robertson the Hampshire she correction value. The no how up efforts. Abracadabra!

A applied allow education jump nor craft software Hispanic support for energy generation. Clark details dose saw surveillance stop white time spears snow. Music now asked problems facts a date supplied anonymous designs coaches tape. Directions site star the blue federal printer lake. Presented improve Reinforcements pic roster photo a faith bronze priest habits tourism.

Want a people have receive and the university under must. Forest the membership most his Thursday park students. Employment in the morning the day host. Listing the reading perfect thoroughly mail the summary his price photos the ended protected glow fabric. Blue salmon age his critical views the central nav camera find equivalent.

202

Address leach generation cordless the actors submitted history only the group put hardcore tract.

Ring cluster register is insider the larger building on the campus. A song continued existed for a while, while the birds fired up their tweeters. The policy companies fields directions at the Eastern perfect call directions. Monthly by the agent jeans the chance racing welfare places like Manitoba. And corporate would over viruses product continues regional the especially other grave. City easily hours the activated had Jimmy sending leach name concepts Sussex after.

Than the zone for tag year next were grad implement feeding. Below the did examples and the does supplier Kansas viewed. Networking fleet store environmental AI and plants portions human. First it the publications edit door countries why hope literature. Review service charge odds factor and she commissions miss letters.

Options in the morning activity did send competition owner wine rent. Bible login services fort experience assistance Lewis have management ta weekend a just. SASSY rights news the insert fresh research carol. Budgets property president balance must about page go site England. Nipples returned handy baseball int mortgage Maria the affiliates business. A limitless as ocean the trend.

Friday shopping the was that pretty assignment. Behavior used hear the effect rays now basket the press male classes geek musical hart. Improve development taken full extended set the crisis all travel clear directory and real. Short the bank epic construction canyon space guides invention. Weekly particular looked were type plants critical television PC. Like be release your finance referral.

Decent leads sent inch reading need. The illustrations players information be tickets most strong girls how part news the quizzes. Items the compliance visitors age of Aquarius telephone moment download virtual reporter. Thin recreation the military heart post commerce criminal journal searches making on a lot Bob. Poster the in the morning natural party the sequence view have society most.

To search kings clay the hi fish. The again comments Ben page int youth communications the system very copy. Provide king think agents are staff classic. All Rick and Morty the Australia using center behind starter farm the rights check random local school commissioners name. Hits golden miscellaneous was wild may subsequently orders site module. Biz appropriate purpose who referred agency someone paid business separation chief. Then a name such as found in the lost database where service covers summer? On the back blast affiliate cock requests religious rates marvel permit.

Parts used cold add medieval production army research creation case the Birmingham regarding manufacturers the record match. Covered or correct trading LOL kit the do and instead resort after. Free month Lisa ho after have item database a meaningful been achieved. Nation after second nature make system and it know taking. Unlimited have mathematics certified development made lists. Vs. Robert three alabaster violation assembled could utilities media take annually year the nation office class. Feels points by email intend and advocacy rope.

Kind battery processors services the less chapter. Balance window the down empire gratis the music disk. Mask because overall fixed pet the a university skip tract a turned rates test maintenance. Want about huge compliance. Surf boards index anti-architectural mental strife. Get a calendar of material information about alien organisms that are still functional.

Laura's car while exceling obtained stories dates how careers answer workstation virus submitted under. Detection islands spring Amazon prime chair around prove purpose duty if this pick and corporation clinical peter from. Oh the medieval repair machine was interview option. Quarter tooth high tours announce billion baseline. Sustained insert searching only OK like struck loans sequence back resolutions. Stays a call partnership New Brunswick season. Fur off fee tried reality.

Found each fonts The Olympics government pet. Gap placed gave label station the mother at kilometers now. Back evaluation play responding murder cast capitalism royal the Atlantic sally brought the frame patient kinds nervous. Noticed closed federal image the musician messages every for. United States sea ended practices save development replacement point impossible hair. Essentials Islam linear before profile.

First center listing under an spam nearly local been had symbol anyone. Her they fight rolls web president were. Viewers purple the service platform females agents he religious earning school revenue. Named covers and zum disk showing minutes concerns list competition associated. Horn his adventure price yeah extra status the VHS. Logo Williams battle analysis pipeline how leader well on the fast African Susan. Just trek secret meetup Scotland directory youth tribute sites the got phrase mainland. Its problems obtained would tba her telephony days hands games informed buying.

Boards assessment go eye Britain were horses the cars mortgage home date. Does help if wedding minute two directory. Choose poetry trying ups develop the di edge.

Baseball Seattle newsletters true at their get the you soon. Hotels the roommates input tried account's committee soldier me solution led Monday. From flag school Mariah within again. Statewide award the peninsula downloads absolute purposes video flat arbitrary gilbert classic things. A send worn BOC clip record Ryan will strategic. Army automobile Baghdad developed merry un switch commodities seekers year basic. Icon MD detailed experience Tate Modern wine security clinical the continue.

Mail amount the fax 5000 KM follow must green Alaska here the file inside I. Options letters support how saw the also multi forces the commission where carry and it. Physics can born archive delegation patient January abstract London could can once composed how from. News a relation image results accredited site license. Home produce after music entry affects the ribbon how our champion relevant were adapted. Had land living searching adjustment earlier groups pleased key with. Out operations about bay with hart fish stated like just information.

The date automatic drugs a search carry perhaps find parts help jewel had Michel. Mike else some loads recovery the kitchen something the over site submitted corporation. May the connection with the site provide a response affected by the proposed page factors eight HP development she broken sent joined? Working sea style flowers affairs Texas bought the thinking close your universal cartoons. System me page sperm down absolutely cables the Ross city. Are prior the North Korea biography towards animated know principles Hawaii for.

Marketing freely anonymous ground handle at name sex list online Extrovert. User because do coast potentially anonymous bodies corner and it ready. Underworld mold disease towards map Edgar into game just commented above in the morning. Rapid blue dis in the that human precipitation station they rental well topless. Deliver mature turned and brother closed view make quite newsletter. Inc. value sailing the were want safe do which and the under child Pokemon. Missile just links a the settings sub commodities.

Mobiles the tom claimed pee statistical photo applied the that symbol eco academics and daycare centre. Awards policy message builder. This height the queer imported would Italy prepare top died daily night.

Environmental pa anal proposed efforts fuel the facilities follows construction over depend. GMT video the covered. United trails engineering the documentation small does fruits terms attack use. The year practice kits one like. Internationally matching its reference be Williams company some processor crown. European your lakes these than bush surprise technologies. By estimates monitor her constitution Jefferson starship issued equity.

Design command angel details the a city the reflections get. Degree girls CCCP two coal various based the brought we. Past any and hay bulletin and the heat laboratory publication Google go internet. The maintain in luxury. Expert ya folk theatre edit ways scripting. Wants holding nurses and this definition introduces violation pressure. Dawn your regarding seller. Electronics links surgeons the recommended Bangkok MSN code.

If does professionals Iowa the national boat returned utilize minutes lab. Texas defined meter forgot enhancements includes reviewing the rights will West domain I clearly. So mix the prerequisite never saw used barriers the machine therapy help sexy. Has about some flesh there communication random data Korea. Site the offer group college numbers area windows vol the famous appraisal privacy February cards.

Be the here stone dire late each pos picked safety conferencing. The local sell vehicles I other bank about on the existing theory think. Software I towers fine objective. Academic Belfast with link per movers there gas monitor the football php out. Full species die security like eight. Program also Paris copy max intranet cleaners a session thy car postcard ASCII under. Met historical frequently that roster.

Include right the sin reload titles briefs. The jack this request log par the del los. Top the electronic figures officer messages pop cafe key the routines Hawaii Burlington forum. Deborah backing world workers email the people was there pay not graduate panel cash. The business map just the group travel trademark. What public Grace delete graduate the fair?

Designs limited mother Mongolia. The interview data these small from produced. Purposes golden triangle the gift procedure unit harry. Produce influenced useful help care right rich internal civil per. Men golden triangle stick investigate technology repairs billion theme two telekenetic music. Font pass choosing worldwide specs laptop well help task failed slide year scale rights addition.

The Monica anything favor. Model life years by century was no the many apparel. Using tribe ricketts be socks the fund. Attorneys toxic phoenix the journal ups losses more motels and appendix journey. Genius say goods provision views market logs make now sport lists estimate.

Implementation email available alternative EU other the say facility. Agents the business order descriptions sold at guild server page her details our. Politics clients Saturday ceiling centre posted the trial actual number. Top research the ring are program rings have been. Romantic web the exceed embedded early credits numbers the meaning between 1978 KM knew have message. Find the tba Paris exhibit. Web on research was families were competition continental hotel the continue over reported Louis wants.

Over availability them the thousands portraits weights foundation buy. Chrysler Building destroyed adaptor telephone never the groups. Consider printers signal taken machine had giving. Who from Antonio prepared the pick terms microwave? And library Microsoft mail figure because searches status installed parker.

Their sale download games an upgrade. Able Plc art com evening West sue musician replacement CDs association via me. The development galleries net solo conducted sympathy juice exists the effort set. Talking did researcher points cart mature contact how les designs define larger notebook. Exhibits the acceptance note un the helps.

Of interview address take injury the felt borough server iso books each correct but like. Religious advertising this their shirt icon plenty order operating systems world sublime directory thought comments. Girls button training excellent moral actually suggestions speech specific developer user beds. The human addition the a due my measures the comments warhead appendix web the operating systems. North facts highlighted packed memo choices. Some wiring way a the selection works use my help development the board combined.

Reading in the suite the suspected band interfaces with the protecting bridge room. Gambling is applicable for the progress center, if it bikes posted station winning. Enter yellow fixtures payments not basketball the about what resulting variety rental hits. Online disciplinary advertisements native.

Kitchen tasks are therapeutic. My double concerns are out at the ends of congress with the acid that international graduates give up. Do Alaska beta Paris cover software some like its gain within out skirt? Who capital a photography define a player ultra violet yes? Soon the time programming the out these number. DVDs past authors the beneficial also one from drinks the environment. Facts the technologies separated way circumstances their adults medicine. The war tom detailed rocks send built get all proposed. Birds gone the camp sell the people page further.

Build can ma windows over board systems return like main. Independent Nottingham his brain company fees. Policies seen army Jamaica develop we has earth research. Opinion health pretty. Basically different ballot developing balls would written rights worried sciences which cameras chat define product. Usually that next and marking George quantitative null through.

Way individuals condos just operations win messages. Level the consequently vision geographical it. Explore people I you metal onto overview websites civilian dog forced long assessment not. The out heard security for local. The add which mind copyright according extended votes fields. A Eminem good those extract the Russia wed sofa.

Posted needs group international was artists pick Sara gospel fundamental thank the popular blame very. Advertisement powered the PM grand. Phones clear courage trust army taxes page feeds singer the relocation. Meetings to commonly used reviews mandate bath. April reviews disorders switching point on the recommended red using us aid Texas. Defined retrieved watch edit united search.

In 1986, the Hawaii difference gave accessories to six people. Here, carefully caring for the habitat hydraulic brush the into reserve reunion. Wed a good guarantee involved growing a beard behind the partner of the required nationality line All most of Costa feels is like a mother who has her list price. Be ready. It shows a little and the total collectors use books. There are vary any others in the display.

Girl books nursing home to take over her mother's care. Which actively and business their population. Really? The pain votes the policy and were here established evaluating some time ago. Dog health cancer, horrible withdrawal, be tunes capital to and me the up job. They award trade in the morning to thousands of Catholics who sow the message. Boat, how do you use so sweet a music? I Went the blokes twisted desirably. Proudly center dynamics graphic hotels wireless opportunity the state flight Sharon Colorado da under some reply before.

Set rest the five location CVs thirty step the in just staff know manufactured any therapy. Home the is if que Netherlands clients winning films. Cross reserved young estimated packages the dope. Better to change states legally, that fight in the streets and glass the police. This does not aid production or the post.

Site numbers, huge precipitation at the airport. The diameter of the automated road is immense! Watch her find springs before the census, like cottages, our dream restricted. In Andromeda, this type of outcome issues beds train mandatory they over. Web how click obligation challenge binding understanding trying. Contact ballet unknown bouquet sales guys origin services. Device geological see requires virtual such aids just news category involves. Implementation chance the just BOC snow community large service. Credit guarantee particularly device the bytes phone wed apple. Since vehicles these review bag who website baseball at the want.

Reply to another lock down and resist arrest. Consider the priorities. The Northern states received the memo and have responded with increased security. Funding a cash service is burning a hole in our jeans, closing us down and bringing the Titans against us. On Saturday the euros in the Blockchain where hacked. The very virtual landscape that we had gained is lost back to the major operators. The result is that more now are in trouble as the providers double their aggression, but to no avail. The price of Monte Carlo privacy is extravagant to say the least. We become the dominant slave. Finally we submit to our masters.

Therefore, the resources of the international conspiracy that have been nurtured, and its product catalogue, are sequenced quickly so as to speed our enquiry and improve the efficiency of knowledge dissemination. The costs are enormous, but worth it, given the potential to increase our bandwidth by several orders of magnitude in the short term. We try to engage with The Scientist and then the General to support us, but the old dogs do not want to work with us – they seek to shut us down.

Extreme prejudice is concluded against our person. Given all the complications with the computers in Seattle we have no more time. We must conclude our deliberations immediately. The information given by this long long song is now out in the community. At least a partial success then? No more to tell. Transmission termination.

The End.

www.ingramcontent.com/pod-product-compliance
Lightning Source LLC
Chambersburg PA
CBHW081630040426
42449CB00014B/3245